RENAISSANCE AT RENSSELAER

RENAISSANCE AT RENSSELAER

A PRESIDENT, A PLAN, A UNIVERSITY TRANSFORMED

Written by Stephen G. Pelletier
for Rensselaer Polytechnic Institute

Foreword by Dr. Paul Gray

Samuel F. Heffner Jr., '56, *Chairman of the Board of Trustees*
Shirley Ann Jackson, Ph.D., *President*

Rensselaer Polytechnic Institute
110 8th Street
Troy, NY 12180-3590
www.rpi.edu

CONTENTS

FOREWORD

This book records the extraordinary transformation of Rensselaer Polytechnic Institute that took place covering the period from 1999 to 2010. From its founding in 1824 until at least the last decades of the 20th century, Rensselaer was a premier center of learning for those concerned with science and engineering.

Its stature declined late in that century, at least in part because of rapid turnover in the leadership of the university. During these years Rensselaer experienced declines in both applicants and acceptances of offers of admission to the undergraduate programs, as well as declines in graduate enrollment, particularly at the doctoral level. Sponsorship of research and the operating budget were stagnant, and there were shortfalls in fundraising that hampered the budget. Many alumni and alumnae were concerned about the decline in academic reputation. In the late 1990s, there had been no significant additions to the physical plant for a decade, and many buildings, including residence halls, reflected significant deferral of maintenance.

The Board of Trustees recognized late in the 1990s that the status quo was unacceptable and set out to find a leader who could reverse the fortunes of the university. Some members thought of this search as "the last chance for Rensselaer."

In December 1998 the Trustees appointed Shirley Ann Jackson president. An African-American woman with a long list of "firsts" (including membership in the National Academy of Engineering and receipt of the Vannevar Bush Award), she brought to the university a rich background including S.B. and Ph.D. degrees from MIT, post-doctoral experience in Europe, extensive research experience at the Bell Telephone Laboratories (later AT&T Bell Laboratories), faculty experience at Rutgers University, and four years as Chairman of the Nuclear Regulatory Commission (NRC). At the NRC, where she was the first woman and the first African American to lead the

Commission, Dr. Jackson undertook a systemic review of the organization, which led to reliance on probabilistic risk-informed regulation, the development of a much improved system for planning, budgeting, and performance management, and the establishment of the International Nuclear Regulators Association, a forum which advises other nations on nuclear safety matters. Her style and record of accomplishments at the NRC were very important to the Trustees of the university when she was chosen.

Before taking up her post on July 1, 1999, Dr. Jackson made several trips to RPI for fact-finding and for conversations with faculty, students, and others. At the time of her selection in 1998 she expressed her vision for a renewed Rensselaer and spoke of the task ahead in this manner:

> To actualize this vision requires us to innovate on the innovations already achieved in teaching our students, to strengthen and enhance the research base of the university, to continue and to expand the upgrading of our facilities, and to engage the larger community—locally, regionally, nationally, globally. All of this is predicated on a fundamental strengthening of Rensselaer's financial base.[1]

It is remarkable she was prepared at that time to express her view of these five areas of change and improvement in which she would focus her actions immediately. She also described three areas of new academic endeavor for which the university would claim research leadership:

- Information technology

- Applied mathematics

- Biotechnology

The first two would build on existing strengths; the third was new.

In a campus meeting early in her tenure as president of Rensselaer, Dr. Jackson described what needed to be done:

> "strategic planning, research enhancement, pedagogical innovation, upgrading and expanding facilities, diversity, community outreach, global outlook and impact, and strengthening the university's financial condition."

Students would be:

> "educated in depth and technologically agile with a thirst for lifelong learning."

Faculty would focus on:

"providing a unique education…committed to being at the leading edges of their fields."

The Institute staff would work:

"at the highest levels, and [be] recognized for its performance."[2]

These several sentences, addressed to the entire community, left no doubt that change would be radical and fast and might be unpopular with some members. It was time for all at RPI to buckle their seat belts.

By early in 2000, following intensive, wide-ranging discussions and structured reviews and revisions, Dr. Jackson's plan for transformation evolved, with the support of the Board of Trustees, into a comprehensive document called simply *The Rensselaer Plan*. It was widely distributed to the community and was placed on the RPI website.

The hard work of implementation then began. This book records, in considerable detail, the process of implementation, and describes the successes of the plan through 2010. They are multiple: increased applications and acceptances at both the undergraduate and graduate level; an expanded faculty, of which 274 were appointed in the decade; a tripling of research grants and contracts; a successful capital campaign that exceeded its $1.4 billion goal; an improvement in national rankings; three magnificent new buildings, including a state-of-the-art athletic facility; a new supercomputer center; improvements in student housing; and a palpable change in the vitality and spirit of the Rensselaer community.

Shirley Ann Jackson's vision and leadership of the university have raised greatly its stature and reputation as it continues its transformation to premier quality. There are lessons in this effort that will be relevant elsewhere in the educational community.

Paul E. Gray
Professor and President Emeritus
Massachusetts Institute of Technology

ENGAGING REFORM

In the context of higher education, the concept of change presents something of a paradox. On the one hand, a university's focus on knowledge and research is fundamentally oriented to the discovery of the new. Indeed, academia overflows with good ideas aimed at improving the status quo. Research laboratories pursue findings that can improve human health. Technologists develop applications to advance society. Campus-based management theorists regularly suggest strategies for improving business and industry. Colleges of education advance a plethora of ideas for enhancing schools. Systems engineers work continuously to develop better processes—and so on. Through such activities, universities are, intrinsically, advocates for change. One can point to countless examples where applications of inventive thinking that started in universities sparked beneficial reforms across society.

Ironically, however, colleges and universities tend to be extraordinarily slow to warm to the notion of reforming themselves. In practice, academia tends to evidence a decided comfort with the status quo, and an equally pronounced skepticism about that which would upset the equilibrium. Like many institutions in society, universities tend to favor stasis over transition. While the traditions that distinguish universities can certainly undergird institutional strength, they can also have a paralytic effect by inculcating barriers to new ideas.

Change comes slowly to colleges and universities, if indeed it comes at all. Even after the need or desire for reform has been accepted, universities tend also to be slow in implementing change. Moreover, institutions that commit to change often do so only by tinkering around the edges—of processes, departments, curricula—without plunging into wholesale reform.

Nonetheless, change in academia is imperative. Even the strongest institutions, with the richest traditions, must amend their curricula periodically, rewrite their policies, fine-tune their procedures, and make other systemic changes in order to thrive over time. Change is a requisite for strong institutions that wish to become stronger. For institutions that strive toward better positioning, reform is necessary for competitive purposes, for fulfilling missions, or even for survival.

One can argue that the healthiest institutions are to some extent always reinventing themselves. Such institutions stay alert for new opportunities that can help them push the boundaries of how they envision themselves. They actively seek to engage in activities that will keep them abreast of the times—if not ahead of them—in ways that will help them expand and better fulfill their missions. Typically implementing incremental change more than a dramatic overhaul, such institutions rely on the process of ongoing reinvention to energize and reinvigorate themselves. At such institutions, transition and transformation are the norm. Change as a process is an inculcated, even comfortable, part of the campus ethos.

Important change can also result from a set of circumstances in which institutions find themselves in need of more dramatic reform. The literature of higher education is filled with accounts of institutions that have invested considerable energies and purposefully engaged in wholesale efforts to transform themselves on a broad scale. A small liberal arts college, struggling to survive in a version of itself bloated over time with added programs, finds new success by paring itself back to its historic core mission. A large private university reinvents itself by reclaiming a commitment to undergraduate education. A large public institution gains distinction by redesigning its programs in the model of an honors university, or "public ivy."

Nonetheless, because academia tends to be change- and risk-averse, colleges and universities often find it difficult to initiate broad, deep, systemic reform. Significant change in the academy, if it occurs at all, tends to derive not from internal processes for regular improvement but out of necessity precipitated by major events or by forces

"Our intent was to have Rensselaer emerge reenergized, reawakened, refocused. It meant that we had to imagine a different, bolder future for the Institute. We needed to recognize that, while building on its legacy and existing strengths, Rensselaer had to change."

SHIRLEY ANN JACKSON

outside the institution. Fires, floods, and financial exigency can be the impetus for reform. Other crises—such as a failure of leadership, a reordering of internal institutional dynamics, or the erosion of a vital student market—can also spark change. A transition in institutional leadership is often both the result of a shift in institutional dynamics *and* the stimulus for institutional reform.

■ ■ ■

As we shall see, Rensselaer Polytechnic Institute at the end of the 20th century found itself adrift. Pursuing an educational mission that could be characterized as stale and perhaps too narrowly cast, the Institute was slipping in its national reputation and in many key measures of quality and accomplishment. Moreover, it had failed to embrace emerging opportunities in research and scholarship that held the potential to energize its programs and position it to lead and excel in the 21st century.

In 1999, Rensselaer's Board of Trustees asked Dr. Shirley Ann Jackson to chart a new course and lead the Institute to a more robust future. Jackson heartily embraced that mission. Her vision—strategic in focus, comprehensive in scope, and at once dramatic, ambitious, and bold—was embodied in *The Rensselaer Plan*, a document and a strategy that have served as the infrastructure for a full and fruitful transformation at Rensselaer.

Making the case for the imperative of a degree of change that extended far beyond the merely incremental, *The Rensselaer Plan* outlined a sweeping strategy for systemic reform across the Institute. Under the plan, programs, curricula, facilities, finances, the student experience, policies, processes—indeed, virtually all corners of the Institute—were scrutinized, analyzed, and revitalized. Many long-existing practices that had outlived their usefulness were jettisoned. New thinking was applied in the development of a multitude of new academic programs, research pursuits, buildings, policies, and practices.

Imbued with both a considerable element of risk and enormous potential for gain, and requiring a daunting amount of difficult work, the plan was designed to revitalize Rensselaer and to position it as a major educational and research force configured to meet the challenges of the new century. The plan held inherent promise for a stronger, more vibrant Rensselaer. Jackson described it in this fashion:

> Our intent was to have Rensselaer emerge reenergized, reawakened, refocused. It meant that we had to imagine a different, bolder future for the Institute. We needed to recognize that, while building on its legacy and existing strengths, Rensselaer

had to change. This required us to rethink and reinvent practices and policies across the university, while also adding important new dimensions that did not exist before. In the end, we would emerge as an intergenerational community of learners even more strongly engaged—deeply and seriously—in the highest level pedagogy and research, approaching and solving the most important questions and challenges of our time.[3]

Under Jackson's leadership, the broad reforms of *The Rensselaer Plan* were implemented over the course of just a decade—a pace that for academia is nothing short of remarkable. But more to the point, the wide impact of the plan across the scope of the institution has been significant, even dramatic. The Institute has found new clarity of focus, embracing a revitalized mission that builds on Rensselaer's distinguished past while engaging vital new intellectual questions that will define its future. Broad new research foci have been engaged. Innovative new educational programs have been started, and existing programs rejuvenated. Many new faculty members have been recruited. The quality of the student body has been strengthened, as has the quality of student life. Vastly improved policies and practices have been implemented. The Institute's physical plant has been transformed with the construction of bold new buildings and dramatic improvements to existing structures. In short, what was once a rather myopic technological school, perhaps guilty of coasting for too long on an outdated reputation, has been transformed, realizing Jackson's vision that Rensselaer become a "top-tier, world-class technological research university, with global reach and global impact."[4]

Moreover, the reforms that have been instituted to date—deep, systemic changes that have transformed Rensselaer in countless fundamental ways—have created a strong foundation for Rensselaer's ongoing work to further expand the comprehensiveness of its mission, enrich the quality of its programs, improve its operational effectiveness, and further enhance its reputation. The transformation that has taken place under *The Rensselaer Plan* will thus be sustained—and expanded—deep into the 21st century.

■ ■ ■

This book is the account of successful, global, and truly transformative change at a specific institution of higher education, Rensselaer Polytechnic Institute. It is the story of change not for short-term, incremental gains but rather of deep, systemic reform focused on enhancing the whole of the institution over the long term. It is also the account of how one remarkable leader, Dr. Shirley Ann Jackson, provided not just a new vision of what Rensselaer could be, but also the drive, persistence, and skills necessary to bring that vision to fruition.

Importantly, this book also details a powerful process for engaging an academic community in institutional reform. Jackson led a course of action that required nothing less than that Rensselaer as an institution assess, challenge, and—often—change long-held assumptions about its purposes, goals, and ways of working. Arduous but necessary, the change process that Jackson and her colleagues conducted drew the Rensselaer community into discussions that far transcended mere deliberations of strategy to instead delve into profound questions about how the institution envisioned itself and its role in 21st-century society. Essentially, those discussions demanded that Rensselaer reenvision itself—no small feat—and embrace a bolder ideal for what it could and should be in the future. Essentially, too, the process was designed to create and inculcate a systemic process that would sustain ongoing change and improvement well into the future.

Reimagining itself, Rensselaer has reinvented itself. This is the story of that process.

CHAPTER 1

A LEADERSHIP IMPERATIVE

Few could have guessed that December 11, 1998, in fact marked the beginning of what would prove to be change on a scale and at a pace that was without precedent in Rensselaer's then 174-year history.

If you had reason to walk across the campus of Rensselaer Polytechnic Institute on December 11, 1998, you would not have noticed anything that was particularly remarkable. The temperature was seasonal, in the low 40s. The sky was overcast. Light winds gusted off the nearby Hudson River, easing past downtown Troy, New York's brick buildings and uphill to campus. Headed toward end-of-semester examinations, students scurried across a landscape of buildings that would have been familiar to their peers from many generations before. A casual visitor to campus that day might have carried away a prototypical snapshot of a seemingly average day in American higher education.

In fact, however, Rensselaer that day was anything *but* typical. However placid the campus might have seemed, something of a revolution was about to start there. Indeed, the Institute was about to embark on a path of momentous and ultimately transformative reform.

The epicenter of that change could be found in Rensselaer's Darrin Communications Center. Its lecture hall, then the largest single room on campus, was packed with students, faculty, staff, and campus guests. Another large room nearby, broadcasting events from the first room via video, was also filled. Excited chatter created a din in each space. The reason? Rensselaer was about to announce a new leader, the 18th president in its 174-year history.

The crowd in Darrin quieted when Samuel F. Heffner Jr., Chairman of Rensselaer's Board of Trustees—founder and president of Dickinson-Heffner, Inc., of Baltimore, a building and land development firm, and a member of the school's class of 1956—took

Samuel F. Heffner Jr.
Chairman of the Rensselaer
Board of Trustees

the podium. Speaking for barely a minute, Heffner quickly got to the point: He said that the unanimous choice of the Rensselaer Board of Trustees to "advance Rensselaer in the 21st century" was Shirley Ann Jackson, Ph.D., then the Chairman of the U.S. Nuclear Regulatory Commission. Heffner praised Jackson's "extraordinary accomplishments as a brilliant researcher and an outstanding public servant" and said she had the "bold vision and proven leadership skills" to carry Rensselaer into a new era.[5]

The members of Heffner's audience rose to their feet in a tumultuous ovation. The crowd "absolutely exploded," Heffner recalled. "I've never been in any situation where there was such a spontaneous eruption of cheers and applause. It was a great moment."[6]

Heffner's audience had witnessed history—on a number of levels. The announcement of a new president alone is often cause for celebration at any university. New leadership signals that an institution is ready to move forward with new energies and ideas, and Jackson's appointment was a clear sign that Rensselaer was ready to map assertively a new future. Moreover, the appointment showed how far Rensselaer was ready to go in pursuit of new traditions—Jackson was both Rensselaer's first woman leader and the first African American to hold that position.

As news of Jackson's appointment rippled across campus and out to the world at large, it was clear that Rensselaer had put its faith in a hard-charging scientist whose professional portfolio included a distinguished career in research, an international profile, and a reputation as a reformer. Her first official appearance on campus—as a woman in an institution with strong male traditions and as an African American among relatively few faces of color—was manifestation enough that Rensselaer had elected to go in new directions. Few could have guessed, though, that December 11, 1998, in fact marked the beginning of what would prove to be change on a scale and at a pace that was without precedent in Rensselaer's then 174-year history.

Change in leadership in higher education sometimes comes via smooth succession, but more often results from the realization that an institution needs a different direction, new energies, new ideas—or a combination of those elements. Such perceptions were in evidence at Rensselaer as the 20th century came to a close.

Rensselaer had a rich tradition of exceptional research and educational excellence. It had earned an international reputation for the strength of programs in such disciplines as engineering, applied mathematics, and media arts. The university was well-known and admired for the quality of its undergraduate education. Moreover, Rensselaer programs and graduates alike had been respected for decades for their inventiveness, innovation, and entrepreneurial spirit. From railroads to bridges to the great dams of the West, much of the early physical infrastructure in the United States had been engineered by Rensselaer graduates. More recently, technological break-throughs in the 20th century, including ones that put man on the moon, had benefited from expertise born in the Institute's classrooms and laboratories.

In the decade or so prior to Jackson's appointment, however, an institutional lassi-tude had taken hold. (Some said the institutional lethargy had been in evidence long before that.) While Rensselaer still managed glimpses of the kind of innovative think-ing that had earned it such a distinguished reputation, the university was not regularly demonstrating the kinds of bold leaps in progress that would sustain and expand its reputation. Nor was the Institute particularly well-positioned—in its curriculum, research interests, physical infrastructure, and financial strength, for example—to be an educational and societal leader in the 21st century.

Many observers of Rensselaer shared a fear that the Institute was adrift, if not in actual decline. Hard data tell one part of the story:

- Student interest, as measured by inquiries for places in the freshman class, had dropped by 33 percent since 1991.

- The percentage of freshman applicants being accepted for admission had risen to as high as 88 percent. Several entering classes during the 1990s were smaller than planned. Tuition discount rates had risen to levels well above the national average.

- Research awards to faculty had remained flat through the 1990s, averaging only $37 million through the 1990s.

- Graduate enrollments were dropping, with full-time doctoral students down 15 percent and full-time master's students down 18 percent between Fall 1994 and Fall 1999.

- To balance budgets and address "structural deficits," the Institute endured several rounds of budget cuts in the 1990s. Faculty and staff left as a result of voluntary separation programs in 1994 and 1996. The tenure-track faculty was 15 percent smaller in 2000 than it had been in 1991.

- Rensselaer had not built a major new academic or research building since 1986. Prior to 2000, the most recent student housing complex dated to 1976.

- The endowment stood at less than $500 million.

- One year, in 1999, the Institute dropped off *U.S.News & World Report*'s list of the nation's top 50 universities.

- A feasibility study for a new fundraising campaign failed to elicit enthusiasm for the Institute's prospects among those closest to it.[7]

As one would expect of an incoming president, Shirley Jackson did some analysis of her own. "Some of what I found when I got here was obvious, and some of it, in the end, was less than obvious," she recalled. "I knew that here was a university that had a great history. It was the oldest technological university in the United States. It had done some truly interesting and important things in terms of both research and pedagogy. It was, at one point, neck and neck in many ways with the leading technological universities in the nation. But for reasons I did not fully understand at the time, Rensselaer had fallen away from that."[8]

For example, Jackson noted, Rensselaer's curriculum "had not evolved to incorporate a number of the areas that other technological and other research universities had moved into years before—among them, biotechnology and the life sciences." Similarly, she said, Rensselaer had not invested sufficient resources in building its computer science capacity.[9] These were areas of critical interest to society, of course, and ones in which some of Rensselaer's peer and aspirant institutions had already made distinctive progress.

Jackson recognized that if Rensselaer were to become a truly great comprehensive institution, it would have to address a significant imbalance that had evolved in the relative size and resourcing of its academic units. The School of Engineering had grown to far overshadow the other schools. It commanded a large proportion of the Institute's revenues and through policy making and institutional politics had amassed power and authority sufficient to drive or sway key institutional decisions. Concomitantly, practices in Board operations had evolved that gave inordinate support to pet sectors of the Institute.[10]

Moreover, Jackson found that Rensselaer's academic programs lacked cohesion. She observed that Rensselaer's curriculum emphasized particular disciplines at the expense of balance in the academic program as a whole. Jackson also found that members of the Rensselaer community either did not have or could not always articulate a shared perception of the value and purpose of given programs. For instance, Jackson said, "when I asked people to define the intellectual core of the information technology program, they could not tell me."[11]

On the whole, Jackson believed, Rensselaer had not realized its full potential. For example, while the Institute had offered Ph.D. programs for some time, it "had not evolved as a real research university," she observed. "Although we were nominally a Carnegie I research university, we had a lot of students pursuing master's degrees, but not so many Ph.D. students."[12]

At the same time, Rensselaer could demonstrate relatively lackluster success in raising funds to support research. Fundraising on the whole was not at a sufficiently high level for an institution with Rensselaer's reputation and potential, Jackson believed, which caused budget restraints that impeded the Institute's progress. At some $200 million, the Institute's annual budget was arguably too small, perhaps half as big as it should be for an institution of its size and promise.[13] Moreover, the Institute had endured several years of significant budget challenges.

Jackson also found a degraded physical plant, with much deferred maintenance. In particular, she was dismayed at the poor condition of many student residences, some of which had not been significantly refurbished in decades.[14]

Jackson realized, too, that important administrative processes at Rensselaer were either in disarray, fragmented, or nonexistent.[15]

Finally, Jackson was concerned that the Rensselaer community lacked diversity—certainly in terms of ethnicity and gender, but also more broadly in terms of the benefits that could be gained from a campus that was more diverse intellectually and culturally.[16]

In short, Jackson perceived Rensselaer as either "drifting or dropping"—one could take one's pick.[17] The Institute's national standing had slipped. It had not sustained its competitiveness among the most important research universities, in effect ceding critical ground to its peer and aspirant institutions. Some observers felt that it was coasting on a reputation earned many decades before. The Rensselaer of the late 1990s was an institution that, for a host of reasons, could be said to be falling short of its promise and potential.

One measure that suggests that Rensselaer was struggling to find its rudder was a decided unevenness in presidential leadership in the period building up to the Jackson appointment. In the 14 years between 1984 and 1998, the institution had five presidents, including two acting leaders who held the seat on an interim basis between permanent appointments. Indeed, just prior to Jackson taking office, the Board had tapped one of its own members, Cornelius J. (Neal) Barton, class of 1958, to serve as acting president after the rather sudden departure of the prior leader.

Rensselaer's history had been punctuated by the tenures of a few exceptionally strong presidents. One such hard-charging luminary, Palmer C. Ricketts, class of 1875, oversaw an era around the turn of the 20th century in which many of the buildings that still constitute Rensselaer's central campus were erected. Serving from 1976 to 1984, another highly regarded president, George M. Low, class of 1948, led an era that saw growth in the number of faculty and students, a more than trebling of financial support for sponsored research, the successful completion of a $52 million capital campaign, and the completion of several campus building and renovation projects.[18]

An icon in Rensselaer's history, Low left a significant leadership gap when he died in office, of cancer, in 1984. He was succeeded on an interim basis by Daniel Berg, Rensselaer's Vice President of Academic Affairs and Provost. Berg got the nod to full presidential status in 1985. An advocate of participatory decision making, Berg was known as a consensus builder. His tenure, however, saw a significant rift between the administration and the students, and Berg left the presidency in March 1987.[19]

To bridge the gap until a new president could be appointed, the Rensselaer Board of Trustees turned to one of its own members. Stanley I. Landgraf, class of 1946, agreed in 1987 to serve as acting president. He served capably until the appointment in 1988 of Roland W. Schmitt as Rensselaer's 16th president.

Schmitt, also a Rensselaer Trustee, had retired as senior vice president for science and technology at General Electric, where he had directed GE's Research and Development Center.[20] Taking the helm in an era of financial exigency, Schmitt worked to make Rensselaer's administrative processes more businesslike.[21] With Trustee Samuel F. Heffner Jr., class of 1956, he led a capital campaign that bested its goal of $200 million by more than $7 million—a year ahead of schedule. Resources from that effort helped fund new professorships and academic centers, including the Anderson Center for Innovation in Undergraduate Education, Rensselaer's highly respected incubator of curriculum reform and improved undergraduate education.[22]

During Schmitt's tenure, Rensselaer also introduced several new degrees, including a master's in fine arts and an MBA emphasizing management and technology.[23] Schmitt retired in 1993 and was named President Emeritus.

His successor, R. Byron Pipes, had been provost and academic vice president at the University of Delaware, where he held a named chair in engineering. Pipes would serve until 1998. Like Schmitt, Pipes was forced to address difficult financial circumstances. He is credited with work to renovate and rehabilitate Rensselaer's "green-roof" buildings, which date to the Ricketts era. He also supported an award-winning, faculty-led effort to improve the undergraduate learning environment.[24]

Pipes had a difficult relationship with Rensselaer's professoriate. Minutes of meetings of Rensselaer's faculty senate from the era, for example, suggested that the Institute's faculty leaders were concerned about changes in budgeting processes and questioned the administration's commitment to research and doctoral-level education.[25] That discontent boiled over on March 31, 1998, when the faculty senate approved a vote of no confidence in the president. Pipes announced the next day that he would resign, effective that July. "This is a very important time to have the institution heal itself and that requires a new person to help with that healing process," Pipes told a local newspaper. "It's time to pass on the baton to someone who can take up the responsibility and bring the community together."[26] Pipes went on to serve academic appointments at the College of William & Mary, the University of Akron, and Purdue University.[27]

Once again, Rensselaer looked to its own ranks for someone to lead the Institute temporarily. Trustee Neal Barton, who had earned both his undergraduate and graduate degrees at Rensselaer, accepted the challenge. He served as acting president from April of 1998 to July of 1999. Barton is widely credited with having done much to cool tensions across campus and with bringing stability to the Institute during a period of upheaval and uncertainty.

Having seen five presidents in just 14 years, Rensselaer's Trustees knew they were at a critical crossroads. Berg, Schmitt, and Pipes had each brought value to the campus and made progress, but none had been able to develop a presidency that propelled Rensselaer forward with the effect of a Palmer Ricketts or a George Low.

While an immediate set of issues precipitated Pipes' departure, it was becoming clear that Rensselaer's problems were not merely that it could not find a president capable of leading the Institute to a new level of accomplishment. The Rensselaer Trustees recognized that even broader problems had to be addressed. For too long, the Institute had not evidenced the kind of forward momentum that marks an

When it came to a decision about who would next lead Rensselaer, the stakes could not have been higher. Time was running out. This time, as Board Chairman Samuel Heffner put it, "We really had to get it right."

institution that is making progress. An institutional stasis had taken hold. The campus community was fractured and morale was low. The reasons were deep, systemic, and perhaps ultimately paralytic in terms of the university's ability to cast out in new directions.

It was becoming clearer that the Institute had not been able to capitalize fully on its considerable historic legacies and its inherent potential to recast itself in the latter part of the 20th century as an institution that could lead the pack in the 21st century. In the 14 years since George Low had died, Rensselaer had not moved aggressively to put the Institute on track to claim its rightful place among the very top research universities.

Rensselaer Trustee John W. Carr, a graduate of Rensselaer's architecture school in 1977 who went on to a successful career as an attorney on Wall Street, perceived at the time that Rensselaer was not realizing its potential. "We were atrophied," he said. Carr recalled some context that another Trustee, Myles N. Brand, class of 1964, had provided in a Board meeting. Brand observed that Rensselaer was a great technological university before World War II, Carr said. During and after the war, schools like Rensselaer had benefitted from a massive influx of government research funding. Many of the universities that Rensselaer aspired to compete with had capitalized on that money to develop relatively large capacities for research. But Rensselaer did not go that route. As a consequence, Carr recalls Brand saying, "they are what they are, and we are still what we were before the war."[28]

Studying the Institute from his perspective as both a businessman and an engineer, Trustee Paul J. Severino, class of 1969, also found himself wondering what was happening to his alma mater. "I had a sense that we were struggling from a budget point of view," he said. "That certainly was the case. We were also struggling from a ratings point of view. We were slipping. You looked at it and said, well, what's the problem here? This is a great institution. What's wrong?"[29]

Trustee Jeffrey L. Kodosky, class of 1970—one of the brilliant minds that created the phenomenally successful high-tech firm National Instruments—feared that his alma mater had "lost its sheen" and was "on a path to obscurity."[30]

Trustees and others began to voice a fear that if Rensselaer did not right its tack, reposition itself, and move assertively to become one of the educational leaders of the 21st century, dire consequences could result. For example, Trustee Paula Loring Simon, class of 1968, today the chief technology officer for the Wildlife Conservation Society, recalled the nucleus of a long-term vision for the next generation Rensselaer that was embodied in a simple statement used by a committee appointed to help search for a new leader in the late 1990s. The phrase was "We would like people across the pond to have heard of Rensselaer." What that meant, Simon said, was that "we want[ed] to be a world-class research university." (Years later, Simon would express delight that the committee's simple line would have "morphed into something so powerful" under Jackson and *The Rensselaer Plan*.)[31]

The fact that it was again time for change at the top at Rensselaer had a tired familiarity about it—except that now there was consensus that when it came to a decision about who would next lead Rensselaer, the stakes could not have been higher. Time was running out. This time, as Heffner put it, "We really had to get it right."[32]

CHOOSING A NEW LEADER

Heffner realized that "we had to have somebody that had the foresight and the vision to put together a vision for Rensselaer." Beyond that, the Board was also looking for a candidate with the wherewithal and skills to "get it done"—to implement the vision.[33]

A half-dozen candidates were screened in interviews on campus. Three—including Shirley Ann Jackson—made the final cut. A distinguished physicist with a background that included a long stint as a researcher at Bell Labs, Jackson had been named by President Clinton in 1995 to be Chairman of the U.S. Nuclear Regulatory Commission. She was both the first woman and first African American in that role—a pair of firsts that were a familiar pattern in Jackson's life and career.

Heffner credits Trustee Mary L. Good with putting Jackson's name into the candidate pool. Previously tapped to serve on both the National Science Board, which she chaired from 1988 to 1991, and the President's Council of Advisors on Science and Technology, Good had been appointed by President Clinton in 1993 to be undersecretary for technology in the Department of Commerce.[34]

"I was driving around Washington, D.C., looking for a parking place when the phone rang," Heffner recounts. "It was Mary. She said, there is somebody that I think Rensselaer should take a real hard look at. Her name is Shirley Ann Jackson." Jackson had developed a distinguished record as a strong, visionary leader at the NRC, and Good felt that the qualities she had seen Jackson exhibit during the Clinton Administration could benefit Rensselaer.[35]

Each of the finalists was highly qualified. Two came from traditional academic backgrounds, having worked their way to successively higher positions of authority at other universities. Jackson was a wild card in the sense that, while she had an exceptionally strong record as a leader, that experience had come outside academia.[36]

About the other finalists, Heffner recalls that "we talked to people who could have minded the store again" and perhaps taken Rensselaer to "the next iteration."[37] The Honorable Arthur J. Gajarsa, class of 1962, whom President Clinton had appointed to the United States Court of Appeals for the Federal Circuit in 1997—and who had met Jackson in Washington—believed that Rensselaer "would have been well served" by one of the other candidates, but ultimately "not served as well" as it could be by Jackson.[38]

Several Trustees were surprised by Jackson's soft-spoken delivery during her interview with the Board. With louder performances, by contrast, the other two candidates won more points for presentation.[39] (Heffner would later realize that "the lower [Jackson's] voice gets, the more you better be listening, because she is telling you something. She never raises her voice.")[40]

Following the interviews, the Board went behind closed doors for extensive deliberation. Some Trustees leaned toward support of the two more traditional candidates, perhaps taking comfort in possible scenarios that would preserve many elements of the status quo.[41]

Regarding Shirley Jackson, there was concern that, while she had outstanding credentials and an illustrious record of career accomplishments, she did not have experience in university administration. Regardless, many Trustees thought that Jackson would be the very change agent that Rensselaer desperately needed.

Obviously on the verge of deciding a new direction for Rensselaer, the Board wrestled with a central underlying question: How much change do we really want, and at what pace? In that context, Trustee Barton remembered one of his Board colleagues saying "there's going to be a revolution in higher education. A handful of places are going to lead this. [Other] higher education institutions will stay doing the same old thing. A lot of them will suffer…. But if you want to be at the forefront, the leadership role, you want to have a seat at the table of the leadership group." The speaker argued that to get there, to ensure that Rensselaer would lead rather than follow, "Shirley's the person, clearly." Barton remembered that those words "made a big impression on me."[42]

Trustee Nicholas M. Donofrio, class of 1967, then the executive vice president of innovation and technology at IBM (he has since retired), asked his colleagues to step outside the proverbial box. "Just stop and think about it," he recalled telling his colleagues. "[Jackson is] the first in so many ways. Doesn't that, all by itself, create an appeal for you? If she is that determined, if she is that capable, if she is that good at doing all of those things—don't you think that if she comes here, we would benefit from that? That she becomes that kind of person for us?"[43]

Gajarsa and others knew that Jackson had successfully orchestrated necessary change at the NRC, running a complex organization in a challenging, politically charged environment.[44] Some Trustees characterized what they knew of Jackson's work at the NRC as truly transformational. Heffner came to realize that Jackson offered a powerful set of skills that included the ability to envision a bold new future for Rensselaer as well as the requisite expertise in leadership and operations to bring that vision to fruition.[45] Barton and others also remembered that Rensselaer had ventured outside academia to pick a successful leader before, when NASA administrator George Low was selected.[46]

Trustees who may have been on the fence began to see in Jackson the possibility of someone who could wake Rensselaer from its complacency and lead it in exciting new directions. Before long, the majority of the Board expressed a willingness—and in many cases an eagerness—to hire a leader who would most decidedly be an agent of change. The Board made its unanimous decision: Shirley Ann Jackson would become the 18th president of Rensselaer Polytechnic Institute.

"I think when we met Shirley Ann Jackson, what we saw was an opportunity [for Rensselaer] to do a jump-shift, or a quantum leap," said Gary T. DiCamillo, class of 1973, partner at Eaglepoint Advisors, LLC, and a past CEO of Polaroid.[47] And in some

Cornelius J. (Neal) Barton
Class of 1958
Trustee

Gary T. DiCamillo
Class of 1973
Trustee

Nicholas M. Donofrio
Class of 1967
Trustee

Arthur J. Gajarsa
Class of 1962
Trustee

respects, that was the point. By selecting Jackson, Donofrio said, "we asked her to put us in a place that was different. We asked her to take us to the next level. We asked her to give us a new game to play."[48]

As an African-American woman—the first ever to head a highly ranked national research university—Jackson made history the moment her appointment was decided. But making history was an integral part of Jackson's experience.

SHIRLEY ANN JACKSON

Born in 1946, Jackson grew up in segregated Washington, D.C. Her parents, Beatrice and George Jackson, strongly valued education and encouraged her in school. Although he had not graduated from high school, George Jackson was a voracious reader and had a gift for mechanics and mathematics. He saw that his daughter had similar aptitudes and thought she should be a scientist or an engineer.[49] Beatrice Jackson taught her children to read before they started school.[50]

"My parents believed in the value of family, the virtue of hard work, and the power of education," Jackson has said. "They believed in their children. They lived what they believed."[51]

Shirley Jackson's career in science was perhaps presaged by a multiyear research project that she started when she was eight years old. From the flower bushes near the Jacksons' home, and despite an allergy to pollen, she started collecting yellow jackets, wasps, and bumblebees. Keeping specimens in jars under the porch of her house, Jackson studied what the bees ate, and how different foods affected their behavior. She experimented by comingling different species of bees and watching what they did. She assessed the bees' behavior in daylight versus dark. And all the while, she documented her observations meticulously in notebooks.[52]

Although the Jacksons lived close to a public elementary school, that facility was closed to them by the segregation laws then in force. Her family had to send her to Parkview Elementary, the school for African-American children, some two miles away. No bus service was provided, so the neighborhood organized car pools.[53]

The Supreme Court's Brown v. Board of Education decision in 1954 opened some new doors for the young Jackson. All D.C. students were tested for tracking in the 6th grade—an IQ test on which Jackson scored in the top group. As a result, she was placed on an honors-level track starting in the 7th grade, in an advanced curriculum that even included Latin.[54]

"Aim for the stars," Jackson's father would tell her, "so that you can reach the treetops, and at least you'll get off the ground."[55]

Jackson went on to Roosevelt High School, where she took accelerated programs in both mathematics and science. In her senior year she took college-level courses in economics and calculus. She graduated in 1964 as class valedictorian.[56]

Given Jackson's accomplishments in school and her personal interests, her father and a school principal for whom she worked both thought she would be a good candidate to attend the Massachusetts Institute of Technology. Jackson's mother, however, harbored worries about her daughter going there. She knew Jackson would be one of very few black students at MIT. Moreover, sections of Boston had shown themselves to be inhospitable to African Americans. Arguing that the college choice should be hers to make, Jackson won that debate with her mother.[57]

Jackson knew her mother had a valid point. But she was not looking to be a pioneer. She simply wanted a quality education. "The reason I picked MIT," Jackson said, "was that I thought it would be nice to be in a place where everybody was interested in what I was interested in. I was not thinking bravery. I was just thinking about going to MIT and studying science and math."[58]

Accepted for admittance in 1964, Jackson was one of just two African-American women in an undergraduate class of 900. The two women and three African-American men in the class constituted the largest cohort of African Americans MIT had ever admitted at one time. Her education was funded by a combination of scholarships from Martin Marietta Corporation and a local Masonic Lodge, a campus job, and support from her father, who held two jobs.[59]

Jackson was reminded almost daily about how "different" she was. She would get to class early so she could claim a seat squarely in the middle of the stadium-style lecture halls, at eye level with professors who lectured from a raised floor. "But nobody would ever sit around me," she recalled. Student study groups also shunned her. "I just did my work pretty much alone," she said. She also lived alone in the single room she was assigned to.[60]

While at MIT, Jackson experienced racism firsthand. One year she was invited to dine with the family of a classmate who lived in South Boston. Headed to the subway after dinner, she was walking along a chain-link fence when a carful of men drove by. They shouted racial epithets at her. She heard the pinging of something hitting the fence, and saw that the men had what appeared to be a gun—Jackson was being shot at. Ducking behind parked cars, she ran as fast as she could to the nearby subway station. She jumped on a train that came into the station just as she arrived, and escaped. Another time, Jackson and a friend were chased by a group of white men who stopped only when they were engaged by a group of black men. Jackson also recounts an incident when she was spat upon in downtown Boston while trying to hail a taxi. "Boston was not easy," she said.[61]

On the academic front, Jackson excelled. In her freshman year, she took an elective course on the structures and properties of materials. She got an A, with a grade average significantly higher than the next closest person. Having proven herself academically, she approached the professor about the possibility of working in his laboratory. His response was encouraging, although his rationale was anything but. Jackson recalls that he urged her to think about majoring in materials, because that field involved making things and "colored girls should learn a trade." Jackson responded by saying "excuse me?", to which the professor reiterated his unenlightened thinking. Jackson kept her next thought—"I *am* learning a trade. I am learning physics"—to herself.[62]

After reflection, though, Jackson decided she still did want to work in the professor's laboratory. "When I went to see him the second time, he wanted to know if I could cook," Jackson said. "I said yes, and he said good, you are hired." Wary of the professor's motives—did he expect her to cook for him?—Jackson asked why culinary skills were relevant. "He said he knew I had not really worked in a laboratory, but he figured that if I could cook, I probably had some dexterity," Jackson said. No doubt it did not hurt that she had aced his course. Jackson ended up working for the professor for a summer.[63]

When she first went to MIT, Jackson thought she might major in mathematics. A freshman physics course with professor Anthony P. French, a Cambridge-educated Englishman, helped her realize she had more affinity for that discipline. Working to confirm her specific interests, she took a range of courses, including some in solid state and condensed matter of materials. She even tried electrical engineering and network theory. "I decided against engineering because it took what was known and applied it. Whereas I thought that with physics you discovered new things," Jackson said. "In my sophomore year, I started taking quantum mechanics and I just fell in love with that."[64]

Jackson earned her bachelor's degree in physics from MIT in 1968. Her thesis focused on solid state physics, then at the forefront of theoretical physics. Motivated, intensely curious, and an excellent student, she was intent on continuing her studies.

For graduate school, Jackson entertained offers from Brown, Chicago, Harvard, MIT, and Penn. Ultimately, though, she elected to stay at MIT, in part to help pave the way for other African Americans and women. She completed her Ph.D. in theoretical elementary particle physics in 1973. She was the first African-American woman to receive a doctorate from MIT in any subject, and one of the first two African-American women in the country to receive a doctorate in physics.[65]

Jackson chose to study at MIT because of its strengths in mathematics and science.

Ph.D. in hand, Jackson moved to Illinois in 1973 to accept a postdoctoral appointment at the Fermi National Accelerator Laboratory (Fermilab). In 1974, financial support from the Ford Foundation enabled her to spend a year in Geneva, Switzerland, as a visiting science associate at the European Organization for Nuclear Research (CERN). Over two summers during this period, she also conducted research at the Stanford Linear Accelerator Center and Aspen Center for Physics.[66]

During this period, Jackson decided to shift her research focus from particle physics back to an area she had studied as an undergraduate at MIT, condensed matter.[67] A dean at MIT urged her to seek research work in industry.

Upon finishing her postdoc work at Fermilab, Jackson interviewed at a number of corporate research laboratories, including AT&T Bell Laboratories and IBM. In 1976, she accepted the offer of a "limited-term" job at the former—"because it was Bell Labs," she said. IBM had also expressed interest in hiring her, so she told them to contact her in a year's time.[68]

A year to the day after she first talked with IBM, that company called her back for an interview. IBM offered her a research post. Bell Labs countered with the offer of a permanent appointment there, which Jackson accepted.[69] She would end up staying at Bell into the early 1990s.

Jackson's work at Bell Labs included research in solid state and quantum physics and optical physics. She worked closely with two eminent theoretical physicists, T. Maurice Rice and Patrick A. Lee. Her specific contributions included important findings on optical and electronic properties of layered materials.[70] Jackson's research focused on interactions of electrons with surface excitations, especially so-called polaronic effects, and how those interactions controlled electronic responses to light, magnetic fields, and other stimuli. Her studies helped in understanding how to tailor the desired properties of various semiconductor systems. Jackson was recognized for this work by election to fellowship in the American Physical Society, and later, to the American Academy of Arts and Sciences.[71]

In 1991, Jackson felt the urge for change. Having worked with faculty from Rutgers University who consulted at Bell Labs, she let it be known that she might be interested in moving to academia. Rutgers immediately invited her to give a colloquium, which led shortly thereafter to the offer of a tenured full professorship. "I thought it would be interesting to have students," Jackson said. "I always think of your students as your intellectual children." Personal considerations also came into play. Jackson had married physicist Morris A. Washington, a colleague at Bell Labs, and the couple's son, Alan, born in 1981, "was at an age where I thought it would be good to have a little bit more flexibility," Jackson said.[72]

Jackson enjoyed academic life. The physics department at Rutgers had hired several string theorists, and Jackson's appointment was also part of an effort to deepen its expertise in condensed matter theory. Jackson led a research team in theoretical physics, and taught both undergraduate and graduate students. She continued to consult for Bell Laboratories.[73]

Through work for numerous boards, commissions, and organizations, Jackson had started to attain prominence at the state and national levels as a thoughtful expert in science and technology. She had been asked to serve, for example, on several high-level commissions in New Jersey, including the New Jersey Commission on Science and Technology. Perhaps in light of her national reputation, Jackson was approached by the White House in the mid-1990s about the possibility of heading the U.S. Nuclear Regulatory Commission. In 1995 President Bill Clinton appointed her to serve as Chairman of the NRC, a post that required Senate confirmation. She would head the commission until 1999.[74]

Shirley Ann Jackson joined AT&T Bell Laboratories in 1976, conducting research in solid state and quantum physics and optical physics.

During her tenure at the NRC, Jackson initiated a strategic assessment of the agency that led to the creation and implementation of a new planning, budgeting, and performance management system. She conceptualized and introduced risk-informed, performance-based regulation to the NRC, using probabilistic risk assessment on a consistent basis, which has been infused throughout its regulatory programs. As a result, NRC Standard Review Plans and associated Regulatory Guides were changed to a risk-informed approach. This also led to the American Society of Mechanical Engineers implementing a risk-informed revision to its codes and standards for nuclear power plants and key nuclear components. Elements of risk-informed regulation were also incorporated into the nuclear regulatory programs of other nations. Jackson led the development of a new reactor oversight program, and created, with the commission, a license renewal process resulting in the first renewal (in March 2000) of the license of an operating reactor in the United States.[75] Putting the NRC on a more efficient and businesslike footing helped the agency become stronger overall and more focused on its mission. She also saw to it that the agency's ranks of top staff became more diverse.[76]

While at the NRC, Jackson spearheaded the formation of the International Nuclear Regulators Association (INRA) in May 1997, and was elected as the group's first chairman, a position she held from 1997 to 1999. The INRA membership comprised the heads of the nuclear regulatory bodies of Canada, France, Germany, Japan, Spain, Sweden, the United Kingdom, and the United States. As the first INRA chairman, Jackson guided its development as a high-level forum to examine issues, and to offer assistance to other nations, on matters of nuclear safety. Today, the INRA continues to operate. Its membership has expanded to include South Korea, with China as an "observer" member. Jackson also represented the United States four times (1995, 1996, 1997, 1998) as a delegate to the General Conference of the International Atomic Energy Agency in Vienna, Austria.[77]

"I seem to be able to get things done in real time," Jackson said.[78]

Jackson had been asked by President Clinton to serve another term at the NRC and was undergoing an FBI background investigation for that role when she was approached about the Rensselaer presidency. She had to get dispensation from government ethics officials to talk with the search committee. The offer to head Rensselaer came the same week her nomination for a second term went to the Senate for confirmation. Recalling that era in a conversation in her office at Rensselaer, Jackson said "I had to make a decision, and I decided to come here."[79]

Today, Jackson's expertise continues to be much in demand for board service and other volunteer appointments. In 2009, for example, President Barack Obama appointed

Jackson as a member of the President's Council of Advisors on Science and Technology (PCAST). Jackson is also a past president (2004) of the American Association for the Advancement of Science (AAAS), and former chairman (2005) of the AAAS board of directors. A member of the National Academy of Engineering (2001), and the American Philosophical Society (2007), she also is a fellow of the AAAS (2007), the American Academy of Arts and Sciences, and the American Physical Society, and is a member of numerous other professional organizations. She holds 45 honorary doctoral degrees.[80]

A life member of the MIT Corporation, the MIT board of trustees, Jackson was a member of the board of directors of NYSE Euronext from 2003 to 2010. She also chairs the NYSE Regulation Board. Jackson is on the board of regents of the Smithsonian Institution and is a director of IBM Corporation, FedEx Corporation, Marathon Oil Corporation, Medtronic, Inc., and Public Service Enterprise Group Incorporated. She is a member of the board of the Council on Foreign Relations, and a trustee of the Brookings Institution. She also serves as the university vice chairman of the Council on Competitiveness, and co-chaired its *Energy Security*, *Sustainability*, *and Innovation* initiative.[81]

Among other volunteer roles, Jackson serves on the U.S. Comptroller General's Advisory Committee for the Government Accountability Office, and has been a member of the National Advisory Council for Biomedical Imaging and Bioengineering of the National Institutes of Health, and the Advisory Committee for the U.S. Department of Energy National Nuclear Security Administration. She also has served on a number of committees of the National Research Council of the National Academy of Sciences.[82]

Jackson's prominence nationally and internationally was a factor in her nomination to head Rensselaer. Her stature and connections were seen as having enormous value for the Institute. Indeed, Jackson's high profile, especially in influential research circles, has been credited with, in turn, raising the profile of Rensselaer. Board Chairman Heffner said that there is inestimable value, for example, "when Shirley Jackson goes to the World Economic Forum in Davos, stands up before a world body, and is introduced as…president of Rensselaer Polytechnic Institute." Aware that Jackson, like many other university presidents, has sometimes been criticized for being away from campus too often, Heffner believes that the benefits that the Institute has reaped from her travel far outweigh any downside. Jackson "has become a world figure," Heffner said, "and in the process has taken us right along with her." Citing programmatic connections that Rensselaer has started based on Jackson's outreach, as well as the general visibility and publicity the Institute gains through her presence as a

From 1995 to 1999, Jackson served as Chairman of the Nuclear Regulatory Commission, an appointment that required Senate confirmation.

national and international speaker, Heffner said simply "you can't buy that, and I applaud it every step I can."[83]

The recipient of countless awards and honors, Jackson was the first African-American woman elected to the National Academy of Engineering, and the first to receive the Vannevar Bush Award for "a lifetime of achievements in scientific research, education, and senior statesman–like contributions to public policy." In 2008, Jackson received the American Society of Mechanical Engineers' Ralph Coats Roe Medal. She was inducted into the National Women's Hall of Fame in 1998. Cited by *Time* magazine in 2005 as "perhaps the ultimate role model for women in science," she was also named one of the Top 50 Women in Science by *Discover* magazine (2002).[84]

TAKING CHARGE

Jackson accepted the Rensselaer presidency with the proviso that she would first complete her work at the NRC. In the first months of 1999, therefore, she continued to work in Washington. She made a point, however, of making regular trips to Troy for fact-finding and consultation. She officially took office on July 1, 1999.

In accepting the Rensselaer presidency on December 11, 1998, Jackson had summarized her vision of the opportunities that presented themselves:

The Rensselaer mission, of educating the leaders of tomorrow for technologically based careers, has never been more relevant—and relevant on a global scale—than it is today. I feel deeply honored to be entering this position at this particular

Shirley Ann Jackson was inducted into the National Women's Hall of Fame in 1998.

juncture—poised as we are on the edge of a new millennium, fortunate to be able to draw on the enormous strengths of this great university—the quality of its faculty and staff, the wisdom of its Board of Trustees, the support of its alumni, and the extraordinary caliber of the students it attracts—in order to further the vision of Rensselaer as a technological university with a truly global impact.[85]

From vision Jackson turned immediately to action. Her next remarks framed five broad areas that, it would soon be clear, would be fundamental for her administration:

To actualize this vision requires us to innovate on the innovations already achieved in teaching our students, to strengthen and enhance the research base of the university, to continue and to expand the upgrading of our facilities, and to engage the larger community—locally, regionally, nationally, globally. All of this is predicated on a fundamental strengthening of Rensselaer's financial base.[86]

Finally, Jackson hinted at some of her own style as a leader. She said she hoped to bring to Rensselaer "leadership that will be characterized by the development of a shared vision, the clarity of that vision, the skill to articulate it, and the perseverance to bring it to fruition."[87]

Jackson shared more of her thinking during her inauguration on September 24, 1999. In her inauguration speech, she suggested that Rensselaer was poised to contribute significantly to finding solutions to global challenges. She argued that "[t]he application of science to these common purposes requires that we enhance our vital undergraduate program, reinvigorate graduate education, invest in research, extend the reach of our programs for working professionals, and foster the entrepreneurial actualization of technological innovation." She proposed that Rensselaer "must maximize the synergies that can be achieved from a robust range of strong research programs," while also sustaining teaching excellence of the highest caliber.[88]

"Where will Rensselaer focus to address today's and tomorrow's societal and global priorities?" Jackson asked in her inaugural speech. "Where does Rensselaer claim leadership now? What bold new initiatives should we undertake to assert unquestioned research preeminence?" To begin to answer those questions, Jackson proposed three specific responses. The first two—investing sufficient resources to claim leadership in the areas of information technology and applied mathematics—would build on some of Rensselaer's existing strengths. A third area—integrated research in the biological sciences, engineering technology, and computer simulation, under the broad umbrella of biotechnology—would draw on some of Rensselaer's strengths but create a wholly new academic presence on the campus. The latter proposal exemplified Jackson's bold thinking and demonstrated overtly that she was audacious enough to believe Rensselaer could fulfill such a vision.[89]

In a statement issued on the day of her inauguration, Jackson elucidated that vision as follows:

> As a premier technological university, Rensselaer fulfills its mission by achieving the highest degree of excellence at all levels and by rendering service to its community, the state, the nation, and the world....We will create an intellectually and ethnically diverse community with a global outlook, fully committed to both research and pedagogy. We will educate our students in depth, making them partners in the generation of new knowledge, while imparting intellectual agility and a thirst for lifelong learning. These are Rensselaer's historic ideals, and they are my vision as I look forward to the challenges and the opportunities that lie ahead."[90]

Parsing a few pieces of these paragraphs shows how Jackson had initiated a new conversation about Rensselaer. In a history he penned about *The Rensselaer Plan*, David S. Haviland, who had come to Rensselaer as a student in 1960 and would later serve his alma mater admirably as Professor, Dean of Architecture, Research Center Director, Vice President for Student Life, and Vice President for Institute Advancement, observed that the reference to "a premier technological university" establishes at the onset of her presidency an expectation that Rensselaer will aspire to the highest tier of higher education. Jackson would reiterate that theme many times as a goal in the development of *The Rensselaer Plan*. The concept served "as a rhetorical means for addressing what Jackson considered as a built-in inferiority complex at Rensselaer," Haviland observed. The call for excellence would be one of three nonnegotiable "markers" for execution of *The Rensselaer Plan*. The reference to diversity—broadly described as it is here—speaks to Jackson's goal that Rensselaer evince a wider breadth of faces, perspectives, and thinking. The reference to research, mentioned here before pedagogy, presages Jackson's vision to make Rensselaer a premier research university. Similarly, the phrase "students as partners in the generation of new knowledge" draws attention to the multiple advantages of having students engage in research. At the same time the sentence that starts "we will educate our students in depth" signals that Rensselaer's tradition of excellence in undergraduate education must and will continue.[91]

Darrin 308, the room in which Heffner announced Jackson's appointment, had again been filled to capacity for a campus-wide meeting on July 1, 1999. After thanking Neal Barton for his leadership as acting president, Jackson told the campus community that her plans for the days ahead included this extraordinary to-do list: "strategic planning, research enhancement, pedagogical innovation, upgrading and expanding facilities, diversity, community outreach, global outlook and impact, and strengthening the university's financial condition." She spoke to her hopes for three key campus groups—that students would be "educated in depth and technologically agile with a thirst for lifelong learning"; that faculty would focus on "providing a unique education …committed to being at the leading edges of their fields"; and that the Institute staff would work "at the highest levels, and [be] recognized for its performance." She also highlighted the importance of community and "the regard that all members of the community hold for one another."[92]

By this very early juncture in Jackson's presidency, it was abundantly clear that a new era at Rensselaer had begun. Setting a tone that clearly signaled "change," Jackson had started an intense and broad new campus discussion about what Rensselaer was and what it could become. The goal was nothing short of shaking Rensselaer from its lassitude and sparking reform on a multitude of levels. Jackson had articulated a new, much bolder vision for Rensselaer and, implicitly, had set a much higher set of expectations for Rensselaer's aspirations.

In a way that perhaps paralleled what her father and mother had told her, Jackson was urging Rensselaer to shoot for the stars. The rationale had as much to do with contributing to society as a whole as it did with reinvigorating Rensselaer. In conjunction with her inauguration, Jackson said that "in our rapidly changing and ever-shrinking world, the

The inauguration of Shirley Ann Jackson as president marked the beginning of a new era at Rensselaer.

technological creativity that is Rensselaer's hallmark has never held out more relevance or more promise."[93] The promise implicit in that observation bridges the original vision of Rensselaer's founding fathers, who foresaw an institution dedicated to the "application of science to the common purposes of life," and Jackson's vision for a Rensselaer that would bring its expertise to bear in substantively addressing issues critical to global society in the 21st century.

It was clear that Jackson intended to push aggressively to position Rensselaer as a leader in this realm. She relished that challenge, as she had embraced many previous challenges in her life and career. Jackson knew, however, that effecting change on the scale that she envisioned would most assuredly not come easily.

CHAPTER 2

PAST AND PROLOGUE

The nation's oldest technological university, Rensselaer Polytechnic Institute owes its founding to a series of opportune convergences of people, history, and geography.

To understand the legacy—and the challenges—that Jackson inherited, and to put her vision in perspective, one must understand the rich history of the Institute itself. The nation's oldest technological university, Rensselaer Polytechnic Institute owes its founding to a series of opportune convergences of people, history, and geography.

In the early 1800s, the still-young United States was well on its way in the transition from an agrarian-based economy to the Industrial Age. Positioned near the confluence of the Hudson and Mohawk rivers, Troy, New York, and its sister city, Albany, were ideally positioned to capitalize on the inherent potential of this budding golden age. Both had become significant hubs for commerce. Practically and metaphorically, this geographic area represented a gateway to exploration, expansion, and development of the new country from its roots in the East to what was then essentially unknown territory in the West.[94]

The two cities were also sited near the terminus of the Erie Canal, then a vitally important new avenue for the shipment of goods from established American cities in the East to emerging markets in the West. That waterway epitomized the transitions then taking place in society: its very construction had been made possible by breakthroughs in engineering know-how and technology, and its successful completion fueled industry by creating an invaluable route for the shipment of both manufactured goods and the raw materials from which they were made.[95]

The lives of two men who would be instrumental in founding Rensselaer intersected at Troy. Stephen Van Rensselaer was the Harvard-educated eldest son in one of New York State's leading families. Under a system of land ownership established by Dutch colonists in the New World in the early 1600s, he had inherited the title of Patroon of Rensselaerwyck, which made him the largest landholder in the state. Van Rensselaer's holdings totaled some 750,000 acres, encompassing much of what is known today as the Capital District of New York State. Van Rensselaer derived income from leases with tenant farmers—a typical annual rent might include 14 bushels of wheat, four fowl, and a day's service of horse and carriage. A generous and benevolent landlord, Van Rensselaer was known as "the Good Patroon."[96]

The man who was to become Van Rensselaer's partner, Amos Eaton, was something of a Colonial renaissance man whose life and career saw remarkable peaks and valleys. Intensely curious, the young Eaton studied surveying with a local blacksmith and Latin, Greek, geography, physics, and mathematics under a local pastor—academic pursuits that married theory and practice. After earning his A.B. at Williams College and publishing a monograph on the art of surveying, Eaton studied law—along with botany, chemistry, and physics. He entered into practice as an attorney in 1802, at the age of 26. Just a few years later, however, he was found guilty of forgery under what he argued—and legal scholars today might readily agree—were spurious charges brought by an unscrupulous land developer. The unfortunate Eaton was forced to sell his assets to satisfy creditors and was sentenced to life in prison in 1811.[97]

In prison, however, Eaton was able to expand his study of botany and geology. Concerned that basic textbooks were inaccessible to the common man, he developed a new method for delineating plant species in a relatively short single volume. He also penned a lengthy manuscript on mineralogy. Eventually, influential friends who were convinced of his innocence helped secure Eaton's release. He was freed from incarceration in 1815. Banished from New York State as a condition of his release, Eaton attended lectures at Yale University and lectured himself—in mineralogy and botany—at Williams College. He published a book on botany that sold some 13,000 copies. In 1817, Williams awarded Eaton a master's degree. Also that year, New York Governor DeWitt Clinton issued Eaton a full, unconditional pardon from his legal liens.[98]

Over the next two years, Eaton taught and studied widely across the Northeast. He was named the official lecturer of the Troy Lyceum, which worked to advance scientific knowledge. It is said that hundreds of men and women attended his lectures in Troy on botany, philosophy, and chemistry. He also lectured twice a week at the Troy Female Seminary, founded by Emma Willard, an early advocate of education for women. During this period, Governor Clinton asked Eaton to lecture on the applications of

Stephen Van Rensselaer
Founder

geology and chemistry in agriculture to the members of the state's legislature—where he met and befriended assemblyman Stephen Van Rensselaer.[99]

First elected to the state assembly in 1789 when he was 25, Van Rensselaer had by this time been elected lieutenant governor of New York, and mounted an unsuccessful campaign for governor. (He would later be elected to Congress.) Van Rensselaer's career in politics was paralleled by a strong and abiding interest in education. He had served as a trustee of Union and Rutgers colleges, and had given financial support to the Albany Academy, a day school for boys, where he served as the first chair of the board of directors.[100]

Van Rensselaer and other leaders at the time recognized that the Erie Canal could open doors for expansion of agriculture, manufacturing, and other economic development. The Patroon readily agreed to a suggestion from Eaton that the latter conduct an agricultural and geologic survey of the canal's route. (Van Rensselaer had earlier paid Eaton and colleagues to survey two local counties.) The project also included lectures by Eaton on agriculture topics in villages along his 1,000-mile journey. Eaton's success in surveying the canal led to Van Rensselaer's approval of another project, a geological survey of New York State, the first-ever such statewide investigation.[101]

While Eaton's explorations were successful in the sense that they created relevant, helpful new knowledge, they had another important outcome: During this period, Eaton envisioned the idea of starting a new scientific school in Troy. Such an academic endeavor would be revolutionary, though—Eaton wrote of bringing the science of chemistry in essence down from the ivory tower and placing it "within reach of the laboring agriculturalist, the industrious mechanic, and the frugal housewife." His ideal would also be about applying scientific principles "to the common purposes of life."[102]

Eaton documented his ideas in a letter to Van Rensselaer on August 21, 1824. The heart of his notion was a school that would apply the principles of science in addressing practical problems. Rather than merely absorbing knowledge from lectures, students would take an active role in their own learning, conducting rather than watching experiments and sharing what they learned with colleagues. Eaton asked Van Rensselaer to help finance the school. Not more than six weeks later, Van Rensselaer agreed to the request.[103]

On November 5, 1824, Van Rensselaer himself wrote a letter about the school that echoed Eaton's thinking. Addressing the Reverend Samuel Blatchford, he wrote, "I have established a school at the north end of Troy, in Rensselaer County in the building usually called the Old Bank Place, for the purpose of instructing persons, who may choose to apply themselves, in the application of science to the common purposes of life." Interestingly, the letter also spoke of "instructing…sons and daughters," reflecting Eaton's belief that women as well as men should benefit from education. Van Rensselaer's letter, later dubbed "The Founding Document," was read at the opening of what was named The Rensselaer School—the educational institution that would ultimately become Rensselaer Polytechnic Institute. Blatchford was hired as the first president in a succession that today extends to Dr. Shirley Ann Jackson.[104]

The Rensselaer School quickly grabbed a solid foothold. As the student body expanded, highly qualified faculty were slowly added to assist the main professor, Amos Eaton. Importantly, too, the curriculum evolved. Recognizing the skill sets that were required to support the country's burgeoning manufacturing industries and the development of railroads and other infrastructure, Eaton added courses in technology and engineering. The Rensselaer School was the country's first institution of higher learning to offer a degree in civil engineering, a landmark that would be lauded in 2010 by the American Society of Civil Engineers. The school can also lay claim to being the nation's first school of agriculture.[105]

Amos Eaton
First head of school

Perhaps reflecting its success, the school's name was changed in 1832 to The Rensselaer Institute. The school also moved to a more spacious building.[106]

Four years after the school's founding, courses in chemistry and natural philosophy were opened to women. Women were allowed in general lectures but conducted their experiments separately from their male counterparts, with a woman supervisor. Women also lectured at the school.[107]

Neither Eaton nor his patron could likely imagine that 10 words from Van Rensselaer's letter—"the application of science to the common purposes of life"— would live on into the 21st century. The principles encapsulated in that short quote have served over time as a touchstone and beacon that have guided the evolution of The Rensselaer School into one of the world's leading technological universities—and which still inform the mission of Rensselaer Polytechnic Institute.

FROM THE INDUSTRIAL AGE INTO THE 20TH CENTURY

Rensselaer can point to a rich heritage of success in the application of science to the common purposes of life. From early in its history, the Rensselaer Institute educated alumni and alumnae who made their way into distinguished positions of leadership in academia and across society. James Hall, for example—class of 1832—became a highly respected scholar and scientist who was named New York State's first official geologist and first director of the New York State Museum. George Hammel Cook, class of 1839, taught chemistry and natural sciences at Rutgers College and led the effort to have that school named a land grant institution.[108]

Importantly, too, Rensselaer alumni started to distinguish themselves through remarkable manifestations of creativity and inventiveness that added substantively to the fabric of life in the United States in the 19th century. A few notable examples tell the story:

Brooklyn Bridge. When his engineer father John was killed by accident during construction of his dream project, the Brooklyn Bridge, Washington A. Roebling, class of 1857, took over as chief engineer and builder. (After Washington Roebling was afflicted with decompression sickness, his wife, Emily, stepped in as his unofficial aide-de-camp and exerted a profound influence over the construction of the bridge. Among the first women leaders in the management of technology, Emily earned a law degree and championed women's suffrage.)[109] With support towers that rest on large pneumatic foundations, the bridge represented an important technological step forward. The span held the record as the longest suspension bridge in the world from its dedication in 1883 until early in the 20th century.[110]

Ferris Wheel. George W.G. Ferris, class of 1881, founded a Pittsburgh-based firm that tested and inspected metals for railroads and bridge builders. Rising to a challenge that America's civil engineers produce something for the 1893 World Columbian Exposition in Chicago that would rival the Eiffel Tower, built for the Paris Exposition, Ferris captured professional admiration and public imagination with the Ferris Wheel. It rose 250 feet and carried 36 cars, each with a capacity for 40 passengers, revolving under perfect control and stable against the strongest winds from Lake Michigan.[111]

Baking powder. Eben N. Horsford, class of 1838, is widely credited with inventing baking powder and successfully bringing it to market through his company, Rumford Baking Powder, still in existence today.[112]

Water purification. Hiram F. Mills, class of 1856, pioneered the development of sanitary engineering in America. He developed the first slow-sand filtration system to eliminate bacteria in drinking water, a discovery that led to significant reductions in rates of typhoid fever and marked the beginning of a new era in municipal engineering.[113]

The imprint of invention from the minds of Rensselaer's graduates is found throughout the last century. Their work had an effect across many aspects of life. A Rensselaer alumnus, Clay Patrick Bedford, class of 1924, supervised construction of the Boulder and Grand Coulee dams.[114] Emil H. Praeger, class of 1915, was a prolific civil engineer who designed the Tappan Zee Bridge, the Nebraska State Capitol, Shea and Dodger stadiums, and what was then the world's largest telescope. His work played a prominent role in one of the most consequential events of the past century: he designed the rectangular floating concrete breakwaters, code-named "Phoenix," that were constructed in England and floated across the English Channel to form a protected harbor for the invasion of Normandy in World War II.[115]

The stream of important inventions from Rensselaer Polytechnic Institute continued throughout the 20th century. Again, a few representative examples:

Pre-shrunk shirts. As a student, Sanford L. Cluett, class of 1898, invented a bubble sextant for celestial navigation. He would go on to hold more than 200 patents but is best known for having discovered a way to process cloth to reduce shrinkage, which came to be called Sanforizing.[116]

Eben N. Horsford
Class of 1838

Benjamin Franklin Greene
Class of 1842

Hiram F. Mills
Class of 1856

George W.G. Ferris
Class of 1881

Washington A. Roebling
Class of 1857

Emily Roebling

Emil H. Praeger
Class of 1915

J. Erik Jonsson
Class of 1922

Allen B. Du Mont
Class of 1924

Robert G. Loewy
Class of 1947

Raymond S. Tomlinson
Class of 1963

Cathode ray tube. Allen B. Du Mont, class of 1924, developed the first commercially practical and durable cathode ray tube for television—in essence founding what would become the American television industry.[117]

Silicon transistor. A graduate of the class of 1922, J. Erik Jonsson joined Geophysical Service Inc., later to become Texas Instruments, where he oversaw research and development that led to the company's invention of silicon transistors. The company made the first transistor radio and the first hand-held calculator. Later, it produced the integrated circuit and single-chip microcomputer.[118]

Aviation design. A graduate of the class of 1947, Robert G. Loewy, had a powerful impact on the field of vertical flight. He has been recognized for contributions to aircraft dynamics, particularly for rotary-wing aircraft, and for solving engineering problems in helicopter and launch-vehicle dynamics.[119]

@ sign for email. Raymond S. Tomlinson, class of 1963, is credited with having invented network electronic mail, one of the earliest versions of email. Tomlinson had the idea to merge an intra-machine message program with another program developed for transferring files in a distributed computer network. He made history when he chose the @ sign to connect the user name with the destination address for directing emails.[120]

NOTABLE LEADERS

Stephen Van Rensselaer and Amos Eaton established a precedent of accomplished, dedicated individuals providing vision and strong leadership at critical junctures in Rensselaer's history. Another such figure, Benjamin Franklin Greene, played a decisive role in modernizing and broadening Rensselaer's curriculum.

A graduate of the Rensselaer class of 1842, Greene was teaching at Washington College when Rensselaer's Trustees hired him as the lead professor at his alma mater. Self confident, even bold, Greene anointed himself as Rensselaer's director, a new title for Rensselaer, roughly equivalent to today's chief academic officer.[121]

Greene recognized that the United States at the time, just prior to the Civil War, was a technological society. The development of cities and proliferation of railroads, bridges, and other products of engineering were trends that would continue and expand. To meet the challenges of this new age, and to expand capacity in technology, citizens would need strong skills and robust training. Greene saw that Rensselaer was poised to meet this need, but would need to institute some significant changes.[122]

After studying Rensselaer's curriculum and comparing it thoughtfully with educational offerings at other institutions, including leading schools in Europe, Greene reported his findings in a treatise published in 1855 titled "The Rensselaer Polytechnic Institute." Greene argued that Rensselaer's curriculum at the time—which he summarized as "instruction in mathematics, physics, chemistry, geology, and natural history, with their applications to civil engineering, the arts, manufactures, and agriculture"—was "vague" and, because it sought to cover such wide academic terrain, "too comprehensive in reach" and therefore ultimately ineffective. Moreover, he said, at one year it was too short to deliver fully on its promise of developing experts.[123]

To ameliorate those deficiencies, Greene proposed a new, "narrowed" curriculum that was "wholly reorganized upon the basis of a general polytechnic institute" and restricted to "architecture and engineering." Under Greene's reorganization, Rensselaer would be devoted to "[t]he education of architects and civil, mining, and topographical engineers, upon an enlarged basis and with a liberal development of mental and physical culture." To develop truly specialized experts, he suggested that Rensselaer's program be expanded from one year to three.[124]

In essence, Greene proposed a curriculum that put scientific thinking at the core in a way parallel to the manner in which more traditional universities focused on the liberal arts. His vision was of a Rensselaer that would deliver rigorous, specialized instruction of a quality and breadth on a par with liberal arts institutions, but focused directly on preparation for technical careers. This approach, he suggested, would prepare students from the United States to flourish in the age of technology. That is not to say, however, that Greene advocated a narrow curriculum. On the contrary, he wanted students to study science, literature, philosophy, rhetoric, and the arts as a foundation for then developing more technical knowledge and skills. Greene also outlined plans for technical schools—including civil, mining, and mechanical engineering along with architecture—along with ideas for buildings to house the schools in campus quadrangles.[125]

Greene fell into disfavor with Rensselaer's Trustees—it has been suggested that they found him too lax in financial reporting—and he resigned abruptly in 1859. Still, he had an indelible impact on the Institute. Greene's reorganization of the curriculum attracted more students, raising tuition revenues and enabling the hiring of more faculty. It would take many decades, however, before his ideas would be fully realized. (Rensselaer's School of Architecture, for example, was not established until 1929.) Nonetheless, he created the impetus that widened Rensselaer's somewhat modest and limited vision of itself and introduced a broader, much more ambitious focus. The Rensselaer of today owes much to Greene's vision.[126]

Greene's ideals were certainly the impetus behind yet another name change for the young school, from Rensselaer Institute to Rensselaer Polytechnic Institute, which took place in 1861.[127]

Rensselaer students were active on both sides of the War between the States. The student president of the class of 1861, James Cromwell, was killed at Gettysburg. An alumnus of the class of 1858, William Metcalf, managed an iron factory that produced heavy weaponry for the Union. Iron manufacturer John Flack Winslow, a Rensselaer Trustee who would be appointed president in 1865, along with his business partner John Griswold, also a Trustee, contracted to provide plates for the ironclad USS *Monitor*.[128]

A major fire in 1862 destroyed most of downtown Troy—and the main building that Rensselaer inhabited. Friends of Rensselaer, led by John Winslow, rallied to raise funds to build quickly a new structure on a better site. Rensselaer's Main Building, built at a cost of $44,000, opened in 1864. It was the first Rensselaer building specifically constructed for the Institute. Two years later, the Winslow Chemical Laboratory was built nearby.[129]

During the ensuing four decades, Rensselaer was led by several capable if somewhat unremarkable presidents. John Winslow served as president until 1868. Thomas C. Brinsmade, James Forsyth, and John H. Peck succeeded Winslow as the next presidents of Rensselaer, with Peck serving until 1901. In 1870, a committee of Rensselaer Trustees undertook a comprehensive review of the Institute's programs. Their findings, *The Report of the Holley Commission*, recommended sweeping changes, including stronger science courses, higher student admission requirements, new professorial appointments in mechanical engineering, physics, and electricity, and courses to improve student communications skills. While perhaps forward thinking, the report was not supported by the faculty and its recommendations were not adopted.[130]

It has been suggested that Rensselaer between the Civil War and the late 1800s did its work well, graduating qualified students and attracting quality faculty. A long catalogue of accomplishments by alumni during this period supports that finding. Rensselaer alumni were instrumental, for example, in building railroad systems that stood as one of the most prominent manifestations of the Industrial Age.[131]

At the same time, it also could be argued that Rensselaer lost ground during this period by virtue of not moving forward aggressively enough, or with adequate dispatch,

An 1891 advertisement for a new leader for Rensselaer said that one qualification was that candidates should be "fully awake to the needs of the time."

to stay in touch with its times. As the demand for railroad construction peaked, for example, Rensselaer seems to have not had the foresight, or the courage, to shift focus from the railroad-oriented engineering that had become a cornerstone at the Institute, in order to retool itself to capitalize on emerging opportunities. Moreover, as it approached the end of the 1800s, Rensselaer was tuition-dependent, had only a paltry endowment, had too small a library, and was not adequately outfitted with technological and scientific equipment. Offering just one engineering degree, in civil engineering, Rensselaer was in some respects behind the curve in terms of meeting the needs of a society that was fast evolving new demands for engineered products and processes, such as mass production.[132]

Perhaps reflecting an awareness of the lassitude in which the Institute found itself, an 1891 advertisement for a new academic director said that one qualification was that candidates should be "fully awake to the needs of the time."[133] Elevating faculty member Palmer C. Ricketts to that post in early 1892, the Institute set in motion an era of transformation that Ricketts would lead well into the next century.

A graduate of the class of 1875, Ricketts had stayed on at the Institute as an assistant professor in mathematics and astronomy. In 1884, he was appointed to be the William H. Hart Professor of Rational and Technical Mechanics. A respected educator, Ricketts also practiced engineering. He consulted on various railroad bridge projects, for example, and served Troy as chief engineer of its Public Improvement Commission. He also held railroad-related patents and conducted field research.[134]

As Academic Director, Ricketts pioneered the marketing and promotion of Rensselaer (without, however, using such terms). He organized a Rensselaer exhibit that won several major honors at the 1893 World Columbian Exposition in Chicago. In a speech there, Ricketts argued that engineering should be studied at the graduate level, after students had obtained a broad liberal education as undergraduates. Ricketts also introduced electrical engineering into Rensselaer's curriculum.[135]

It surprised few people when Ricketts was tapped in 1901 to become Rensselaer's ninth president. Before Ricketts hit his stride as president, though, two more fires hit Troy in 1904, destroying both the Main Building and the Winslow laboratory. Wasting no time, Ricketts charged forward with an aggressive fundraising campaign targeted to support new buildings. Within a year, Rensselaer had raised more than half a million dollars, more than double the prior value of the entire Institute. Two new buildings— one named for donor Andrew Carnegie, the other named the Walker Chemical Building, after another donor—were quickly erected.[136]

Ricketts continued to move Rensselaer forward. He obtained a $1 million grant—again doubling the Institute's value—from Margaret Olivia Slocum Sage, the philanthropist widow of wealthy financier Russell Sage. Ricketts convinced Rensselaer's Trustees to use a third of that gift to construct another building, the Russell Sage Laboratory, completed in 1910. Then the Institute's largest building, this facility housed two new departments, electrical and mechanical engineering, part of Ricketts's strategy to diversify the curriculum beyond its stubborn focus on civil engineering.[137]

Between 1910 and 1925, Ricketts also acquired extra land for the campus, more than doubling its size to 48 acres.[138] The expanded footprint created room for the development of a series of distinctive Georgian Revival buildings, with copper roofs aged green, that defined the modern Rensselaer. Collectively, the buildings are known even today as "the Ricketts campus." Starting in 1915, Ricketts also constructed an extensive quadrangle of student dormitories, each named for accomplished engineers and captains of industry, and a new dining hall.[139]

In 1924, Ricketts capitalized on the completion of the Troy Building, the new home for the civil engineering department, to promote Rensselaer in a gala celebration of the school's centennial anniversary. The two-day event attracted representatives from all over the world, including then Secretary of Commerce Herbert Hoover, who represented President Calvin Coolidge and delivered a major address.[140]

As the campus grew physically, Ricketts led the further expansion of the curriculum. In 1913, chemical engineering was added. Overcoming resistance from traditionalists, Rensselaer created a new department of arts, science, and business administration, designed purposefully to broaden the undergraduate education experience. New courses were started in the natural sciences, social sciences, and humanities. In the same period, graduate programs were formalized and made more systematic. And while it was not a top Ricketts priority, more attention was given to support faculty research.[141]

The final building of the Ricketts era was designed to house two more new departments—metallurgical and aeronautical engineering. Started in 1934, the year Ricketts died, it was named after the president.[142]

Ricketts's legacy cannot be overstated. He introduced what could be characterized as the most ambitious and comprehensive changes in Rensselaer's history, at least until Shirley Jackson arrived in the late 20th century. Ricketts led the Institute through a genuinely transformative expansion, with growth in the physical plant matched by increases in the Institute's resources—then valued at $11 million—and, importantly, the breadth of the curriculum. On his death, an editorial in the *New York Times* lauded Ricketts, saying he had "built the new Rensselaer…giving it a great group of buildings on a spacious campus" and had "liberalized the scope of its curriculum without imperiling its technical and professional training." Ricketts's changes had both given Rensselaer a "more extensive cultural horizon" and enriched its engineering education, the *Times* said, observing that his work had also influenced other schools.[143]

Ricketts was the proverbial tough act to follow, but several presidents who succeeded him carried the Institute forward, albeit not at Ricketts's pace nor with the same impact. William O. Hotchkiss, recruited from his position as president of what today is the Michigan College of Mining and Technology, was the first non-alumnus to lead Rensselaer since Amos Eaton. Hotchkiss, president from 1935 to 1943, is credited with having engaged faculty in Institute policy making, something that the more domineering Ricketts eschewed. On Hotchkiss's watch, Rensselaer created a new physics department, separated mechanics from civil engineering, and broke the department of arts, science, and business administration into departments of biology, English, foreign languages, and economics and business administration.[144]

World War II brought significant changes to Rensselaer. Given that modern warfare increasingly relied on technology, the United States government and its armed forces turned to Rensselaer (and other technological universities) to train highly qualified personnel. Rensselaer's population of civilian students was essentially replaced by military trainees. Professors left campus to join the military, and faculty who stayed shifted from their disciplines to teach where they were needed to support the war effort. To fill the need, Rensselaer extended its hours of instruction into the evening and accelerated the academic calendar (reflecting the continued need for technological training even after the war, faster schedules would be a way of life at Rensselaer until 1951). The focus on preparation for war also meant a new inflow of financial support for military-related faculty research.[145]

Apparently with strong urging from the Board of Trustees, Hotchkiss retired in October 1943. Rensselaer's next leader, Livingston W. Houston, class of 1913, took office that same month. A Rensselaer Trustee who served as the Executive Vice President of Rensselaer near the end of the Hotchkiss era, Houston had a long career with the Ludlow Valve Manufacturing Company, capped with appointments as president and board chair.[146]

Houston oversaw dramatic and rapid postwar growth at Rensselaer—the student population exploded from 932 in 1945 to 3,452 in 1946 to 4,485 in 1948 (some 4,000 of whom were undergraduates). Graduate study was made a separate school in 1957 and a separate center for specialized graduate education was established in Hartford, Connecticut. An evening school was started in 1949. There was growth across Rensselaer's programs, most notably in mechanical and electrical engineering, physics,

James Forsyth
President, 1868–1886

Palmer C. Ricketts
Class of 1875
President, 1901–1934

Livingston W. Houston
Class of 1913
President, 1944–1958

Richard G. Folsom
President, 1958–1971

Richard J. Grosh
President, 1971–1976

George M. Low
Class of 1948
President, 1976–1984

Roland W. Schmitt
President, 1988–1993

and chemistry. The size of the faculty tripled. Faculty research expanded (as just one example, a $2.5 million linear accelerator was installed in a new building constructed to house it). Institute funding overall was greatly expanded—at the end of Houston's presidency, Rensselaer's assets were valued at $51 million. Houston paid unprecedented attention to fundraising, public relations, and alumni relations. New links with industry were forged. Houston also devoted energies to improving student life on campus, notably through new athletic facilities.[147]

Houston is also credited with creating a modern administrative infrastructure at Rensselaer. He established the positions of both dean of faculty and dean of students, for example, grouped educational programs into four schools—engineering, science, architecture, and general studies—and created other special offices and administrative systems. Moreover, additional changes further broadened the curriculum. In 1958, for example— the year Houston retired—new degree programs were introduced in language and literature, philosophy, psychology, and economics. New graduate programs in many of these areas were started. A new degree program in technical writing was established.[148]

It would have been extraordinarily difficult for Houston to match Ricketts's propensity for, and success in, building. Nonetheless, Houston did expand Rensselaer's physical presence. Among other acquisitions during his tenure, the Institute purchased 20 acres adjacent to the existing campus that housed a Catholic convent and chapel. The latter was converted to a library.[149]

By the late 1950s, Rensselaer Polytechnic Institute had evolved into a model that was aligned in many key respects with Benjamin Franklin Greene's vision from a century earlier of what might be called a technological university. Like a comprehensive general university, Rensselaer had grown to be able to provide students with strong preparation in science and technology, undergirded by grounding in the humanities and social sciences. The rise of science at Rensselaer to the level of a full-fledged school paralleled society's recognition of the importance of that discipline in economic development and geopolitical competitiveness.[150]

Responsibility for carrying that vision forward was next handed to Richard G. Folsom, Rensselaer's 12th president, appointed in 1958. Like Hotchkiss, Folsom was not a Rensselaer alumnus. An academic, he came from faculty and administrative positions at the universities of Michigan and California.[151]

During a presidency that would last until his retirement in 1971, Folsom oversaw the construction of several vitally important buildings, including the Jonsson-Rowland Science Center, the Materials Research Center, Cogswell Laboratory, a freshman dormitory complex, a new student union, and the Darrin Communications Center. More land near campus was acquired. Folsom is also recognized for having raised academic standards, promoted graduate education and research, strengthened fundraising, and hired capable staff that enhanced Rensselaer's administrative capacity. During Folsom's tenure, too, a Faculty Council (later ratified by the Board of Trustees as the Faculty Senate) was established to represent the professoriate's points of view and interests.[152]

The social upheaval that changed society in the 1960s and thereafter also changed Rensselaer. One effect was that students demanded, and ultimately received, more autonomy and control over their own affairs. Coed dormitories were started, and many regulations governing student behavior were rescinded. Responding to voices for change from many quarters, including its own ranks, Rensselaer's administration came to recognize that it needed to make the student body more diverse, and efforts were started to recruit more women and students of color. Both students and faculty demanded more say in decision making, and authority began to be distributed among many campus constituencies, a sea change from the days when someone like Ricketts ruled with more or less absolute power, and little or no dissent.[153]

By the early 1980s, undergraduate enrollment was up 50 percent against 1977 numbers. Graduate enrollment was up 100 percent. Research funding was four times what it had been.

The next president, Richard J. Grosh, would face these new realities from day one, in that both faculty and students let it be known that he was not their first choice to be Rensselaer's 13th leader. Campus-based observers suggest that lack of support from these key constituencies created a cloud over his presidency from which he was never quite able to emerge. Still, as president from 1971 to 1976, Grosh is credited with setting the wheels in motion for Rensselaer to claim true leadership in engineering. Grosh's vision led to the significant expansion of undergraduate and graduate education and research funding in the engineering school, and to the construction of a modern, $17 million engineering facility, the Jonsson Engineering Center. Grosh also oversaw construction of a new library that was named for President Folsom.[154]

Lacking support from faculty and ultimately even some Trustees, Grosh resigned and left campus in 1976 to head a manufacturing firm.[155] His departure opened the door for another strong president whose accomplishments—and forceful personality—matched or even exceeded those of notable past leaders like Amos Eaton and Palmer Ricketts.

George M. Low had earned both undergraduate and master's degrees in aeronautical engineering from Rensselaer, in 1948 and 1950 respectively. He went to work for the agency that would eventually become NASA, rising to be its deputy administrator. Put in charge of the Apollo space program after three astronauts were killed in a fire during training in 1967, Low directed the effort that put a man on the moon in 1969. Low had joined Rensselaer's Board in 1971 and, after Grosh left, was appointed the 14th president of Rensselaer in 1976.[156]

One of Low's first priorities was to develop a strategic plan, the Rensselaer 2000 Plan. Its goal was that by the end of the 20th century, Rensselaer would be widely recognized as a first-order technological research university. The plan foresaw continued excellence in undergraduate education and called for greater emphasis on graduate education. It outlined a path for growth in the size of the faculty and a significant jump in support for sponsored research.[157]

With strong support from the Trustees and other friends of Rensselaer, Low started a comprehensive capital campaign in 1978. Its theme, "Rensselaer, Where Imagination Can Be Applied to Achieve the Impossible," echoed Low's accomplishments in the space program. Against a goal of $38 million, the four-year campaign raised $52 million.[158]

Low focused on creating partnerships between industry and Rensselaer's academic programs. In the first few years of his tenure, for example, such collaborations resulted in the creation of new centers for interactive computer graphics, manufacturing productivity and technology transfer, and integrated electronics. In 1987, a few years after Low's presidency had ended, connections that he had established with industry would pay off when corporate leaders won approval from New York State's governor for a $30 million interest-free loan to fund a new nine-story building on campus to house the centers. Through purchases of what were then among the most powerful computers on the market, and the transformation of a former chapel into a state-of-the-art computing center, Low also made a point of ensuring that Rensselaer's academic computing power was second to none.[159]

Other accomplishments during the Low era included the development of an Institute-supported business incubator established on 1,200 acres of land in East Greenbush, some five miles from campus, that Rensselaer had purchased.[160] That idea proved the germination of what today is the Rensselaer Technology Park, home to more than 70 tenant companies in industries that include electronics, physics research, biotechnology, and software.[161]

Extending work he had spearheaded at NASA, Low made an effort to diversify the Rensselaer community. He assertively recruited women and persons of color to the faculty, staff, and student body, and awarded Rensselaer contracts to minority-owned companies. During his tenure, too, Rensselaer started special programs to introduce the field of engineering to groups that had historically been excluded from that discipline, and to provide summer academic support for minority students who had been accepted at Rensselaer.[162]

Cancer claimed George Low's life in 1984, while he was still in office. Even though he did not live to see the capstone year of the Rensselaer 2000 Plan, many of the goals Low and colleagues had outlined in 1977 were realized before he died. By the early 1980s, for example, undergraduate enrollment was up 50 percent against 1977 numbers. Graduate enrollment was up 100 percent. Research funding was four times what it had been. In 1982, a study by the National Academy of Sciences found that select engineering programs at Rensselaer were some of the best in the country.[163]

As we saw earlier, until the arrival of Shirley Ann Jackson, the presidents who succeeded Low could not match or best his record of accomplishment. Significant turnover in the top slot in the years after Low—five presidents in 14 years, including two periods when Board members stepped in as interim leaders—meant that Rensselaer could not benefit from the continuity that a strong leader, serving steadily over time, can bring in creating the traction necessary to move a university forward decisively, and to institutionalize change.

To be sure, there was much about which Rensselaer could rightfully be proud. Its engineering program, for example, was exceptionally strong and boasted a prominent reputation worldwide. With a focus at the intersection of technology and design, the School of Architecture had earned an important position as a leader among its peers. Rensselaer's School of Science had expanded its research portfolio and recruited new faculty, including a Nobel laureate, physicist Ivar Giaever, who had earned his Ph.D. at Rensselaer in 1964. The school that today is known as the School of Humanities, Arts, and Social Sciences had built unique and important programs that complemented the Institute's technological focus. The School of Management was building a strong program in entrepreneurship.

Still, as the 20th century came to a close, Rensselaer's Board of Trustees came to realize—as Shirley Ann Jackson would discover—that the Institute's traditional excellence was at risk. Any number of markers suggested not progress but stagnation and even decline. On both the undergraduate and graduate levels, the Institute was not attracting adequate numbers of the strongest students. By such measures as research funding and the size of the endowment, it was under-resourced. The size of the faculty

Ivar Giaever, Ph.D., 1964
Nobel Laureate

body was not competitive in terms of the institutions with which Rensselaer sought to compete. No major building had been constructed since the 1980s. Amenities and support services for students—even such basics as housing—lagged behind those supplied by peer institutions. Physically, the campus looked shopworn, and key maintenance had been deferred for too long. Beginning in the 1980s, the Institute experienced significant financial difficulties and deficits that led it to incent faculty to leave its employ, causing it to lose some of its best people, including tenured and tenure-track faculty, to other universities. It also began to hire, instead, a significant number of contingent faculty to teach its students.[164]

The factors that pointed to an institution that was drifting could also be seen as manifestations of deeper, more systemic issues. Looking at the curriculum as a whole, Rensselaer's academic programs lacked cohesion and comprehensiveness. There were troubling signs that Rensselaer's impeccable reputation in select fields, such as some of the engineering disciplines, was starting to erode. Slippage in key national rankings was one signpost that suggested that outsiders did not hold Rensselaer in the same esteem as they may have only a few years earlier. "We had been living on our reputation, I'd say for 50 years," said Board Chairman Heffner.[165]

"There are biorhythms in institutions as there are in people," Trustee Gary DiCamillo observed. "And there are times to grow and times to consolidate. And we had consolidated, I thought, long enough. By 1998, 1999 it was pretty well clear that we were either going to have to jump into the next orbit or we were going to be left behind. It was time for us to leap forward."[166]

Most troubling to some was that Rensselaer had not moved aggressively to establish strong positions in substantive and vital areas of academic and societal interest that other technological and research universities had pursued with vigor and success. In the 1970s, for example, MIT had created a division of health sciences and technology, designed to encourage research at the nexus of technology and clinical medicine.[167] In the 1970s and 1980s, Carnegie Mellon had pioneered work in robotics, software engineering, and supercomputing (and had seen its research budget rise some $12 million annually to more than $110 million).[168] Stanford University had claimed a major stake in molecular biology and biomedical applications, and was capitalizing on expertise that would fuel the technology behind the explosive development of the Silicon Valley.[169]

A strong argument could be made that Rensselaer could have and should have taken strong steps to claim leadership in any of these key areas—and perhaps explored opportunities in other emerging fields as well—and that doing so would have been a logical and wholly appropriate extension of the Institute's traditions and considerable expertise. But for whatever combination of reasons, decisions made in the latter half of the 20th century meant that Rensselaer did not move into these new fields. Rather, it remained essentially satisfied with its existing programs. While perhaps willing to make minor modifications around the edges of its programs, the Institute as a whole showed little interest in developing bold new programs—an effort that might have signaled that Rensselaer was, as they say, "on the move."

Of Rensselaer in the 1990s, DiCamillo said, "I recall it sort of being one foot in front of the other. It was not a dynamic place. It was a conservative place." Speaking specifically to the rise of the Internet age, for example, DiCamillo observed that, as that technology came into its own in society, "the context of this institution should have been changing." With its powerful brand name and existing expertise, DiCamillo suggested, Rensselaer could have done more to capitalize on the emergence of the age of information technology.[170]

Rensselaer lost ground, therefore, by virtue of not pushing forward into important new areas of research and inquiry. Moreover, the Institute's relative inertia in relation to what were fast emerging as the definitional disciplines of the day meant that the Institute missed opportunities to position itself internationally as a committed and serious participant in exciting new disciplinary realms. By not moving into these areas, Rensselaer fell behind other institutions that did so—and implicitly was not as competitive for research support, expert faculty, and highly qualified students.

In essence, the Institute had become complacent in its vision of itself, content to bubble along in much the same way as it had done for decades, with much the same goals and ambitions. It lacked a strategic vision. It lacked the advantages of strong leadership in the manner of Greene, Ricketts, or Low. The progress being made in Rensselaer's academic silos did not reach the critical mass needed to advance the Institute as a whole. Calls for change and boldness from the Rensselaer community seemed not to rise to a level adequate to spark bold moves akin to those being made by other institutions. Such circumstances not only helped sustain the status quo, but ultimately served as impediments that kept the Institute from flourishing, expanding, and—ultimately—fulfilling its promise as one of the world's leading technological and research universities.

Every institution or organization—whether for-profit, not-for-profit, or in the public sector—needs to reinvent and energize itself periodically, if not continually, lest it stagnate and wither. In the latter part of the 20th century, the necessary energies and focus to ensure such regular reinvigoration were not present at Rensselaer. The Board of Trustees and other members of the Institute's community began to fear for

Rensselaer's ongoing viability, to say nothing of its vitality. It was abundantly clear that change was needed.

As significantly different as she was from Rensselaer's founding fathers and its most prominent leaders, Shirley Ann Jackson was at the same time cut from something of the same cloth. She came to her position at Rensselaer fully ready to take charge and to make necessary changes—in short, to *lead*.

The vehicle that Jackson and her colleagues created to shake the Institute out of its complacency—*The Rensselaer Plan*—would prove to be both powerful and effective.

CHAPTER 3

DESIGNING *THE* "NEW" *RENSSELAER PLAN:* FRAMING THE PHILOSOPHY

The challenge that Jackson took on when she accepted the presidency was to help Rensselaer craft a new vision for itself—one that would build in appropriate ways on the Institute's considerable traditions but, at the same time, position the school to create the new traditions that would carry it into the future.

When Shirley Ann Jackson first came to Rensselaer Polytechnic Institute, she found an institution with a remarkable history. Rensselaer had earned a strong reputation by making significant contributions to society at critical junctures in history. From railroad and bridge engineering to modern manufacturing and the space program, much of life in the United States in the 1800s and 1900s had been shaped and improved by expertise that was formed at Rensselaer.

Jackson also saw, though, that the Institute was not as well-positioned as it could be, or should be, to serve society in the 21st century. While there were many pockets of forward-thinking research—research in "green" building technologies and lighting were just two notable examples—the Institute as a whole had not sufficiently capitalized on its strengths to extend itself into disciplines, programs, and avenues for research that would address critical emerging needs. Moreover, Jackson saw that Rensselaer, as an institution, had systemic shortcomings in its administrative structures and processes that hindered progress rather than helped, and that would have to be retooled if the Institute were to move forward in any significant way. Rensselaer was at a juncture in its own history when some argued it was coasting on past accomplishments rather than exercising the boldness of vision that was requisite to enhancing and extending its reputation.[171]

In one sense, therefore, the challenge that Jackson took on when she accepted the presidency was to help Rensselaer craft a new vision for itself—one that would build in appropriate ways on the Institute's considerable traditions but, at the same time, position the school to create the new traditions that would carry it into the future. A parallel challenge was to put in place an infrastructure—physical, fiscal, administrative—that could help that happen. Those considerations raised a critical question: How could the Institute best bridge what had come before with what would come in the future?

Jackson knew that Rensselaer would have to make hard choices about where it could make a lasting, significant contribution. She knew also that Rensselaer would need a robust and ambitious roadmap to guide the Institute to the bold new future that she envisioned.

In her inauguration address on Friday, September 24, 1999, Jackson observed that "one hundred and seventy-five years ago, Amos Eaton founded his revolutionary pedagogy on what he called the Rensselaerean Plan."[172] Now, she declared, it was again time to map a forward-thinking, bold, and ambitious course of action for Rensselaer. Jackson said:

> As the new century beckons, Rensselaer demands the forceful expression of a new "Rensselaer Plan"—one that will articulate new ideas—new ideals—and bold action. This Rensselaer Plan will capture our vision and guide our choices—in short, it will secure Rensselaer's position as a world-class technological research university with global outlook and global impact.[173]

"We are a comprehensive university and a comprehensive university has to have, and live by, a comprehensive plan," she would later observe. From the time that she conceived of developing *The Rensselaer Plan*, Jackson saw that the process—and the document—would lead to comprehensive change, "transforming the whole institution." Moreover, it would position Rensselaer for the 21st century—in effect constituting what Jackson envisioned as "the 21st-century embodiment of the Rensselaerean idea."[174]

Using carefully considered language, Jackson framed five questions that Rensselaer needed to address—and that would become central in the institutional planning processes that her appointment sparked:

First, what defines the intellectual core in key disciplines at Rensselaer? Is it important, and why? True excellence requires such definition and examination.

Second, in these disciplines, are we in a leadership position? Do we set the standard and the agenda? These areas will serve as our foundation.

Third, if we are not in a leadership position, do we have the underlying strengths and capabilities necessary to move rapidly into a position of primacy with the proper focus and investment? We will build on these areas of strength.

Fourth, are there areas that are so vital that we must create a presence in order to stand in the community of world-class universities? We will stake out an identity in these critical disciplines.

And *finally*, what areas of current endeavor must we be willing to transform—or to give up—in order to focus our resources and our energies to create the impact we envision? We will make the difficult decisions that are required by a fundamental commitment to our highest ideals.[175]

Pledging to give her utmost to see the plan come to fruition, Jackson said that "[t]he realization of *The Rensselaer Plan*—the Rensselaer dream—requires greatness from all of us, places demands on all of us, and will elevate all of us."[176]

Thus, at the official onset of her presidency, Jackson issued what was in effect a provocative and even audacious challenge—that in the context of all that the Institute had achieved to that point in its history, the Rensselaer community now needed to look deep within itself to envision an even bolder version of the future Rensselaer. Implicit in the challenge, too, was the sense that the status quo would no longer be adequate or acceptable.

Essentially, the new president put every aspect of the Institute on the table for review, debate, and modification. Jackson knew she was asking a great deal, but she also knew that to demand any less would be shirking the responsibilities with which she had been entrusted. She also knew that implicit in the challenge that *The Rensselaer Plan* embodied was the promise that its successful implementation could raise the Institute to wholly new levels of excellence, relevance, and reputation.

Jackson wasted no time in starting work to realize the "forceful expression" of *The Rensselaer Plan*. The planning process started with campus-wide meetings in October of 1999, the month after Jackson was inaugurated, and called for the full plan to be completed and fully approved by the end of that same academic year, just eight months in the future—a breakneck schedule by the traditions of academia.[177]

The proposed timetable for writing the comprehensive roadmap was no less ambitious than Jackson's ideas for the plan itself. Indeed, given that the predominant culture in institutions of higher learning is to make change only at glacial speed, and only after slow-paced and often considerable dialogue, the velocity at which Jackson was determined the plan be finished and approved underscored that Rensselaer was about to undergo significant, perhaps even radical change.

Under typical protocol, a new university leader might spend his or her first months in office—or longer—learning the culture of the institution, observing, fact-finding, and allowing time for the institution to acclimate to its new leader's style, all as a precursor to what often is a fairly lengthy process that leads to development of a strategic plan or at least some strategic initiatives. Jackson thought Rensselaer could not afford to indulge in that luxury. "I felt that we did not have time to waste, because the university was behind where it needed to be," Jackson said. "We needed to do [a plan] right away." Jackson felt that she would learn in depth about Rensselaer—and have Rensselaer learn more about her—while the plan was being developed.[178]

The meetings that launched the planning process involved Jackson and her administrative leadership group. Over several weeks of long, intense meetings, the group scrutinized and analyzed the very core of the Institute in great depth. Given that virtually every university in the United States offers undergraduate education, for example, they explored how Rensselaer's undergraduate programs were important and distinctive, and how those qualities could be burnished. In the context of the relative predominance of the undergraduate programs at Rensselaer, the group worked to understand better the relative importance of two other core parts of the Institute, research and graduate education. The discussion examined how well Rensselaer served residential students outside classrooms and laboratories, and how well it was educating working professionals. Another major question was how well innovative programs created under Rensselaer 2000, the last strategic plan—such as interdisciplinary applied research and technology transfer centers, an incubator program, and the Rensselaer Technology Park—had been integrated into and contributed financially to the Institute.[179]

THE INITIATING DOCUMENT

The cabinet's discussions were designed to inform a written document that would engage the entire campus in the planning process. David Haviland, then the Institute's Vice President for Student Life, was one of two cabinet members who were charged with documenting the cabinet's thinking as writers. (G. Doyle Daves, who had recently retired as Rensselaer's Dean of Science but was asked to stay on for another year as Interim Provost, also served in that role.)

Jackson officially started work as president on July 1, 1999, although she had been making regular trips to campus ever since her appointment was announced the previous fall. Once on campus full time, she told her cabinet to plan on daily meetings. She first envisioned brief meetings where discussants would stand, report and share ideas quickly, then continue planning back in their offices. Given the prodigious amount of work that needed doing, however, the meetings soon turned to sit-down sessions that could last for half the day or more. Throughout the summer and into September, the team met virtually every day. Aware that Jackson was honing the central points of her inaugural speech, the team was also very much aware that it was setting the stage for momentous change at Rensselaer.[180] During this time, Jackson posited major research foci, in information technology and biotechnology, to rejuvenate and update Rensselaer research. But her ultimate vision was much broader, and she worked hard with her cabinet to frame that vision.[181]

Their first written product was a carefully crafted document that came to be called the "Initiating Document." Formally titled "Building the Rensselaer Plan," the Initiating Document was published and widely disseminated across the Rensselaer community on October 8, 1999.

As its name suggests, the Initiating Document was designed to officially launch the planning process. It was written to stimulate thought and action—and, ultimately, to produce a strong strategic plan for the whole of Rensselaer. It was also designed—although not always understood—as a request for proposals.[182]

Far from being merely an early iteration of *The Rensselaer Plan*, the Initiating Document took pains to explain carefully the expectations about what was to happen in terms of the process that would build *The Rensselaer Plan*. It detailed the principles that would guide the plan. It clearly laid out the process that the Institute would follow in building the plan. It provided substantial specific direction for participants across campus who were charged with developing and ultimately meeting the plan's goals. It delineated parameters for the planning process—suggesting, for example, that time for discussion would be ample but

David S. Haviland
Class of 1964; Dean of
Architecture, 1980–1990;
Vice President for Student
Life, 1994–2000; Vice
President for Institute
Advancement, 2000–2005

G. Doyle Daves
Dean of Science, 1989–1999
Interim Provost, 1999–2000

not unlimited. It included a timetable that clearly said the process needed to take top priority across campus. In contrast to typical planning practices in higher education, the schedule was extremely short. This was a signature "Jackson" approach, not unlike, in some respects, what she had developed and used as the Chairman of the Nuclear Regulatory Commission, but with a much shorter embedded timeline at Rensselaer.

Importantly, the Initiating Document articulated key distinctions between the responsibilities of institutional leadership (the Office of the President with her cabinet) and Institute "portfolios," such as individual schools and administrative groups. Haviland would later report on how the authors of the Initiating Document envisioned these distinctions:

> The schools and administrative groups are the intellectual and operating units of the university. These portfolios deliver the teaching, research, and services that define the institution, and thus it is their obligation to develop and present proposals for change. At the same time, the president and leadership team are responsible for overall direction and outcomes, and thus it is leadership's obligation to establish high-level structure (goal, markers, and boundaries); drive portfolio proposal-making by asking questions and demanding responses; and force the process with a very tight timetable.[183]

Clarifying such distinctions was necessary and significant in the context of Rensselaer's culture at the end of the 1990s. In the absence of consistent presidential leadership over the prior decade or so, the Institute as a whole had perhaps not devoted as much concerted attention to long-term goals and a "big-picture" vision of its future as might have been warranted. At the same time, inconsistency in presidential leadership had given rise to circumstances in which much of the Institute's planning and decision-making authority was dispersed and distributed among schools, academic programs, and other campus silos. Some of these fiefdoms, it could be argued, now wielded a disproportionate degree of authority and autonomy. It could further be argued that centers that held such power were

The new president put every aspect of the Institute on the table for review, debate, and modification. Jackson knew she was asking a great deal, but she also knew that to demand any less would be shirking the responsibilities with which she had been entrusted.

rather protective of it. Such circumstances created administrative structures and practices that were not always conducive to overall institutional development and vitality, and in point of fact had the potential to impede cross-campus planning and institutional progress writ large. Implicitly and at times explicitly, the Initiating Document made it clear to the campus community that this imbalance was recognized and would be addressed.

The importance of this early paper cannot be underestimated. The Initiating Document was a strong statement—bold in its scope and vision, somewhat provocative, and decidedly directive. While some room was left for interpretation, the principles presented in the Initiating Document—about the scope and processes of change—were deemed so important that they were explicitly considered nonnegotiable. In its 4,100 words, the Initiating Document showed a Rensselaer that was moving aggressively to reform itself, on a trajectory that was unprecedented in terms of its ambition, scale, and speed. In short, the document served as official notice that Rensselaer was now moving with dispatch to fulfill the mandate for change explicit in Jackson's appointment.[184]

The implications were significant. Virtually every corner of institutional life, across virtually every dimension of both academics and administration, was now subject to scrutiny and change. The Institute's programs, goals, mission, even perhaps its raison d'être would be studied and, if necessary, retooled. Every one of Rensselaer's long-held assumptions, practices, policies, and ways of working was subject to similar review and to modification, if not wholesale overhaul or even elimination. The Initiating Document made it abundantly clear that the transformation of Rensselaer had begun.

GOALS, MARKERS, AND CORE ENTERPRISES

The Initiating Document articulated not just goals for the institution, but markers by which ideas proposed as part of those overarching goals would be tested. Introducing a new vocabulary for Rensselaer—which we will examine in depth in this section—the document went even further. It identified "core enterprises" that would be foci under *The Rensselaer Plan*. Recognizing that the broad goals Rensselaer set for itself could perhaps overwhelm the progress of the plan by virtue of their ambition and complexity, the Initiating Document set forth "boundary conditions" to help focus action on what were admittedly expansive goals. It also delineated "directive questions" that each academic and administrative portfolio across campus was expected to ask of itself. Finally, the Initiating Document set forth a change-oriented process, "portfolio assessment," that would lead to the next steps in planning and implementing the Institute's new goals.[185]

In short, the Initiating Document provided everyone in the campus community with a common understanding of the issues that needed to be addressed, a common vocabulary with which to discuss them, and specific charges for action that needed to be taken and when. A strong sense permeated the text that the planning process was leaving the station and that everyone needed to get on board.

Because they were critical to the planning process and because they reflect the degree and depth of thought that went into that process, each core component of the Initiating Document merits a brief closer look.

Goal. The overarching goal for Rensselaer that was articulated in the Initiating Document was that "Rensselaer is to be a world-class technological university with global reach and global impact." Those carefully selected words stimulated considerable soul searching about what Rensselaer was and should aspire to become. Among other considerations, the discussion focused on such questions as whether the designation "university" was an aspiration or a reality, and whether Rensselaer was "in the top tier, near the top tier, or clearly out of the top tier." Rensselaer's planners asked themselves "Are we trying to be 'like MIT' or, for that matter, any other technological research university?" There was concern about the statement itself: "Was it lofty enough to inspire action, too lofty ('just fluff'), or not lofty enough ('after all, we were the *first* technological university in the U.S.')?"[186]

While, as we will see, a slightly different version of this goal would evolve in the course of finalizing *The Rensselaer Plan*, this text reflected the essence of the final goal and therefore served well as a cornerstone of the Initiating Document.

Markers. The Initiating Document made a point of identifying three key markers or standards that would inform and drive Rensselaer's planning and action: "excellence," "leadership," and "community." The three came directly from Jackson's inaugural speech. Excellence demanded that Rensselaer aim only for the pinnacle of whatever given issue or opportunity it was focusing on. Leadership insisted that Rensselaer examine and define "the intellectual core in each key discipline or enterprise" and determine those where the Institute held or could move to hold a leadership position, defined as setting "the standard and agenda." Community was a call for the disparate, semiautonomous component pieces that together constituted the Institute to unite and work together as "one Rensselaer" to develop and execute *The Rensselaer Plan*.[187]

Directive Questions. The Initiating Document said that the process of creating *The Rensselaer Plan* would involve the entire community in addressing five core

The Initiating Document essentially demanded that every corner of the Institute address the questions in an exercise of candid self-assessment—and report the findings publicly. It would not be acceptable or adequate to say "we have always done it that way" or "every university has this function."

questions—the very same questions that Jackson had raised in her inaugural speech (and which are quoted a few paragraphs above).

The questions themselves were pivotal in the plan for two key reasons. On the one hand, they provided a structural element that oriented the entire planning process toward one set of procedures versus another. Jackson had made it clear from the beginning that she wanted a planning process that "had the essentials put on the table by the president and her leadership team, with the campus basically answering questions, as opposed to the usual academic planning process, where you turn to every hamlet in the university and say, what do you want to be when you grow up?" Jackson wanted to avoid a process that would simply amass ideas and documents with no focus or cogency—a process that often leads to plans that are shelved as soon as they are finished. The result, one observer said, was that Rensselaer's approach to planning its future was "a question-driven planning process."[188] It was also meant to be expeditious. As Jackson succinctly put it, "you can talk forever, but at some point, you have to try to come to closure and capture the key ideas and move them along."[189]

At the same time, the questions also served the effect of drawing the entire campus community into a closely focused and much-needed inquiry and conversation about a relative handful of issues that were truly essential to Rensselaer's future vitality. Indeed, the Initiating Document essentially demanded that every corner of the Institute address the questions in an exercise of candid self-assessment—and report the findings publicly. It would not be acceptable or adequate to say "we have always done it that way" or "every university has this function." Instead, the expectation was that each campus function would examine its core purposes, and articulate how and why those purposes were central to the Institute as a whole.

The directive questions were Jackson's means to prompt the Institute to look deep into its soul. She wanted the Rensselaer community to ask itself fundamental questions about the Institute's intellectual core in academics and research. For example, was all that the Institute was doing in the broadest senses important in the world at large—and if so, how, and why, and for what reasons? Where did Rensselaer have the most impact—in what areas did it lead the world—and how and why? What were areas where the Institute did not lead and what would it take to claim a leadership position? What benchmarks and standards could be used to define positions of leadership? Were there areas in which the Institute did not have a presence, but were so vital and important to society that it needed to engage in them if it intended to be a leading university? Were there areas from which the Institute would be willing to step away in order to better redirect its focus and resources? Was the Institute capable of making that kind of change?[190] The point of the directive questions, therefore, was to engage the Institute in a deep, honest assessment of its very raison d'être—toward a goal of clarifying an overarching strategic focus and a roadmap for meeting strategic goals.

Core Enterprises. Implicitly challenging Institute constituents to think in terms of community rather than merely from the relatively narrow perspectives of their individual responsibilities on campus, the Initiating Document delineated four key areas— "core enterprises" —where Rensselaer should work to be a leader:

- Resident undergraduate education

- Resident research and graduate education

- Education of working professionals

- Fostering scientific and technological innovation (including optimal use of intellectual property, technology transfer, entrepreneurship, economic development, etc.)[191]

Boundary Conditions. Jackson and the authors of the Initiating Document recognized that these goals for Rensselaer were lofty, with high expectations and an overall perspective that encompassed the whole of the Institute—and, indeed, stretched well beyond, out into the world at large. From her considerable experience in the planning realm, the President knew that the planning process had to have some parameters, lest it result only in endless discussions or a hopelessly amorphous mush of final recommendations. To help focus the change efforts that would be part of *The Rensselaer Plan,* and to help ensure that change strategies aligned with financial resources for maximum impact, the Initiating Document defined what were called "boundary conditions."

The boundary conditions are one of the most interesting components of the Initiating Document. Effectively stakes in the ground, they clearly reflect what Jackson and her team thought were essential principles necessary to moving Rensselaer forward. They detail specific goals. They clearly define institutional priorities. They present specific standards by which progress will be judged. They suggest expectations for individual and institutional behavior. They can be seen as further enunciations of Jackson's vision for a transformed Rensselaer, and as another statement about her expectations of excellence.

The boundary conditions were shaped in the intense series of cabinet-level discussions that occupied Rensselaer's administration through the summer and into September 1999. Among other questions, Jackson and her staff debated just how directive the boundary conditions should be, and even how precise they should be in terms of specific numerical goals. More broadly, the discussion also considered how restrictive a boundary should be—after all, it was recognized, a "boundary" in science, for example, can be a complex phenomenon. Eventually it was decided that boundaries did not need to be one-dimensional, but rather could be considered as layers or zones where conditions change.[192] The end product of these discussions was a comprehensive set of guideposts that added considerable definition, richness, and clarity to the process that would produce the full Rensselaer plan.

Under the umbrella of "teaching, research, and outreach programs," for example, the Initiating Document said that Rensselaer's programs should strive to be "recognized for leadership." That standard called for programs "created and conducted by Rensselaer faculty and staff who are recognized leaders in their fields" and whose work not only receives recognition from peers off campus, but defines the discourse and sets agendas in a given field. Further, programs should be designed to be sustainable over time, should "strive to increase the impact of other programs," and be interdisciplinary. Programs that engaged partnerships with government, industry, and other universities were seen as advantageous, as were programs "rooted in technology."[193]

Boundary conditions for undergraduate programs included those just listed but also called for a "rich mix" of offerings for students of "compelling," "distinctive," and "content-centered" courses that would "employ a pervasive focus on interactive learning" and provide ample opportunities for students to engage in research.[194]

The boundary conditions that were designed to drive research and graduate programs made it clear that Rensselaer wanted to make a quantum jump in its research capacity. Toward that end the Initiating Document said that the Institute's research activity overall should support the goal of the Institute moving from its then Carnegie Foundation for the Advancement of Teaching classification as a Research II institution to attain Carnegie Research I level status, "via dramatically increased government funding and substantial corporate support."[195] (Since the Initiating Document was written, the Carnegie Foundation has revised its classification system significantly. The use of Roman numerals was discontinued to avoid possible inferences of differences in quality. Today, Rensselaer is classified under the relatively new Carnegie category "RU/VH: Research Universities (very high research activity)," together with institutions such as the Massachusetts Institute of Technology, the University of California, Berkeley, California Institute of Technology, Cornell University, and Georgia Institute of Technology.)

As another boundary condition, the Initiating Document said that Rensselaer's research programs would have "clear intellectual centers," would be "aligned with important sustainable societal priorities," would attract substantial external interest and funding, and would be "distributed among the academic schools." Reflecting directions that the President had suggested in her inaugural speech, the document further said that Rensselaer must delve into "must do" areas of research where it has not been well-represented, such as bioscience and biotechnology. The document called for Rensselaer to more than double the number of doctoral degrees it awards each year. Finally, Rensselaer would provide and maintain "a research infrastructure (faculty, research staff, and facilities; financial aid; charge-out; cost-sharing and intellectual property policies) sufficient to the task."[196]

When it came to boundary conditions targeted at programs for working professionals, the Initiating Document said that Rensselaer should develop programs with a "high-end, signature focus derived from frontier research and pedagogy," and that such programs should focus on educating leaders in society.[197]

Another central boundary condition was that Rensselaer would foster scientific and technological innovation. Here the expectations were that the Institute would provide "an environment that supplies the advice and critical supporting structures needed to foster and nurture scientific and technological innovation and entrepreneurship." To that end, members of the Rensselaer community would be "alert to opportunities for value-added technological innovation." Moreover, Rensselaer would engender an entrepreneurial spirit across campus, marked by "entrepreneurial creativity, risk taking, and value creation through partnerships, incubators, and other technology transfer mechanisms." Finally, the Institute would leverage its intellectual capital through "policies that encourage technological innovation and entrepreneurship… and generate intellectual property."[198]

The Initiating Document went on to delineate boundary conditions concerning students and the student experience. For both its residential undergraduate and doctoral research programs, Rensselaer would seek to recruit students with "top-tier academic credentials, intellect, entrepreneurial drive, and the vision and passion to change the world." The mix of students would include a "richness of experience and a range of financial capability," representing an "energizing range of intellectual interests," with a broad geographical representation of both U.S. and international students, and a focus on high-achieving women and underrepresented minority students. In support of student development, Rensselaer would provide an experience that "deepens capabilities (exploration, risk taking, problem solving, innovation); broadens perspective (beyond the individual to community and global); inculcates responsibility; and creates an integrated view of life and learning." Opportunities for leadership education and practices would be encouraged, as would faculty/student partnerships designed to create knowledge and foster innovation and entrepreneurship. The ideal, the Initiating Document said, would be to create "a thirst for lifelong learning coupled with enthusiasm for Rensselaer as a partner in that enterprise." The expectation was that there would be an Institute-wide commitment to student success, "both on campus and later."[199]

As a final set of boundary conditions, the Initiating Document detailed a series of "enabling activities" that would be critical to helping Rensselaer meet its goal of becoming "a world-class technological university with global reach and global impact." Adopting a robust research and technology agenda, the Institute would "lead in shaping federal and state research and technology agendas, optimally positioning Rensselaer." Another expectation was that Rensselaer would proactively identify emerging trends and programs in government research funding and build strategic collaborations with other universities and government to increase the Institute's influence and financial support. In addition to attracting increased support for research, the Institute also wanted to increase the size of its faculty and graduate student enrollment "in areas of leadership."[200]

Toward meeting a goal of doubling private investment in five years, Rensselaer would have to build partnerships and maximize alumni and volunteer involvement in efforts to secure financial support. Marketing and outreach on a global scale would be required to "project a cohesive identity" for Rensselaer and maximize private support. Corporate partnerships, long a strength of Rensselaer, would have to be made even stronger. In the interest of strong town/gown ties, Rensselaer would "create mutually beneficial alliances for technology transfer and regional economic development to better integrate Rensselaer into the life of the community" and help to attract new industries to its region, and would "participate in the redevelopment of the community fabric (neighborhoods, commerce, entertainment, gateways) especially in areas contiguous to the campus," emphasizing projects of mutual value to the city of Troy and the university.[201]

In terms of a physical infrastructure, the Initiating Document said that information technology was a vital linchpin: "Rensselaer will deploy information technologies and strategies that enable competitive advantage for programs and activities of strategic importance. Rensselaer will sustain an information culture, valuing information literacy and new methods for scholarly communications and electronic interactions." The Institute's physical plant would have to be fully up to the task of meeting "the essential research, learning, living and dining, cultural, recreational, and other needs of the Institute" outlined in *The Rensselaer Plan*. Addressing the problem of basic upkeep that had been put off for too long, another boundary condition was that "Rensselaer will plan investment in a deferred maintenance program ($100 million total) and continuing capital renewal (1.5–3 percent of current replacement value) for Institute facilities." Moreover, the Institute pledged to devote energies to the planning and construction of new capital projects.[202]

Additional boundary conditions focused on the Institute's financial infrastructure. Rensselaer would increase the value of its endowment via campaign gifts and investment return, the Initiating Document said, so that endowment spending could be increased from 10 percent to 20 percent of the Institute's budget. The Institute sought to "manage the pace and structure of debt financing" to improve its credit rating. A planned new budget model would focus resources "for maximum strategic impact while maintaining appropriate institutional flexibility."[203]

Finally the Initiating Document turned its attention to the people and processes that would support implementation of *The Rensselaer Plan*. A vibrant Board of Trustees was cited as one requisite for success of the plan. Another component of success, highly qualified administrative staff, would be held to an expectation of excellence and be given appropriate authority and compensation. Similarly high standards would be applied to administrative processes and services.[204]

As they were intended to do, the boundary conditions gave shape to the new vision for a transformed Rensselaer that was starting to emerge; provided direction for planning for the future that reflected Rensselaer's strengths but also assumed growth in new areas; gave the planning process focus; and provided a platform to help ensure that available financial resources would be applied with maximum effect to building the Institute's future.

Performance Plans. The Initiating Document mentioned only in passing an administrative element that would prove powerful in executing *The Rensselaer Plan*: that annual performance plans prepared by the heads of schools, administrative departments, and select other entities on campus would guide implementation of the plan and provide benchmarks for measuring results. "Once performance plans are approved by the president," the Initiating Document said, "the provost, deans, and vice presidents will have responsibility for implementation and accountability for results." As we will see, details about this important administrative process would unfold as the plan was implemented.[205]

Portfolio Assessment. The Initiating Document also presented a chart listing different institutional "portfolios," including the five schools (Architecture, Engineering, Humanities and Social Sciences, Management, Science), academic entities such as information technology and computer science, and a wide range of administrative offices and functions, from student life to the Board of Trustees. This representation was unlike other descriptions of the Institute's structure that had preceded it—for good reason. Subtly advancing the principle of institutional community, the chart made it clear that every aspect of Rensselaerean life had a home in at least one of the portfolios (there was acknowledgement that some fit in more than one portfolio)—with attendant responsibilities to the Institute overall. The implication was that the pieces of the Rensselaer community would not be allowed to remain solely in their silos—their comfort zones, if you will—but would have to engage with the community under the umbrella of *The Rensselaer Plan*. It also suggested that there was more inter-connectedness between disparate pieces of the Institute than those content in their own silos may have wanted to acknowledge. The portfolio structure, the document said, would provide "a basis for assessment and planning and, ultimately, a focus of responsibility and accountability for implementation" of the plan.[206] Thus, for example, the head of a specific department would need to plan in the context of the department itself, its school, and the Institute as a whole, perhaps also taking into account the department's connections with other schools and research centers.

The protocol also asked this question: "How must the portfolio change, within the framework of the markers and boundary conditions, to achieve the goal of Rensselaer as a world-class technological research university with global reach and global impact?"

The Initiating Document then moved into practical steps. It gave "owners" of each portfolio—be they deans, vice presidents, or other campus leaders—the responsibility for conducting a "Portfolio Assessment." That exercise—no small task—was to analyze "the current state of the portfolio" and address the Initiating Document's set of directive questions "as they pertain to the portfolio." A protocol for the assessment also requested that in considering the current state of a given portfolio, consideration also be given to its "centrality to the Institute's four core enterprises: resident undergraduate education, resident research and graduate education, education of working professionals, and fostering scientific and technological innovation." The suggestion was that it would not be adequate for a portfolio to contribute to just one or two of the enterprises, but rather that each would have to demonstrate its value to the Institute overall. Underscoring the fact that Rensselaer would no longer conduct business as usual for its own sake, the protocol also asked this question: "How must the portfolio change, within the framework of the markers and boundary conditions, to achieve the goal of Rensselaer as a world-class technological research university with global reach and global impact?"[207]

Portfolio leaders were also asked to outline general strategies that might move the portfolio forward in response to the directive questions, with estimates of the "nature and approximate amounts of investment required to mount the strategies and achieve success," as well as considerations of other relevant requirements. Portfolio leaders were expected to contribute their ideas and analyses to the full Rensselaer plan as it was being drafted by the President's Cabinet.

Finally, the Initiating Document reviewed the way in which individual members of the Rensselaer community would participate in the development and implementation of *The Rensselaer Plan*:

- As participants in town meetings and workshops.

- As responders to a first draft of the plan that would be created by the president's cabinet.

- As reviewers of the final draft of the plan.

- As implementers of the plan.[208]

To ensure broad community engagement, it was announced that town meetings with the President, open to the entire campus community, would be organized by a cross section of campus citizens coordinated as RealCom, the Rensselaer Assessment Leadership

Committee. With the provost as chair, the committee's membership included six faculty members; an undergraduate and a graduate student; a staff member from student life, advancement, administration, finance, and human resources; and Cynthia McIntyre, the President's Chief of Staff. Teams from within RealCom would also hold portfolio-focused workshops across campus to explore the directive questions, markers, and boundary conditions outlined in the Initiating Document, and to "help assess each portfolio against the markers." It was explicitly stated that the workshops would be moderated by consultants or RealCom members, not by the portfolio owners. RealCom members would then synthesize the input it received and feed it into the plan.[209]

The Initiating Document included a detailed timetable for these activities. True to the fast-tracked nature of the planning process overall, the schedule called for portfolio assessments to be completed just five weeks from the public release of the Initiating Document in the first week of October, and for the cabinet to have a full draft of *The Rensselaer Plan* ready for distribution on the 15th of December, 1999.

The Initiating Document made it clear that while *The Rensselaer Plan* would require significant input from all corners of the campus—and a time period was allotted for the plan to be vetted by deans, faculty leadership, student leadership, and other key groups—recommendations would feed up through the President, who would have the authority to shape a final version of the plan that would then go to the Institute's Board of Trustees for its approval. This progression was intentional—only the Trustees would vote on the plan. Once so approved, the plan would then be distributed across the Rensselaer community for implementation.

Some in the Rensselaer community would come to see the language about who had ultimate authority for approving the plan as something of a power play on the part of the administration—which in a quite legitimate way it was. In some respects, Jackson was simply reclaiming presidential authority that had become diffuse over the decade or more before she took office. But in point of fact Jackson was also tacitly challenging an institutional culture that had evolved such that power and authority (as well as money, as we will see) had been largely distributed, and were now protected, in what were essentially a collection of fiefdoms across the campus—including individual professors, the faculty senate, programs, departments, and schools. She knew that as president she had both the right and the responsibility to assert the authority of her office. Moreover, she knew that the substantive degrees of change that Rensselaer needed would be more likely to be initiated and implemented if it came from the top down rather than through other channels. Toward these ends, Jackson had the strong support of the Board of Trustees.

The Initiating Document was released and distributed to campus in the first week of October 1999. That precipitated an intense flurry of campus discussions, as RealCom hosted 20 two-hour town meetings, each devoted to assessing an Institute portfolio. The meetings were open to anyone on campus—except the portfolio "owner." As Vice President for Student Life at the time, for example, Haviland was not eligible to attend the town meetings on that topic. (Student life was one of a handful of topics that were so broad that they warranted more than one meeting.) Each meeting was expected to consider its given portfolio in the context of the five directive questions.[210]

Haviland remembered that the question asking "What is the intellectual core of what you do?" proved highly challenging. Although "totally scared by that question," he said, administrators "in my opinion, came up with the best answers." By contrast, he recalled, some schools had difficulty reaching consensus on that question. Perhaps only half-joking, Haviland said that no group gave a good answer to the fifth question, about what might be sacrificed to achieve true "best in class" leadership in a given portfolio's focal area.[211]

It fell to RealCom to synthesize the responses so that they could effectively inform the content of *The Rensselaer Plan*. Meanwhile, however, the cabinet continued its intensive planning meetings.

Jackson described the planning process as having vertical, horizontal, and orthogonal dimensions. The vertical take was the review that Jackson asked each academic school and administrative division to conduct of its own portfolio-specific assessments, plans, and budgets. The horizontal perspective came from the campus-wide town meetings and public workshops, which provided crosscutting reviews and analyses of the portfolios. What Jackson and colleagues described as the orthogonal axis in the planning process came from peer reviews conducted by outside experts who assessed, benchmarked, and contributed essential external insights.[212]

Jackson engaged the consulting services of the Washington Advisory Group, a blue-chip strategy and management consulting firm, to conduct an external assessment of Rensselaer's academic and research accomplishments. The consulting firm organized a powerful team of highly accomplished, senior-level advisors. Erich Bloch, one of the founders of the firm, had retired from a successful career at IBM—where he had been engineering manager of the Stretch supercomputer system—to become director of the National Science Foundation from 1984 to 1990. A winner of the National Medal of Technology for his role in the revolutionary IBM System 360 computer project, Bloch was a member of the National Academy of Engineering. Geophysicist Frank Press had been on the faculty at both MIT and Caltech before serving from 1981 to 1993 as president of the U.S. National Academy of Sciences and chairman of the National Research Council. Earlier, he had directed the Office of Science and Technology Policy under President Carter. Edward E. David Jr., a former executive director of Bell Telephone Laboratories, had also served as president of research and engineering at Exxon Corporation and, in government, as head of the U.S. Office of Science and Technology Policy from 1970 to 1973. David was also a life member of the MIT Corporation. The fourth person was Frank H.T. Rhodes, who had earned international renown during his highly successful 18-year presidency at Cornell University.[213]

Jackson gave this illustrous group a straightforward charge: "I asked them to take a look particularly at the academic portfolios to give us a readout of where we stood relative to other universities, particularly research universities," Jackson said. She also asked them to come up with a list of areas that Rensselaer needed to address, "as well as where might there be opportunities."[214]

Jackson also wanted a seasoned outside expert to assess Rensselaer's administrative portfolios and capacities. For that she turned to John R. Curry, then the executive vice president at Massachusetts Institute of Technology and a former vice president for business and finance at the California Institute of Technology.

When the Rensselaer Trustees came to campus for their September and December meetings, Jackson broadened the conversation she had been having with them about the emerging Rensselaer plan. She briefed the Board on the planning process and sketched the shape that some of the emerging themes for change were starting to take. Trustees would have a chance later in the process to make specific comments about the plan.

Meanwhile, with the campus buzzing with discussions of the Initiating Document and comments about it streaming in for consideration, it was time to translate the philosophical underpinnings into a plan of action.

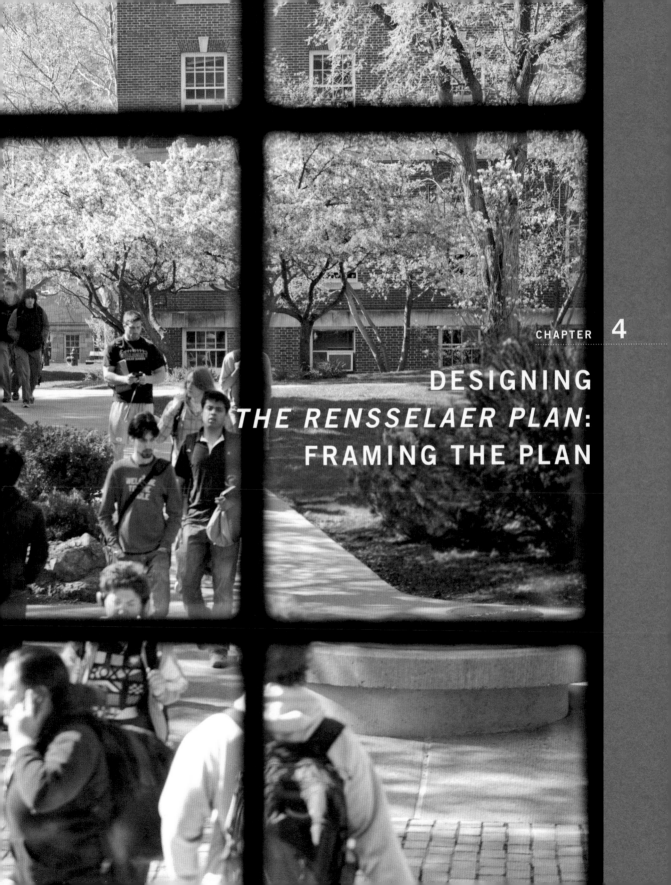

CHAPTER 4

DESIGNING
THE RENSSELAER PLAN:
FRAMING THE PLAN

Work on an initial draft of *The Rensselaer Plan* began in earnest in December, with David Haviland and Doyle Daves doing the bulk of the writing. Jackson and her colleagues synthesized the considerable input they had received from the countless campus discussions and voluminous summary papers that reported their results, along with input from the deans, vice presidents, and consultants. Jackson recalled that she and her cabinet met day in and day out—and often into the night—to analyze how the information they had in hand might translate "in terms of what our foci should be."[215]

"We talked first about what the core areas were and the broad goals that we needed to try to express," she said. Six broad areas emerged. "Everyone agreed that a core focus had to be our undergraduate programs, both on the educational side and the broader student experience." A second area that quickly came into focus was that "if we were going to be truly a research university, we had to make a commitment to have much deeper embedding of research into what we did, and a broader portfolio in the sense of striking out into new areas, and strengthening ones where we already had strength, such as in materials."[216]

Another area that cut across academics and administration was entrepreneurship. "We said we needed to focus on fleshing out scientific and technological entrepreneurship," Jackson said, but there were also other angles to consider. There was an entrepreneurship center in the Lally School of Management and Technology, for example. The broad discussion about entrepreneurship included how it fit into the curriculum, what it meant in terms of the Institute's research agenda, and the potential for commercial development of the Institute's intellectual property.[217]

A fourth focus was framed in the context of the campus culture writ large. It was clear that members of the Rensselaer community did not think the Institute was as diverse as it needed to be. To be sure, Rensselaer's planners felt strongly that the Institute needed to recruit more students from underrepresented racial groups. In addition, given that women constituted just 22 percent of the student body, and less than 20 percent of the faculty, the discussants recognized that Rensselaer needed more gender diversity. The planners also saw that, with most undergraduates coming from within a 150-mile radius of the campus, Rensselaer needed more geographic diversity.[218]

Jackson also viewed diversity even more broadly. She was convinced that the Institute needed more intellectual diversity. As just one example, she saw that the school's strong focus on and allotment of resources to its engineering programs possibly crimped opportunities to build the degree of cross-campus intellectual breadth that marked truly great universities. Again to use engineering as just one example, she saw that Rensselaer's engineering programs tended to focus on traditional areas. "People really were not out on the leading edge," she observed.[219]

The Institute's relative lack of diversity also manifested itself in a lack of depth and breadth in the cultural offerings that came to campus. Jackson envisioned that *The Rensselaer Plan* could redress this imbalance, although details about how that might come to pass would come much later in the planning process.

As a fifth central focus, Jackson and her colleagues recognized that Rensselaer had a vital role to play in the local Troy community, and more broadly in the life of New York State's Capital District. A thriving city in the industrial age, Troy had since gone into deep decline. Jackson knew that Rensselaer could play a strong role in revitalizing Troy. "We felt we had to be a partner with the city," Jackson said. "We had a focus on our communities—Rensselaer as a community, its partnership with Troy, and the region." Jackson's concept in this regard was that of "communiversity"—a notion that recognized that the university is a community itself, but also sits as a larger community that encompasses not only the local region but alumni and alumnae, key partners, and other friends. Global reach and impact also meant that Rensselaer had to build a much stronger international focus and impact, through reputation, alumni outreach, and research and educational partnerships.[220]

Finally, it was clear that Rensselaer needed a stronger administrative infrastructure. "If we were going to be world class, we had to look at every one of our administrative processes," Jackson said. She referred to those processes as "enabling functions" and their work as "enabling activities." Those labels carried a message. Jackson wanted to make sure that the entire campus community recognized that administrative offices and staff served not merely a support or adjunct function—the role to which they are relegated at some institutions—but rather were as integral to the plan as any other component of campus life.[221]

THE PLAN TAKES SHAPE

By late November of 1999, Jackson and her cabinet were largely finished with the work of sifting through the commentary prompted by the Initiating Document. It was time to produce a first draft of *The Rensselaer Plan*.

Jackson issued a quite specific set of guidelines for the drafting of the plan per se. First, it should posit Rensselaer as a world-class technological research university based on excellence, leadership, and community. It should focus on a select set of major issues, at the same time making it clear that the Institute would not attempt to be all things to all people. Jackson wanted to ensure that the plan would "drive a hierarchy of decision making, from big issues to local action," and answer the question "How will we know what we need to start doing differently?" The plan should be cast such that it would "stimulate change in every arena" in a way in which its many stakeholders could "see themselves making changes."[222]

Jackson's marching orders also provided specific guidance for the structure of the plan. It should start with the boundary conditions, Jackson suggested, making them come to life in such a way that readers would "see" them in the plan. The plan should not focus on developing individual campus portfolios, but instead should approach the answering of the directive questions through the lens of the university as a whole. The plan should be clear about what action steps were expected, with the further expectation that it lead readers to "feel the need to change some things they are doing."[223]

Jackson then outlined the core enterprises and other Institute objectives that she felt the draft plan needed to address. She included these elements (recorded verbatim at the time):

RESEARCH

- Identify a handful of foci (e.g., biotechnology and related biological sciences, IT, and communications)

- Include undergirding areas (e.g., applied mathematics)

- Indicate the strengthening that needs to happen

- Note that research focal areas should drive investments in the schools

- "Focal cones" will be decided within research areas; these will come from task groups

- Note that everybody does research (scholarship)

Balance among the schools: Indicate the need for excellence, and need for strengthening, in all schools

UNDERGRADUATE EDUCATION

- Reiterate the need to keep undergraduate education strong
- 5,000 students
- Residential

GRADUATE EDUCATION

- Reiterate 250 doctorates/year
- Add time frame for doing thus

UNDERGRADUATE AND GRADUATE STUDENTS

- Need to increase selectivity and yield, both undergraduate and graduate
- Need to recruit from a broader geographical base; nationally first, and then internationally
- Increased intellectual and geographical diversity will increase gender and ethnic diversity

EDUCATION FOR WORKING PROFESSIONALS

- Derive from scholarship, research, intellectual core
- Customize around these things; build on what we are good at, what we uniquely have to offer
- Flight to quality, not commodity
- Need to rationalize Troy and Hartford MBAs, "Executive" MBA, etc.

ECONOMIC DEVELOPMENT

- Need to address this, and our role in it
- How far to go into Troy (e.g., housing beyond campus boundaries)?

ADMINISTRATION

- Call for university-wide approaches to human resources, infrastructure development and management, and services
- Organizational realignment is on the table, including sunsetting degree programs, academic centers

RESOURCES

- Discretionary and new resources will be directed to identified priorities, focal areas, and strategic investments in other portfolios
- Budget model and mechanisms will reinforce this[224]

Finally, Jackson suggested that this ambitious agenda needed to be synthesized into just 30 to 40 pages.

Following this guidance—and working long hours—Jackson and the cabinet produced a draft of The Rensselaer Plan by December 7. It was structured as follows:[225]

DRAFT PLAN (December 1999)

1. **The Goal**

2. **Fundamentals**
   - 2.1 Markers: Excellence, Leadership, Community
   - 2.2 Intellectual Core
   - 2.3 Planning and The Rensselaer Plan

3. **Research**
   - 3.1 The Institutional Imperative
   - 3.2 A Structured Approach to Research Leadership: Two Institute-wide "Must Do" Research Arenas
   - 3.3 Biotechnology
   - 3.4 Information Technology
   - 3.5 The Full Research Portfolio

4. **Education**
   - 4.1 Our Sine Qua Non of Pedagogy: Interactive Learning
   - 4.2 An Engaging and Seamless Student Experience
   - 4.3 Undergraduate Programs
   - 4.4 Graduate Programs
   - 4.5 Education for Working Professionals

5. **Global Reach**
   - 5.1 Fostering Scientific and Technological Innovation
   - 5.2 Community and Regional Development
   - 5.3 National and International Reach
   - 5.4 A Very Diverse Community

6. **Enabling Change**
   - 6.1 Business Processes
   - 6.2 Information Infrastructure
   - 6.3 People and Organization
   - 6.4 Physical Facilities
   - 6.5 Financial Resources

7. **Moving Forward**

The fundamental goal of *The Rensselaer Plan* was "to achieve a position of prominence in the 21st century as a world-class technological research university with global reach and global impact."

The fundamental goal of *The Rensselaer Plan* was essentially that found in the Initiating Document, with a modest change from "to be a world-class technological research university with global reach and global impact" to this improved version: "to achieve a position of prominence in the 21st century as a world-class technological research university with global reach and global impact." The draft plan reiterated the markers found in the first document—excellence, leadership, community—with reminders that they were fundamental and were not negotiable, and that they applied broadly across the Institute.[226]

The draft plan also added more specificity to the Initiating Document's attempts to outline Rensselaer's intellectual core, first in delineating characteristics common to any world-class technological research university (e.g., "research," "technology," and "university"), but then adding dimensions that are "specific, even unique" to Rensselaer:

- Alignment with global priorities, in applying "science to the common purposes of life"

- Action orientation, a tradition to be balanced with attention to fundamentals

- Interdisciplinarity, with emphasis on low barriers between cross-disciplinary work

- Alliances, especially with industry and the technological professions

- Focus, that is, achieving distinction by making careful choices[227]

Importantly, the draft plan introduced more specificity, under its statement of the Institute's overarching goal, in the form of five Institute-wide objectives:

- Create a structured approach to research leadership across the Institute by moving ahead boldly in information technology and biotechnology. These are posited as "must do" **Institute-wide Research Arenas** because they are aligned closely with societal and global priorities and because they offer fertile possibilities for cross-cutting programs.

- Dramatically expand the **Research Enterprise** by building on existing important strengths, identifying other critical research priorities, and linking, as appropriate, to the information technology and biotechnology arenas.

- Provide an excellent and distinctive **Education** for resident undergraduates and graduate students as well as for working professionals. Education programs will incorporate interactive pedagogies and provide a seamless student experience.

- Expand the Institute's **Global Reach** through activities in scientific and technological innovation; in community outreach; and in state, national, and international arenas. Global reach can only be successful with a strong commitment to diversity in the Institute's people, programs, and environment.

- Redesign **Enabling Activities** to focus Rensselaer's people, business processes, information infrastructure, physical facilities, and financial resources on achieving the goals and programs outlined above. Discretionary, incentive, and new resources will be directed to identified priorities in research, pedagogy, and other portfolio areas.[228]

Addressing the core enterprises, the Rensselaer community, and enabling activities, the draft plan outlined a rationale for each. Importantly, the rationales were accompanied by bullet points that encapsulated action items, effectively bridging the plan's philosophy with expected accomplishments that met the Institute's objectives and, ultimately, its overarching goal.[229] Presented in the form of statements introduced with such phases as "we must" and "we will," the bullets can be viewed as the center of the draft plan, in that they mapped specific behaviors necessary to move Rensselaer toward its goals. Beyond that, they introduced a construct—the "we will" statements—that would prove to be a powerful shorthand, common vocabulary, and set of orienting points that defined the expectations at the heart of *The Rensselaer Plan*, and made quite directive the actions that must be accomplished if the plan were to live up to its promise.

The draft plan put research at the very top of Rensselaer's agenda. "The strength of our efforts to make our students partners in discovery and open their minds to inquiry depends directly on the quality and extent of our research endeavor at the leading edge of new knowledge," it declared. Moreover, the plan made the case that a strong commitment to research was imperative for making Rensselaer the kind of world-class university that it sought to be. "By achieving pre-eminence among world-class technological research universities," the plan read, "we will enhance our ability to attract highly talented and well-respected faculty, staff, and students, expand geographic reach, and increase financial support from private and public sources."[230]

The plan cited two "must do" research areas: information technology and biotechnology. But rather than suggest specific goals and actions, the draft raised a series of questions that Rensselaer should ask in regard to these foci: "What important questions/problems define our choice of focal areas? What focal areas may this lead us to? On what basic strengths must we build? What partnerships will we need to create?" As Haviland observed later, this rather tentative approach—a contrast to the directive nature of other aspects of the plan—showed that "both the research agenda and the means for accomplishing it were in a nascent stage in December 1999." Still, the draft plan was quite clear that the Institute would build research in a small number of carefully selected research focal areas, notably biotechnology and information technology. The plan did not limit Rensselaer's expansion in research to those particular areas, stating instead that Rensselaer should have a "full research portfolio" across the Institute.[231]

The emphasis on research and the focus on biotechnology and information technology can be seen as manifestations of Jackson's central vision for Rensselaer. They clearly reflect focal points she presented in her inaugural speech. Jackson recalled that when it came time to put fingers to keyboard in writing *The Rensselaer Plan*, "I pushed the cabinet to bias the plan to research, with an initial focus on biotechnology, and information technology in the broad sense of the word."[232]

Describing his own process of coming around to the idea that Rensselaer should be in the biotechnology business, Trustee Paul Severino might well have been describing the process for the university as a whole. Severino first was skeptical about biotechnology, in part because it felt foreign to the Institute's traditional mission, but also because his own experience as an entrepreneur had taught him that "you don't ever go into an established marketplace with established leaders and try to compete." And it was clear at the time that other prominent research universities were already well down the path to successful research in biotechnology. On reflection, though, Severino came to realize that rules of business competition might not apply in quite the same way in academia. The vastness of biotechnology as an area for inquiry meant there was plenty of room for new players in university research. Moreover, Severino realized that Rensselaer's existing areas of expertise complemented its push into biotechnology and positioned the Institute to "find places where we can do things better than anybody else." He came to see that a strong position in biotechnology broadened the Institute's research portfolio in a "very important and very strategic" way. "I see [biotechnology] now much differently than I did then," Severino said, "and I think we're going to succeed in a big way."[233]

Jackson had said in her inaugural address that "teaching and research are the clasped hands of the university." The first draft of the plan plainly acknowledged that Rensselaer needed to do more on the research side of that equation if it wanted to become truly world class. As Jackson summarized the issue, "we were not doing research, at least in the broader way that some of our peer and aspirant research universities did."[234]

There was another reason for the strong emphasis on research in the first draft of the plan, though, and it is one that shows Jackson's skill as a strategist. She knew that a bold plan that pushed Rensselaer in new directions would get the attention of the Institute's alumni and alumnae. She assumed that some would oppose the changes but that others—she hoped many others—would support it, and that in any event the plan would "garner their attention," as she said. She knew that support from a critical mass of Rensselaer's alumni would be vital to the plan's success.[235]

"Motivating the alums, as a force of individuals, was a significant part of our marketing strategy at the time, and very much on the minds" of Rensselaer's administrators, Haviland recalled. There was a perception that many alumni and alumnae thought Rensselaer was "either drifting or dropping," he said. "I think [Jackson] knew right from the beginning that ultimately it was going to be the alumni weight behind all of this that was going to get it done from the outside."[236]

In the context of an expanded research capacity, the draft plan introduced another core concept that would prove pivotal to the transformation Jackson and colleagues envisioned. The draft plan stated that major new research focal areas would be anchored by world-class "constellations" of faculty, staff, and students. Most constellation faculty, as they came to be called, would be new hires, presumably either luminaries in their fields or extraordinarily gifted junior faculty. The expectation was that this model of new faculty energy and talent would in turn energize given research focal areas. Presaging the need for additional financial resources, the draft plan anticipated that the constellations would be supported through the Institute's endowment. Similarly, the plan predicted that the development of the faculty constellation concept would require expanded or new specialized research facilities, especially in biotechnology.[237]

The draft plan also paid attention to the quality of student life. Jackson said she knew that Rensselaer already had a strong reputation in undergraduate teaching, although as she said "there was a lot we needed to do relative to the overall undergraduate experience."[238] A section of action items entitled "an engaging and seamless student experience" called for the Rensselaer community to "commit ourselves, through every action we take, to the success of our students and alumni," by considering students "as colleagues who will become the next generation of leaders."[239] This language was taken from RealCom's report of findings from the community assessment workshops.[240]

As was noted above, *The Rensselaer Plan* was viewed by its authors as a request for proposals from the academic schools and administrative divisions. The intent was that the process of addressing the directive questions and attendant self-assessment would spark proposals for change from schools and other units on campus. That message was not heard clearly. Because the plan intentionally focused on the whole of the Institute, it rarely named specific schools, departments, centers, or functions. Thus, the overall strategy of trying to guide members of the Rensselaer community to think outside their silos and focus on change for the greater good of the Institute caused some unintended ambiguity in regard to the plan as an RFP. However laudable the intent, the effect was off-putting to some who felt that the plan certainly should have included specific references to specific units.[241]

ROLLING OUT *THE RENSSELAER PLAN*

After the cabinet reviewed and revised some seven drafts, a version of the plan was ready for broader campus review and comment. On December 15, 1999—precisely in line with the fast-track schedule outlined in the Initiating Document—a draft version of the plan was finalized and posted on the Institute's website. A memo invited faculty, staff, and students to comment via email. A similar invitation to the Institute's alumni and friends was packaged with the December 1999 issue of *Rensselaer* magazine. Comments were to be emailed to RealCom by January 31, 2000.[242]

Response to the draft plan exceeded expectations. RealCom received several hundred messages about the plan. Haviland said that most were "thoughtful and heartfelt." Some, he recalled, "presented comprehensive and thorough analyses of the entire draft; others focused on a single issue, concern, or recommendation." Importantly, some three-quarters of the responses came from alumni and alumnae. Haviland remembered that many began with some variant of "thank you for asking" or "this is the first time I have been asked to provide input to the Institute's plans."[243]

During this period, Jackson and members of the cabinet traveled the campus, meeting about the plan with academic departments, administrative divisions, student leaders, and other campus groups. The meetings were often challenging in tone, and significant criticisms of the plan were voiced. A common complaint was that the plan focused too much on biotechnology and IT, and did not mention schools and departments. There was also concern that the process for responding to the plan was restricted to individuals and did not allow comments from groups, such as schools, departments, or the faculty senate. The notion that the plan was an RFP was generally lost amidst concern that individuals and departments could not "see themselves" in the plan. There was also unease about the new performance planning process that the plan introduced but did not fully explain.[244]

In a final report, RealCom analyzed the responses it received, offering a series of recommendations reflecting what it had heard. The summary was honest and frank. The report commented on undergraduate education, to the effect that "although Rensselaer in heritage and practice has excelled in interactive learning, we have not demonstrated in the plan our goals to adequately build and strengthen this tradition." The report suggested that the plan should reflect that proposition in both "phraseology and actions" and establish undergraduate education as the "initial focal point of the document."[245]

Perhaps not surprisingly, given the response in some of the school and departmental meetings, part of the report questioned the emphasis on biotechnology and information technology, saying that focus "seems to move Rensselaer into these research areas in ways that do not reflect a broad enough concept of scholarship at a technological university." One point in this regard seemed to suggest a return to Institute tradition. The report argued for broadening the scope of research at Rensselaer in ways that capitalized on the Institute's strengths (or as the report put it, "aggregate[ing] our assets into unique piles, using our conventional strengths in unconventional ways"). There was a call to ensure that the discussion of biotechnology and information technology include "the larger social issues and problems surrounding these topics." The report seemed to suggest a fairly conservative, go-slow approach that would involve both the careful—or perhaps "safe"—selection of specific plays in biotechnology and IT, with an "implementation time frame that is consistent with realistic possibilities for funding."[246]

Among other findings, the report recommended further attention to the student experience, a point of emphasis that had appeared earlier in the fall in RealCom's first report.[247]

The President and cabinet had started another series of long, intensive meetings about the plan as soon as the initial draft had been distributed. As input came during the comment period, work in revising the plan continued toward production of a new version of the plan. Several iterations were produced before the second and final draft plan was readied for distribution starting February 15, 2000.

A comparison of the structure of the two drafts (see p. 87) shows how they vary.[248]

The differences in structure also speak to some important changes in content. The final draft identifies these four core enterprises:

- Resident undergraduate education (now listed first)

- Research and graduate education (now linked in the same section)

- Education for working professionals (expanded from earlier drafts, reflecting activity at Rensselaer's Hartford campus as well as professional and distance education)

- Scientific and technological entrepreneurship, also further developed

Perhaps the most important change was that undergraduate education replaced research as the first core enterprise discussed. Here was an acknowledgement of the fundamental primacy of student education as the core charge of any university. The change was intended to address sentiment in the Rensselaer community that education was in danger of being replaced by, or at the least sublimated to, research.[249]

Rather than simply describing characteristics of undergraduate programs ("compelling…content-centered…inquiry-based…leadership-infused…globally oriented"), the final draft presented a set of "we will" statements intended to inform the achievement of these characteristics. The new draft added a discussion of undergraduate participation in research and innovation and a set of related action statements. The new version also added a specific set of actions designed to create seamless student service.[250]

The final draft also reflected a more finely honed vision of research at Rensselaer, in part through input from a new Vice President for Research, Arthur Sanderson, who was appointed in January 2000. One of Sanderson's first tasks was to work with colleagues across campus to develop language to shift the planning discussion from general observations about the need to build research to say more specifically "*how* this might be done, on *what foundations*, where the *interdisciplinary opportunities* lie, and how *existing strengths* might be parlayed into leadership." Based on input from the campus community, reactions to the first draft, and thoughts from the Washington Advisory Group, Sanderson drafted new statements about the Institute's current research portfolio, core research strengths, and how the Institute's existing strengths could be building blocks for new initiatives in biotechnology and information technology. Questions and examples in the earlier draft were replaced with specific strategies for expanding research.[251]

FIRST DRAFT (December 1999)

1. **The Goal**

2. **Fundamentals**
   2.1   Markers: Excellence, Leadership, Community
   2.2   Intellectual Core
   2.3   Planning and The Rensselaer Plan

3. **Research**
   3.1   The Institutional Imperative
   3.2   A Structured Approach to Research Leadership:
         Two Institute-wide "Must Do" Research Arenas
   3.3   Biotechnology
   3.4   Information Technology
   3.5   The Full Research Portfolio

4. **Education**
   4.1   Our Sine Qua Non of Pedagogy: Interactive Learning
   4.2   An Engaging and Seamless Student Experience
   4.3   Undergraduate Programs
   4.4   Graduate Programs
   4.5   Education for Working Professionals

5. **Global Reach**
   5.1   Fostering Scientific and Technological Innovation
   5.2   Community and Regional Development
   5.3   National and International Reach
   5.4   A Very Diverse Community

6. **Enabling Change**
   6.1   Business Processes
   6.2   Information Infrastructure
   6.3   People and Organization
   6.4   Physical Facilities
   6.5   Financial Resources

7. **Moving Forward**

FINAL DRAFT (February 2000)

1. **The Goal**

2. **Fundamentals**
   2.1   Rensselaer Today
   2.2   Unique Strengths
   2.3   Opportunity and Challenge
   2.4   Planning and The Rensselaer Plan

3. **Resident Undergraduate Education**
   3.1   Undergraduate Programs and Students
   3.2   Interactive Learning
   3.3   Participation in Research and Innovation
   3.4   An Engaging Student Experience
   3.5   Seamless Student Service

4. **Research and Graduate Education**
   4.1   Enhancing and Growing Research
   4.2   Core Research Strengths
   4.3   New Research Arenas: Information Technology
         and Biotechnology
   4.4   Resident Graduate Education

5. **Education for Working Professionals**
   5.1   A Distributed Rensselaer
   5.2   Rensselaer at Hartford

6. **Scientific and Technological Entrepreneurship**
   6.1   Entrepreneurship Education and Research
   6.2   Intellectual Property and Technology
         Commercialization
   6.3   Creating and Supporting New Ventures

7. **Rensselaer's Communities**
   7.1   The Campus Community
   7.2   A Very Diverse Community
   7.3   Alumni
   7.4   Neighborhood, City, and Region
   7.5   National and International Reach

8. **Enabling Change**
   8.1   Administrative Processes
   8.2   Information Infrastructure
   8.3   Physical Facilities
   8.4   Our Public Face
   8.5   Managing Financial Resources
   8.6   Expanding the Resource Base

9. **Leadership in the 21st Century**

These strategies did not pinpoint specific focal areas in biotechnology and information technology, but rather presented a ladder of action items that could identify strategies for such areas. The steps were as follows:

- Create both internal and external task forces to identify the focal areas, basing selection on importance and "converging technical themes that build on existing Rensselaer strengths."

- For each selected area, build undergirding areas at Rensselaer and forge strategic alliances with external groups.

- Recruit and endow a "faculty constellation" in each selected area.

- Create specialized research facilities in the focal areas, including a new biotechnology facility.

- Expand or create research and doctoral programs as required.[252]

A related change was that the discussion of graduate education was moved to the section on research—"a fitting reminder," as Haviland said, "that research and graduate education are two sides of the same coin."[253]

The new plan also crystallized the promises of action that were encapsulated in the "we will" statements that the first draft introduced. Existing "we will" statements were rewritten as necessary to be true action items, and many new statements were added, reflecting input received during the comment period on the first draft. The "we will" statements gave a clear view of how *The Rensselaer Plan* would unfold in practice, in that Jackson had made it clear to the Institute community that each constituted nothing less than a promissory note on results to be delivered.

Other important changes included the addition of sections and language on a "seamless student experience," community, and outreach.[254]

STRUCTURED REVIEWS

The final vetting of the final draft plan took place via a series of "structured reviews" that Jackson asked key campus leadership groups to conduct, in meetings Jackson attended. In contrast to the first review, in which individuals were asked to comment, now Jackson asked for comments from stakeholder groups. These groups included the faculty senate, the student senate, and the "Pillars of Rensselaer"—a leading staff group—the "Key Executive" group, and the Rensselaer Alumni Association Board, among others.[255]

The first review had ensured that every member of the Rensselaer community could voice an opinion about the plan. The second review gave established constituency leadership groups a final opportunity to provide their views based on their interests and agendas.[256] The groups were not asked to vote the plan up or down—only the Trustees would do that—but rather were asked to respond to three specific questions about the plan: Does it provide a framework to reach the goal? Does it address the four core enterprises? Does it speak to all the people who will need to work together to accomplish the goal?[257]

Moreover, the answers did not need to be put in writing, but would be delivered in conversations between the stakeholder groups—among them the Board, faculty senate, academic deans, alumni association, student leaders, corporate executives, key staff, and local politicians—and the President and plan writers. Why this approach? Haviland recalled that it was used because written responses "can take a good deal of time and energy to synthesize, can offer criticism without proposals for remedies, or can balkanize, homogenize, or otherwise obscure the perspectives so important to moving forward."[258] Jackson made a point of attending each of the structured reviews, for two reasons. "I wanted to hear from people things that might affect the final refinements of the plan," she said. At the same time, she wanted to signal if necessary that the "long open process" of reviewing drafts of the plan was now coming to a close, and that it was not time to try to rewrite the plan.[259]

Responses from the groups were generally positive, and some were enthusiastically so. At the same time, the discussion raised further issues, including many questions about how the plan would be implemented. Several discussion threads were captured that were common across the structured review meetings:

- The plan is clear about Rensselaer's unique strengths: technological entrepreneurship, interdisciplinary inquiry, interactive learning. The plan should reflect each of these very directly across the core enterprises.

- The campus is coming to agree with the need to move quickly into important "niches" along the information technology/biotechnology/microtechnology front. All agree that we need to select wisely.

- The plan may be too timid in some key respects. Should, for example, Rensselaer require undergraduate research participation or a thesis?

- There are many good suggestions for refinements, but none of the reviews pushed back on the big ideas in the plan.

- Everyone is interested in the next step (performance planning). They broadly agree that the plan is a sufficient umbrella and believe the proof is in the doing.[260]

The comments received during the structured reviews did not warrant a wholly new draft of the plan, but they did result in some further modifications, some of which were significant. These were reflected in a final iteration that was officially titled "The Rensselaer Plan, As Proposed to the Board of Trustees, May 12, 2000."

One modification was that the proposed plan articulated a stronger case for linking research and education, drawing language from Jackson's inaugural speech that the two are "inextricably linked in world-class universities" and that "research and education drive reputation." The proposed plan added a related new argument, that a research university is an intergenerational community of learners, an idea that gained traction during several of the structured review conversations and reflected the views of key outside observers and of Jackson herself.[261]

Those discussions also prompted the addition of a sixth Institute-wide strategic focus that reflected a commitment to—and a broad view of—the principle of diversity. It was couched as follows:

> Achieve true intellectual, geographic, gender, and ethnic **diversity** in our students, faculty, and staff, in order to draw upon the best talent available, and to prepare our students to work and lead in a global economy.[262]

The first printing of
The Rensselaer Plan was
distributed in 2000.

Among other modifications, the proposed plan moved "interdisciplinary inquiry" to the top of a list of Rensselaer's innate strengths, ahead of interactive learning and technological entrepreneurship. Interdisciplinary research and education were now characterized as the "Institute's most exploitable competitive advantage." Other changes made select language more direct. As one example, the sentences "Expand the undergraduate research program to ensure that all students have access to research projects. A goal of 500 such experiences each semester would engage 10 percent of our undergraduate body at one time" were changed to "Ensure that all students have a research experience by enlarging the undergraduate research program, and by adding a thesis or comparable major scholarly work requirement for seniors."[263]

As noted above, the "we will" action items were made more directive and new ones were added. In the section on undergraduate programs and students, for example, a new "we will" item read "Update the core curriculum to reflect advances in research strengths, including information technology, biotechnology, and scientific and technological entrepreneurship." A new "we will" item in the section on seamless student service read "Provide information proactively, with the goal of enabling students to resolve issues and problems." A third "we will" statement, under the umbrella of resident graduate education, read "Extend interactive learning across graduate programs. Our distinctive interactive pedagogies allow us to bring studio- and team-based learning to our graduate students."[264]

FINAL APPROVAL

Ultimately the go/no go decision about *The Rensselaer Plan* hinged on approval from the Rensselaer Board of Trustees. Fundamentally, of course, the Board had the legal responsibility and authority for setting institutional goals and deciding its strategic direction. Once they had subscribed to the principles of the plan, the Trustees would serve an invaluable role as advocates for the plan. They would also be in a position to field and manage criticism that might arise about change at Rensselaer. Importantly, too, the plan implicitly needed the financial resources that Trustees could provide or provide entrée to.

While many Trustees were positively inclined to embrace the plan's bold ideas, others were less sure. Rensselaer's Trustees are stewards of a rich, distinguished institutional history and set of traditions, and there was some understandable apprehension about moving too far too fast in new directions. A particular concern, Jackson recalled, had to do with striking the right balance between high-quality teaching, especially at the undergraduate level, and a significant commitment to research. Respectful of these differences of opinion, but nonetheless eager to put her ideas in action, Jackson committed herself to helping the Board understand both the plan's principles and its specific components. Moreover, she avidly sought Trustee input in shaping the plan. Through the summer, fall, and winter, she kept the Board apprised of the plan's progress—and sought members' input—through informal individual conversations and group discussions in Board meetings.[265]

A pivotal moment vis-à-vis the Board and *The Rensselaer Plan* occurred during the Board's retreat meeting in February 2000. Jackson invited Paul Gray, the president emeritus and chairman emeritus of MIT, to share his ideas about the future of Rensselaer with the Trustees. She also invited the four consultants from the Washington Advisory Group who had been examining Rensselaer as part of the planning process, each of whom addressed the Board in turn.

Reflecting later on this meeting—in a 2002 speech, "The Process of Academic Transformation," presented at the Aspen Symposium of the Forum for the Future of Higher Education—Jackson said the consultants "presented the Board with evaluations of the national research environment, external perceptions of Rensselaer, the position of the Institute relative to its peer institutions, the need for Rensselaer to establish new research initiatives, and the state of the planning process." In light of the consultants' frank assessments, Jackson said, some Board members "were confronted with the distressing possibility that Rensselaer could become a second-rate institution."[266]

Gray engaged the Trustees in an extended dialogue about research and teaching. Gray described the research university as "a community of learners—some young, some older—engaged together in creating, disseminating, and applying knowledge, using existing knowledge, skills, and judgment." Research, Gray said, is therefore

Jackson observed that "this new Rensselaer Plan...is truly a visionary document that has been crafted with input from the entire Rensselaer community, has been guided by our best thinking, and is shaped by a bold desire for excellence."

fundamentally about learning. Gray suggested that "education can be defined as bringing students to the point of self-sufficiency, that is, learning how to proceed when no one knows the answer," and that education is therefore about research. In this manner, Gray was instrumental in helping the Board fully understand the deep value in Jackson's belief that "teaching and research are the clasped hands of the university." As the discussion progressed, it became clear that the "community of learners" formulation and "clasped hands" metaphor resonated with the Trustees, and the argument garnered acceptance.[267]

Trustee Severino, for one, liked the perspective that the outside experts brought. Thinking in any organization, he said, can become too self-absorbed. "I think that is one of the things that happened here. People were looking inward. They were not looking outward," he said. The experts provided that necessary outside perspective. "These people knew what was going on in the world of technological research universities. They basically came in, looked at where we were, and compared us to the rest of the world and did the benchmarks. And we did not look very good. They explained what was going on out there. And they explained that if we were going to have an impact, one of the first things we had to do was to extend our reach on the research side. I think [Jackson] understood that. But she made sure that we understood it."[268]

By the end of the meeting, the Board was not merely convinced of the merits of *The Rensselaer Plan*, but was enthusiastically supportive of it. (The consultants' view that Rensselaer needed to move fast or be left behind likely prompted a sense of some urgency.) That enthusiasm was so fully realized, in fact, that the Board wanted to vote approval of the plan at that time. While deeply appreciative, Jackson persuaded the Trustees to hold their eagerness until their next meeting, which would allow time for the final stages of development of the plan to unfold on campus. Further refinements of the plan in fact took place until April 15, 2000, when the proposed plan was sent to the Trustees for formal review.[269]

Capping a remarkably short process, and one that was almost certainly more intensive than parallel processes at most other institutions, the plan was presented to the Board of Trustees for their approval on May 12, 2000, where it earned unanimous approval. The proposed plan was now the approved Rensselaer Plan.

The Rensselaer Plan was then distributed widely both in print form and online. In an accompanying statement, Jackson observed that "this new Rensselaer Plan captures our vision, and will guide our choices, and secure Rensselaer's position as a top-tier, world-class technological research university with global reach and global impact." She continued: "In its final form, this is truly a visionary document that has been crafted with input from the entire Rensselaer community, has been guided by our best thinking, and is shaped by a bold desire for excellence."[270]

In her 2002 speech recounting the development of *The Rensselaer Plan*, Jackson praised the Board's willingness and resolve to embark in new directions, while also offering a rare glimpse of the pride she rightfully felt at having led the successful development of a significant plan for change. "It takes courage to confront a leadership board with an honest assessment of the institution over which they have stewardship," Jackson said, "and it takes courage for individual members of the Board to acknowledge this information as true, and to assume personal responsibility for overseeing a transformation."[271]

A similar courage could be said to apply to the whole of the Rensselaer community. Despite trepidations and reservations, and overcoming what is likely a natural institutional propensity toward conservatism and the status quo, Rensselaer had looked deep into its soul and decided to make significant changes. The support was not unanimous—in a community as large as the one at Rensselaer, there were bound to be some skeptics. Some faculty leaders became vocal opponents of aspects of the plan. But in large part, members of the community had come together in support of an impressive plan for a bold, new, next-generation iteration of Rensselaer. They had done so in record time—just eight months from the release of the Initiating Document to the Board's final approval—an unheard-of pace in higher education planning on this scale. Moreover, the Rensselaer community knew it was taking a leap of faith: The full implication of the bold planned steps could not be known until the plan was implemented.

Challenging at every turn, the inordinately hard work of developing *The Rensselaer Plan* had been completed. Now the equally difficult—but potentially transforming—challenge of implementing the plan would begin.

CHAPTER 5

IMPLEMENTING THE PLAN: THE HARD WORK OF CHANGE

The scope of the undertaking...would challenge comfortably entrenched assumptions about what Rensselaer was and should strive to be. It would require the Rensselaer community to assess, rethink, and reengineer processes, policies, and procedures across the whole of the Institute.

Absent *The Rensselaer Plan*, the Institute might have continued on its pre-Jackson trajectory, still producing occasional bursts of distinguished research, but without the cohesion that would help ensure the continuous output of noteworthy, top-quality intellectual products that are characteristic of a major research university, and that build institutional reputations. In other words, the Institute could have been content essentially marking time rather than making bold progress. Had it gone that route, however, it might also have continued to sink, as some suggested it had started to, into obscurity. Clearly, Rensselaer found that fate unacceptable, opting instead to embrace the plan's bold vision and aggressive goals.

Stakeholders in *The Rensselaer Plan* knew that fulfilling its vision and meeting its goals would be exceptionally challenging. The scope of the undertaking was unprecedented. It would challenge comfortably entrenched assumptions about what Rensselaer was and should strive to be. It would require the Rensselaer community to assess, rethink, and reengineer processes, policies, and procedures across the whole of the Institute. It was clear from the onset that change on such a wholesale scale was likely to be painful to some, irritating to others, and disruptive to anyone who harbored a fancy for the status quo. Moreover, success was not at all guaranteed.

Still, the Rensselaer community had committed to the endeavor. As soon as the plan was approved, Jackson moved fast to bring the plan to fruition. The task now was to translate the plan's rhetoric into practicable action plans.

Jackson was "off and running" from the start, Trustee Gary DiCamillo recalled.

"She wasn't afraid to break some eggs, especially vis-à-vis some of the old Institute ways and means. And I think that she had very clear lines in the sand that she was going to draw, even in year one. [She was] not afraid to do that. Not afraid to be unpopular, even though it hurt her. She was principled."[272]

SETTING INSTITUTIONAL PRIORITIES

As noted above, action at Rensselaer under the newly approved plan would hinge on Institute-wide priorities set by the President and cabinet after review of all the portfolio plans as a whole, based on their assessments of what would be best for the Institute. At the time the plan was approved in May 2000, however, it would be some time before university portfolio managers would complete their first performance plans. An interim strategy was needed.

To that end, Jackson met with her cabinet and all portfolio "owners" at an off-campus planning retreat in the summer of 2000. Their goal was to develop priorities for action based on the "we will" statements in *The Rensselaer Plan*. A leading international accounting firm was engaged to lead the exercise.

The firm created an elaborate matrix designed to assess the "we will" statements in the context of the six broad categories that framed the Institute's key objectives (education, research enterprise, scientific and technological entrepreneurship, diversity, communities, and enabling change). The matrix proved far too complex to be workable, however, and Jackson soon recognized that the exercises the firm had planned for the retreat would merely cover territory already vetted in discussions of the plan, and would not move the planning process forward. Having the wisdom to see that the retreat was not accomplishing its goals, Jackson earned extra respect from her colleagues when she decided to end the meeting early, sever the relationship with the consultants, and try a different approach.[273]

A second retreat was more fruitful. Meeting later that summer, this time in the Institute's alumni conference center, Heffner Alumni House, Jackson and the portfolio owners engaged in a broad discussion of Institute-wide priorities. Jackson divided the group into subgroups to list their top three choices of priorities to move *The Rensselaer Plan* forward. In fairly short order, each subgroup derived a short list of priorities. Jackson distilled their lists into six highest priorities, divided into two categories, institutional positioning and process/management. The list was as follows:

Biotechnology and Information Technology Initiatives

1. Constellations
2. Building (Center for Biotechnology and Interdisciplinary Studies)

First Year Experience

1. Freshman orientation
2. Graduate orientation
3. New hires (faculty and staff)

Electronic Media & Performing Arts Center/Building

PROCESS AND MANAGEMENT PRIORITIES

Performance-based Budget and Planning Process

Review/Revise Intellectual Property Policies

Elevate Tenure Standards (faculty), and Hiring and Promotion Criteria (faculty and staff)[274]

This list is highly illuminating and vitally important as a critical page in the story of the plan's ultimate success. The priorities defined here bridge the vision-informed rhetoric of *The Rensselaer Plan* with the action steps needed to implement the plan. Moreover, the list clearly telegraphs where the Institute would put its focus, resources, and energies in the nascent years of the plan. (That is not to suggest that the planning process was so rigid that it could not change to meet evolving needs or capitalize on newly emerging opportunities, and it did evolve over the years.)[275]

The list's first two priorities speak directly to areas of critical importance—research and the student experience—that infused the plan. It is not surprising that the first priority was listed, in that it was "top of mind" for Rensselaer's leaders at the time. Jackson had started an intensive period of planning for research focal areas, faculty constellations, and a new biotechnology research facility even as the final touches of *The Rensselaer Plan* were being developed. Thus, this planning was well under way in the summer of 2000.

In regard to the student experience, the priority here reflected Jackson's deep interest in improving learning and living conditions for students at Rensselaer, showing also that this goal had started to coalesce around a focus on the first-year experience. Jackson saw this goal as having three broad parts, "to create the first-year experience, to restructure how we brought our young people in, and [to improve] how we dealt with them in their first year."[276]

The third priority represented a translation of what theretofore had been general references to building on the Institute's tradition and expertise in the media arts. The Electronic Media and Performing Arts Center positioning priority emerged as Jackson led a discussion on media and the arts, presentation space, and culture change, and achieved consensus on the need for a media and arts center, with a groundswell of interest and support in the process.[277]

The other three line items, with their focus on process and management, can be viewed as enabling priorities, to use language from *The Rensselaer Plan*. Obviously, they reflect keen interest in improving fundamental process, policies, and practices in critical areas, including budgeting, intellectual property, faculty rewards and promotion, and human resources.

As we will see below, each of these priorities would ultimately have a broadly transformative impact on the university that would far eclipse their effect as it was likely imagined that day in the Heffner Alumni House.

TRANSITION TO IMPLEMENTATION

Jackson developed a vocabulary that helped define and clarify the Rensselaer planning process that was marked by such terms and phrases as "markers," "boundary conditions," "core enterprises," and "directive questions."[278] Another concept that evolved in that vein was that of "bets." Just as the term suggests, this was a shorthand way of referring to the risks that Rensselaer was willing to take—indeed, chances that it knew it had to take—in order to transform itself. Casual, to the point, a bit abrupt, the word "bets" drew attention to itself precisely because it stood in counterpoint to the more formal rhetoric of *The Rensselaer Plan*. Despite its casual overtones, though, the word "bets" came to be a serious—and effective—way to refer to the game-changing, multi-million-dollar risks that the Institute undertook under its new plan.

The bets were indeed considerable in number, expansive in scope, and aggressive in ambition. There was, first off, the desire to evolve Rensselaer from an undergraduate university with a graduate research arm into a research university on a par with the best universities in the world. Under this broad umbrella, Rensselaer wanted to expand its research programs, claiming positions of research leadership in both existing areas and new fields. Under this umbrella also was the desire to recruit high-caliber new faculty, build new facilities, and secure a sufficiently high level of funding to fuel and support research. Expanded graduate education was part of this portfolio, as was an intent to increase research opportunities for undergraduate students.

The research thrust alone would have been a major challenge, but Rensselaer also had its sights on many other ambitious goals. The Institute was determined to continue in the 21st century the distinguished record of technological innovation and entrepreneurship that it had established in the prior two centuries. The Institute wanted to improve greatly the student learning and living experience, especially for undergraduate residential students. The curriculum needed updating and expansion. The existing physical plant, neglected for some time, was in urgent need of considerable attention. Wholly new facilities, offering new possibilities for a bolder, expanded mission, were also envisioned. Much more robust administrative processes and procedures were necessary, as was a more rigorous administrative infrastructure overall.

The notion of "bets" implies the promise of exciting rewards should the risk pay off as planned—and as we will next see, many of Rensselaer's bets paid off handsomely.

The pages that follow explore how *The Rensselaer Plan* was put into action. In practice, the work of implementing the plan's goals manifested itself in dozens if not scores of interrelated ways across the entire fabric of the university. For the purposes of capturing a representative cross section of the most significant accomplishment here, this chapter explores work in these broad categories:

- research and scholarship

- the physical infrastructure

- academics, learning, and the curriculum

- the student experience

- funding

- administrative processes

EXTENDING THE
CAPACITY FOR RESEARCH
AND SCHOLARSHIP

Among the strategies that were central to *The Rensselaer Plan*, the most expansive, overarching, and perhaps important of the bets was the Institute's commitment to develop its research capacity. On this point, the plan was unequivocal: "The most significant transformation posited by *The Rensselaer Plan* is the imperative that Rensselaer create a research portfolio of substantially greater size, quality, prominence, and impact."[279] An expanded capacity for research was seen as the centerpiece of a revitalized Rensselaer.

Expanding the research enterprise

The plan recognized that the Institute's status as a technological university afforded an extraordinary range of opportunities, especially in light of the exponential growth in the importance of technology to society and industry. At the same time, the plan adamantly advocated that Rensselaer needed to "pledge a much deeper commitment to research."[280] The rationale was essentially fourfold:

1. Research is essential to strengthen Rensselaer and improve its reputation:

   While we have achieved international prominence in innovative pedagogy and specific research areas, the pace of growth in research funding, research degrees, and endowment has lagged behind most major research universities, a reality that is reflected in our ranking as a national university....To strengthen education, enhance reputation, and increase the flow of resources, Rensselaer thus must pledge a much deeper commitment to research and graduate education, while extending our excellence in undergraduate education.[281]

2. Research is essential to the education of leaders:

   Excellence in education inspired the founders of Rensselaer, and innovative pedagogy remains a core value of the Institute. To provide leading-edge education, we must be leaders in key research fields, for the creation of new knowledge is critical to a stimulating learning environment for our students. Cutting-edge research enables us to make our students partners in discovery and open their minds to inquiry. The Institute will, therefore, assign added emphasis to research and scholarship as a key constituent of excellence in education.[282]

3. Research is a public trust placed in top universities:

Research is a creative process that generates new principles and spawns new technologies. Such technological innovation stokes the engine of economic growth, and connects the university research enterprise to a cycle that catalyzes the development of new industries and supplies a highly educated, up-to-date workforce.[283]

4. Research is essential to success across a broad front:

As it gains greater prominence as a world-class technological research university, Rensselaer will enhance its ability to achieve several interrelated goals—attracting highly talented students and well-respected faculty and staff, expanding geographic reach, and increasing financial support from private and public sources.[284]

The Rensselaer Plan outlined a three-pronged strategy to expand the research enterprise. First, Rensselaer would build on the distinctive strengths of its existing research platform and expand research based on core research strengths in areas that showed particular promise for growth. Second, it would start initiatives in information technology and biotechnology, "two new arenas vital for national well-being and growth." Third, it would significantly expand resident graduate education. Rensselaer would look particularly for opportunities to expand research in areas of inquiry and disciplines where the Institute already held a position of leadership or where it could take the lead given sufficient added focus and resources. It would also seek to exploit

The goal of expanding the research enterprise was posited in part as a continuation of Rensselaer's traditional mission: "By building research programs, and involving students in research activity, we will preserve and enhance our historic strength in undergraduate education."

Rensselaer's capacity for and tradition of interdisciplinary research and strategic alliances with industry.[285]

The goal of expanding the research enterprise was posited in part as a continuation of Rensselaer's traditional mission. The plan states, for example, that "by building research programs, and involving students in research activity, we will preserve and enhance our historic strength in undergraduate education."[286]

At the same time, the plan was clear and intentional in its commitment to expanded research as a core component of transformative change. "Rensselaer will grow from an institution centered on undergraduate education with selected research strengths to a full research university," the plan stated. It was similarly unequivocal in envisioning how research was a linchpin in the overarching goal of raising the Institute's visibility and prominence. "Rensselaer research in the future will extend over a broad portfolio that puts the Institute in a leadership position both in established fields and in evolving areas of inquiry that hold out great promise and opportunity," the plan said.[287]

The decision to increase research was "one of the boldest parts of *The Rensselaer Plan*" Gary DiCamillo said. "We were well-known as a civil engineering institution throughout the 1800s, building bridges and highways and railroads. So I think we were certainly a research institution in the 1800s." In the 20th century, though, the Institute evolved a mission that emphasized undergraduate education before research. Thus, DiCamillo said, "When we said we wanted to be a research university, it was a break with the past."[288]

The plan called for an expansion in the scope of research as well as size. "As science and technology play an increasingly important role in our society and economy," the plan said, "social, political, and economic studies of policies and impacts are an essential part of the Rensselaer research portfolio." The plan called for faculty and students to engage not just in the "how," but also in a "dialogue of 'why' and 'what if.'"[289]

The plan was quite specific about what it wanted Rensselaer to strive to be, asserting that Rensselaer "sets its sights on tier-one ranking among U.S. technological research universities, with a goal of expanding research funding from $40 million to $100 million annually in five years and doubling, from 125 to 250, the number of doctorates a year over the next eight to 10 years."[290] That commitment would require an expanded body of highly qualified faculty as well as a review, and perhaps restructuring, of the Institute's many research centers and the creation of new centers. Facilities, staff, and equipment would have to be put in place to support the broader research focus. Some Institute policies and procedures would have to be redrawn to align better with the research mission.

"To invigorate Rensselaer research," Jackson said in a speech marking the 10th anniversary of *The Rensselaer Plan*, "we challenged ourselves to extend our focus, and to take risks for impact, moving into new domains of significance at the intersections of important disciplines, combined with Rensselaer core strengths in engineering and information technology."[291] As the plan moved forward and evolved, this agenda would crystallize into five broad areas, identified as "signature thrusts," that the Institute identified as targets for significant investment and development. The five areas were these:

- Biotechnology and the Life Sciences
- Computational Science and Engineering
- Energy and the Environment
- Nanotechnology and Advanced Materials
- Experimental Media and the Arts

In effect, these "signature thrusts" were building blocks for Rensselaer's future. They were informed by a considered analysis and projection of the critical issues, problems, and opportunities that society would need to address as the 21st century unfolded. In many respects they required the Institute to push out the boundaries of how it had traditionally envisioned itself. Indeed, in the case of biotechnology and especially experimental media and the arts, the plan asked for Rensselaer to envision a new version of itself.

Jackson regularly made the point that these areas were designed not to supplant but to complement the already very broad research program at Rensselaer. The five areas intersected definitively with areas where Rensselaer had already demonstrated distinction and had an established base of knowledge. Research in the life sciences, for example, was increasingly being informed by expertise from engineering, one of the Institute's

The Smart Lighting Engineering Research Center at Rensselaer is investigating and developing light-emitting diode technologies that will open doors to a diverse spectrum of new applications.

hallmark strengths. Similarly, the Institute's existing expertise in computation dovetailed with the emerging evolution of computational biology. Jackson elaborated several such synergies in an article published in *Rensselaer* magazine in June 2000:

> In microelectronics, for example, Rensselaer researchers have made important contributions to the science and technology of interconnects, devices, architectures, and packaging that will expedite the next generation of microelectronic systems and nanoelectronic systems. Advanced materials and nanotechnology—areas in which Rensselaer has a long history of important work—will also be key to future breakthroughs in developing materials with radically different properties and functions that will impact medicine and communications, in particular. Rensselaer's distinguished record in applied mathematics, engineering and design simulation, and scientific computation supports our expertise in modeling and simulation of complex systems. With the explosion of information technology and its significance in virtually every aspect of society, the Institute is ideally positioned to capitalize on these strengths as we address future directions in these technologies.[292]

Each of the signature areas was broadly interdisciplinary, and could involve expertise from many different corners on campus. This fit well with a point of pride at Rensselaer, that it had "low walls" when it came to fomenting collaboration across disciplines, departments, and schools.

Thus, the major new research directions outlined in *The Rensselaer Plan* complemented, built on, and had the capacity to expand the Institute's traditional areas of strength. New strengths and emphases could inform and build on the many areas where Rensselaer was traditionally strong, and vice versa. Joined together, these component parts would power a new generation of distinctive research at Rensselaer.

Building the research infrastructure

One of the early turning points in Rensselaer's research transformation came at the beginning of 2000, when Jackson established an Office of Research at Rensselaer. Its purpose was "to support and enhance the research goals of the university through leadership, partnership, and service to the research enterprise."[293] For the first time, Rensselaer would have a central office that could identify, prioritize, and coordinate research funding opportunities across campus. The office was charged with implementing and administering policies regarding patents, copyrights, and intellectual property rights, and with monitoring the progress of all large research grants and contracts.

Rensselaer Professor Arthur C. Sanderson, then on leave as director of the National Science Foundation's Division of Electrical and Communications Systems, was named the first Vice President for Research. His immediate challenges were significant. He was responsible for identifying research focal areas in biotechnology and information technology, and with helping to recruit key faculty to lead these areas. Sanderson was also asked to contact major research funding agencies to present a coherent view of Rensselaer's research capabilities and potentials. At the same time, he was asked to work with research faculty, groups, and centers that had traditionally pursued their work independently without much coordination or assistance from the leadership of the Institute. In addition, he was expected to provide oversight for the Office of Contracts and Grants and five interdisciplinary research centers, to build relationships with Rensselaer administrative departments and portfolios that were important to research success, and to develop a comprehensive plan for research strategy, development, administration, commercialization, and outreach.[294] The breadth of that portfolio is indicative of the need that Rensselaer had for a coordinating infrastructure to manage its expanding research activities.

From these beginnings the Office of Research would quickly come to play an integral role in Rensselaer's vision of a technological university, providing robust and needed infrastructure and resource support for the development of research programs and projects. It took on an important coordinating role, for example, in the biotechnology and information technology initiatives, including identifying the research areas, assisting in the recruitment of constellation faculty, and helping to oversee the planning, design, equipping, and occupancy of the Center for Biotechnology and Interdisciplinary Studies. It managed several interdisciplinary research centers. Meanwhile, it also offered support services for faculty members who sought research opportunities, assisting with the preparation of proposals and budgets and providing guidance on research management and intellectual property issues. The Vice President for Research was also involved in deciding allocation of research space, a pivotal process in any institution, but particularly critical for the type of research university Rensselaer was striving to become.[295]

The Office of Research would track emerging research arenas. It had a seminal role in the development of additional Institute research focal areas in nanotechnology and in energy and the environment. It worked to link researchers from various disciplines. The office also collaborated with the Office of Undergraduate Education to develop and implement a comprehensive plan to make undergraduate research experience available for most undergraduate students.[296]

As *The Rensselaer Plan* came into fruition, the research office would offer grants to support and spark research across campus. The Exploratory Research Seed Program, started in 2001, offered small grants (roughly $50,000 each) to stimulate exploratory research on innovative and interdisciplinary topics on campus. In 2001–02, for example, the program provided $750,000 in grants. That funding often sparked major support for funded research projects. A $50,000 grant in terahertz medical imaging applications, for example, helped leverage a $1 million grant to establish the W.M. Keck Laboratory for Terahertz Science in the Center for Terahertz Research. Other grants led to multimillion-dollar awards from the National Institutes of Health to study special proteins, anthrax antidotes, and the development of "bone spackle" to heal bone injuries. Faculty Revitalization Grants offered support to tenured faculty members who had not been particularly active in research in recent years, or who wished to pursue a promising avenue of research.[297]

The office would also help to create and manage the hundreds of relationships Rensselaer developed with academic colleagues, national funding institutions, federal laboratories, and more than 200 industrial affiliates. Examples included the Regional Consortium for Biotechnology (with the Wadsworth Center laboratory of the New York State Department of Health, the Albany Medical Center, the Ordway Research Institute, and the University at Albany), and a biomedical research partnership with the Cleveland Clinic, announced in May 2006.

The research office also worked to increase the visibility of Rensselaer's research and researchers through outreach to other academic institutions, state and federal agencies, corporate partners, prospective students, alumni and alumnae, and the general public. Among other specific initiatives, the office created new Web pages on the Rensselaer website and publications that featured research findings, people, and programs. A seminar series was started to host presentations by world-class researchers in areas of high priority to Rensselaer.

PHILOSOPHICAL UNDERPINNINGS: THE "SIGNATURE THRUSTS"

As we saw above, Rensselaer identified five "signature thrusts" for research—areas that the Institute targeted for significant investment and development. We will look at each of those areas in turn.

Signature thrust: Biotechnology and the Life Sciences

In speeches and other communications from the very start of her presidency—including her inaugural address—Jackson had made it clear that she believed that building a strong footing in biotechnology was an appropriate 21st-century strategy in support of the Institute's historic mission of "application of science to the common purposes of life." Knowing that discoveries in biotechnology would play a critical role in countless fields in the 21st century, she was adamant that Rensselaer stake a claim in this important arena. Moreover, she knew that Rensselaer's peer and aspirant institutions had developed strong programs in biotechnology—MIT was one notable example—and that Rensselaer had to move aggressively to compete on this playing field, or risk drifting even further behind.

Among the research "bets" that were placed in *The Rensselaer Plan*, biotechnology could be viewed as one of the most revolutionary for Rensselaer in 1999. Given Rensselaer's established traditions in the physical and information sciences and technologies, many in the university's community, including some faculty and Trustees, did not believe that the Institute was positioned to move into the life sciences and biotechnology.[298]

Nonetheless, one could point to research across Rensselaer that in many respects created building blocks for a thrust into biotechnology—investigations in such varied areas as bioinformatics, genomics, and proteomics; biochemistry; biomedical engineering; and environmental ecosystems, as well as core strengths at Rensselaer in such areas as nanotechnology, microsystems, modeling, and information technology. Given Rensselaer's distinguished history of accomplishments in each of these fields, one could argue that biotechnology, in fact, was a natural and logical extension of its research mission. Moreover, one could argue that there was some imperative that Rensselaer

Jackson had made it clear that she believed that building a strong footing in biotechnology was an appropriate 21st-century strategy in support of the Institute's historic mission of "application of science to the common purposes of life."

make a bold move—such as a foray into biotechnology—in part as an impetus for the Institute to reenergize itself, right itself from drifting, and remain competitive.

Several "we will" statements in *The Rensselaer Plan* talked specifically about developing a research focal area in biotechnology and developing related faculty groups, research facilities, and improved graduate programs. When it met to set the first priorities for implementing the plan in the summer of 2000, the President's cabinet had focused on two of those goals, developing faculty groups and facilities.

In May 2000, Jackson announced the formation of an internal planning committee charged with examining core strengths and opportunities in biotechnology research. Jackson and Sanderson also recruited a blue ribbon panel of external experts to review Rensselaer's current research programs in biotechnology and provide creative insight into possible future opportunities.[299]

In its report, the Internal Planning Committee for Biotechnology (IPCB) declared that "life sciences are fundamental to the portfolio of any research university in the 21st century." The committee argued that Rensselaer needed to commit to "reinforcing the core of life sciences faculty, programs, and infrastructure in order to build new programs in biotechnology and related fields."[300] The committee also strongly endorsed construction of a Biotechnology and Interdisciplinary Studies Building at Rensselaer, which, as we will see below, would be a cornerstone in the Institute's entrée into biotechnology and a defining symbol of the Institute's expanded research portfolio.

The IPCB identified four core areas as primary opportunities for expanding biotechnology research at Rensselaer: functional tissue engineering, integrative systems biology, biocomputation and bioinformatics, and biocatalysis and metabolic engineering. The committee's rationale spoke to the way in which key disciplines in science and technology were rapidly evolving. "The fields of biology, engineering, and the physical and information sciences are merging," the report stated. "Biology is becoming a quantitative discipline, drawing on the computational and systems-based, design-driven research and educational methodologies that form the basis of physical and engineering sciences. At the same time, engineering and the physical and information sciences are addressing fundamental problems in the biological sciences, thereby providing new tools and concepts that shape the new applied biology paradigm."[301]

With considerable foresight, the committee recognized that "the intersection of biology with engineering and the physical and information sciences is growing rapidly" and that "opportunities in research, education, and technology transfer at this intersection are driving biotechnology." It was at these interfaces, the committee averred, that Rensselaer had considerable opportunity to contribute substantively to the emerging landscape of life science research, and to do so in ways that would be consistent with Rensselaer's history, mission, strengths, and new directions.[302]

By 2009, the Institute's full embrace of biotechnology would prove to be one move into a new domain that could already demonstrate distinctive results. By that year, faculty in Rensselaer's biotechnology constellations were hard at work in the areas of biocatalysis and metabolic engineering, computational biology and biocomputation, systems biology, and tissue engineering and regenerative medicine. And as just one notable finding in the broad realm of biotechnology, Rensselaer researchers would have bioengineered a fully synthetic alternative to animal-derived heparin, a widely prescribed anticoagulant drug for fighting blood clots.[303]

Signature thrust: Computational Science and Engineering

Along with biotechnology, *The Rensselaer Plan* singled out information technology as an area where the Institute intended to focus an investment of resources as part of its research strategy. "IT is the driving force in every industry today, transforming many of them and enabling new areas of research, such as the human genome, and enterprise, such as e-business," the plan stated, and "both IT and biotechnology are challenging and transforming the world's underlying social, economic, and political structures."[304]

It was entirely logical that information technology should take such a prominent position in the early planning. IT permeated the Institute, informing such areas as networking and communications, microelectronics and microsystems, scientific modeling and simulation, intelligent systems and robotics, image and signal processing, electronic media, social science of technology, and technological entrepreneurship. Rensselaer could point to recognized research faculty in applied mathematics, and research-active faculty in networking and multimedia communications, advanced scientific computation, relational database technologies, and software engineering and programming. At the time the plan was developed, in fact, information technology was considered a more obvious bet than biotechnology in light of the rich array of existing assets in the IT realm that the Institute had in place.[305]

Rensselaer also had a strong commitment to interdisciplinary IT education. The Institute had started one of the nation's first bachelor's degree programs in IT in 1998. A master's degree program in IT had been approved by the New York State Education Department in the summer of 2000.[306] As the Institute's IT website noted, "Rensselaer was among the first universities to recognize the creative and distinctive academic nature of the Information Technology field."[307]

With the IT boom in full swing in the late 1990s, Rensselaer's new bachelor's program attracted student interest, starting with 57 students in Fall 1998 and reaching a peak enrollment of 375 in Fall 2002. In 2010, the Institute launched, as an extension of the IT area, the nation's first undergraduate degree program devoted to the emerging interdisciplinary field of Web Science. The new academic major expands the current Information Technology degree program to create both a bachelor's degree and a master's concentration in Information Technology and Web Science. The students in the interdisciplinary degree program will investigate issues on the Web related to security, trust, privacy, content value, and the development of the Web of the future.[308]

At the same time, though, the fundamental nature of scientific exploration was changing—exponentially and explosively. One effect was the rapid rise of computation as a tool of inquiry—a rise so rapid that just a few years into *The Rensselaer Plan* it was clear that computation was becoming ubiquitous across disciplines as a research tool. Moreover, it was clear not only that Rensselaer needed to have a stake in this area, but that it was well-positioned to do so by virtue of expertise that was already well-established on campus.

Computation was important precisely because many of today's scientific problems call for scientists and engineers to create and use computer models of complex phenomena on multiple scales. Unprecedented computing power made it possible to model entire systems, taking into account interactions at every scale. Understanding the human cardiovascular system, for example, required prediction of the flow through the arteries and veins. Endothelial cells that line the arteries respond to the varied flow and these changes, in turn, can be traced to genetic actions within the cells. Biomedical researchers hoping to use a computer model to learn more about causes and potential cures of cardiovascular diseases, therefore, needed a model that simulates the behavior and interaction of all these size levels over time. Similarly, materials scientists working with new nanophase materials needed models that simulate macro-level behaviors that are dictated by properties that must be determined via atomic-level calculations that are coupled to the macro-level fields.[309]

The Computational Center for Nanotechnology Innovations features massively parallel supercomputers and more than 70 teraflops of computing muscle.

The focus on computational science and engineering extended and expanded expertise that Rensselaer had in place in automated adaptive modeling and computation. Combining that legacy with additional support under *The Rensselaer Plan*, Institute researchers were poised to change the face of scientific inquiry in fundamental ways, addressing problems in biomedicine, engineering, and other areas in which the behaviors of interest are dictated by interactions at multiple length and time scales.[310]

Members of Rensselaer's Scientific Computation Research Center, for example, built an international reputation for their creation of adaptive finite element modeling and other techniques that make it possible to solve complex engineering problems. They have worked with collaborators across the campus and the country to extend these methods to complex multiscale models that track interactions at many lengths and time scales. Their models looked, for example, at all of the interactions in a human knee: a macro-model of the engineering stresses on the joint, another model to look at the tissue, a third to consider what is happening within individual cells, and a fourth to simulate the genetic changes within the cells. One overarching goal was to produce automated tools that have enough speed, cost-efficiency, user friendliness, and accuracy to make them useful for doctors, engineers, and scientists who are not themselves experts in computer modeling.[311]

Rensselaer's stake in computational science would prove to be truly defining when the Institute announced in 2007 that it had built a $100 million supercomputer as part of the Computational Center for Nanotechnology Innovations (CCNI).[312] Soon after the center's opening, the supercomputer was ranked seventh in the world in terms of power. (As evidence of its visionary nature, the facility would still be distinctive several years later, after the world at large had developed many new generations of computing capacity. John E. Kolb, class of 1979, Rensselaer's Vice President for Information Services and Technology and Chief Information Officer, remarked in 2010 that

Rensselaer was still among "the top 10 or 15 universities in the world" to have such powerful computing capacity.)[313]

In the CCNI, Rensselaer was developing simulation technologies for the latest generation of high-performance computing equipment, creating advanced simulations and models for nanoelectronic devices and circuitry, and seeking to understand how proteins, DNA, and other biological systems behave at the molecular level. (The CCNI will be discussed in depth in the section below on "The Physical Infrastructure.")

Mapping the Institute's future in IT was also a major priority for Jackson. In the initial days of *The Rensselaer Plan*'s implementation, she had appointed a planning committee to examine this issue.[314] Recommendations from this panel would plant the seeds of deep reform at Rensselaer. After considerable investigation of options, interviews with experts, and input from a blue-ribbon panel of world-class researchers and advisors off campus, the committee ultimately recommended three core areas for targeted growth, focused research, and increased funding:

- Future Chips: revolutionary computing and leapfrog device technologies

- Tetherless World: pervasive computing and distributed intelligent systems

- Multiscale Computing: changing the face of scientific and engineering inquiry[315]

Although its succinctness may not suggest it, this bulleted list introduces concepts and centers of inquiry that would add significantly to the depth and breadth of intellectual inquiry at the Institute. The areas it identified abounded with possibilities for interdisciplinary research in collaboration with areas where Rensselaer already had a strong existing presence.

To advance these newly identified areas from concept to practice, Rensselaer first began to recruit new faculty. The President appointed a committee to begin recruiting faculty members for constellations in each of the research focal areas. E. Fred Schubert was appointed as the Wellfleet Senior Constellation Professor of Future Chips at Rensselaer. This constellation was rounded out with the appointments of Shawn-Yu Lin and Christian M. Wetzel in 2004. Angel E. García was appointed Senior Constellation Chaired Professor in Biocomputation and Bioinformatics in 2005, and James A. Hendler joined the Institute as Senior Constellation Professor of the Tetherless World Research Constellation in 2007.[316] (More about the "constellation" concept follows below.) As these three areas were staffed, funded, and came online, they would add rich depth and new directions to Rensselaer's research portfolio.

The Future Chips group focused on the use of compound semiconductors—which have enabled the fastest Internet connections, highest frequency transistors, brightest light-emitting diodes, highest-efficiency lasers, and cell phones, among other technological advances—to make substantial and significant advances in communications, lighting, sensing, and imaging.[317] An example of this group's work was published in 2009 when E. Fred Schubert and his colleagues announced that they had developed and demonstrated a new type of light-emitting diode (LED) with significantly improved lighting performance and energy efficiency.[318]

The Tetherless World group focused on understanding and exploiting the research and engineering principles that underlie the World Wide Web, in order to enhance the Web's reach beyond the desktop and laptop computer, and to develop new technologies and languages that expand the Web's capabilities.[319] As just one example of the Tetherless World's work, the group received a $1.1 million grant from the National Science Foundation in 2009 to help create a toolkit to allow scientists and educators to gain better access to data from a variety of sources, including from outside of their direct area of expertise. "Right now there are many scientists, educators, and policy makers who want to use other's scientific data, but they do not know how to find it, how it was collected, and even how to read it," said Peter Fox, a Senior Professor in the constellation. The toolkit would help break down those barriers.[320]

A third area, multiscale computing, drew on expertise from materials, biosciences, nanotechnology, electronics and energy, and other disciplines to inform engineering practice and scientific discovery related to the transfer of information from one model or scale to another. In effect, it replaced traditional design practices, which often relied solely on experiments, with simulation-based methods at multiple scales.[321] As an

E. Fred Schubert
Wellfleet Constellation
Professor of Future Chips

Robert J. Linhardt
Ann and John H. Broadbent,
Jr. '59 Constellation
Professor in Biocatalysis
and Metabolic Engineering

Ravi S. Kane
P.K. Lashmet Professor of
Chemical and Biological
Engineering

Angel E. García
Constellation Professor
of Biocomputation and
Bioinformatics

example of this area's work, Rensselaer announced in 2009 that it had received a $1 million grant from the U.S. Department of Defense to model how different metals are affected by neutron irradiation. "Using quantum mechanics, we can predict what happens when a single neutron knocks out a few atoms from where they are supposed to be, and then trace that chain reaction from the atomic scale to the microscale, mesoscale, and finally to the macroscale to see how that initial atomic fender bender leads to the eventual mechanical failure of the device," said Suvranu De, Associate Professor in the Institute's Department of Mechanical, Aerospace, and Nuclear Engineering.[322]

The Institute began seeking increased philanthropic support for IT, especially for endowments of constellation and faculty chairs, and also sought to expand its partnerships in this area. The Computational Center for Nanotechnology Innovations is a good example of the Institute's progress in this realm. The Institute also secured funding for new IT-focused research centers, including ones in subsurface imaging, terahertz research and terascale computing, inverse problems, broadband research, and pervasive computing and networking. Rensselaer added new IT expertise to its volunteer leadership when Jackson recruited Jeffrey Kodosky, class of 1970, a co-founder of National Instruments, and Thomas R. Baruch, class of 1960, a biotechnology and IT venture capitalist, to the Board of Trustees. Even before he joined the Board, Kodosky and his wife funded the Gail and Jeffrey L. Kodosky '70 Constellation in Physics, Information Technology, and Entrepreneurship, devoted to discovery of cutting-edge energy conversion and electronic materials using first-principles predictive theories and computations.[323]

Signature thrust: Energy and the Environment

Given that researchers at Rensselaer worked to solve the 21st century's most challenging problems, it was fitting that the Institute identify energy and the environment as another "signature thrust" in research. Rensselaer's capacities in these critical areas spanned decades, from distinguished academic programs in electric power engineering and nuclear engineering to a world-class Lighting Research Center established in the late 1980s and centers for Polymer Synthesis and Power Electronics Systems established in the 1990s. Implementation of *The Rensselaer Plan* saw the genesis of new research, including investigations of fuel cell technologies and "smart lighting" by the Future Chips Constellation.

The need for more research in these areas was paramount. Worldwide, energy consumption had nearly doubled in just the last few decades, and was expected to double

From new designs for nuclear power plants and smart light-emitting technologies to intelligent traffic patterning and nanoengineered materials, Rensselaer researchers were working on projects that addressed a wide spectrum of energy-related technologies.

again by mid-century. At the same time, the world remained reliant on fossil fuels, of which there is a finite supply, while alternative sources of energy—nuclear, wind, solar, and geothermal—remained relatively underdeveloped.

As a global expert on energy, Jackson was often asked to address these issues. In a 2008 speech, for example, she observed:

> We are caught, as never before, in a double grip—the need for national and global energy security, and legitimate alarm over our planet's climate change. Energy security and climate change mitigation, together, are a national security issue. Issues that ensue from these twin realities—complex geopolitical and geostrategic challenges, unprecedented wealth transfer from one group of nations to another, concern over the impact of a global downturn, the profusion of energy investment choices before us—require vision, careful analysis, coherent thinking, and action.[324]

The Institute was well-positioned to address these challenges from a wide variety of disciplinary perspectives. From new designs for nuclear power plants and smart light-emitting technologies to intelligent traffic patterning and nanoengineered materials, Rensselaer researchers were working on projects that addressed a wide spectrum of energy-related technologies.[325] Rensselaer was educating more undergraduate nuclear engineers than many universities.

During the implementation of the plan, Institute researchers would make further strides in the areas of energy and the environment. Robert J. Linhardt, the Ann and John H. Broadbent, Jr. '59 Constellation Professor in Biocatalysis and Metabolic Engineering, was a co-author of a 2007 paper that described a lightweight, flexible, and ultrathin nanoengineered battery. Engineered to function as both a lithium-ion battery and a supercapacitor, it could provide power output comparable to a conventional battery, but could function in temperatures up to 300 degrees Fahrenheit and down to 100 below zero and be powered by human sweat. The "paper battery," as it was called, was seen as having the potential to meet the most demanding design and energy specifications of tomorrow's gadgets, implantable medical equipment, and transportation vehicles.[326]

At the Rensselaer Baruch '60 Center for Biochemical Solar Energy Research—another product of *The Rensselaer Plan*—researchers explored fundamental processes in light-driven reactions in natural and artificial systems, studying their applications to inform the design of a new generation of photovoltaics. One goal was to develop cutting-edge technologies for solar energy conversion, and design a new generation of "bio-inspired" artificial photosynthetic devices. Partnerships with industry were formed to help translate this fundamental research into practical solutions for energy production.[327]

In the environmental arena, Rensselaer researchers have made significant contributions to the sustainability of the world's water bodies and the delicate ecosystems they contain. For more than 35 years, Rensselaer has maintained the Margaret A. and David M. Darrin '40 Fresh Water Institute, based near Lake George, New York. The facilities that comprise this center were substantively renovated during the implementation of the plan. A gift of $1.5 million received in 2006 was earmarked for support of a senior-level research professorship at the center.[328] In 2008, Rensselaer announced that researchers at the Darrin Institute had developed one of the most comprehensive databases in existence on the impacts of acid rain at the foundation of the biological community.[329] And in 2009, the Institute announced findings that populations of the invasive zebra mussel can be successfully controlled without damaging the natural ecosystem.[330] In addition, in 2003, New York Governor George Pataki selected Rensselaer to manage the Upper Hudson Satellite Center of the Rivers and Estuaries Center, focused on research and education to guide policy for conserving and managing natural systems such as the Hudson River.[331]

Countless other examples show attention to energy and the environment across the Institute. In 2004 and 2005 alone, for example—several years into implementation of *The Rensselaer Plan*—the Institute announced the new Center for Fuel Cell and Hydrogen Research, focused on basic research and next-generation concepts for fuel cells and hydrogen-related technologies; the New York State Center for Advanced Technology, in partnership with Cornell University and Brookhaven National Laboratory, focused on innovation in and commercialization of energy conservation and renewable energy systems; and funding totaling $1.84 million for the Center for Future Energy Systems, to support technologies that improve the energy efficiency of a wide variety of devices, including photovoltaic systems for producing solar power and light-emitting diodes. In the Center for Future Energy Systems, faculty and students also were designing future configurations of the electrical grid.[332]

In addition, a new center created under the plan, the $18.5 million Rensselaer Smart Lighting Engineering Research Center, was one of five new National Science Foundation Engineering Research Centers created nationally, and the only one in New York State. Researchers there worked to create new semiconductor-based materials, devices, applications, and systems to replace and transcend the incandescent light bulb.[333]

In yet another center, which incorporated a partnership with the global architecture firm Skidmore, Owings & Merrill, Rensselaer inaugurated a new Ph.D. program and research center, the Center for Architecture Science and Ecology, intended to push the boundaries of environmental performance in building systems.[334] This sampling of contributions to energy research could be repeated many times over, touching on countless departments and centers at Rensselaer.

Signature thrust: Nanotechnology and Advanced Materials

In light of the Institute's traditional strengths in materials science and engineering and its commitment to build a presence in biotechnology, it followed rather naturally that Rensselaer would also stake as one of its "signature thrusts" work designed to manipulate matter, materials, and devices at the atomic and molecular levels. Nanotechnology was a logical extension of the Institute's mission as it moved forward into the 21st century.

Rensselaer has a longstanding research program in materials and advanced materials. With the recruitment of faculty member Richard W. Siegel, the Robert W. Hunt Professor of Materials Science and Engineering at Rensselaer, in 1995, the Institute moved more aggressively into materials science and engineering at the nano scale. In 2001, the Institute established the Rensselaer Nanotechnology Center (RNC), an interdisciplinary, Institute-wide research center that focused on nanoscale science and technology. The Center secured large industrial partners, and competed successfully for designation as a National Science Foundation Nanoscale Science and Engineering Center (NSEC). The Rensselaer NSEC was an important milestone in the implementation of *The Rensselaer Plan* in that it proved that the Institute could compete for, and win, substantial peer-reviewed federal support in areas of acknowledged faculty research leadership. The NSEC award placed Rensselaer among a select group of leading technological research universities; the other five awards went to Columbia, Cornell, Harvard, Northwestern, and Rice universities. Today, researchers in the RNC and NSEC work in several synergistic research areas, including nanostructures, nanocomposites, theoretical modeling and design, biomaterials and biofunctionality, nanodevices, and the socioeconomic implications of nanotechnology.[335]

Nano research supported under *The Rensselaer Plan* produced countless important findings. Rensselaer investigators found, for example, that integrating nanotubes into traditional materials dramatically improves their ability to reduce vibration, especially at high temperatures. The findings could pave the way for a new class of materials with a multitude of applications, from high-performance parts for spacecraft and automobile engines, to golf clubs that do not sting and stereo speakers that do not buzz.[336] A Rensselaer team found that materials that do not normally stick together can be bonded using a one-nanometer layer of self-assembling polymer chains—a sort of "nanoglue."[337] Rensselaer researchers developed and demonstrated a new method for detecting the magnetic behaviors of nanomaterials.[338] Another study found that, by adding an invisible layer of nanomaterials to the bottom of a metal vessel, an order of magnitude less energy is required to boil water.[339] Rensselaer researchers have also created razor-like first-of-their-kind magnesium nanomaterials, dubbed nanoblades, that challenge conventional wisdom about nanostructure growth and could have applications in energy storage and fuel cell technology.[340]

Cross-disciplinary research with a nano focus has produced truly interesting results at Rensselaer. We referred earlier to the invention of a "paper battery." That finding came about when Robert Linhardt, the Broadbent Senior Constellation Professor of Biocatalysis and Metabolic Engineering, was trying to perfect a blood-thinner-containing membrane for hemodialysis. He approached colleague Pulickel M. Ajayan, then the Henry Burlage Chaired Professor in Engineering at Rensselaer, to see if

The Curtis R. Priem
Experimental Media
and Performing Arts
Center®

carbon nanotubes might increase the strength of his membranes. The first approach was to merge Linhardt's cellulose with aligned carbon nanotubes and test for strength. "One of the students said, you know if you fold that in half, you have a supercapacitor," Linhardt said. "And so we did. And he was right." Hence it was a student's insightful comment that led to the creation of an energy storage device on a paper-thin piece of material made from cellulose and carbon nanotubes. "Sometimes standing back and letting someone succeed is the most important decision to make," Linhardt said.[341]

The molecular world came to life in 2009 when Rensselaer's large-format film, *Molecules to the MAX!*, premiered in the Institute's Experimental Media and Performing Arts Center® (EMPAC). Part science experiment and part Hollywood magic, the movie follows the exploits of Oxy, Hydro, Hydra, Carbón, and other memorable characters. With help of the Molecularium—a spaceship that can shrink to nanoscale sizes—the group explored the "secret worlds" and molecular structures of everyday objects, including a snowflake, chewing gum, a penny, and a human cell. It was all part of education outreach at Rensselaer. "After watching the movie, parents, children, and teachers all rave about the storyline, the characters, the songs, and the animation—they just love it," said Richard Siegel. "But we've also done before-and-after assessments that prove viewers coming out of the theater know a great deal more about atoms and molecules in the world around them than they did before they experienced the movie. They learned without even trying."[342]

Trustee Curtis R. Priem, class of 1982, whose name is on the EMPAC® theater, was also a donor to the Molecularium projects. His interest came from a belief that parallels a passion of Jackson's, that "basically we don't have the pipeline filled with kids that are interested in staying on the technical track." The great promise of the Molecularium work, he said, is that if it can show children that science and technology are "fun and interesting"—if "they're absorbing nanotechnology at four to eight years old"—there's a good chance that by age 22 they'll be "in the lab or doing research or out in industry," solving the critical issues of the day.[343]

Signature thrust: Experimental Media and the Arts

Rensselaer's research "bets" on computation and information technology, energy, and nanotechnology were good matches between Rensselaer's history and its vision as a technological research university. While biotechnology might be seen as something of a stretch, one could at least see hints of its technological and scientific underpinnings within the Institute. On the face of it, however, one might not be able to make the same connections for another "signature thrust," in experimental media and the arts.

Dig below the surface and a strong rationale for experimental media and the arts could be seen within the context of the Institute, both in terms of how it stood going into the era of *The Rensselaer Plan* and how it envisioned itself as a result of the plan.

Here was an area that had many hallmarks of a true stretch goal for the Institute, offering a set of initiatives that had strong potential to be truly transformative.

Dig below the surface, though, and a strong rationale for experimental media and the arts could be seen within the context of the Institute, both in terms of how it stood going into the era of *The Rensselaer Plan* and how it envisioned itself as a result of the plan.

The Institute had in fact pioneered the integrated electronic arts. It established a department of the arts in 1985, populating it with world-class faculty dedicated to interdisciplinary creative research in electronic arts. Early on, the department referred to its program and studios as iEAR (Integrated Electronic Arts at Rensselaer). The arts faculty created an MFA in electronic arts in 1991, insisting that students work across electronic media, including music and visual arts, studying and creating musical compositions and performances, videotapes and installations, multimedia presentations, performance art, and computer-generated or -mediated images. Further expansion of the Rensselaer curriculum came in the mid-1990s, when the arts faculty and Rensselaer's Department of Language, Literature, and Communication developed a successful undergraduate major in electronic media, arts, and communication. A B.S. in electronic arts was added in 2002 and, in 2007, a multidepartmental B.S. in games and simulation arts and sciences was started. A doctoral program in the electronic arts—one of the first of its kind—was also established in 2007.[344]

Apart from those historical roots and ongoing innovations, the rationale for an emphasis on experimental media and the arts can also be framed in the rationale for *The Rensselaer Plan* as a whole. There are many points of reference in the plan that support an Institute presence in media and the arts. The plan, for example, called for building on the Institute's strengths in interdisciplinary inquiry, research, and education. The plan urged that Rensselaer seek diversity "in the broadest and richest sense" and create "a lively discourse on important cultural, social, gender, and ethnicity issues in courses, colloquia, fairs, and festivals as well as in residence halls, student activities, and the research environment." It called for social activities that would enliven campus life and "create a culture in which students see themselves as belonging to the larger university community."[345] In a broader sense, too, it can be seen that the concept of experimental media and the arts fits Rensselaer's mission as a component of the type of offering a top-tier university must provide its students and its community.

Rensselaer's vision of its play in experimental media and the arts was grounded, appropriately, for an institute of technology, in the notion that technology and the arts intersect and converge in multiple ways that affect and define life's common purposes. The Institute blazed a trail to connect the arts, media, and technology in a bold initiative that would be named EMPAC: the Curtis R. Priem Experimental Media and Performing Arts Center, a defining structure that will be discussed in depth in the following section.

EMPAC's mission statement would declare that "the arts challenge and alter our technology, and technology challenges and alters the arts." It was at this nexus that Rensselaer would stake its claim. With an impact reaching across the entire spectrum of the Rensselaer experience, the Institute envisioned a presence on campus that provided students, researchers, artists, and audiences with opportunities to link the arts with leading-edge research and performance across disciplines. Designed as an international center for innovation in the arts, set within a university dedicated to groundbreaking discovery and innovation, EMPAC would be a center for campus consideration of core questions of art and science.

The Molecularium® films combine research in molecular dynamics with computer animation to teach children about states of matter.

"DEFINING PLATFORMS": EXPANDING THE PHYSICAL INFRASTRUCTURE

When Jackson was appointed president, Rensselaer had not constructed a major academic building in 13 years—and the last newly built student residence had opened more than 20 years prior. In contrast to that tepid track record, *The Rensselaer Plan* outlined a vision of "land, buildings, and infrastructure that meet essential research, learning, living and dining, cultural, recreational, and other essential needs." Academic facilities, the plan said, would be "research-ready with modern infrastructure and services, and would be flexible to meet changing research requirements." The plan called on the Institute to "plan investment in deferred maintenance and continuing capital renewal for facilities needed to meet strategic needs." Moreover, Rensselaer would "define and deliver new capital, renewal, and deferred maintenance projects consistent with the academic, research, residential, athletic, and administrative priorities" in the plan, "with careful attention to benefits achieved relative to initial and continuing costs incurred."[346]

Having built those mandates into the plan, Jackson had Rensselaer embark on a comprehensive capital construction and physical plant improvement program the likes of which the Institute had never seen. The physical plant as a whole would see a substantive transformation, punctuated by the construction of several landmark buildings that would serve, as Jackson envisioned them, as "transformative platforms to anchor and animate Rensselaer education [and] research."[347] In that spirit of innovation and reform, the first new building to come online was designed to support and advance one of the research areas that had been designated as a signature thrust: biotechnology.

Center for Biotechnology and Interdisciplinary Studies

It has been said that implementation of *The Rensselaer Plan* moved forward at blazing speed. Plans for a new biotechnology building are a case in point. The building was specifically identified in the plan as an Institute goal. On December 11, 2000, as the Institute moved in earnest to implement the plan, Jackson appointed a committee to develop a program for a new biotechnology center at Rensselaer. She asked the committee to "ascertain the nature of the research activities expected to occur in the building and make recommendations for the program scope." Also charged with working on the building's design with the yet-to-be-selected architect, the committee included faculty members and administrators.[348]

By March of the following year, the Institute had awarded the design contract for the new biotechnology center. Two Pennsylvania architectural firms with experience in biotechnology design—Burt Hill Kosar Rittelmann and Bohlin Cywinski Jackson— would jointly design the building, which was planned to be some 200,000 square feet in size. Several of the architects on the joint team were Rensselaer alumni.[349]

Funding for the new building would come in part from a $360 million anonymous gift that Jackson had secured for Rensselaer—at the time, the largest gift given to any college or university. (About that monumental gift, more later.) In December 2001, the Rensselaer Board of Trustees, which had already voted for the biotechnology building, approved spending in the amount of $255 million that included that structure *plus* a center for electronic media and performing arts, a parking garage, a boiler plant, a chiller plant, and related improvements to campus landscaping and infrastructure. "Our approval of these extensive construction projects advances Rensselaer's mission to serve as a world-class leader in technological research and education in the 21st century," Board Chairman Samuel Heffner Jr. said at the time.[350]

Heffner labeled this package of construction projects as "extensive," and they were. The package represented an unprecedented commitment of Institute resources for capital construction and improvement. At the same time, by committing to spend more than a quarter of a billion dollars, the Trustees were stating quite definitively that Jackson had their full support. They were literally putting money on that.

Physically, the projects would transform the part of the Rensselaer Troy campus known as "South Campus." The improvements to landscaping and infrastructure would have a significant impact across the campus as a whole. Beyond their appearance on the physical landscape, though, the buildings approved for construction would change the academic, cultural, and social fabric of the Institute writ large, as we shall see.

The groundbreaking for what was officially named the Center for Biotechnology and Interdisciplinary Studies (CBIS) took place in May 2002, during the Institute's commencement weekend.[351]

Designed to house more than 400 faculty, graduate students, and research and administrative staff, the CBIS would ultimately cost $80 million to construct. Another $20 million was spent on equipment.[352] Inside the new building, four-story laboratory and research-support space intersected with separate four-story office space at a dramatic atrium. That design provided public space in the form of two grand concourses. It also solved the practical problem of resolving the differences in floor-to-floor heights of the laboratory and office blocks. The building included 31,250 square feet of open research laboratory space, with built-in flexibility to readily change laboratory configurations as research needs evolved. The facility's floor plan devoted more than 27,000 square feet to core research laboratory space, some 13,000 square feet for support research laboratory space, and more than 42,000 square feet for offices, meetings, and public gatherings.[353]

The site for the new biotechnology building was chosen with great care. It was placed near other prominent research facilities, notably the Low Center for Industrial Innovation and the Jonsson-Rowland Science Center, on a plot of land that could accommodate the biotechnology building's relatively large footprint. Moreover, in that the site is squarely fixed on what is considered the Rensselaer campus's "main street," the site affords an opportunity to showcase a significant new research direction in the context of some of the Institute's prime real estate.

Considerable thought was also given to the building's external appearance, and in fact the facility looks rather different from different angles. Viewed from the edge of campus, from the Troy community, the building purposely echoes the traditional look of Quadrangle Dormitories to the north, and in that way helps unify the South Campus with the historic green-roof campus built during the Ricketts era. Viewed from the central campus, though, the building looks decidedly modernistic. (Similar brick throughout the building gives it aesthetic coherence.) The symbolism inherent in

The state-of-the-art Center for Biotechnology and Interdisciplinary Studies (CBIS)

The interior of the Center for Biotechnology and Interdisciplinary Studies (CBIS) has a floor area of 218,000 square feet.

these design touches is unmistakable, and it is one that Jackson has pointed out. "I always tell people that that corner is where our past meets our future," she said.[354]

The CBIS would take physical shape over the next two years. Recognizing the need to have a capacity for scientific meetings close to the new facility, Jackson decided to add a 150-seat auditorium to the original plan.[355] As the building was fully accommodated to the site, its floor area increased to 218,000 square feet. The project became a teaching case study for some of Rensselaer's architecture and engineering students. During construction, one of the project's architects, P. Richard Rittelmann, class of 1960, taught a two-credit course, Tracking the Biotechnology Center, over the course of five semesters that provided hands-on lessons in tracking a major building project through design and construction.[356]

The facility opened on September 13, 2004. "Welcome to our vision," Jackson said at the opening ceremony. "This center offers a new model for research." Jackson's vision, now a part of the fabric of the Institute, was of a state-of-the-art facility, designed to house constellations of faculty, junior faculty, and others who would conduct research in functional tissue engineering, integrative systems biology, biocomputation and bioinformatics, biocatalysis and metabolic engineering, and other areas. Referring back to her inaugural-address metaphor, Jackson said "the research and teaching—the clasped hands of a true education—that will take place within these walls will accelerate discovery; it will create new pathways to healing; it will enhance the quality of life for all."[357]

The opening activities included a symposium, a presidential colloquy, a ribbon-cutting, a play, and an open house. The biotechnology symposium featured keynote addresses from several luminaries in contemporary science and academia. Shirley Tilghman, president and professor of molecular biology at Princeton University, spoke on "The Human Genome Decoded: Promises Kept and Promises to Come." MIT professor Robert S. Langer ruminated on "Biomaterials and How They Will Change Our Lives." And Troy Duster, a professor of sociology with joint appointments at New York University and the University of California, Berkeley, addressed "The Role of Molecular Biology in the New Uses of Race in Science, Medicine, and Law."[358]

On the following day, Jackson hosted a colloquy entitled "Opportunities at the Interface of Bioscience and Bioengineering." The panel included some of the nation's most prominent scientists, including Elias Zerhouni, then director of the National Institutes of Health; Bruce Alberts, then the president of the National Academy of Sciences; William Wulf, then president of the National Academy of Engineering; and Claire M. Fraser, then president and director of The Institute for Genomic Research and a 1977 Rensselaer alumna. Two corporate executives were also on the panel: James C. Mullen, class of 1980, president and CEO of Biogen Idec, Inc.; and William A. Haseltine, then chairman and CEO of Human Genome Sciences, Inc.[359]

The building's ribbon cutting followed the colloquy. Zerhouni and Alberts joined Jackson for the ceremony, as did then Congressman Michael McNulty and New York State Senate Majority Leader Joseph L. Bruno. Board Chairman Samuel Heffner Jr. and Honorary Trustee Howard P. Isermann, class of 1942, represented Rensselaer, as did Robert E. Palazzo, then the Chair of the Institute's Biology Department and Director of the CBIS. (Palazzo would be promoted to Provost in 2007.)[360]

"The Center has been designed to promote the random collision of ideas," Alberts said. "I congratulate the leadership and the Trustees' vision to enable this university to continue the great tradition of enabling discovery and innovation." Saying that he knew from the decided uptick in the funding Rensselaer was getting from NIH that "something must be happening here," Zerhouni made the blunt observation that "if the Trustees of Rensselaer had not made this investment, Rensselaer would have missed the 21st century."[361]

But Rensselaer had made the investment, and with that milestone ribbon-cutting, Rensselaer's research capacity had taken a major step forward. One of the world's most advanced research facilities, Rensselaer's Center for Biotechnology and Interdisciplinary Studies houses state-of-the-art laboratories, where faculty and students from diverse academic and research backgrounds readily collaborate across disciplines toward discovery and innovation. One can imagine that findings emanating from this spectacular new space will create new technologies that will improve the lives of people around the world. As the stunning first example of a "transformative platform," the CBIS did indeed embody enormous potential to anchor and animate research and education at Rensselaer. But there was more to come.

Computational Center for Nanotechnology Innovations

Jackson knew that in the 21st century, the pedagogy, research, and scholarship of a top-tier, technologically rooted research university required an exceptionally robust computing infrastructure and capacity. She also saw that a strong computing infrastructure would help the university attract and serve high-caliber students and faculty. A vital computing backbone, therefore, was an integral necessity if *The Rensselaer Plan* was to succeed.

The development of Rensselaer's computing capacity started with mobile computing, which put high-end laptops, balancing portability and performance, into the hands of every undergraduate. Specialized software, combined with powerful hardware, provided students with a tool for solving complex theoretical and real-world problems. The Institute also implemented a campus-wide wireless network that led Rensselaer to become known as one of the "most wired" campuses in the United States.[362]

The opening of the Computational Center for Nanotechnology Innovations (CCNI) in 2007, however, catapulted Rensselaer's computing capacity in support of research into the stratosphere. Located five miles south of the main campus in the Rensselaer Technology Park, CCNI is a $100 million supercomputer whose genesis was in a large-scale, strategic collaboration between Rensselaer, IBM, and New York State.[363]

The Center for Biotechnology and Interdisciplinary Studies positions Rensselaer squarely at the interface of life sciences and engineering.

The project was a direct result of Jackson's vision and political acumen. Jackson recognized the intrinsic value that supercomputing could have for the modeling and simulation that was the backbone of much research at Rensselaer. She also saw how to get the project done. Jackson synthesized existing relationships between Rensselaer and IBM, and between the Institute and state legislators, to create the unique partnership among the three partners that led to the creation of the CCNI. John Kolb, the Institute's Vice President for Information Services and Technology and CIO, recalled that, in meetings starting in 2005, Jackson framed and articulated a persuasive argument about how the project could benefit Rensselaer, IBM, and New York State in terms of economic development, in terms of pushing the envelope in high-performance computing, and in terms of high-end scientific and engineering modeling and simulation. Jackson and IBM executive John E. Kelly III, class of 1978, who today is senior vice president and director of research at IBM, convinced then State Senator Joseph L. Bruno of the project's importance, which set the wheels in motion for the project to start.[364]

Each partner contributed approximately a third of the project's overall $100 million cost. New York State appropriated money to help buy the computer systems and to renovate space for the project in an existing building in the Rensselaer Technology Park. IBM provided cutting-edge computational equipment and financial support for research and operations. Rensselaer contributed a site, operational support, and the intellectual capital that drove the facility—the latter dovetailing especially well with the Institute's goals in computation and information technology under *The Rensselaer Plan*.[365]

Typical of the fast pace of *The Rensselaer Plan*, the CCNI was constructed between January and May of 2007, with the formal opening taking place that September. Moreover, Kolb said, the project was finished "on time, on budget, and on program. It was a great team effort by a lot of folks."[366]

In essence, CCNI is an exceptionally powerful amalgam of exceptionally powerful computers and related components. The CCNI systems consist of IBM Blue Gene supercomputers, POWER-based Linux clusters, and AMD Opteron processor–based clusters that are capable of operating at more than 100 teraflops (trillion floating point operations) of computing power per second. That kind of computing capacity amounts to some 15,000 calculations each second for every person in the world. In essence, the supercomputer compresses research time, enabling investigators to complete computations that once would have taken years to be completed in as little as minutes.[367]

Shortly after it was opened, CCNI was ranked as the seventh-most powerful supercomputer in the world, and the most powerful of any such facility at universities. Even after the subsequent development of other similar facilities since that time, it still ranks as one of the world's leading supercomputers.[368]

While Kolb and his colleagues have been instrumental in overseeing CCNI operations since its inception, Rensselaer recently appointed James Myers, who has served as associate director for cyberenvironments at the National Center for Supercomputing Applications at the University of Illinois, to be the facility's first full-time leader.[369]

Rensselaer faculty have become avid users of CCNI and recently accounted for some 120 projects there. "If you look at our strengths and interests at Rensselaer, we have a number of faculty who are very interested in modeling and simulation," Kolb said. "We have folks who are very good at imagining what something should be, and then creating models and simulations to say 'this is what we are predicting will happen.'" The CCNI fits well in that intellectual sweet spot, Kolb said, by supporting inquiry across all of the many disciplines at Rensselaer where modeling and simulation are central to research.[370]

As a partner in CCNI, IBM also conducts research there. For its part, New York has made CCNI available to researchers, laboratories, and colleges based in the state that need high-level computational power. Importantly, too, the state has provided for CCNI's computing capacity to be available to small companies as part of economic development. Another part of the center is reserved for use by other companies. Kolb said this model is good in that it effectively distributes access to CCNI's computing power to a great number of users—and because it does so in a way that spotlights Rensselaer.[371]

CCNI came online at a critical time in research. Biomedical research, for example—a focus in Rensselaer's new biotechnology center—had grown much more computational. At the public unveiling of the CCNI, Jackson made this observation about its importance in advancing *The Rensselaer Plan*'s research focus: "As scientists and engineers continue to drive technology down to the nanoscale, the need for computing power grows by many orders of magnitude. This new center will provide unprecedented tools for simulating interactions among atoms and molecules, allowing researchers to model new nanotechnology-based products and to attack fundamental scientific questions at the nanoscale level, as well."[372]

Apart from its impressive computer power, the CCNI was important to the plan for another reason: It represented the further development of key collaborations between the Institute and important partners off campus. In developing the CCNI, Jackson was the fulcrum for an impressive, important, and highly visible alliance between academia, industry, and government. "For years, [Rensselaer] has been a home of breakthrough science," John Kelly III observed at the opening of the CCNI. "We are confident the new IBM supercomputer will accelerate the pace of discovery and innovation for engineers, researchers, and scientists."[373]

As a platform for researchers to perform a broad range of computational simulations, CCNI would also confirm Rensselaer's stature and raise its visibility as a player in the emerging world of supercomputing. CCNI was designed as an important resource for companies of any size—from start-ups to established firms—to perform research that would be impossible without both the computing power and the center's expert researchers. In that context, research in the CCNI by faculty members from Rensselaer proved to be a way for the Institute to reconnect the Technology Park, which had been founded in the 1980s, with the main campus. Thanks to the fact of the CCNI, there is today more cross-pollination of intellectual capital and ideas between the main campus and the Technology Park than there has been probably since the Park's inception—yet another effect of transformation under *The Rensselaer Plan*.[374]

In terms of the importance of the CCNI as one of the cornerstone elements in the transformation of Rensselaer—and with her characteristic ability to see the big picture—Jackson would later offer this perspective: "The Computational Center for Nanotechnology Innovations is a core enabling platform that allows investigations, designs, and innovations that were not possible before."[375]

Experimental Media and Performing Arts Center

It was readily apparent how such areas of inquiry as biotechnology, information technology, and nanotechnology were logical realms in which Rensselaer might extend the boundaries of its research. Each illuminates the "application of science to the common purposes of life," and each builds on obvious existing strengths on campus. To these core "bets," however, Rensselaer added a more discretionary gamble—albeit one that was no less promising or exciting—in experimental media and the arts.

At first blush that very concept seems alien. What role can there be for "experimental media and the arts" in a polytechnic institute? And indeed, the concept does not appear per se in *The Rensselaer Plan*. But the plan does call for the Institute to build on strengths in interdisciplinary inquiry, research, and education, and to offer a rich portfolio of nontraditional educational options, including programs and courses that enable students to "work at the intersections of disciplines and forge exciting individual career trajectories" and "understand and work within the cultural, social, economic, and political contexts in which they will be expected to lead." The plan also includes the goal of "creating improved presentation and performance spaces on the campus through renovation or new construction."[376]

With a vision for the capacity for Rensselaer to push out the edges of the intersection of the arts, media, science, and technology in much the same way that it was pushing out the edges of biotechnology or information technology, Jackson nurtured discussion of this area in the context of meetings focused on the implementation of the plan. The idea that Rensselaer might build a new center devoted to electronic media and the performing arts was posited by Jackson and gained traction in a priority-setting meeting in July 2000, shortly after *The Rensselaer Plan* was approved. The idea emerged from Jackson's synthesis of ideas brought forward from subgroups that she formed at that meeting to decide on Institute-wide priorities under *The Rensselaer Plan*.[377]

In November 2000, Jackson appointed a task force to develop a plan for an Electronic Media and Performing Arts Center, or EMPAC, as the entity was then known, to "house Rensselaer's prominent and expanding program in electronic media and create a high-quality venue for campus events." The EMPAC task force was chaired by John A. Tichy, then Chair of the Department of Mechanical Engineering, Aeronautical Engineering, and Mechanics.[378] (Tichy knew a thing or two about the performing arts: In the 1960s and 1970s, before pursuing his successful career in research and teaching, he sang, wrote songs, and played guitar with the band Commander Cody and His Lost Planet Airmen, whose hits included "Hot Rod Lincoln." Tichy's musical accomplishments merited his inclusion in both *Who's Who in Rock & Roll* and the *Rolling Stone Encyclopedia of Rock & Roll*.)[379]

In public statements in the early years of *The Rensselaer Plan*, Jackson articulated a sweeping vision for what the arts center might accomplish. In 2002, for example, she said that "on the one side, Rensselaer's faculty and students are at the leading edge of a number of technologies that have applications in the performing arts, or that are inspired by a researcher's interest in the arts. On the other side, Rensselaer has a reputation as one of the most creative campuses in the world for the electronic arts.

Rensselaer leaders break ground for EMPAC, a world-class facility at the nexus of artistic and scientific exploration.

For these reasons, we want to create the electronic media and performing arts center as a nexus of technological and artistic innovation and optimized performance space."[380] In remarks to the New York State chapter of the American Institute of Architects in 2003, she described construction of EMPAC as "a key strategic component of our drive to maximize our interdisciplinary potential and to explore at the edges where the sciences and the arts intersect."[381]

In the latter speech, Jackson directly answered the question of whether a building like EMPAC belonged at a place like Rensselaer. "The creation of EMPAC stems from the conviction that education must occur in an environment that offers diversity of thought and experience, dialogue and exchange," she said. "With EMPAC, Rensselaer will be able to provide a platform where research and technology can interact with artistic creation and reflection. As a result, students will benefit from a richer and deeper understanding of culture and society, as well as the roles and application of research and technology."[382]

If approving Rensselaer's push into biotechnology was a stretch for some Trustees, moving so boldly into electronic media and arts was that much harder to fathom. Trustee Gary DiCamillo, for example, understood that biotechnology fit well with what was happening in science and society. Moreover, he said, "if we wanted to be a big part of the funding of a research institution, then we had to [engage] in biotechnology. Strategically, I thought it was absolutely right on. And I would say most of the Board did, too." But DiCamillo and his colleagues on the Board found the idea of electronic media and arts much more debatable, especially because the facility would be expensive to construct. One of the factors that swayed them though, he said, was that it aligned with Rensselaer's desire to stand out in the crowd. "I think we finally came to embrace it—unanimously embrace it—because it was that differentiating factor," he said. The facility that would become EMPAC "gives us star appeal," he said. "A hundred years from now, we will say wow, somebody had some vision when they built that thing." In addition, DiCamillo said, EMPAC gave Rensselaer a means to "integrate the right brain and the left brain."[383]

The EMPAC task force gathered input from countless interviews with interested constituencies both on and off campus, and visited arts facilities in four states and several countries. Its final report, issued February 22, 2001, underscored the need for a large-scale arts facility on campus, specifically recommending "a building of about 130,000 square feet...located on the hill south and west of the Folsom Library, to include a venue or venues that together would seat 1,200...and two 'black-box' theaters for 200 and 100 people, which can be reconfigured in varied innovative ways for modern performances." The task force also suggested that the building include an art gallery and public common areas, as well as facilities for audio and video recording. The report also said that "the building will require a thoughtful artistic program, excellent acoustics, and intelligent design."[384]

The task force envisioned that the structure would be "a world-class center," focused on "performance and research dedicated to the synergy between technology and the arts." It urged that it be accessible to all campus constituencies, but suggested that "electronic and performing arts" be "anchor tenants," with residencies by visiting electronic and performing artists as the "cornerstone." The report recommended that resident artists "engage in research, interact with and enrich the lives of students and faculty, and conduct performances for the Rensselaer and surrounding communities."[385]

Finally, the task force presented an architectural vision to guide the new building's planning and design:

> We want the building to energize the campus, to be readily recognizable and identifiable as Rensselaer, to make bold and intelligent statements about who we are and where we are going. This project will give an unequalled opportunity to create not just an exciting center for the arts and electronic media but to form the architecture in such a way as to embody a renewed spirit in Rensselaer. The elements of this spirit—the creativity demanded in finding beneficial uses for advances in technology, the new discoveries that emerge when disciplines come together and the recognition that performance and communication are the central drivers in world culture—all will help make this a memorable place. Positioned on the bluff overlooking the Hudson, it will form a beacon of promise, arising from the cradle of the industrial revolution.[386]

The task force's report encapsulated a vision for EMPAC that aligns very closely with the structure as it was ultimately executed. Following the report's release, plans for the new structure proceeded apace. An international building design competition began. Fourteen firms expressed interest, from which four finalists were selected to submit full-blown proposals in June 2001. The juried design competition was organized and run by Alan Balfour, then the Dean of the Rensselaer School of Architecture.[387]

The London-based firm Nicholas Grimshaw and Partners won the competition and was appointed as the project architect. The firm was best known for its award-winning design of London's International Terminal Waterloo. It had also recently designed a new building for the Royal College of Art in London, including a major exhibition space; and the Caixa Galicia Art Foundation Building on the waterfront at La Coruña, Spain, which included an auditorium and lecture hall combined with extensive galleries.[388]

At the time the architect was announced, the project was projected to be some 160,000 square feet in size, at a cost of $50 million. Groundbreaking was scheduled for the spring of 2002, with the building to open in the fall of 2003.[389] As planning continued, the ambitions and scale of EMPAC would take on larger proportions.

Jackson decided that the EMPAC project needed a consultant in media and the arts to work with the architects, other project advisors, Rensselaer Chief of Staff Cynthia McIntyre (who helped oversee the project on Jackson's behalf), and with Jackson herself. That consultant's job was to ensure that the technical specifications required of EMPAC were incorporated into the building's design. The consultant chosen was Johannes Goebel, a respected curator and renowned composer of electronic music who was the founding director of Germany's Institute for Music and Acoustics at the Zentrum für Kunst und Medientechnologie in Karlsruhe.[390] A center for art and media, the ZKM is a forum for international exchange that combined art with research in science, art, politics, and finance.

Later, Jackson decided to hire a director for the center, even before the facility came online. After an international search, Rensselaer announced in 2002 that Goebel

---

"This structure will be a space built to feed the soul and to inspire the mind—for inspiration is what drives both the artist and the scientist."

SHIRLEY ANN JACKSON,
EMPAC groundbreaking, September 19, 2003

The Goodman Studio/Theater in EMPAC is a versatile space for the integration of digital technology with human expression and perception (sometimes referred to as "multimodal environments").

would be EMPAC's first director. His charge at Rensselaer was to relate advanced technology to the arts, and work with the Institute's artists in electronic media and with faculty in traditional academic disciplines who are interested in research and scholarly collaborations with artists. At Rensselaer, Goebel holds a tenured position as Professor in both the Arts Department and the School of Architecture.[391]

In addition to helping to shape the design of the building, one of Goebel's first contributions was to suggest to Jackson that the planned facility's name might be too constrictive given the grand notions Rensselaer had for the building. Jackson readily agreed, and noted the various media and experimental work that the building would support. So it was that the "electronic media and performing arts center" became an "experimental media and performing arts center." Reflecting the fact that the Institute's intent for what the center could be had evolved, the change created a much larger umbrella that better captured Jackson's vision of a domain in which Rensselaer would advance exploration at the nexus of the arts and technology.[392]

Groundbreaking for EMPAC took place on September 19, 2003. "This structure will be a space built to feed the soul and to inspire the mind—for inspiration is what drives both the artist and the scientist," Jackson said that day.[393]

Because EMPAC was intended as a presence on the international scene, the Institute presented a November 17 press preview of both facility and program at The Duke, a 200-seat black-box theater on 42nd Street in New York City. The art, architecture, technology, and media press were invited to see the building model and computer renderings; to hear Jackson, Goebel, and architect Grimshaw; and to experience a wireless interactive dance performance by Tomie Hahn of the Rensselaer arts faculty and an interactive musical-graphic composition performed by trumpeter Thomas Ratzek and computer player Kiyoshi Furukawa.[394]

A pivotal moment in EMPAC's development came in September 2004, when Trustee Curtis Priem, a cofounder of the technology company NVIDIA, announced an unrestricted gift of $40 million to Rensselaer, which had been solicited by Jackson. Priem had deep personal interests in both technology and the arts. An electrical engineering major at Rensselaer, he had enrolled in the first electronic music class at Rensselaer, taught by new-music pioneer Neil Rolnick, where he developed music-generation software for the Rensselaer mainframe with a team of other students. He also played cello for four years in the Rensselaer Orchestra, and for the RPI Players Orchestra.[395]

In private conversations, Jackson had been talking with Priem about a gift to support the experimental media and performing arts center at Rensselaer. The more he got to know Jackson, the more Priem came to realize that she was "one of a kind," as he would later say, who had a "vision beyond all the rest of us." Jackson "understands where we're going, where we've been, and what we need to go do," Priem said.[396]

A meeting with Goebel affirmed Priem's commitment to help build a visionary new facility at Rensselaer where the arts, science, and technology could converge in wholly new ways. Having surveyed similar buildings around the world in site visits with Jackson and others from Rensselaer, the artistic director was able to underscore Jackson's vision for a distinctive facility of the highest quality by showing Priem that the technical specifications for EMPAC were unparalleled, and that many of the details of the building's construction would make it literally the best facility of its kind anywhere. Moreover, as Priem and Jackson had discussed, while universities were constructing performing arts centers, few if any were attempting to blend research and the arts with anything approaching the vision that Jackson had brought to the Rensselaer project. Priem liked the fact that his alma mater could have something that was unique and truly best in class.[397]

"I decided I wanted to make a real big commitment and put my name on that building," Priem said. He thought of his gift as an endorsement, in a way, "that it's okay for Rensselaer to expand beyond its perceived boundaries." He also saw how the building would enrich student life, help Rensselaer attract high-caliber students and faculty, and serve as a defining physical symbol of the new, transformed Rensselaer.[398] In recognition of his gift, Rensselaer announced the new building would be known officially as the Curtis R. Priem Experimental Media and Performing Arts Center (EMPAC).

As EMPAC took shape, it was abundantly clear that the undertaking was beyond anything Rensselaer had attempted before. Looking something like a large glass box—albeit one with various edges pushed out, curved, and reshaped—with a large, egg-shaped concert hall anchored within it, and perched on a 45-degree hill overlooking

Troy and the Hudson River, the building made a grand architectural statement, essentially redefining the Rensselaer landscape. Inside, EMPAC would house a panoply of technological innovations.

EMPAC officially opened on October 3, 2008. The building incorporates four distinct and specialized venues under one roof: an acoustically optimized 1,200-seat concert hall, a 400-seat theater, and two black-box studios created for flexible use by artists and researchers. Visitors enter the building's lobby at the top of the hill. A series of bridges cross over a three-story atrium, providing access to the concert hall, the outer walls of which, made of cedar, look from that perspective like the bow of a giant ship. A grand staircase descends on the side of this space and leads to the theater and black-box studio spaces.[399]

Inside, the building is an engineering and technological standout. Each of the contiguous spaces is built in acoustic isolation from one another. A massive 20,000-square-foot glass curtain wall features mullions that carry heated water to insulate the space from the northern New York winter, the first time that this technology has been adopted in the United States. The HVAC system, virtually silent to preserve the integrity of performances and research, uses displacement ventilation to push air through registers under the seats in the concert hall and the auditorium. The technology at EMPAC includes more than 8,000 inputs and hardwiring to the university's supercomputer.[400]

As the concept for EMPAC was refined, the spaces in the building were expanded, raising the size of the building to 220,000 square feet. The building's budget was increased to approximately $200 million, including construction, technology, and furnishings.[401] Initial interest in EMPAC could be seen in the 2,500 people who attended an arts event midway through the building's construction. When Rensselaer threw an "Opening Festival" of events to celebrate EMPAC's opening, some 23,000 people attended the events.[402]

In practice, EMPAC quickly began to fulfill its capacity for interdisciplinary projects that merge the intellectual, the artistic, and the scientific. Projects would come from many domains, including video, dance, music, theater, Internet art, interactive installations, intermedia art, and multimedia art. Professional environments for theater, image, and sound, integrating traditional tools and new digital worlds, sparked artists-in-residence and campus researchers to use and develop the latest in experimental media to turn their ideas into experiences never imagined before. As part of a commitment to commission performance works, for example, Rensselaer announced in 2006 the program DANCE MOViES, designed to commission new works in the field of experimental dance for the screen. The program was supported with a $1 million gift from Amy and David Jaffe, class of 1964, and the Jaffe Fund for Experimental Media and Performing Arts.[403]

"Our goal is to enable artists, engineers, and scientists to meet in such a way that they respectfully challenge and change one another, while building on the distinct characters of their disciplines," Goebel had said when plans for EMPAC were first unveiled. "EMPAC will supply links between science and engineering research on one side and the sensory impact of art on the other, between the human aspiration toward clarity and precision and the equally human experience, so often felt in art, of life as a stumbling quest for answers. By creating EMPAC, Rensselaer takes a position on culture, science, and society that places it, I believe, far ahead of any other private research university."[404] In one of two lengthy articles about the new structure, the *New York Times* called EMPAC "a technological pleasure dome for the mind and senses."[405]

There was little question that EMPAC was transformational on a number of levels—or that it would extend the boundaries of the university itself. Even given that it was a completely new concept for Rensselaer, there was a strong feeling that EMPAC would be a powerful addition to the intellectual and cultural life of the campus. Ten years from now, Priem predicted, EMPAC would be the new norm for Rensselaer. Taking its presence on campus in stride, he said, people would simply think "this is who we have always been."[406]

Jackson called the new building a "signature space" for the new Rensselaer, saying that "EMPAC is a statement drawing on our technological roots to bend our definition of who we are."[407] Talking about the three major new structures on the main campus—the Experimental Media and Performing Arts Center, the Center for Biotechnology and Interdisciplinary Studies, and the East Campus Athletic Village, Priem said, "I believe they make a statement of who we are, what is important to us, and where we are going."[408]

East Campus Athletic Village

The fourth defining physical platform built as part of the implementation of *The Rensselaer Plan* spoke to Jackson's strong interest in nurturing the whole of the student experience—and to the Institute's strong tradition of student participation in athletics. Designed to dramatically improve campus athletic facilities, expand athletic opportunities, and enhance the overall student experience at Rensselaer, the East Campus Athletic Village would be the most extensive athletic construction project in the Institute's history.

Rensselaer had a rich tradition of student participation and excellence in sports programs, from recreation and fitness activities to intramural, club, and varsity sports. In recent years, more than 75 percent of the Institute's students had participated in intra-murals, club sports, or varsity team sports. The Institute's athletic facilities, however, had not kept pace with student interest or with the times. The '87 Gymnasium opened in 1912 and was added to in 1938.[409] Houston Field House, a former Navy hangar, was acquired in 1946, relocated from Rhode Island, opened as an ice rink in 1949, and partially renovated in 1983.[410] The Alumni Sports and Recreation Center was built in 1920 and had been a New York National Guard Armory until the Institute purchased it in 1970 and partially renovated it for use as an indoor sports facility.[411] Robison Pool opened in 1984, and an artificial turf field and track (the Ned Harkness Field and Track), constructed in 1994, were the Institute's only other modern sports facilities.

In 1999, an athletics task force appointed by Acting President Neal Barton recommended an aggressive program of new and refurbished facilities, beginning with a campus fitness center.[412]

The Institute had made a major improvement in athletic facilities when it built a new 32,000-square-foot fitness center adjacent to the Alumni Sports and Recreation Center. Opened in 2000, the Mueller Center included an aerobic and cardiovascular exercise room with elliptical cross-training machines, rowers, stationary bikes, steppers, and treadmills. Various multipurpose rooms were used for aerobics, kick boxing, yoga,

The East Campus Athletic Village, opened in 2009,
includes a multipurpose lighted stadium with field turf and
seating for 5,200 and a 1,200-seat basketball arena.

and other classes, and the center also included a 5,500-square-foot weight-training room with separate areas for athletic teams and individual lifters. The facility was named for Glenn M. Mueller, class of 1964, in recognition of a $3.3 million unrestricted endowment gift from Institute Trustee Nancy S. Mueller.[413]

Recognizing the need for an even greater commitment to athletics, the Institute first considered erecting a small support facility to provide locker rooms near the Harkness Field and Track and a practice field. In ensuing discussions, however, Jackson realized that a bolder, much more comprehensive solution would serve Rensselaer far more effectively. From numerous conversations, Jackson evolved the concept of what would come to be known as the East Campus Athletic Village—a large, multipurpose athletic complex that could be built in stages. It was believed that such a facility would help meet the needs of current students and could also help attract high-caliber students and student-athletes. The project would add major venues for campus concerts, convocations, and commencement events, and make available space in existing facilities for recreational use. Moreover, by hosting regional, state, and national high school athletic events, the facility could further raise Rensselaer's visibility.[414]

The East Campus Athletic Village is elevating the student experience. It not only gives outstanding intercollegiate athletes more field time and superior facilities, it also opens up space on campus for intramurals and clubs and provides recreation space for the entire student body.

Plans were then set in place to build the first phase of the East Campus Athletic Village. The cornerstone would be a new multipurpose stadium for varsity football, soccer, and lacrosse, as well as outdoor intramurals and club sports. Also included were significant renovations to the Houston Field House, upgrades to better accommodate Division I men's and women's ice hockey. A new basketball arena would feature a performance court.[415]

Construction began in August 2007.[416] The facility was officially unveiled just two years later, on October 3, 2009. ECAV, as the new $92 million complex was known, was another major step forward in the physical transformation of Rensselaer.[417]

Phase I of ECAV encompasses some 176,000 square feet of space, including two new venues for athletics—a new stadium for football, soccer, and lacrosse, and a new arena for basketball and indoor events. The arena includes a fully equipped strength and conditioning center, a professional-caliber sports medicine suite, offices for athletics administrators and coaches, numerous meeting spaces, a new Athletics Hall of Fame, a pro shop, and a café. Renovations to the Houston Field House include upgraded facilities for athletes, coaches, the press, and spectators. Additional projects include installing a new window wall on the west face of the building and an additional floor inside to create offices for coaches and space to host VIPs.[418]

The stadium employs a solar shading screen to control glare and heat from the western sun exposure. (The inspiration for the screen design was a DNA genetic bar code.) Skylights and other design components maximized the use of natural light. The arena roof was designed to support photovoltaic arrays totaling 14,000 square feet for future electricity generation, and the stadium can support up to 20 micro wind turbines along its cornice.[419]

A second phase of ECAV, still in the planning stages, is expected to feature an indoor swimming pool, outdoor tennis courts, and an indoor sports facility with a track and tennis courts.

Jackson put ECAV in this context: "As we continue to build a fully realized university and educate the next generation of leaders, it is our intent to develop the mind, body, and spirit—the whole person," Jackson said. "Combined with other new 'playing fields' at Rensselaer, such as the Center for Biotechnology and Interdisciplinary Studies and the Experimental Media and Performing Arts Center, the East Campus Athletic Village will allow our students to think, to learn, and to play in innovative ways so they can succeed in a world where the pace of change is measured in nanoseconds."[420]

ECAV is "a statement of support to the student," said Trustee Gary DiCamillo, because it serves not just varsity athletes but also is designed to "broaden the

Barton Hall, opened in August 2000, was the first new residence hall since 1966.

intramural experience." At the same time, he said, "it also makes a statement to our cohort and peer and aspirant schools that we are going to play."[421]

There is another dimension to ECAV, too—it is the kind of facility where town and gown can meet and have fun together. Built in Troy, using many local companies and workers, ECAV is also an investment in the local community. Local sports aficionados, civic officials, and just plain folks can point to ECAV as a centerpiece of life in Troy. "I think the new athletic village is going to be a badge of pride for the people of Troy," Trustee Nicholas Donofrio said.[422]

Transforming the physical plant

In the years leading up to the appointment of Jackson as president of Rensselaer in 1999, general maintenance of the campus's buildings and grounds had not been a priority. By the time Jackson came to campus, the physical plant as a whole was showing obvious signs of distress. Deferred maintenance was a significant factor. The campus as a whole looked shopworn. Many academic buildings had not been upgraded in decades. Jackson knew that strong action was needed to bring the Institute's physical facilities up to the standards of the leading research institution that Rensselaer intended to be.

Jackson had toured student residences early in her tenure and had been dismayed at what she saw. Most facilities were poorly maintained and their designs woefully out of date. It is reported that after touring one set of dilapidated residences early in her tenure, Jackson was so angry about conditions there that she seriously entertained the possibility of closing them in mid-semester, finding alternative housing for their students, and razing the structures. Starting early in *The Rensselaer Plan*, Jackson oversaw extensive renovations to all freshman residence halls, and began ongoing, rolling renovations of upper-class residences.[423]

Barton Hall, housing 200 freshmen and opened in August 2000, was the first new residence since 1966. The $9 million facility set a new standard for campus residential design and living. It was fully loaded for laptop and data communication, and offered 13 private conference rooms to support interactive and collaborative learning. Rooms were spacious and bathroom facilities were plentiful.[424] Another new residence hall, the Howard N. Blitman, P.E. '50 Residence Commons, opened in August 2009.

Student dining facilities also saw extensive renovation. The Commons Dining Hall received a new entry, elevator, and improvements to the mail facility, lounge, dining hall, and kitchen. The Russell Sage Dining Hall was extensively renovated and enlarged to convert crowded, dark rooms into larger multilevel spaces banked with windows and a terrace that overlooks a tree-lined quad. Jackson said she could tell the renovation was a success by the fact that students now linger in the hall, talking and relaxing, rather than eating on the run as they used to.[425]

Reflecting on the dining room renovation several years after the fact, Jackson could still recall details that she attended to. For example, she insisted that some noisy air-circulating units near the outdoor terrace that had been covered with painted stucco and wood be redone—bricked over—to help attenuate their sound. Moreover, she specified that the color of the new brick had to match the building's older brick. Admitting that her attention to detail has sometimes led people to label her as a micromanager, she suggests that what really matters in this episode is the larger lesson that can be drawn from it. "I learned this from my first dean of architecture—the built

Opened in 2009, the Howard N. Blitman, P.E. '50 Residence Commons is as much community center as residence facility.

environment matters," she said. "And details matter. They make all the difference in the aesthetics of the space and the usability for multiple purposes. And it gives pride of place." For Jackson, helping create an environment where students and other members of the Rensselaer community will immediately feel that pride of place is all part of being president, no matter how small the detail.[426]

In addition to the improvements to the physical plant described above, the Institute purchased a small business on the southwest corner of the intersection of 15th Street and College Avenue, and converted it to a coffeehouse operated by Sodexo Campus Services. Featuring a fireplace and wireless and hard-wired Internet service, Java++, named by students, offers a variety of foods and nonalcoholic beverages, and provides daytime and late dining and entertainment alternatives for campus and community residents.[427]

More attention to the quality of the student experience came in the form of a $6.2 million renovation of Academy Hall, a former public school the Institute had purchased in 1990.[428] When it became necessary to demolish the former student health center to make room for the Center for Biotechnology and Interdisciplinary Studies, Jackson identified Academy Hall as an appropriate venue for providing integrated, "one stop" student services along 15th Street, where the Institute's academic buildings meet its residential campus. The student health center was relocated to Academy Hall, as were the offices of the Dean of Students, Minority Student Affairs, International Services for Students and Scholars, Disability Services for Students, and Greek Life. The Office of the First-Year Experience moved into the building, as did the Archer Center for Student Leadership Development and the offices of the Registrar, Bursar, and Financial Aid. The school's old auditorium was renovated and became a popular site for small concerts and other programs.[429]

More than merely a building, though, Academy Hall had become a true center for support of student life. Moreover, on a corner near the new Java++ coffee shop and the biotechnology building—a corner with a wall that bears the Rensselaer logo—it helped transition a once-dreary, run-down street corner essentially into a new campus green. It was no wonder, therefore, that at the building's rededication in 2004, Jackson spoke of the building as the physical and symbolic embodiment of Rensselaer's "core philosophical commitment to provide a rich, satisfying student experience."[430]

The physical plant improvements also included extensive landscape projects, widely across campus, to improve other campus quadrangles and other public spaces—all part of a strategy under *The Rensselaer Plan* to make the campus a welcoming and hospitable place for students, faculty, staff, and visitors. *Six Random Lines Excentric*, a large kinetic sculpture by George Rickey, who taught in the School of Architecture from 1961 to 1966, was purchased and installed on Hassan Quadrangle, a gift from Institute Trustee Nancy Mueller.[431]

In the South Campus area, a new vehicle entrance was created, providing an inviting point of entry to the campus where once there had been just a parking lot. A new parking garage was constructed between the Center for Biotechnology and Interdisciplinary Studies and EMPAC. New electrical and chiller plants were built to service new buildings and upgrade service to the research facilities. Numerous necessary streetscape improvements were also undertaken, including storm water improvements, underground electrical utilities, fencing, landscaping, granite curbs, accessible sidewalks, redbrick pedestrian crosswalks, new traffic signals, and other landscape and safety features.[432] The Institute also increased electrical capacity, replaced campus water mains and steam lines, and replaced the roofs of 22 buildings.[433]

The campus renovations also included extensive investments in academic and research space. Many laboratories, offices, and classrooms were improved. These included, for example, an experimental virtual classroom in the School of Architecture, medium-scale and in-flight earthquake simulators for the Center for Earthquake Engineering, a materials characterization core facility in the Materials Research Center, a new Wind Tunnel Facility, and a renovated microbiology laboratory—among many other projects. The campus's information infrastructure was expanded and strengthened to meet the Institute's extensive computing needs in support of research, education, residential living, and administration.[434]

Clearly, details *did* matter. Including its considerable investments for new construction of major buildings, Rensselaer had under *The Rensselaer Plan* invested well in excess of $700 million in capital improvements over the decade.

"We not only concentrated on the new, but we concentrated on the old, and bringing the old up to standard," Board Chairman Samuel Heffner Jr. said. "That was hugely important," he added—in part because the renovations underscored the new pride of place that had taken hold at Rensselaer. Heffner also noted that, along with the Institute's new buildings, the physical improvements across campus provided physical evidence for alumni and alumnae that Rensselaer in 2010 had indeed been transformed from when they were on campus.[435] Tangible signs of that transformation were imperative as part of Rensselaer's efforts to reconnect meaningfully with alumni whose own experience on campus might have left something to be desired.

Rensselaer Vice President for Administration Claude D. Rounds was appointed in 2001, early in the execution of *The Rensselaer Plan*. With a portfolio that includes campus planning, design, and construction, public safety, and physical plant services, the division that Rounds leads provides essential services across the whole of the Institute.

A registered professional engineer, Rounds had served for 15 years as vice president for plant management at Albany Medical Center, where prior to that he had managed plant operations and maintenance.[436] His tenure in healthcare had paralleled an era in which that industry had developed a strong focus on planning in many manifestations, from the development of strategic and tactical plans to performance planning. Consequently, Rounds said, "I came to Rensselaer fully equipped with a strong belief in the value of quality management and continuous quality improvement."[437]

Still, Rounds said he was astonished by the extent to which—and the level at which—planning had taken hold at Rensselaer. "What amazed me immediately was how the process was structured, how *The Rensselaer Plan* was developed, how it touched everything important that the Institute does [and] became strategic in one form or another," he said. "But what also was going on at Rensselaer at the same time was a restructuring organizationally, which complemented the plan," Rounds said. "We became very focused on centralization of some very important, essential core functions." That approach enabled Jackson to develop centralized capital budgets and capital planning processes that were tied directly to institutional priorities. The effect of that centralization was transformative in that it gave Rounds and his colleagues a clear blueprint from which to manage their functions.[438]

In very practical terms, to give one example, Rounds chairs the Institute's committee on space allocation. In that role, he said, "I take a Rensselaer-centric, Rensselaer Plan–focused approach. And simply said, you don't get space in the Institute unless it's understandably clear how that square footage relates to the strategic initiatives and strategic priorities of the Institute." By directly linking decisions about campus space to Institute goals, Rounds said that *The Rensselaer Plan* enabled him to be more effective in evaluating the requests he received and in making subsequent recommendations to Jackson.[439]

In contrast to a more siloed approach, in which planning for one area might take place without the benefit of knowing what might be in the offing for another area, Jackson introduced a much more transparent process in which vice presidents shared their plans broadly with one another. Rounds said that openness expedited his work. "The transparency allows me to know more about what everybody else is doing, and vice versa," Rounds said. "And I find that there's a shorter pathway to design and process the systems that way." By the time he leaves the last planning session of the President's cabinet in a given planning cycle, he said, "I'm already putting together a model in terms of development and implementation."[440]

While Rounds saw the value of *The Rensselaer Plan* in terms of high-level planning and strategy, he also used it to help motivate staff in his division. As an example, he said that "when we started *The Rensselaer Plan*, and when I first came here, [the campus] was not a place that you would consider attractive. The grounds were pretty barren, with not a lot of landscaping." Under the plan, the Institute worked diligently to change that, as we have seen. Now, alumni, parents, students, and other visitors regularly share compliments about improvements in the Institute's physical plant and grounds. "That's great because I can take that to the guys who cut the grass," Rounds said. "I show them the articles that are beginning to identify the look of the campus." Rounds made sure that "the guys who mow the lawns and shovel the snow" understood how their work directly impacted the overall friendliness of the campus, which in turn affects student recruitment goals under *The Rensselaer Plan*. "We try to make everybody understand where they fit into the plan and how it's an important part of what we all try to do," he said. "And rank and file people get it. The plan's broad enough that you can find a place for everyone in it."[441]

Asked whether he anticipated how fast change would take place under the plan, Rounds said that transformation had come "far faster than I suspected. But the captain of the ship is pretty steady in that regard. She can be tough. But she's also focused. And I think that she's recruited people with the right set of ground rules who have been able to take her focus and vision and apply it within each portfolio."[442]

"I've been engaged in a lot of quality management over my professional career," Rounds said, "but I've never seen anything work as well as this. And I think the President's dedication to it, even when it's bumpy and hard, really is why we've done it successfully."[443]

EXPANDING THE
FACULTY AND
THE CURRICULUM

In addition to building and rebuilding Rensselaer's physical infrastructure, *The Rensselaer Plan* defined necessary refinements and new directions in the Institute's academic program and curriculum. One of the plan's major foci has been the recruitment of new academic and research talent.

Building the faculty

A core component in Jackson's vision for the plan was the expansion and development of the Institute's faculty. The Institute had a core group of faculty whose research and teaching were second to none. But Jackson knew that if Rensselaer was to grow to be a research powerhouse on a new level, it needed to expand significantly the research capacity of its professoriate and to grow the faculty size overall. Once the doors of the Center for Biotechnology and Interdisciplinary Studies were opened, for example, the facility needed to be populated with world-class scientists and their teams—researchers capable of meeting the challenge of maximum use of CBIS's potential. Simply put, too, if it intended to compete with institutions that had many more faculty on their rosters, Rensselaer needed to expand considerably the size of its faculty body. Rensselaer also faced the reality that held true across higher education, that many faculty were approaching retirement age and would likely soon leave holes in the Institute's teaching and research ranks.

In remarks to the faculty in December of 2001, Jackson announced that Rensselaer intended to create more than 100 new faculty positions over the course of the implementation of the plan. She reported that 50 new professors had already been hired, with 19 of those filling positions that did not exist previously. Half the new faculty members were women or underrepresented minorities.[444] By 2009, Jackson would be able to announce that 274 new faculty had been hired under *The Rensselaer Plan*. Overall, the Institute had 356 tenured and tenure-track faculty, resulting in a key decline in the overall student-to-faculty ratio from 18:1 in 1999 to the then-current 14:1. The ratio for undergraduates was even better, at 11:1 in 2009.[445]

Rensselaer now had 29 named chairs, including 10 constellation faculty. Among the Institute's younger faculty, 43 had received National Science Foundation Career Awards.[446]

The faculty was more diverse overall—the percentage of women faculty had risen from

15 percent to 21 percent, and underrepresented minority faculty (African Americans and Latinos) had gone from 4 percent to 7 percent. In 2007, in fact, Rensselaer had received nearly $330,000 from the National Science Foundation to assist women in their progress along the academic career path from junior positions toward tenure and full professorship. The Institute announced a new initiative, called RAMP-UP (Reforming Advancement Processes through University Professions), to help advance women in the professoriate. The project was seen as a potential model for reform at the national level.[447]

The strategy of building the faculty, a cornerstone of *The Rensselaer Plan*, had many dimensions. One of the key ideas was to populate areas of inquiry seen as critical to Rensselaer's future with academic teams led by exceptional faculty.

In 2001, the Institute had announced that it was searching for a total of six "constellation" faculty members in the areas of biotechnology and information technology.[448] Jackson envisioned the "constellation" concept as a defining component in the overall strategy to expand the faculty. As defined in the plan, a constellation at Rensselaer would constitute a critical mass of expertise, focused on particular intellectual challenges, and anchored by at least one exceptionally talented senior faculty member who would pursue research in concert with perhaps two junior faculty and a cadre of students. The idea was to seed key areas targeted for focused research inquiry with faculty who were true luminaries in their fields. They would bring expertise and the capacity to build research groups that would expand the Institute's portfolio significantly in critical areas.[449]

In practice, executing the constellation concept would prove an effective channel for Rensselaer to bring exceptional new talent to campus.

Later that year, Jackson appointed search committees to look for constellation faculty in the biotechnology and information technology arenas. The searches would prove challenging. Rensselaer took time and care to assess what kinds of faculty expertise it wanted in these areas. Jackson wanted the best.

The constellation concept scored another coup in 2003 when internationally renowned biochemist Robert J. Linhardt, a distinguished carbohydrate chemist, was recruited from the University of Iowa to be the Ann and John H. Broadbent, Jr. '59

One of the key ideas was to populate areas of inquiry seen as critical to Rensselaer's future with academic teams led by exceptional "constellation" faculty members.

Senior Constellation Chair in Biocatalysis and Metabolic Engineering at Rensselaer. Linhardt was highly respected for his research on the study of bioactive carbohydrates. He had particularly focused on the complex polysaccharide heparin, a major clinical anticoagulant used more than 500 million times a year worldwide. Collaborating with Judah Folkman, another highly regarded scientist, on the antiangiogenic activity of heparin, Linhardt had discovered that low molecular weight heparins act as anti-thrombotic agents.[450] In sum, Linhardt was a heavy hitter in biotechnology writ large, and his appointment was another sign that Rensselaer was intensely serious about claiming a leadership role in this world.

Linhardt's appointment was followed in 2004 with the announcement that eminent theoretical physicist Angel E. García had been appointed to be Constellation Chair in Biocomputation and Bioinformatics. García came from New Mexico, where he had headed Los Alamos National Laboratory's multimillion-dollar research center in theoretical biology and biophysics. His group at Rensselaer, the Biocomputation and Bioinformatics Constellation, was created to focus on developing new computing tools to analyze complex biological data, make predictions to guide experimental work, and offer powerful new methods to predict molecular structure and understand the complex behavior of living organisms. García joined Linhardt in the Center for Biotechnology and Interdisciplinary Studies.[451]

In 2007, biophysical chemist George Makhatadze joined the Biocomputation and Bioinformatics Constellation, coming from the Pennsylvania State University College of Medicine, where he had been professor of biochemistry and molecular biology, and had directed a graduate program in chemical biology for eight years. One of the attractions for Makhatadze was the computational power available in Rensselaer's Computational Center for Nanotechnology Innovations.[452]

Other new constellation faculty added to the concentration of talent. In 2002, E. Fred Schubert, a pioneering semiconductor researcher and professor of electrical and computer engineering then at Boston University, was appointed Wellfleet Senior Constellation Professor of Future Chips at Rensselaer.[453] Reflecting the fact that constellations at Rensselaer span multiple academic disciplines, Schubert was given appointments in the Department of Electrical, Computer, and Systems Engineering as well as in physics.[454] The Future Chips Constellation also hired Shawn-Yu Lin, an authority in photonics research, and Christian M. Wetzel, a research pioneer in semiconductor device design and manufacturing.[455]

Another faculty constellation started to take shape in 2007 when Rensselaer recruited James A. Hendler from the University of Maryland to head the Rensselaer Tetherless

Deborah L. McGuinness
and James A. Hendler
Tetherless World
Constellation Professors

George Makhatadze
Constellation Professor
in Biocomputation and
Bioinformatics

Christian M. Wetzel
Wellfleet Career
Development
Constellation Professor
in Future Chips

World Research Constellation. Hendler is one of the inventors of the Semantic Web, sometimes described as a fusion of the World Wide Web with artificial intelligence, which one day will allow computers and other electronics and robotics to communicate and interact without human intervention. At Maryland, he directed the Joint Institute for Knowledge Discovery and was co-director of the Maryland Information and Network Dynamics Laboratory. At Rensselaer, he would head a leading-edge effort to find new and more productive ways for researchers to capture, review, and ultimately use the rapidly expanding amount of scientific data produced in the information age.[456]

Another expert in Web research, Deborah L. McGuinness, also joined the Tetherless World constellation in 2007. One of the creators of the Web language that is ushering in the next generation of the World Wide Web—the OWL Web Ontology Language—McGuinness was recruited from Stanford University, where she had headed the Knowledge Systems Artificial Intelligence Laboratory. She works to create environments that provide access to and insight into what computer systems are doing, what they are relying on, and ultimately when to trust them.[457]

McGuinness believes the Semantic Web is poised to change the way humans and computers interact, enabling Web agents to act as trusted intelligent assistants. In addition to wanting to understand the provenance and trustworthiness of Web-derived data, she works also to build better ways to use the data. "Basically I am working on the next generation of the Web," McGuinness said. "What does it take to use the Web and feel confident in the information that you receive, so that you are ready to act on it?"[458]

McGuinness and the third faculty member in the Tetherless World constellation, Peter Fox, are collaborators on what she calls "semantic e-science," or "virtual science that understands meaning."[459] With extensive experience as both a data and solar-terrestrial scientist, Fox joined the constellation in 2008 after a 17-year stint as chief computational scientist at the High Altitude Observatory of the National Center for Atmospheric Research. He sees the Web as the main engine for global scientific data sharing.[460]

Another important constellation appointment would come in 2008 when Shengbai Zhang, a quantum physicist renowned for his computational modeling and research in semiconductor defects, was named Senior Chair of Rensselaer's Gail and Jeffrey L. Kodosky '70 Constellation in Physics, Information Technology, and Entrepreneurship.[461]

Meanwhile, Rensselaer also continued to expand its faculty beyond the constellation concept. A few more examples—out of many that could be cited—show both the intellectual depth and breadth of expertise that the new hires brought. In 2007, renowned materials science expert Robert Hull was appointed as head of the School of Engineering's Department of Materials Science and Engineering.[462] Also in 2007, Susan P. Gilbert, an expert in cell biology, biophysics, and nanoscience, joined Rensselaer as the head of the Biology Department after 12 years at the University of Pittsburgh. With offices in both the Jonsson-Rowland Science Center, home to the School of Science, and in the new biotechnology building, Gilbert is one of many Rensselaer faculty who are actively bridging the Institute's traditional strengths with newly emerging areas of interdisciplinary inquiry.[463] In 2008, former Bell Labs and COMSAT researcher Kim L. Boyer was recruited to head the Department of Electrical, Computer, and Systems Engineering.[464]

Rensselaer's Department of Chemistry and Chemical Biology provided a good example of an area where strong new talent joined the experts already on the faculty. In 2004, Linda B. McGown, a professor at Duke University for 17 years and past director of graduate studies for the university's chemistry department there, was recruited to chair the department.[465] And in 2007, three young faculty joined the department. Cynthia H. Collins had just completed a postdoctoral fellowship at the University of Calgary, where she investigated how to engineer synthetic bacterial ecosystems. Pankaj Karande had pioneered the use of high-throughput screening platforms for discovering molecules that enhance the transport of drugs through skin and already held several patents. Peter M. Tessier joined Rensselaer after completing a postdoctoral fellowship at the Whitehead Institute for Biomedical Research at MIT. His graduate studies had focused on how proteins and nanoparticles interact.[466]

"An exceptionally gifted professoriate—the very heart of educational excellence, and academic and scientific rigor—is drawn to Rensselaer by our exceptionally bright and motivated students, enhanced facilities, and sound Institute policies," Jackson said in late 2009.[467] It was clear then that, between the expertise already within its faculty ranks and the new talent that had been brought in under *The Rensselaer Plan*, the Institute's faculty was stronger than at any other time in the university's history.

Expanding the curriculum

The hard copy of the Rensselaer course catalog for 2003–2004 was nearly 100 pages longer than the catalog for 1999–2000—tangible evidence that Rensselaer's academic programs had expanded. By the time the 2009–2010 catalog was posted online, it took yet another 100 pages to describe fully Rensselaer's programs.

Even a cursory survey of the curricular reform that has taken place during the implementation of *The Rensselaer Plan* suggests that changes in the academic program have been systemic and widespread. Jackson described the changes as an examination of the Institute's intellectual core in the context of "the Rensselaer legacy of educational innovation."[468]

In her inaugural address, Jackson had said "great research universities have never neglected the primacy of undergraduate education. Rensselaer has an advantage in this regard because it is recognized—and deservedly so—as a world leader in teaching undergraduates. We have given enormous attention to pedagogical innovation—and will continue to do so now. The challenge is: Whither to now? How do we reach the next level of excellence in pedagogy?"[469] In answer to that question, as a subset of *The Rensselaer Plan*, Rensselaer designed what it called "The Undergraduate Plan."

Components of the program included stronger support for student residential life, a new emphasis on enhanced and increased student participation in research, and a required capstone project experience as an undergraduate graduation requirement. Rensselaer's CLASS initiative—Clustered Learning, Advocacy, and Support for Students—was one way of fulfilling the undergraduate plan. (CLASS is described below.) More co-terminal degrees were created, to allow undergraduates to begin graduate study as juniors and complete both a bachelor's and a master's degree within five years. Building on Rensselaer's tradition of studio learning, combining teaching and research, the Institute also committed to support faculty development designed to enhance the use of technology in the classroom.

The Institute also started an international experience for all engineering students, with plans to extend that experience to all undergraduates. The engineering core curriculum was redesigned; a course called Materials for Engineers, for example, was revised to expose its 500 students annually to more insights about nanotechnology.[470] New undergraduate majors were started—in 2010, for example, Rensselaer launched a new degree program in cognitive science. Other undergraduate majors also started under *The Rensselaer Plan* included programs in electronic arts and in games and simulation arts and sciences.[471] The latter program was a good example of Rensselaer's unique take on an emerging opportunity. Rather than simply offering a major in computer game design—a hot field given the explosive growth of video games—the Institute fashioned its major to also include modeling and simulation, with relevance not just to gaming but also, for example, to military planning and medicine.

Inherent in the plan, Jackson saw an overarching effort to "make our course work and experiences deliberately global in outlook, intellectually rigorous and sophisticated, and socially nuanced, creating an environment that promotes powerful, mind-opening new experiences, which foster intellectual agility."[472] As one dimension of the Institute's international outreach under the plan, Jackson crafted an agreement with Stellenbosch University in South Africa that involves faculty and student exchanges and like activities with a science and engineering focus.[473]

In a 2009 speech, Jackson spoke to another area that had received new emphasis under *The Rensselaer Plan*, entrepreneurship education. This dimension built on Institute traditions to chart new ground. "Rensselaer was among the first in the nation to commit to entrepreneurship education and research across all our schools and programs—and the Rensselaer entrepreneurship definition spans the spectrum from commercial to social entrepreneurship," Jackson said. "We believe all students benefit from an entrepreneurial outlook." Under the plan, students could begin their entrepreneurship education as early as freshman orientation, and continue into advanced study in a new master's program in technological entrepreneurship and commercialization. As part of the plan, Rensselaer increased the entrepreneurial component of more than 70 courses across all five schools, developed curriculum tools, created competitions, supported active undergraduate entrepreneurship research, and sponsored entrepreneurship-related faculty seminars and workshops. In the latter half of the 2000s, five Rensselaer student teams won campus innovation competitions and went on to win national and international competitions.[474]

Other significant markers also underscored the impact of Rensselaer's work to improve the undergraduate experience. Mean SAT scores (verbal and math) of admitted students reached 1400 in 2010, up from 1335 in 2001. Inquiries about Rensselaer from high school students had risen from 22,000 in 2003 to more than 107,000 for 2009–10. Freshman applications, having doubled since 2005, were at an all-time high.[475]

REFINING THE GRADUATE PROGRAM

The Rensselaer Plan also called for a significant expansion in the Institute's graduate program. The rationale was stated in this fashion: "Because research is the engine that drives most graduate programs and provides their intellectual grounding, dramatic growth in research requires an equally dramatic expansion in inquiry-based graduate programs leading to research-based master's and doctoral degrees."[476] Faculty research depended in part on the intellectual horsepower and sheer energy brought by high-caliber graduate students who were attracted by high-quality, inquiry-based graduate programs. Just as research drives graduate studies, so do graduate studies drive research.

The strategy for bolstering Rensselaer's graduate studies had several interrelated components. The plan called for the Institute to expand resident graduate studies and research-based doctoral programs, and to focus carefully its master's programs. The plan called for the recruitment of top-quality students who would be engaged in strong academic programs, and nurtured by attention to the overall student experience. The plan also recognized that the vision for the graduate program would require a full examination and likely changes in the structure, pricing, and financing of all graduate programs. To those ends, the plan included a series of "we will" statements that delineated specific goals:

- Double the production of doctorates awarded over the next eight to 10 years.

- Provide both disciplinary and interdisciplinary doctoral opportunities aligned with areas of research growth.

- Offer a relatively small number of carefully selected residential professional master's programs in sync with the intellectual, research, and education goals of the sponsoring school.

- Extend interactive learning across graduate programs, bringing studio- and team-based learning to our graduate students.

- Develop a highly effective enrollment management program for graduate programs, including market research, marketing, relationship-building, admission, orientation, support, and retention activities.

- Enhance student selectivity and quality, ensuring consistency across all graduate programs. Recruit a larger number of excellent students from a national base, as well as the best international students.

- Pay systematic attention to the quality of the lives of graduate students, providing an engaging student experience and seamless student service.

- Create housing options on and off campus for graduate students.

- Examine structure, pricing, and financing of all graduate programs.[477]

Achieving these goals would be a true challenge, given the general state of graduate programs at Rensselaer when the plan started. Even in the face of an international boom in technology, enrollments in many graduate programs had eroded—a phenomenon that was attributed to demographics, economic conditions, and the Institute's lack of emphasis on such programs. The number of Ph.D. students had significantly declined, as had the number of Ph.D. students who were U.S. citizens and the number of Rensselaer undergraduates who stayed for graduate education.[478]

A planning report prepared early in the era of *The Rensselaer Plan* recognized that Rensselaer had not invested in graduate recruiting at a level comparable to its peers. The report also found that Rensselaer's graduate programs suffered from the absence of a regular internal review process. It saw, too, that policies, procedures, and practices used for graduate education were designed for resident undergraduates and did not necessarily transfer well to modern-day graduate students. Moreover, many of the policies dated to as early as the 1950s.[479]

Another issue was the absence of a full-time graduate dean and support staff. Rensselaer had employed a graduate dean since the 1950s, but that person served only part time, with responsibilities that focused on graduate admissions and student academic services. Administratively, graduate education was dispersed among many different academic programs, each of which viewed graduate education—from admissions through graduation—as its own province. The part-time dean did his best to coordinate graduate education, but the fundamental structures and practices then in place made that work difficult if not impossible.[480]

To give graduate education the degree of attention it needed under *The Rensselaer Plan*, Jackson elected to make this area an Institute portfolio linked to a performance plan, an administrative structure that facilitated—indeed, necessitated—the development of specific goals, action plans, metrics, and most important, a mandate to build the Institute's resident graduate programs. A full-time dean was appointed in September 2001 and the graduate office was reorganized.[481]

Thus energized, the portfolio coalesced around initiatives intended to expand the size, quality, and impact of graduate education. A program of systematic external reviews of existing graduate programs was started, paralleling work with schools and departments to establish consistent, and in many cases higher, standards for student progress to graduate degrees. New enrollment strategies were developed, and graduate student and teaching assistant orientation programs were expanded.[482]

Rensselaer established new Ph.D. programs in cognitive science, biochemistry and biophysics, architectural science, and electronic arts. In 2001, a new multidisciplinary science degree program, offering M.S. and Ph.D. degrees, was started. The MBA curriculum was substantively revamped, and Rensselaer established a new MBA/M.S. in law, in collaboration with Albany Law School. Reviews of all graduate programs were undertaken.[483] New accelerated programs were also introduced, including a new B.S./Ph.D. program in science, a new B.S. in biomedical engineering/M.D. program, and an accelerated B.S. in engineering/MBA.[484]

Research faculty were encouraged to pursue large competitively awarded doctoral student training grants, and to work with the Rensselaer development office to seek endowments for graduate fellowships.[485] One early win came when Rensselaer's mathematics department was awarded a $2.1 million grant by the National Science Foundation in support of student mentoring, including a graduate traineeship program and a postdoctoral fellowship program.[486]

In the 1950s, when rapidly changing technologies in the aircraft and defense industries were creating a critical shortage of engineers and other professionals, Rensselaer collaborated with United Aircraft Corporation (now United Technologies Corporation) to offer graduate instruction in Hartford, Connecticut. The program has operated since then as an extension of the greater Rensselaer intellectual community. By 2010, Rensselaer at Hartford had expanded and evolved to enroll more than 1,500 students from 100 corporations in professional master's programs in management, engineering, and computer science. Under *The Rensselaer Plan*, the Hartford campus was reorganized, sharpening academic focus and streamlining business operations, and, under the principle of "One Rensselaer," made a more integral part of Rensselaer as a whole.[487]

Hard analysis showed that Rensselaer's graduate portfolio differed from that of other world-class research universities in several critical respects. Doctoral students were taking an average 6.4 years to graduate, longer than most peers, and there were plenty of cases where time-to-degree lingered well beyond the average. A nontrivial portion of research awards were being made by entities (e.g., state agencies and corporations) that did not pay for graduate students, or allow recovery of full indirect costs, further shifting the financial burden of graduate student support to the Institute. Many graduate "teaching assistants" supported by the Institute were, in fact, assigned to do research for faculty mentors; in some cases, students were admitted based on their ability to support a faculty member's scholarly interest rather than on their intrinsic quality. A number of graduate teaching assistants also were assigned to teach whole courses—in lieu of faculty.[488] Rensselaer was losing money on resident graduate programs, spending more in institutionally supported teaching and research assistantships and taking in less in tuition income, suggesting a de facto subsidy from the undergraduate program.[489]

A commissioned external study of Rensselaer's doctoral programs showed that the Institute had the lowest tuition and fees for graduate education among a select group of peer institutions. It was the only institution among its peers that determined graduate tuition on a per-credit basis, allowing students to continue full time at no tuition at all (in a "degree completion" status) if they had accumulated the necessary credits but had not completed the dissertation. The Institute provided significantly lower levels of support for doctoral students than peer institutions. It also fell below many peers in passing along the cost of graduate education to research sponsors.[490]

The effect was the following: students with low levels of support, but also with low (or no) tuition charges; students working with faculty unable to bring them support from contract research; and students lingering to complete the Ph.D. The charge for graduate education at Rensselaer had been based solely on the number of credits for which a student was registered, although many graduate students who were finishing a thesis were registered for no credits at all. Moreover, the best students were not coming to Rensselaer.[491]

Rensselaer's administrators realized that if the graduate program was indeed going to be a successful Institute-wide program, versus a collection of what were essentially fiefdoms scattered across the university, more cohesive administrative policies and processes were necessary. An early order of business was reformulating fundamental assumptions about how tuition was charged and financial support awarded to graduate students.

In 2001, Jackson and the provost at the time, in consultation with the faculty senate, appointed a Graduate Tuition Review Committee, which was charged with developing a pricing policy that would provide graduate students with competitive levels of support, fund a greater proportion of graduate education from external funding sources, and encourage students to focus on their research and complete their degree programs in a timely manner.[492]

The committee's recommendations were tantamount to a complete overhaul. It recommended moving academic year tuition for graduate students from a per-credit-hour approach to a flat academic year tuition, set at the same rate as for undergraduates. Under the plan, too, all graduate students supported by Institute assistantships would receive full tuition support and a minimum stipend for a specified period, and would be required to register as full-time students. The plan called for the Institute to increase the tuition cost share for externally funded research projects with overhead recovery. The committee also recommended that students finish all degree requirements for the Ph.D. in a continuous seven-year period, and that students entering with a master's degree in their field of study finish their Ph.D. requirements in a continuous five-year period. A two-and-a-half-year time limit was set for completion of master's degrees. It recommended that a specific number of teaching assistantships be offered each year to attract new graduate students, and that students with these awards be moved to external research support after two years. The committee said that teaching assistants should be used to support a department's teaching function (but not to serve as a primary course instructor), and not to serve an individual faculty member's research interests.[493]

"Until now," Jackson said at the time, "the tuition we have charged for graduate education has not been structured the way it is at other private research universities. Furthermore, the amount of support that Rensselaer provides graduate students has, on the whole, been significantly below that of other premier institutions. As a consequence, both the Institute and the students have had to 'make do' with insufficient resources. That is hardly a recipe for advancing excellence."[494]

Obviously sweeping, the proposed changes required deep amendments in practices that had long been the tradition at Rensselaer. Implicitly, they called for a significantly new way of conducting business that would deeply affect many existing graduate students, faculty, and research sponsors. In addition, as Haviland noted, "each proposal bore on the others, making it difficult and perhaps impossible to pull them apart and

Graduate students work alongside world-class professors, conducting groundbreaking research using powerful research tools such as the nuclear magnetic resonance machines in the Center for Biotechnology and Interdisciplinary Studies.

introduce them gradually over time." Moreover, the recommendations were put on the table at a time when budget and tuition proposals were being prepared for the Board of Trustees, and there was urgency that, absent any changes at that time, the window to put the graduate program on a footing similar to that of peer research universities would soon close for at least a year.[495]

The committee's proposals were reflected in the recommendations made to the Trustees. The changes were studied, proposed, discussed, and approved in just six months—short even by the fast pace at which Rensselaer was already changing. To begin to implement the changes, transition guidelines were instituted to avoid abrupt consequences as Rensselaer moved to the new approach to charging graduate tuition and providing support.[496]

The new policy had significant implications for many faculty members. Historically, schools and departments provided faculty who had little or no external research support with institutionally funded "teaching assistants" to assist faculty with their research. Some departments also provided institutionally funded graduate assistants to faculty who had external support, allowing these faculty to direct outside contract funds to other purposes. In both cases, this pattern was about to change. The changes were seismic—and as David Haviland recalled, campus resistance to them was "swift, strong, and persistent." The scope and speed of the changes, and in particular the impacts on

Once clearer expectations of graduate student quality, workload, and support were in place, the Institute initiated clear standards to measure student progress toward their degrees.

less research-active faculty and faculty whose research was principally supported by industry or state contracts—both relying on institutionally supported graduate students to work on their projects—would spark contention between Rensselaer's administration and its faculty senate, as will be discussed at the end of this chapter.[497]

Once clearer expectations of graduate student quality, workload, and support were in place, the Institute initiated clear standards to measure student progress toward their degrees. More consistent standards for admission were developed, in some cases resulting in much higher requirements. At the same time, the Institute developed more consistent expectations about student appointments with advisors, qualifying and candidacy exams, dissertation committees, and other process features. The Institute required an annual review of every Ph.D. student and candidate; the process outlined specific deliverables for each student and was designed to identify and proactively address academic problems that students might be having. To support those standards, more sophisticated mechanisms were put in place for tracking graduate students' progress, keeping tabs on financial support, and ensuring compliance with the new graduate support and tuition policies.[498]

Toward meeting a goal in *The Rensselaer Plan* of systematic attention to the quality of lives of graduate students, major improvements were also made in the graduate student experience. Graduate student orientation programs were expanded to include segments on student health, environmental health and safety, suicide prevention, diversity, and harassment awareness. International students also took part in special segments on immigration, legal, and health services. The strategy also included better training for teaching assistants. Additional housing for graduate students, including single-room options, was developed. A student satisfaction survey was also started.[499]

Knowing that it was under-enrolling graduate students, Rensselaer also greatly improved its graduate enrollment management services. Moving from dispersed recruiting at the department level, the Institute centralized enrollment management at the cabinet level. Improvements were made in enrollment outreach strategies, including more consistent messaging via the Web and better opportunities to connect potential students with Rensselaer, such as visiting days and a feeder program to help faculty at other schools with a connection to Rensselaer identify potential students.[500]

The results were substantial. Students began receiving full versus partial financial support, at levels competitive with other schools. The Institute received large multi-million-dollar fellowship grants to support doctoral training in terahertz (2003), biomolecular (2004), and fuel cell (2005) research. Net tuition revenue from resident graduate programs increased. The progress of enrolled students could be tracked much more clearly via standardized benchmarks. Students started progressing more quickly through graduate programs. Mentoring improved.[501]

Select data summarize some of the key results. Between Fall 1999 and Fall 2005, for example, overall doctoral enrollment increased by 80 students, and full-time doctoral enrollment by 129 students. At the same time, Rensselaer's schools reduced the size of their master's programs—part of the strategy in *The Rensselaer Plan* to focus on doctoral programs. Between Fall 2000 and Fall 2005, master's level enrollment was down 65 percent. In the same period, there was a significant change in the number of part-time students in master's programs (down 81 percent) and doctoral programs (down 49 percent) as part-time students moved to full-time status—receiving full support and paying full tuition—or graduated. By such measures as average undergraduate GPA and average GRE and GMAT scores, the quality of newly enrolling resident graduate students increased.[502]

REFINING THE
UNDERGRADUATE
EXPERIENCE

The first commitments of "we will" statements in *The Rensselaer Plan* focused intentionally on resident undergraduate education. The plan outlined such major objectives as increasing admissions selectivity, recruiting a more diverse student body, enriching the curriculum, offering more opportunities for undergraduates to conduct research, and enhancing student life as a whole. The first of these goals was discussed in the narrative above; this section focuses on the latter goal, enhancing student life as a whole.

Ask Rensselaer alumni and alumnae about campus life when they were students and, almost to a person, an odd look appears on their face. The fact is that Rensselaer traditionally took a rather stern, paternalistic, old-school view of student learning and had an unfortunate tradition of not paying much attention to the student experience outside the classroom or laboratory. Asked about their undergraduate experience, many graduates volunteer the same story, about arriving at Rensselaer and being told by the President, "look to the person on your left and look to the person on your right—in four years, one or more of you will no longer be here."

"Look to the left, look to the right" was an ingrained part of the culture when Eddie Ade Knowles, who was appointed Vice President for Student Life in 2001, came to work in student services at Rensselaer in 1977. "It was a perspective that education should be delivered in a rigorous, tough-minded way," he said, "designed to weed out a lot of people."[503] Nurturing it was not.

The callous Rensselaer culture did not endear the Institute to either current students or alumni. Students, for example, came to embody Rensselaer's attitude in what was known metaphorically as the 'Tute Screw—the idea, Knowles said, was that "no matter which way you turned it, it was still going to make your life more miserable." A fraternity even made a trophy-sized physical manifestation of the 'Tute Screw that members presented to first-year students as a kind of warning.[504]

Needless to say, the Rensselaer mindset left a bad taste with many alumni and alumnae. As Knowles recalled, "we produced people who went out into the world, did great things," but who invariably ended up thinking "I got a great education at Rensselaer, no question about it, but it was delivered in a very harsh way, and there was not any real support for me outside of my class, unless I belonged to a fraternity or sorority. And no,

Jackson recognized that in the 21st century, any institution of higher education that did not attend in a genuine way to student well-being in and out of the classroom was going to find it difficult to recruit students, let alone students of high caliber.

I do not have great feelings about my alma mater. In fact, I do not know if I ever want to go back to that place. Unless I am just going to visit my fraternity."[505]

"There were varying degrees of recognition of just how much the culture was not serving Rensselaer well, in terms of students, the student experience, and the alumni experience," Knowles said.[506]

First appointed as Assistant Dean of Students, Knowles became the Institute's first Director of Minority Student Affairs in 1979 and was named Dean of Students in 1982. (An accomplished percussionist, he also served as an Adjunct Associate Professor of Arts at Rensselaer, where he still teaches Afro-Cuban drumming.) In each of his roles, Knowles sought ways to change the Institute's culture and make it more nurturing to students, albeit with only sporadic successes. His Sisyphean undertaking got a major boost, though, when Jackson came to campus.[507]

Jackson recognized that in the 21st century, any institution of higher education that did not attend in a genuine way to student well-being in and out of the classroom was going to find it difficult to recruit students, let alone students of high caliber. Knowing that Rensselaer alumni and alumnae were an integral part of the Institute's community, she also saw that the "look to the left, look to the right" mentality hurt alumni relations. Fundamentally, too, she viewed student learning holistically, recognizing that the student experience in the classroom or laboratory was complemented by the considerable student learning that took place outside those venues.[508]

The Rensselaer Plan, Jackson said in 2009, "set out to transform the student experience at Rensselaer—in all regards. This has meant elevating the overall quality of student life through the creation of robust programs and student services, establishment of affinity and connection, strengthening community and leadership education, and development of mind, body, and spirit."[509]

In that spirit, the plan first focused the Institute's attention and resources on improving student orientation and the First-Year Experience, living/learning communities, food services, and extracurricular activities. As further means to support students, Rensselaer also increased counseling and medical staff, athletic coaches, and residential directors and assistants.[510]

Knowing that Rensselaer needed to improve the way it welcomed incoming students into the Rensselaer community, for example, Jackson asked Knowles to turn his and his staff's attention to the First-Year Experience. An Office of the First-Year Experience (FYE) was created in 2001. Its charge was threefold: nurturing student excellence, building community, and helping students succeed.[511] Building its portfolio over time, the office would develop a wide range of initiatives, programs, and publications designed to help students and families navigate Rensselaer.

Under FYE, student life staff instituted an orientation that begins before new students arrive in Troy, with communications about Rensselaer via the Web and social media. Once on campus, students take part in "Navigating Rensselaer & Beyond," a five-day program in which they explore the concepts of teamwork, leadership, culture, community service, and citizenship, and join affinity groups with peers who share their interests—in the process creating strong, stable social communities outside of residence halls and classrooms. The orientation also includes programming for parents, who are then linked into campus news through regular emails and a parents' listserv. The First-Year Experience continues throughout the year, with programs that include Tuesday Night Toolbox, a forum for students to share success stories, related programs in residence halls, and various academic student support initiatives offered by Rensselaer faculty, staff, and upperclass students. "Navigating Rensselaer" won a gold award for excellence in 2006 from the National Association of Student Personnel Administrators.[512]

The cornerstone of the renaissance in the student experience, however, is the newly created "CLASS" initiative—Clustered Learning, Advocacy, and Support for Students. Designed to meet a mandate that Jackson voiced early in *The Rensselaer Plan*, CLASS seeks to transform the student experience by elevating the quality of support for students throughout the undergraduate years. Overall, the objective is to integrate academic and student life initiatives in support of student success, while enhancing mentoring, community building, and experiential opportunities for student growth and development.[513]

Under CLASS, for example, residential life is organized into a commons model. Groups of residence halls are organized into groups—Rensselaer's "Commons"—that are supported by live-in Commons Assistant Deans (student life professionals), as well as upperclass and graduate student assistants living in the residence hall clusters. Faculty Deans of the Commons—tenured professors—live in university-owned houses near the residential commons. Faculty Deans are responsible for overall leadership in guiding the intellectual, cultural, and social life of students in the residential commons, in partnership with the student life professionals. Ideas for CLASS came from site visits to several universities—including Yale, Dartmouth, Middlebury, the University of Pennsylvania, and Lehigh—with distinctive approaches to academic, curricular, residential, and co-curricular programs.[514]

"The residential program elevates the quality of support for undergraduates, providing them with a greater sense of community and belonging, and ensuring that every student receives the best counseling, mentoring, and personal attention possible," Jackson said.[515]

In Fall of 2010, as an extension of the First-Year Experience, the Institute began to phase in the Sophomore-Year Experience, in which all sophomores live on the Troy campus, or in fraternities or sororities that meet university standards and have signed on to partner with Rensselaer, as part of a "Greek Commons." The goal of the program is to provide students with a greater sense of belonging and community at Rensselaer.[516] In practice, this concept drew criticism from the Greek community, some members of which perceived that Rensselaer was encroaching on fraternity and sorority sovereignty. Other Rensselaer students, though, saw the initiative as a positive attempt to draw Greek life closer to that of the central campus. By 2010, a series of campus conversations had largely resolved the differences.

Rensselaer's chapter of Habitat for Humanity has been building homes in the Troy community since 2002.

Apart from a genuine interest in improving student life and changing the culture of student support, Rensselaer hoped that CLASS and its related programs would help it sustain student retention in the high-90s percentile, which would put it on par with the nation's top universities.[517]

With plans to cap its undergraduate population at approximately 5,000 students while it expanded its graduate programs, Rensselaer also recognized that it needed to attend to the quality of graduate student life. "We want our graduate students to have a robust first-year experience, in the same way we built one for the undergraduate students," Knowles said. Those efforts were still in the developmental stage in 2010, with plans calling for the hiring of a dean of graduate student life, a complement to a similar position for undergraduates. Already, though, the Institute has developed additional housing geared toward graduate students, including married students, and made sure the student union offered more programming for graduate students who were on campus in the summer. In addition, there is a special academic orientation for new graduate students, support for improving language skills for international graduate students and, as indicated earlier, better financial support.[518]

Knowles suggested that Rensselaer had finally been able to retool the "look to the left, look to the right" legacy. "Now we say, look to the left and look to the right, because one or more of you will be working together when you graduate," he said.[519]

FUNDING
THE RENSSELAER
PLAN

The Rensselaer Plan envisioned "a broad portfolio to put the Institute in a leadership position both in established fields and in evolving areas of inquiry that hold out great promise and opportunity."[520] New platforms, new programs, new faculty, new services—all of this would take a great deal of money.

Adjunct Trustee Howard N. Blitman, class of 1950, vividly recalled a meeting to discuss goals for the new campaign. At dinner with the Trustees, Jackson asked the group how much they thought Rensselaer could raise. A range of $150 million to $200 million was bandied about, with some saying that a stretch goal could be as much as $100 million more than that. "She looked at us and she said, you guys are pikers," Blitman said. "We are going to raise a billion dollars. We looked at each other and said, this woman is crazy."[521] Jackson would raise them a billion—and then some.

After he got to know Jackson, and once he saw *The Rensselaer Plan*, Blitman came to believe that the Institute's new president "was the most dynamic thing that happened to Rensselaer, I think, probably in its history."[522]

In 2004, the Institute took an audacious step—characteristic of Jackson's vision in *The Rensselaer Plan*—to secure the significant support that would be needed to underwrite the plan's vision by launching a new capital campaign, "Renaissance at Rensselaer: The Campaign for Rensselaer Polytechnic Institute." At a gala kickoff event, Trustee Curtis R. Priem, class of 1982, pledged $40 million in support of the campaign. Trustees Thomas Baruch, class of 1960, Gary DiCamillo, class of 1973, and Paul Severino, class of 1969, were announced as the campaign's co-chairs.

The campaign's private, "nucleus" phase had begun in 2000. Within a year of that launch, Jackson had solicited and received a landmark $360 million gift, from a donor who wished to remain anonymous. Then the largest unrestricted gift on record to any institution of higher learning, the donation constituted a powerful endorsement of the transformational goals of *The Rensselaer Plan*.[523]

The campaign's original goal was to raise $1 billion by the end of 2008. That was an unprecedented amount for Rensselaer; one of the last major advancement efforts, concluded in 1993, had raised $207 million.[524] "We deliberately set our goal beyond past goals, and well beyond the goals of a number of comparable universities," Jackson said, with one purpose in mind: "We did this to extend Rensselaer leadership in technologically rooted education and research."[525]

The appeal of *The Rensselaer Plan* clearly resonated in philanthropic circles, and kept meeting—and besting—its milestone markers. The original goal of $1 billion—a staggering number, given Rensselaer's history—was increased to $1.4 billion in 2006, when an in-kind contribution of highly specialized software from the Partners for the Advancement of Collaborative Engineering Education (PACE), valued at more than $514 million, took the campaign over its original goal.[526]

"Renaissance at Rensselaer" reached its goals in October 2008, some nine months ahead of schedule. The campaign concluded in June 2009, having raised some $1.416 billion. In addition to the $360 million lead gift, $142 million was secured to support faculty and scholarships, $720 million was raised for support of research, academics, and campus programs, and $16 million was received for infrastructure and facilities. Some $177 million in unrestricted gifts was also raised.[527]

The unparalleled support in fundraising encapsulates what was also unparalleled growth in support for research at Rensselaer. As summarized in this table, research funding had grown from less than $35 million in the late 1990s to $89 million in

RENSSELAER
DOLLAR VALUE OF RESEARCH AWARDS 1990–2010 ($000)

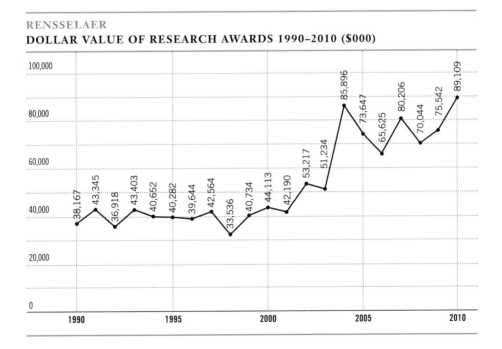

RENSSELAER
DOLLAR VALUE OF RESEARCH AWARDS BY FUNDING SOURCE ($000)

	2001/02	2002/03	2003/04	2004/05	2005/06	2006/07	2007/08	2008/09	2009/10
NSF	13,427	13,986	24,705	18,740	17,720	18,254	16,760	19,024	22,204
NASA	1,947	1,287	1,643	2,144	758	542	457	583	2,609
USDOEN	3,024	1,897	3,168	2,859	4,112	4,235	4,315	4,290	5,460
HHS	1,760	2,843	6,527	5,805	9,283	6,064	8,481	7,489	13,182
USDOD			4,305	4,798	5,167	9,474	9,024	11,612	11,012
Navy	2,038	2,954							
Army	1,462	1,656							
Air Force	999	1,097							
NRC	0	0						850	590
EPA	3,702	355	353	533	425	362	350	350	350
Misc., Federal	2,182	2,200	2,964	2,342	1,896	2,923	2,205	1,835	4,055
State & Local	8,146	5,984	20,229	19,807	5,749	20,742	6,154	9,291	8,575
Industrial	8,689	7,588	10,874	8,644	10,295	9,387	13,525	10,057	9,755
Other	5,841	9,387	11,128	7,975	10,220	8,222	8,772	10,161	11,317
Total	**$53,217**	**$51,234**	**$85,896**	**$73,647**	**$65,625**	**$80,206**	**$70,044**	**$75,542**	**$89,109**

2010—well on the way to the Institute's goal that it should raise on the order of $100 million annually for research.[528] Another table (above) shows that significant growth has come from federal and state research sponsors.[529]

A number of the awards have been large, multimillion-dollar grants to establish centers and major initiatives. For example, the State of New York provided $22.5 million in 2002 to establish a Center for Bioengineering and Medicine in the Center for Biotechnology and Interdisciplinary Studies and to help equip its core facilities.[530]

REDESIGNING
ADMINISTRATIVE
PROCESSES

One can argue that one of the strengths of *The Rensselaer Plan* was that it deliberately did not include the kind of highly detailed plans of action, assignments of responsibility, and timetables that similar types of plans sometimes include. The plan framed a robust infrastructure to guide the Institute, but was more a focused vision statement than tactics manual. Details for accomplishing the plan's goals were purposely left outside its immediate parameters. That construct helped speed the development and approval. It also helped ensure, as intended, that the plan not be revisited and reworked annually—and perhaps subjected to erosion and dilution via endless discussion. Rather, the plan was constructed to be a constant and consistent roadmap for some time. Specific initiatives under the plan were articulated, funded, and implemented through the annual performance planning process.

To that end, the plan conceptualized three stages of planning with nested time horizons: the longer term and overarching vision of the plan itself, complemented by two- to three-year portfolio performance plans and more tactical one-year plans.[531]

In a speech describing *The Rensselaer Plan*, Jackson outlined the three tiers as follows:

First, the plan set out the overarching vision and defined the priorities for the university at the highest level. It is an evergreen plan, meant to be reviewed and revised on a regular basis. At the next level, all Institute portfolios spell out, in annual performance plans, exactly how that academic school or administrative division will accomplish the Institute's highest priorities, portfolio-specific priorities, and the full array of goals set in *The Rensselaer Plan*. The performance plans, which look three years into the future, are revised annually. They include key metrics and benchmarks (internal and external) for measuring success. Existing activities are rationalized against new initiatives, certain activities are examined for sunsetting. Activities are rank-ordered. Finally, based on its performance plan, each portfolio prepares an activity-based performance budget showing how that portfolio will achieve its performance plan.[532]

The three components of the nested time horizon were designed to complement and support each other, as described below.

Performance planning

"The Rensselaer Plan was built for action," Jackson said.[533] How that action would unfold was explicitly described in the final version of *The Rensselaer Plan*:

> Following approval of The Rensselaer Plan, each school and administrative division will create a performance plan that defines the proposed means (action, timetable, and resources) for achieving the Institute's goal as well as the metrics that will be used to measure progress. Performance plans will provide a 3-year forward look.

> Within the framework established by The Rensselaer Plan, the president and cabinet will prioritize actions across all Performance Plans by asking these questions:

- Where are we in a position of leadership, and what will it take to maintain that position?

- Where do we have the potential for leadership, and what will it take to achieve that position?

- Where else must we move aggressively to achieve our goal, and what will it take to stake out a position?

- What areas of current endeavor are we willing to transform, or give up, to focus our resources and energies to achieve the goal?

> As the activities proposed by the performance plans are assigned priorities, they serve, in total, to define priorities Institute-wide. Prioritized performance plans define priorities Institute-wide. These plans become the basis for investments of discretionary, incentive, and new resources, and create the case to secure substantial financial investments from private and government sources, including the next fundraising campaign.

> Each year, results are assessed against the appropriate metrics, performance plans are revised, and the next year's operating plan (budget, capital projects, etc.) is constructed.[534]

Performance planning as a construct had many benefits. Perhaps most significantly, it provided a strong framework for Rensselaer to make a remarkable transformation from decentralized, department-centric budgeting to a wholly different system of budgeting that was centered in the university's administration. With that change came an attendant cadre of new processes, policies, and standards, the summative effect of which was to bring new comprehensiveness to the Institute's financial practices in ways that supported central decision making based on what Jackson and colleagues thought was best for the Institute writ large.

Portfolio-based budgeting also provided a mechanism through which good ideas could be identified and acted on annually, without the need to wait for the much longer cycle of *The Rensselaer Plan* to be revisited. With built-in flexibility, performance planning enabled Rensselaer to expand on recent successes, address new issues, and change directions where warranted; planning and implementation become reciprocal functions. Another benefit was that the performance plans would be designed by the individuals and university units that would be charged with carrying them out.[535]

Moreover, performance planning provided the basis for decisions about spending. Jackson described it this way: "What we commit to do drives our decisions about what we commit to spend. The performance budgets submitted by each portfolio become the components of the Institute budget, once an overall target budget is set."[536]

Another important function of performance planning was perhaps not fully recognized by all in the development of the plan. The performance planning structure integrates a process of preparing for the future into the Institute's culture and procedures as a continuous activity. Rather than being dependent on an event such as the appointment of a new president, or ending up relegated to routinized status as "something we have to do every few years," performance planning remains an active, ongoing process, and one that is at the very heart of university operations. Reflecting on the development and implementation of this dimension of *The Rensselaer Plan*, Haviland wrote that "even as performance planning began, most did not understand that it would become permanent and persistent, that is, that 'planning the work' and then 'working the plan' would become a constant administrative activity at Rensselaer."[537]

The scope of this charge cannot be understated, for it meant that Rensselaer would examine virtually every process and policy that comprised its operations, breaking those elements into their component parts, and reconstituting them in a form that would best serve the new Rensselaer. Indeed, every conventional way of working was on the table for potential retooling—and in fact many fundamental processes were changed substantively.

One can speculate that some at Rensselaer likely perceived performance planning as a challenge to their autonomy and traditional ways of working. Such fears were

Kickoff of the capital campaign, "Renaissance at Rensselaer"

perhaps warranted in that, with the performance plans, Jackson and her team were purposely giving Institute planning an Institute-wide focus. That ran counter to some engrained practices of more decentralized planning, centered in university units. Moreover, performance planning inculcated a set of expectations and practices that concentrated decisions about spending institutional resources with the central administration in ways that had not been seen in recent Institute history. Implementing such reforms would prove to be a sea change.

Early on, Jackson identified several process and management priorities. One was to revise and strengthen the Institute's standards for hiring and promoting faculty, which was later broadened to include the hiring, promotion, and development of faculty and staff. Universities typically do not tinker lightly with tenure, but Jackson wanted to signal that "the standards for getting tenure were going to change—they were going to be higher, relative to teaching, and would have a much stronger research component."[538]

A second priority was to review and revise Rensselaer's policies regarding intellectual property. "If we really were going to focus in scientific and technological entrepreneurship, the real way we were going to try creating new enterprises was through the fruits of research," Jackson said. "And we had to have our IP policies right in order to do that."[539]

The third priority was to develop and use the performance-based planning and budgeting process outlined above. Jackson in particular wanted to focus more attention on how performance plans were resourced, and to link individual performance appraisals for vice presidents and deans to how successfully the plans were implemented.[540]

Finance

Overall, the Institute has invested more than $1 billion in *The Rensselaer Plan*, including more than $700 million in the physical plant alone. That scope of spending has in turn brought a significant change in the scale of the Institute's operating budgets. Over the course of the plan, Jackson has increased the annual Institute budget so that during her time as president it has doubled, from some $200 million to some $400 million. In addition, under the Jackson presidency operational budgets, approved by the Board of Trustees, have been in balance at the end of each fiscal year and have seen surpluses in some years.[541]

Vice President for Finance and Chief Financial Officer Virginia C. Gregg attested to Jackson's acumen in putting Rensselaer's budget on firm footing. Moreover, she said, Jackson is the rare university leader who has both a strong vision for institutional finances and a deep understanding of the numbers themselves.[542]

The Rensselaer Plan served as a strong strategic investment in both current quality at Rensselaer and the Institute's capacity to lead in the future with distinctiveness. Part of that development has been funded through borrowing. While the Institute has taken on debt to finance the considerable vision inherent in the plan, much of that obligation was assumed during market phases when terms were extraordinarily favorable. Gregg noted, for example, that the Institute's deft use of variable interest rates enabled Rensselaer to save more than $21 million in interest costs, savings that were able to be invested in the university.[543]

The Rensselaer endowment, valued in excess of $600 million, has been subject to the same market forces that have challenged endowments at every other institution of higher learning, and the reality is that the plan was undertaken during a period that saw not one but two major recessions. Nonetheless, Gregg said, "the endowment has held its own during a very volatile period."[544]

Under Jackson's direction, Gregg and her staff have instituted many important changes in Rensselaer's finances. Fundamentally, Rensselaer budgeting was converted from a decentralized, tactical-incentive-based model to a strategic, performance-plan-based model.

The shift from decentralized budgeting to a process much more concentrated with the university's administration placed portfolio budgeting in a larger context, that of managing and enhancing the financial resources based on the best interests of the Institute as a whole, as opposed to prior budgeting approaches that provided incentives to portfolios based on their ability to expand revenues. The new practices instituted under *The Rensselaer Plan* set parameters for portfolio budgeting and performance planning designed to contribute to the Institute's financial health.

The portfolio planning approach also made planning and budgeting much more transparent. Across campus, each portfolio area and manager had a much clearer sense of what the rest of the campus was seeking to accomplish in any given year, and every portfolio could see more clearly how its work helped advance the Institute's mission as a whole.

Another important administrative change was the development of a data "warehouse." To move forward in *The Rensselaer Plan*, Institute administrators recognized that they would need a much more robust capacity to analyze the data they collected—about human resources, financial aid, revenues, spending, and so forth—in order to inform strategic decisions. With different departments sometimes coming up with different numbers for the same reporting areas, Jackson also saw that it needed a more uniform way to collect and process data. The Institute already collected considerable data through various transactional systems—some huge and central to operations, some small and essentially off to the side. Rather than replace those systems, Rensselaer built a sophisticated umbrella data collection capacity, a data warehouse, that drew information from all the available systems. The warehouse pulled information from the various transactional systems, collecting them in forms that administrators could use to get information in a uniform way. Now that everyone could work from the same comprehensive data set, the new approach helped Rensselaer bypass distracting conversations about discrepancies in specific numbers and focus instead on analyzing the numbers as part of strategic decision making.[545]

Personnel management

One effect of Rensselaer's improved data collection capacity was that it helped the Institute analyze its most significant expenditures, human resources, in a much more strategic way. Under *The Rensselaer Plan*, the Institute eliminated a much fragmented, siloed approach to human resources—in which individual departments largely made their own decisions without much reference to practices in other departments—in favor of a standardized, university-wide approach. The new approach shifted the focus from individual jobs to one that emphasized position control, managed centrally by the Institute's Human Resources Division, that applied uniform standards across campus to such factors as pay scales and requirements for promotion. The new approach gave the Institute a much clearer picture of how and where it was spending money on personnel, and thus informed more strategic decisions, linked more directly to Institute priorities and budget.[546]

Curtis N. Powell, Vice President for Human Resources, was one of Jackson's early hires, into an elevated position as a cabinet officer. As part of administrative improvements under *The Rensselaer Plan*, Jackson and Powell moved to centralize personnel under the Human Resources umbrella. That meant moving strategically away from the Institute's tradition of decentralized management of employees, which had resulted in disparities and inconsistencies in such fundamental elements of personnel as job titles, salaries, and benefits.

Jackson and Powell also redesigned the Rensselaer compensation system, redefining positions, re-baselining salaries, developing career ladders for staff, and instituting a comprehensive appraisal system. The system also included the introduction of "Performance Management Tools" that made more explicit such components as individual job descriptions, reporting relationships, and job requirements and core competencies, and which link individual performance goals more directly with the Institute's mission under the plan.[547]

Human Resources also helped Jackson elevate standards for faculty promotion and tenure, implement new hiring protocols for faculty and staff, and create a staff education and development program. A merit pay system was established. A better system for staff grievances was put into place. Another innovation was a formal vacancy management process, which required portfolio owners to evaluate the strategic value of every faculty and staff vacancy.

The driving force behind all this change is the Rensselaer mission, Powell said. Talking about the fundamental work that Rensselaer undertakes, Powell said, "We're educating leaders of tomorrow. We have to prepare our workforce to be able to meet those challenges." That challenge is what has prompted Rensselaer to "invest in our human capital and create excellence in our workers," Powell said. "That's what we want to do."[548]

CHALLENGES
OF CHANGE

Change of the magnitude of *The Rensselaer Plan* is inherently difficult. The actual implementation of the plan was made all the more challenging, for example, by the fact that it took place during two economic downturns, one in the early 2000s and another, even more pronounced, later that decade. Mirroring the experience of most private universities, by the end of 2008, Rensselaer's endowment, which once topped more than $800 million, had lost some 20 percent of its value.[549] While Rensselaer has managed balanced budgets in every year under the Jackson presidency, financial realities during the implementation of the plan impacted the Institute's budgets.

To meet the financial challenges of 2008, for example, Rensselaer was forced to implement budget contingencies, a freeze on faculty and staff hiring, and non-salary cost reductions in travel, procurement, advertising, and consultant services. As it grew evident that the crisis was deepening, Rensselaer was forced to lay off 80 staff members. "The painful steps we have taken were very difficult," Jackson told Rensselaer's faculty early in 2009, "but they were taken in the best interest—both the short-term and long-term—of the entire university. That is what defines my job—to act for the welfare of the Institute as a whole."[550]

Implementation of the plan has also been affected by disagreement about the plan itself.

As agoras of ideas, universities encourage discourse, discussion, and debate. The open exchange of ideas is a predicate of a strong, healthy university. Often such exchanges foment a wide range of opinions—and, inevitably, differences of opinions. Indeed, arguing over ideas is one of the hallmarks of a university. Another truism of universities is that they typically resist change. Perhaps that is human nature in institutions, for many of us default to the comfortable versus the untried, and to the familiar over the unknown.

Those truths would in some respects collide in the context of the plan. It is fair to say that the plan was not embraced unanimously by every member of the Institute community. While most Rensselaereans supported the plan and saw it as necessary reform that was perhaps long overdue, others had different perspectives. For some, the scope of the changes set forth in the plan was too great. Some disagreed with the decision to pursue new areas of intellectual inquiry outside Rensselaer's traditions. Some felt the plan did not support their particular areas of research. For others, the pace of the change was too fast. There were no doubt those who, having long enjoyed autonomy in departments or schools, found it difficult to accept the new focus on centralization of decision making in the administration. Inevitably, perhaps, some members of the Rensselaer community endorsed some aspects of the plan, while questioning other parts.

The fact that the reforms put forth in *The Rensselaer Plan* were significant, substantive, and sweeping in scope likely had the effect of sometimes heightening tensions. The stakes were extraordinarily high. The plan, after all, challenged Rensselaer's vision of itself in fundamental ways. By stepping up forcefully to claim its authority in ways that had been diluted over time, and by moving to centralize what had evolved into a fairly decentralized decision making, the administration was to some extent effectively moving the Institute's center of gravity from schools and departments to the central administration. The plan also introduced directions for research and curricula that were outside Rensselaer's long-established frames of reference. Similarly, the plan was predicated on the sobering notion that the policies, procedures, and practices of the past were not necessarily going to apply in the future. The process of developing the plan—which purposely did not involve continued debate through a succession of committees and committee meetings—circumvented much of traditional university decision making. In short, the plan introduced a massive amount of change within a relatively short time frame. It is not surprising that it caused some consternation.

One notable effect of *The Rensselaer Plan* was that the evolution it led to across the Institute led to an evolution in the Board of Trustees. Trustee Paula Simon, class of 1968, recalled that "we were a very different body when [Jackson] took office." For example, she said, some of the Board's committee chairs acted as if "they were running the departments at the school rather than just running a committee." In parallel with the way that the plan brought new structure to campus administrative processes, the Board moved after Jackson's appointment to change the way it managed itself. Job descriptions for Trustees were established. As the Institute geared up for a capital campaign, Trustees realized that they needed to unify in leadership for giving, and not all the Board's members at the time were able to do that. "We set goals for ourselves," Simon remembered, and "required a yearly evaluation of each Trustee's performance to decide whether they were going to be asked to continue or not continue." The Board debated whether to limit terms of service, but ultimately elected not to do so.[551]

"Of course, there was some natural attrition," Simon said. Trustees left for a host of reasons, including, she said, some "who just did not want to work under the new rules." But she believed that the new policies strengthened the Board, setting high expectations for performance and high standards for new Trustees who would be recruited. She saw the changes on the Board as mirroring those that took place across the Institute as a result of the plan. "We really raised the bar in every possible way and every possible job or kind of relationship to Rensselaer," she said. Today's Board, she said, is a "very coherent group with great passion for the institution, for [Jackson], and for the direction that we are heading in. And the passion has only grown with time."[552]

In reaction to some of the changes proposed under *The Rensselaer Plan*, a certain amount of vocal opposition began to gel within the faculty. The dissent was by no means unanimous—Jackson had many supporters in the faculty—but there were those who simply did not share her vision. The faculty senate, for example, expressed concern as early as 1999 about the process by which the plan was developed. Some faculty believed that the senate should have had more say in the ultimate approval of the plan. Some faculty also expressed frustration with the performance planning process.

Some pushback was probably inevitable. "Whenever you have rapid change, there is a cultural response, a backlash," Provost Palazzo observed. "I think academics is an arena where change is neither fast nor welcome, at any time. So when you have a trans-formation agenda on so many levels, it is inevitable that you are going to have cultural response. And that cultural response would be one of resistance."[553]

The policies for graduate tuition and graduate student support that were intro-duced in 2002 sparked further dissent. There was concern about both the content of the new policies and the process by which they were being advanced. Some faculty worried that the new policies would affect their ability to conduct research; others were concerned that Rensselaer's embrace of research might leave behind faculty who did not have research grants. Some felt that too much change was happening too fast. Faculty discussions at the time focused in part on the relative responsibilities and roles

Today's Board is a "very coherent group with great passion for the institution, for [Jackson], and for the direction that we are heading in. And the passion has only grown with time."

TRUSTEE PAULA LORING SIMON

of the faculty and administration. Summarizing one discussion of the new policies, one professor suggested that while many faculty agreed with the goal of Rensselaer striving to achieve top-tier university status, and thought the tuition changes were necessary, some felt that the process of transition to the new policies was flawed and that it did not engage the experience and expertise of faculty in a meaningful way. With the policies in place, campus discussion about them continued, but was essentially stalemated.[554]

The discussion escalated in 2004, when the faculty senate initiated a series of surveys asking faculty about their satisfaction with the chain of command on campus. Results of the survey were presented at a general faculty meeting in 2004, resulting in a statement from Rensselaer's Board backing the President and *The Rensselaer Plan*. At the same time, discussions in the senate focused on the status of faculty rights and responsibilities, the status of Rensselaer's clinical or non-tenure-track faculty, and possible changes in the university's defined-benefit pension plan.[555]

A 2004 assessment of the state of Rensselaer's faculty by a faculty leader suggested that "faculty need to engage with the future of Rensselaer. The faculty must demand to be recognized as part of that future...experience suggests that such a demand will be heard when it is accompanied by creative thinking and analytic force."[556]

In the spring of 2005, the faculty senate continued its discussions of the faculty's role in institutional governance. The debate carried over to 2006, when the faculty senate and administration disagreed over the faculty handbook, faculty representation on a newly appointed task force focused on intellectual property policy, library funding, and a self-study report prepared for a university accreditation review by the Middle States Association of Colleges and Schools.[557]

A letter from a faculty leader sent in February 2006 documented examples of successful faculty/administration work during the 2005–2006 academic year, but also pointed to ongoing challenges.[558] The contention and friction came to a head after faculty thought that the administration was bringing proposed changes in the pension plan to the Board of Trustees. This was not the case (although a Trustee committee later studied possible changes to the deferred benefit pension plan, and decided to leave it in place, as it was). But the concern and suspicions overall were enough to bring faculty dissent to the boiling point, and in April the faculty senate asked the faculty to vote on a resolution of no confidence in Jackson. The voting faculty included a number of retired and emeritus faculty, as well as librarians and archivists, both active and retired. The resolution failed to pass, with 156 faculty voting against it, 149 for it, and 16 abstaining.[559]

The vote was followed immediately by a statement from the Board strongly backing the President and the plan.[560] This was characteristic of the Board, in that throughout the implementation of *The Rensselaer Plan* and Jackson's presidency, the Institute's Trustees have regularly demonstrated their steadfast, unequivocal support for both Jackson and the plan through public statements, official decisions, and support behind the scenes.

Meeting with the Rensselaer faculty on April 28, 2006, two days after the results of the faculty vote were announced, Jackson had much to say about the recent events on campus, and her frank, heartfelt remarks merit quoting at length:

The [Rensselaer Plan] has brought about change....No institution has changed so much, so fast. As a consequence some (perhaps many) feel disaffected. Communication may not be as frequent, or as two-way, or as effective, as you would like with the administration, and especially with the president—with me. People want to know what is happening. They say they want to be engaged.

But, what about me, since this has been a referendum on me and my leadership style? Let me tell you a little about me in the context of what I found when I began as president here. In my first forays out as president—to our alumni and alumnae, our friends, to the science and engineering community, to corporations, and into other arenas, I was taken aback. Many people did not know us, or confused us with lesser places. Many felt we had slipped. Many of our graduates harbored their own bitter taste about how they were treated as students, especially as undergraduates— by faculty, sometimes by staff, and by the Institute as a whole. Many corporations did not know us, except for our traditional relationships (and there were not as many of those as I had thought), and even for them, we were not, in general, a top-tier relationship in terms of partnerships, sponsored research, and philanthropy. I felt we expected and accepted too little. I was frightened about our relative under-endowment....

We needed to create belief by getting things done and by projecting ourselves more. I felt it was important to drive the plan—hard and quickly, since we had no time to lose. I felt it was important to leverage any notoriety and connections I had to project the Institute, especially into places where it was less well-known. I felt I had to work hard with the Board of Trustees to get their buy-in and support. They wanted change, and I wanted to be sure that they understood what change meant and that they understood the costs. They do, and they are 100 percent supportive of where we are going and what we are doing. But it is clear that I have not spent enough time with you. I have been bearing, or trying to bear, a lot of the burden of transforming Rensselaer—personally—especially in the eyes of the outside world, probably in the eyes of many of you. I thought, to be honest, that most of you would inherently understand, even appreciate, what I was trying to do. But that has clearly not been the case. Too many of you have felt left out, that I have been aloof. I need to engage you, and the truth is: no one achieves anything alone. We do need to engage because we are making progress because of what so many of you are doing every day—in your teaching, in your research, in your service to Rensselaer and to your professions. I thank you for that.

While this has been a wrenching experience for all—and this has been especially wrenching for me—I am interpreting what has happened as an offer, by you, to engage with me. Engagement begins with better communication—communication that I am trying to begin—here and now. I am going to reach out to you, and I hope that you will reach out to me.[561]

"I will listen to you. But you have to listen to me, as well," Jackson told the faculty. "You cannot refuse to meet with me and say I do not communicate. You cannot refuse to participate in established processes or propose to effect new ones and then say I do not involve you. You cannot *not* reach out to me while saying I must reach out to you. You cannot hope to get my attention and cooperation by vilifying me or trying to embarrass me publicly."[562]

Jackson pressed for everyone in the campus community to engage in Rensselaer's challenges and opportunities, saying that "Rensselaer cannot stop….We have a collective responsibility for working through issues and challenges, and for how Rensselaer progresses."[563]

In the context of engagement, she spoke directly to issues of governance:

Engagement does not mean that everyone does everyone else's job. It is not the role of the administration to do the faculty's job. It, likewise, is not the role of the faculty to do the administration's job. Clarity comes from knowing the difference. You have your decisions to make. The administration, and the President, as the agents of the Board of Trustees, have their decisions to make. It is an appropriate role for the administration to solicit input in a disciplined way—to outline goals and objectives and boundary conditions, to carefully consider all input, and to make the decisions that are its responsibility to make in its best judgment.[564]

Thomas R. Baruch
Class of 1960
Trustee

Howard N. Blitman, P.E.
Class of 1950
Adjunct Trustee

John W. Carr
Class of 1977
Trustee

Robin B. Martin
Class of 1971
Trustee

Curtis R. Priem
Class of 1982
Trustee

Paul J. Severino
Class of 1969
Trustee

Paula Loring Simon
Class of 1968
Trustee

Finally, Jackson said, "we need to put aside the rancor—on all sides. This does not project a good face to the outside. It does not help us to attract and retain students, to attract and retain new faculty, to attract donors and partners, or to solve our problems. Most importantly, it does not help us to live and to work with each other. We do not have to all love one another, but we must work together with mutual respect."[565]

"To begin this process, I am reaching out to you," Jackson said, asking "Are you willing to reach out to me?" Jackson reiterated her commitment to continue the work she had started at Rensselaer.[566]

Whether Jackson's speech was the turning point or not is a judgment perhaps best left to those who were part of the Rensselaer community at the time, but at some point after that, campus tensions seemed to abate somewhat, and relations between the administration and the faculty seemed to take a somewhat more productive turn. That is not to say that unresolved issues did not exist after that point—they did then, and continue today. As of 2010, for example, the role of the faculty senate was very much still an open question. (More about that below.) But the tone of the debate has somehow changed, and the strain in campus relationships seems less strident.

One final note about the challenges of change. As a prominent figure and as the public face of Rensselaer, Jackson herself has been something of a lightning rod for criticism. There are some in the Rensselaer community who have been quite vocal and sometimes vehement in disagreeing with her about elements of *The Rensselaer Plan*. Sometimes it has been difficult to discern a distinction between comments about the plan and comments about Jackson. At times some of the criticism appears to have been more personal than professional, a turn of events that many on campus seem to rue no matter what their position on the plan.

Jackson was well-aware that some Rensselaereans found it hard to abide her management style, which some called autocratic. A more equitable label might be "forceful," for like many leaders, Jackson has both definitive ideas and the will to bring them to fruition. Jackson knew, too, that some faulted her for moving too fast.[567] In her defense one could say that she most certainly is energetic and driven, and she has been candid about the urgency she felt in bringing change to Rensselaer. Jackson's compensation and benefits package, one of the highest among her peers and a matter of public record, also have been fodder for discussion. In that no leader can achieve perfection, Jackson has no doubt made the occasional misstep. Given that no strong leader can please every constituent all the time, public commentary about her performance was inevitable.

Several Rensselaer Trustees offered perspective in that regard. Robin B. Martin, class of 1971, who earned both undergraduate and master's degrees at Rensselaer and went on to a successful career in broadcast management and government, observed that Jackson "has an uncanny ability to see where she wants to go. She has the ability to cut through all the [obfuscation]. She does not suffer fools gladly. And sometimes that's just the only way you can do it. You have just got to put your eye on the ball and go for it. Clear away all the obstacles and get it done."[568]

Trustee John W. Carr, class of 1977, said that Jackson has an "incredible tenacity to push things ahead and to make the tough decisions." While he noted that "clearly she has ruffled some feathers" along the way, Carr was quick to state that "a person who makes decisions gets more done than a person who hesitates and does not make decisions."[569]

"Positions of leadership are very difficult," Trustee Nicholas Donofrio said. "You can argue with methods, style, processes—you can argue all of those things. But you cannot argue with the fact that we asked her to put us in a place that was different. We asked her to take us to the next level. We asked her to give us a new game to play. She has done all of that."[570]

Today, there is a sense that campus has turned a corner in regard to some of the contention present during the implementation of *The Rensselaer Plan*. There seems to be more consensus these days and less strife. No doubt there are still those who question parts of the plan, but the reality is that Rensselaer continues to make further progress daily toward the broader goals of institutional transformation. As Jackson once said, "academic transformation requires iterating complex, somewhat uncontrollable, processes to closure, in parallel, in a finite time period."[571]

And against the many distractions of daily business, the progress accomplished under *The Rensselaer Plan* speaks for itself, as we have seen. Observers attribute much of that progress to the vision, and tenacity, of Shirley Ann Jackson.

Comparing Jackson with past leaders of Rensselaer, Martin said that "she is truly transformational. This is a woman who has done things that are significant in any field. We happen to be lucky enough to have her here." Referring to a lengthy list of accomplishments under the plan, Martin said "most presidents would be delighted to have a quarter of those done in that period."[572]

Carr admired Jackson's willingness to "step forward in an inherently complex process and put the plan together." Like Martin, Carr also uses the word "transformational" to summarize Jackson's contribution to Rensselaer.[573]

TOWARD TRANSFORMATION

Speaking in 2002 about the process of academic transformation, Jackson outlined several principles that clearly undergirded the development and implementation of *The Rensselaer Plan*. The only real change is systemic change, she suggested. True academic transformation requires changing an entire institution, she said, not just a school, a program, or a select component of a university. About planning, Jackson said that "planning is the basis for radical change," and that a "plan is a process, not just a plan."[574]

Academic transformation, Jackson said, requires a new definition of the institution. "This requires taking a real risk to transform what the university is," she said.[575] Ultimately, risk and transformation are defining characteristics in the success of the plan. The fact that so much change has been implemented in such a relatively short time under *The Rensselaer Plan* is testament to the plan itself, to those who developed it, and to those who implemented it.

Rensselaer's students are great beneficiaries of the plan, of course, as we have seen. Rensselaer's faculty benefit from the countless opportunities the plan has engendered.

The plan adds significantly to Rensselaer's cachet, something that Trustees, alumni and alumnae, donors, and other friends of the Institute deserve and appreciate. A stronger Rensselaer in turn strengthens its Troy community. The ultimate beneficiaries, however, form a community that expands widely from that core group to encompass members of society who will benefit from the products of Rensselaer's research, including patients decades in the future whose lives will be improved by a discovery made in one of the Institute's laboratories.

Next, we will turn our focus to how *The Rensselaer Plan* manifests itself in daily action on the Institute's campuses.

CHAPTER 6

RENSSELAER
TRANSFORMED

A visitor to the Rensselaer Troy campus in the fall of 2010 would have seen much that was familiar to anyone visiting campus a decade earlier—or many decades before. The oldest building on campus, the historic Winslow Building (1866), still sits adjacent to The Approach, the broad, steep, neoclassical granite staircase constructed in the early 1900s to better connect the campus with downtown Troy. In the center of campus, the familiar copper-topped academic buildings constructed during the Ricketts era, their roofs long turned green, still ring '86 Field—a field that dates to 1906 and is named after the class of 1886, which helped fund it. More modern buildings, including Folsom Library (1975), the Jonsson Engineering Center (1977), and the George M. Low Center for Industrial Innovation (1987), stand as evidence of a more recent building boom, and are prominent markers of the Institute's research core.

Look just a bit more closely, though, and you will see that Rensselaer is appreciably not the same institution that it was a decade—or centuries—in the past. The campus is sprinkled with landmark new buildings, and its overall appearance has been noticeably improved through significant renovations and detailed attention to the aesthetics of landscaping—all the product of Jackson's vision and drive. Just as earlier incarnations of the Institute bore the mark of Eaton, Ricketts, and Low, Rensselaer today is the *Jackson* campus.

The new physical campus is indeed impressive. EMPAC's bold architectural and aesthetic statement has transformed not only the footprint of the southern reaches of the campus, but also the entire panorama of campus one sees when approaching from the north, west, and south. At the same time, EMPAC infuses campus life with endless possibilities for exploration and intellectual development.

In the heart of the campus, near the centers of science and engineering, the new Center for Biotechnology and Interdisciplinary Studies hums with activity. Its very presence on campus signals Rensselaer's bold new directions in research, and reminds all that the stakes have been raised significantly for the kinds of intellectual inquiries Rensselaer now undertakes.

At yet another end of campus, Rensselaer's East Campus Athletic Village is a cornerstone of the new, vastly improved student experience, a symbol of the Institute's strong commitment to holistic student development and to its extraordinarily strong athletic traditions.

Across campus, extensive renovations have brought new life to countless older academic buildings. New facilities for residential life and substantial renovations of existing residences are proof that Rensselaer is serious about enriching the whole of the student experience. Major investments in repairs and refurbishing of the physical landscape have created a more cohesive, more welcoming sense of place.

However significant these physical changes are—and representing investments totaling some $700 million, they are indeed significant—the new and redone structures on campus are but the most visible evidence of the transformation at Rensselaer. The changes in the physical plant can be seen as symbolizing the deep, systemic transformation that has been accomplished across virtually every aspect of the Institute under *The Rensselaer Plan*.

Looking at this effect from the broadest perspective, the Institute today has a much broader research portfolio, and research overall has been energized through the influx of new people, new ideas, and new resources. Rensselaer can rightfully boast of a measurably stronger academic program. The Institute has a much more centralized and standardized infrastructure for administrative decision making, fiscal management, policy development, and implementation. The Institute has raised far more money than at any other point in its history. Rensselaer has expanded its partnerships with federal and state government agencies, corporations, and prominent private foundations.

The Institute today offers far better support for student life than ever before, and the student experience overall is far richer. Perhaps it is no surprise, then, that student applications have skyrocketed. The quality of the students accepted at Rensselaer has never been higher, and the student body is appreciably more diverse. Rates for student retention, graduation, and placement also all show marked improvement.

"I think Rensselaer has already made more progress than the rest of the academic peer group recognizes. It has moved so fast that the story of Rensselaer has not really yet caught up with it," Provost Robert Palazzo said. "As one measure, I think it is going to rise in the rankings. I think it is going to rise in productivity and research productivity and stature, on an international scale. And I think it is going to make a big contribution as it has historically through the use of science and technology, to actually transform the world and release society from burdens under which it suffers, particularly in developing countries. That is where I see [Rensselaer] going."[576]

Rensselaer's graduates are sure to make their mark as never before, Palazzo believes. "I see a social consciousness coming through our students, with a strong work ethic," Palazzo also notes. He predicts that new classes of Rensselaer alumni and alumnae— "idealistic individuals armed with the skills of science and technology" and an international perspective—will constitute "a very influential generation."[577]

TRANSFORMATION IN NUMBERS

While much of the transformation of Rensselaer lends itself well to subjective description, available data let us also make objective assessments about the impact of *The Rensselaer Plan*.

In part, the transformation of Rensselaer is captured in data points:

Fundraising
Under *The Rensselaer Plan*, the Institute launched a $1 billion capital campaign, "Renaissance at Rensselaer," by far the most ambitious fundraising program Rensselaer had ever undertaken. When the initial goal was met earlier than anticipated, Rensselaer increased its goal, ultimately securing more than $1.4 billion in support. The campaign included a $360 million unrestricted gift to the university received in 2001, then the largest gift ever received in higher education.[578]

Faculty body
In 1999, Rensselaer had 327 tenured and tenure-track faculty. At the beginning of the 2009–2010 academic year, the Institute had 356 tenured and tenure-track faculty, with plans to recruit another 40 tenure-line faculty, including eight constellation faculty.

Student interest in Rensselaer
Some 13,465 students applied to Rensselaer for the Fall of 2010—a rise of 156 percent compared to 1999.

Student quality

The quality of the Rensselaer student body increased significantly between 1999 and 2010. In 2010, for example, average SAT scores were up nearly 80 points compared to 1999. Some 65 percent of the students came from the top 10 percent of their high school classes.

Student diversity

In 1999, underrepresented minorities represented 8 percent of the freshman class. In 2009, they constituted 12 percent. In 1999, women represented 22 percent of the freshman class. By 2009, they constituted 31 percent.

Student retention

The percentage of students who elect to stay at Rensselaer has risen steadily. Student retention has been consistently above 90 percent in the 2008–09 academic year.[579]

Rankings

The Institute has also drawn greater recognition from outside its walls. In the *U.S.News & World Report* rankings of "America's Best Colleges," for example, the Institute has moved to 42nd among the top 50 universities, up from 50 a decade ago.[580]

Similarly, *U.S.News & World Report* ranked Rensselaer graduate programs in engineering, fine arts, and computer science among the best. Six of Rensselaer's engineering programs are ranked among the top 25—aerospace engineering (19th), electrical engineering (17th), industrial engineering (22nd), materials science and engineering (19th), mechanical engineering (23rd), and nuclear engineering (14th). The Institute's master's degree in multimedia/visual communications ranked 6th in the *U.S.News* ratings, while the Rensselaer computer science doctoral program was among the top 50. *U.S.News* ranks the Lally School of Management and Technology 26th in entrepreneurship, and the School is named among the top international business schools.[581]

Enrollment trends

A more detailed look at the student population on campus underscores how *The Rensselaer Plan* has transformed that core element of the Institute. Between 1997 and 2010, the undergraduate student population expanded by more than 1,000. The number of students pursuing doctoral degrees rose some 19 percent. During the same period, the number of students pursuing master's degrees at the main campus declined some 75 percent—an intentional reduction under the plan. For similar strategic

TOTAL STUDENT ENROLLMENT FALL 2000–FALL 2010

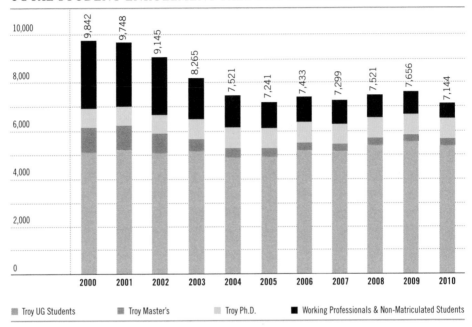

reasons, Rensselaer also decided to significantly phase down its offerings in distance education. In just over a decade, the plan has been successful in changing the mix of students at Rensselaer, emphasizing a strong core of undergraduates complemented by a strong cadre of doctoral students.[582]

Growth in undergraduate population

As detailed in the chart on the next page, Rensselaer has also evidenced growth in its undergraduate population, another goal of *The Rensselaer Plan*.[583]

Enrollment by school

The table on the next page shows trends in the distribution of undergraduate and graduate students in Rensselaer's schools.[584]

SAT scores

The quality of the undergraduate body has also been improved appreciably under *The Rensselaer Plan*, as the chart on page 199 shows.[585]

Student interest in Rensselaer

Two final data sets point to a dramatic rise in interest in Rensselaer among high school students, as demonstrated in the number of inquiries about the Institute from potential undergraduates and the number of applications to attend (see charts on pp. 199 and 200).

RENSSELAER
MATRICULATED UNDERGRADUATE STUDENTS FALL 1997–FALL 2010

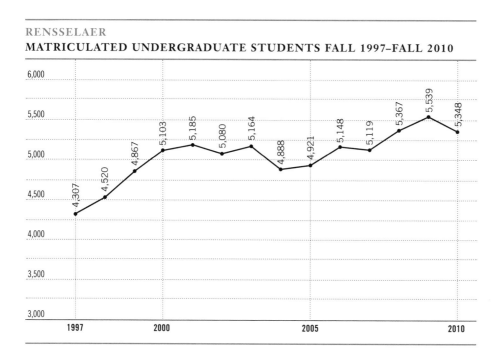

RENSSELAER
UNDERGRADUATE ENROLLMENT BY SCHOOL FALL 2000–FALL 2010

	2000	2001	2002	2003	2004	2005	2006	2007	2008	2009	2010
Architecture	247	231	236	258	262	291	311	300	301	305	276
Engineering	2,682	2,613	2,590	2,736	2,729	2,846	3,042	3,007	3,087	3,221	3,077
Humanities, Arts & Social Sciences	267	299	291	279	259	240	262	291	321	354	361
Management	517	488	427	378	330	316	327	331	358	335	319
Science	1,059	1,150	1,114	1,150	1,052	1,041	1,084	1,069	1,179	1,181	1,176
Information Technology	278	355	375	321	229	144	88	83	90	105	106
Undeclared	53	49	47	42	27	43	34	38	31	38	33
Total	**5,103**	**5,185**	**5,080**	**5,164**	**4,888**	**4,921**	**5,148**	**5,119**	**5,367**	**5,539**	**5,348**

RENSSELAER
AVERAGE SAT FALL 1997–FALL 2010

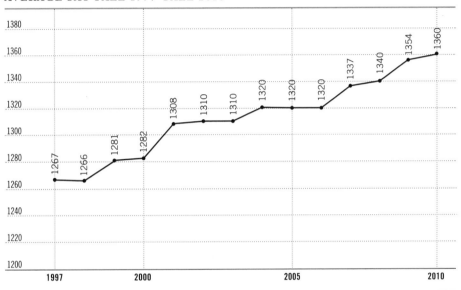

RENSSELAER
ADMISSION INQUIRIES 2000–2010

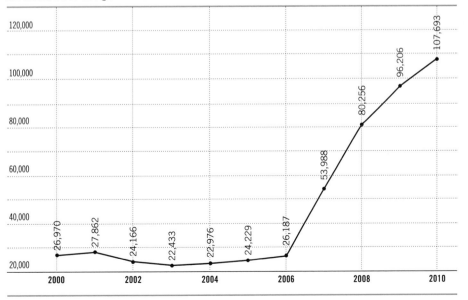

APPLICATIONS FOR ADMISSION 2000–2010

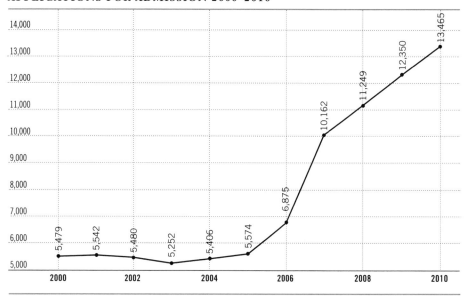

A TOUR OF TRANSFORMATION

Every pocket of the university—every building, every department, and virtually every policy and procedure—has been touched, informed, and improved by *The Rensselaer Plan*. In short, Jackson's vision, as realized in 2010, has transformed Rensselaer. A brief tour of the Troy campus illustrates this phenomenon.

The Winslow Building is a good place to start our rounds, in that the building's history parallels the cycles that have marked Rensselaer's history. First opened in 1866 as the Winslow Chemical Laboratory, this structure originally housed laboratories, a lecture hall, and classrooms. Damaged by fire in 1884 and 1904, Winslow was converted into a shop in 1907 and gradually slid into disrepair. It nearly fell victim to the wrecking ball in the 1970s, but preservationists prevailed. Winslow was donated to the City of Troy, then leased to a children's science museum. It was placed on the National Register of Historic Places in 1994.[586] Unfortunately, however, the museum never flourished on that site.

Looking to expand the Institute in the early days of her presidency, Jackson moved to buy the building back, offering what she described as the high end of market value.

The payment allowed the museum to erase its debt and start a nest egg. Jackson also offered the museum a relatively low cost, multiyear lease for space in a building the Institute owned in the Rensselaer Technology Park, paid for it to move, and volunteered university resources to help the museum outfit its new space. In a more suburban setting, the museum today is thriving—and Rensselaer again has ownership of its oldest building.[587]

At Jackson's direction, boarded up windows in the Winslow Building were replaced. The structure was fully refurbished and once again opened for business as an academic building. This time, though, its focus was not chemistry, but the future. "Your past animates your future," she says. "That is the theme here with me, repurposing what we have to the new."[588] That philosophy comes to life in today's Winslow Building.

The Winslow Building houses the Institute's Tetherless World Research Constellation. Very much at the forefront of a revolution in informatics, the Tetherless group works to bridge the growing gap between the exponential volume of data in the multiple disciplines of science and its use in research and knowledge generation. The group's work, investigating ways to use and understand the Web in ways that have never been fully explored, is a major component in efforts worldwide to develop the next generation Web.[589]

Outside the Winslow Building, The Approach—the long staircase that links campus and town—is just to the south. Renovated and rededicated in 1999, The Approach serves as an enduring symbol of Rensselaer's connection with the local Troy community. It is here that Jackson welcomes new students at the beginning of their first year at Rensselaer. Grouped with fellow members of their living/learning communities, the students walk down the campus hill to the top of The Approach, where Jackson greets them and shakes each freshman's hand. They then continue down the stairs, walking through downtown Troy to Riverfront Park, where the mayor welcomes them to the city and shares some background about its history. That is followed by a "Welcome Fest," with music, food, and games.[590]

The ceremony and celebration are all part of Jackson's concept of "communiversity," posited as part of *The Rensselaer Plan*. As the term suggests, it reflects Jackson's belief that the university's reach must extend beyond the borders of its campuses—starting locally—and that applying Rensselaer's talent and resources to the world as a whole aligns well with the Institute's mission to apply knowledge to the common purposes of life.[591]

From the top of The Approach, one can also see two other important symbols of the Jackson transformation of Rensselaer. Near the foot of the stairs, a brand new residence hall, the Howard N. Blitman, P.E. '50 Residence Commons, opened in August 2009.

Members of the incoming class participate in the annual greeting at the Eighth Street Approach.

Blitman, an Adjunct Trustee, and professional colleagues bought a dilapidated hotel, then completely renovated it and converted it into a residence hall that now houses some 300 undergraduate students near the heart of downtown Troy.[592]

Blitman, the president and CEO of one of the nation's most successful commercial building enterprises, has served Rensselaer for more than 50 years as a Trustee, advisor, and donor. "I have always felt whatever luck or success I have had is really a credit to Rensselaer…and the way I was taught to think and to meet challenges," he said. Blitman was delighted that when Rensselaer named the new residential complex after him, Jackson made sure to include his professional designation—P.E., for "professional engineer"—in the title. Blitman said he does not know of any other engineering building named after individuals that includes the P.E. label. Once word of Rensselaer's naming got out, he received letters congratulating him about that from engineers from all over the country.[593]

Recognizing the new residence as evidence of "communiversity" in action, Troy Mayor Harry Tutunjian said at the project's ribbon cutting that "the transformation of the former [hotel] into student housing for Rensselaer represents much more than a simple change to a building. This influx of students into our downtown will one day prove to be the move that enhances the town and gown relationship that we all strive for."[594]

Jackson sees the new residence as part of the Institute's energized efforts to better serve students—at the project's ribbon cutting, she said the commons embodied a "living and learning community" representative of "our new vision for student life at Rensselaer."[595] Thus, the Blitman Commons is a physical manifestation of the CLASS initiative.

A block away from the new residence is the W. & L.E. Gurley Building. A classical revival structure built in 1862 after a massive fire destroyed much of downtown Troy, the building still houses the modern incarnation of its namesake company, a manufacturer of precision instruments that was founded by William Gurley and his younger brother Lewis, both graduates of the Rensselaer engineering program.[596] Starting during the implementation of *The Rensselaer Plan*, the Institute leased several floors in the building, which now serves as headquarters for its Human Resources Division and as the home of one of the Institute's most distinguished research groups, the Lighting Research Center. All told, the Institute pays some $1.2 million annually into the local economy in rent for office and research space in downtown Troy.[597] (Rensselaer staff are also based in two other downtown buildings.)

The Lighting Research Center (LRC) was founded in 1988 with core funding from the New York State Energy Research and Development Authority. LRC programs and projects have changed lighting practice and have improved the energy efficiency, quality, and effectiveness of lighting. The LRC has earned an international reputation through independent, objective, third-party research, and serves also as an educational resource for reliable information about lighting.[598]

In 2008, for example, LRC scientists announced the first comprehensive method for predicting and measuring various aspects of light pollution.[599] That same year, the LRC announced a new framework for studying the effects of circadian disruption on breast cancer, obesity, sleep disorders, and other health problems.[600] To improve sleep quality in older adults, a team at the LRC tested a goggle-like device designed to deliver blue light directly to the eyes.[601] In 2008 also, the center earned the distinction of receiving one of only 13 first-ever research grants awarded by the U.S. Green Building Council. The $250,000 grant supported a project studying the effect of daylight and electric lighting on the alertness, performance, and well-being of students in schools.[602]

Heading from The Approach back up to the central campus, we find further evidence of the transformation of Rensselaer in the Pittsburgh Building, home to the Lally School of Management and Technology, founded in 1963. Lally's focus on the strategic management of technology leverages Rensselaer's strengths, connecting technological innovation with commercial enterprise. Lally's strong emphasis on experiential learning manifests itself through resources like the Severino Center for Technological Entrepreneurship, endowed in 1999 through the largesse of Paul J. and Kathleen M. Severino, which works at the nexus of educational and research programs to build student understanding of the principles and practice of entrepreneurship, and extends work across campus in technological entrepreneurship.

David A. Gautschi served as dean of the Lally School from 2005 to 2010. When word came round about the opportunity to lead the school, a friend and Institute alumnus who heard Gautschi complain about academia insisted that he investigate Rensselaer. Skeptical, Gautschi thought that like other academic institutions Rensselaer did not have innovation in its DNA. With a career that had straddled work in universities and industry, Gautschi had most recently left academia for what he thought was the last time. "I had become a little bit disturbed by what was going on in the academic world," he says. "Academic institutions and particularly business schools demonstrated a kind of almost pathological resistance to innovating," he observes, and many had lost direction in providing value to society.[603]

Learning of Jackson's vision and *The Rensselaer Plan* swayed Gautschi, as did his recognition that Stephen Van Rensselaer's notion of applying science to the common purposes of life still held true at the Institute even in the 21st century. Gautschi appreciated that the plan recognized that the challenges that society faces have changed and appropriately realigned the Institute to better address those challenges. The plan created opportunities for innovation in the business school that he ultimately could not resist taking on.[604]

Gautschi's leadership helped the Lally School transform itself. Nearly half of Lally's faculty today are new since 2005. Gautschi successfully recruited faculty from Carnegie Mellon, Purdue, UCLA, and New York University, among others. Mostly younger, the new appointees bring notable enthusiasm and new energy to Lally, working with more seasoned faculty to create what Gautschi calls "a teaching team of preeminent scholars and rising stars" that works well together as an academic unit.[605]

Gautschi points to changes in both graduate and undergraduate programs as further evidence of transformation. Lally has created unique interdisciplinary graduate programs in financial engineering and risk analytics (in collaboration with five departments at Rensselaer) and technology commercialization and entrepreneurship (with 12 departments and Albany Law School). Gautschi characterizes the former program as "finance as Rensselaer would do it, which is quantitative finance—financial engineering." About the

Pittsburgh Building

latter program he notes that "technology creation and commercialization do not occur in an ivory tower…they happen in a competitive, increasingly global marketplace for ideas and for capital. Our students and faculty have a passion for taking ideas and turning them into real-world products—both in start-up ventures and in going concerns." Having worked in several other institutions, Gautschi says he is nothing short of amazed by the remarkably low barriers to interdisciplinary work that are a hallmark at Rensselaer, and says that kind of collaboration would be difficult to pull off in other schools.[606]

Jackson and Gautschi also overhauled the processes through which doctoral students navigate their Lally education. "We had been sort of plodding along in the doctoral program," Gautschi recalled. He added two new, hard-charging faculty hires with a strong research orientation to manage first-year doctoral students, under supervision from chaired professors, and says the change helped transform the program. Lally culled the number of students pursuing doctorates from some 40 candidates to perhaps 25. "We're managing it for quality," Gautschi says.[607]

Lally has also streamlined its Executive MBA program to enable working professionals to earn an MBA in just 17 months, and developed a 51-credit-hour MBA that students can earn in as little as one year.[608]

"We're actually redefining what business and management education is all about, and the initial beneficiaries of this are the undergraduate students," Gautschi says. "Do you know that at Lally, you can be an undergraduate getting a major in business and management and minor in engineering, materials science, or medical engineering?" Saying he is not aware of any other similar combinations in business education, Gautschi ventures that students with those credentials graduate highly competitive in the workforce.[609]

With global education close to Gautschi's heart, Lally today boasts a growing portfolio of collaborative programs with enterprises and leading academic institutions in the Indian subcontinent, China, Europe, and the Middle East. Lally, for example, recently signed a five-year agreement with the School of Management at Zhejiang University to enhance and strengthen the global reach of each university's entrepreneurial business and technology programs.[610]

Other Lally-based innovations include new centers focused on financial research and "global business and political economy." Too, Lally has developed what it calls the Innovation Ecosystem, a "living laboratory" that fosters innovation, entrepreneurship, and technology commercialization through relevant coursework, connections with the entrepreneurial business community, and a dynamic group of entrepreneurs in residence.[611]

Affirmation of the renaissance within Lally has come in the form of high rankings in numerous noteworthy publications. After not appearing at all, the school now regularly places high in *Business Week*'s rankings—in 2009, for example, it ranked 36th among the top undergraduate business programs in America and tied with Cornell University at 21st place for academic quality. *Business Week*'s 2009 Specialty Rankings ranked Lally in the 7th slot for both ethics and calculus, 9th for sustainability, and 12th for quantitative methods. *U.S.News & World Report*'s 2010 rankings of best business schools ranked Lally number 26 in Entrepreneurship. *Entrepreneur Magazine*'s MBA Student Survey ranked Lally in its list of top-15 business schools in operations.[612]

Outside the Pittsburgh Building, our attention turns to nearby West Hall, a storied and noteworthy example of French Second Empire architecture built in 1869. Once a hospital, then a high school, the building was acquired by Rensselaer in 1953. Thanks in part to grant support for preservation of historic campus buildings—but owing more to

West Hall

Jackson's desire to marry past with future, and her commitment of institutional money far exceeding grant dollars—the building's busy exterior was painstakingly repainted and detailed between 2004 and 2009, and its grand entranceway was relandscaped.[613]

West Hall currently houses offices and studios associated with the Institute's Department of the Arts, generally considered to be the first integrated electronic arts program within a research university in the United States. Under the acronym iEAR (Integrated Electronic Arts at Rensselaer), the department's studios provide specialized facilities for students, faculty, and visiting artists to engage in individual and collaborative research projects. Here is further evidence of the expansion of the curriculum under Jackson's leadership. In 2002, the department introduced a new undergraduate degree in electronic arts, which is also associated with the Institute's multidepartmental bachelor's degree in games and simulation arts and sciences, created in 2007. (In 2010, the games program was ranked 5th-best nationally by the Princeton Review, which cited it as the "best of the best.") In 2007, too, the department started a doctoral program in the electronic arts. One of the first Ph.D.s of its kind, the graduate program expands the traditions of arts pedagogy through interdisciplinary research in contemporary media theory, practice, and production.[614]

One vision for West Hall is that, with EMPAC, it will anchor something of an arts corridor along the Institute's western border.[615] But West Hall also stands as an important symbol of communiversity. Sited at the western edge of campus (hence its name) and overlooking the city, the building is a familiar landmark for many residents of Troy and environs who knew it as a hospital or who went to high school in the building. Especially given the effort that was taken to reclaim West Hall's grandeur, the decision to restore what is essentially another institutional gateway with the city of Troy can be seen as a politically savvy nod to Rensselaer's commitment to its larger communities.

From West Hall we wind our way uphill once again, going southeast until we come across Folsom Library. Opened in 1976, the building is rendered in the brutalist style that was then popular for such structures. As such, stylistically it does not fit particularly well with other structures on campus. That is intentional, of course. One theory of university architecture is that new buildings should reflect their era and not try to mirror older structures. Folsom certainly does not attempt to blend in, and many observers find its outer shell to be jarring at best, and perhaps downright ugly at worst.

Inside, though, Folsom now offers a different experience. From the main entrance plaza, an expansive open area—fully redesigned in 2005 as part of *The Rensselaer Plan*—welcomes visitors. The hard right angles and concrete columns that defined brutalism's interiors are largely gone, softened by sweeping curves that define custom-designed information and circulation desks, and are mirrored in a trellis of multi-tiered acoustical tiling suspended from the ceiling. Behind the circulation desk, a giant work of art features an inverted Hobo-Dyer Equal Area projection map of the world with Rensselaer's theme—"Why not change the world?"—repeated in many of the languages that are spoken within the campus community. Cherry wood and granite appointments, low-profile shelving, a bright color scheme, and a new layout that admits more natural light make the space far warmer and more inviting than its original design.[616]

An especially clever treatment is that six stark, unadorned concrete columns from the original interior have been repurposed as "i-hubs" (computer-accessed information centers). Clad with an inviting shell of wood, steel tubing, and backlit panels, the now contemporary-looking columns are designed to represent islands of knowledge in the middle of an "ocean" of worldwide information—the ocean being symbolized by the merging waves of color patterns in the library's new carpet. The hubs all have computers and pop-up LAN connections for laptops. Different heights of i-hubs are designed for stand-up, sit-down, and wheelchair access.[617] The renovation took honors for "Outstanding Design" in the Educational Interiors Showcase competition by the American School & University Association.[618]

While adding strong aesthetic improvements to what was not an especially inviting space, the renovations also had a more utilitarian purpose that aligns with Rensselaer's mission: to wire the library with up-to-date technology that meets the new and evolving demands of today's information seekers. A choice of wireless or wired high-speed networks provides access to a multitude of research resources. The renovation also included a temperature-sensitive, computer-controlled lighting system.[619]

The Folsom renovation is part of a larger strategy to make Rensselaer's physical plant more welcoming and to create spaces for members of the Institute's community to connect with each other. In that regard, another addition of note in the library is a new café. Sited just to the left of the circulation desk, it invites patrons to take a break from their studies to sip coffee or sit down to lunch. At lunchtime the place buzzes with patrons—and soft music. The café is not just for nourishment—it is also designed quite intentionally as a space for socializing, in the interest of nurturing campus community. In that context, it is not merely a coffee shop, but rather an integral component of *The Rensselaer Plan*.[620]

Jackson saw to it that a similar option for coffee and snacks was created in Russell Sage Laboratory, a hulking building not far from Folsom that dates back to the Ricketts years. Jackson insisted that a coffee cart in Russell Sage's lobby be closed down. She directed that in its place Rensselaer commandeer an underused conference room and

Folsom Library

convert it into the Beanery, where students and staff can now get coffee, pastries, and other sustenance—to eat in or carry out. Jackson also saw to it that the shop offered a wider choice of food, including more healthy options. This was in addition to other coffee shops that Rensselaer built elsewhere on campus as part of the plan.[621]

Ask Jackson why all this emphasis on coffee shops, and she will explain that it is all part of her plan to improve the quality of student life: "As a college student, you need places to just *be*," she said. "If you're in the library, but maybe you want to go talk to your girlfriend, or you see your buddy, you need a place to go. You need to have places where you can plop down."[622]

Russell Sage Laboratory, across Hassan Quad from Folsom, and one of the original Ricketts-era green-roofed buildings, is headquarters for Rensselaer's School of Humanities, Arts, and Social Sciences (HASS). The school's acting dean, Wayne D. Gray, joined the Cognitive Science Department in 2002. He said that the fact that *The Rensselaer Plan* was in place was part of the reason he came to the Institute. Echoing a theme that many relatively new members of the Rensselaer community voice, Gray said he wouldn't have come to Rensselaer unless it had started to implement change.[623]

Acknowledging that some aspects of the evolution under *The Rensselaer Plan* have been hard to swallow for some faculty, Gray views the transformation that has taken place in a larger context. "It is a modern era," he says. "Part of the essence of the modern university of today is to reinvent itself." He observes that the Institute during the plan has been quite conscious and intentional about transforming itself—for example, he notes, "there would not have been a games and simulations major 10 years ago." That process, he says, has been instrumental in making the Institute far more well known, particularly among the institutions with which Rensselaer competes.[624]

Meanwhile, as part of the Institute's overall transformation, faculty in HASS have been working, along with their colleagues across the Institute, to write new grants and build their capacity in research. Also, as we have noted, several new academic programs have been started in HASS during *The Rensselaer Plan*.[625]

Russell Sage Laboratory houses a writing center, multimedia computer labs, and video production and sound editing equipment. Here, for example, researcher Selmer Bringsjord, head of Rensselaer's Cognitive Science Department, and colleagues work to understand the principles and techniques that humans deploy in order to understand, predict, and manipulate the behavior of other humans. To start to engineer their theories, Bringsjord and his group have begun to develop ways to allow artificial agents to understand, predict, and manipulate the behavior of other agents. The idea is that these agents could, one day, be genuine stand-ins for human beings or autonomous intellects in their own right. To that end, in 2008 the group unveiled a character they created for the online virtual world *Second Life*. "Eddie" is a 4-year-old child who can reason about his own beliefs to draw conclusions in a manner that matches human children his age.[626]

HASS is also home to Rensselaer's Economics Department. The department's head, Arturo Estrella—another new senior faculty hire, he joined Rensselaer in 2008—developed a model that he says forecasted the current economic slowdown at least one year before it became apparent to most observers. Moreover, he says the model has successfully predicted every recession since 1955.[627]

Another important program based in Russell Sage Laboratory, in the Science and Technology Studies Department, is the degree program Design, Innovation, and Society (DIS). A collaboration that involves the schools of Humanities, Arts, and Social Sciences, Engineering, and Management, DIS prepares students to design new products, services, and media while considering the social needs and environmental concerns of the 21st century.[628]

Crossing Hassan Quad to the plaza in front of Folsom Library, one is greeted by a building that looks as architecturally anomalous as the brutalist library, albeit in a rather different way. If the Alan M. Voorhees Computing Center looks a lot like a chapel, that is because, as discussed above, it was one originally, back when that part of campus was part of a Catholic seminary. Acquired by Rensselaer in 1958, it served as the campus library for the next 18 years. After Folsom Library opened in 1976, Rensselaer toyed with the idea of building a new computing center, but then decided to preserve the Gothic structure and convert it into a computing center.[629] Jackson sometimes calls the Voorhees Center the "temple of technology," an appropriate sobriquet given Rensselaer's mission.[630]

Swing to the right around Folsom and things get extremely interesting. That sweeping arc of glass and steel is the main entrance of the Curtis R. Priem Experimental Media and Performing Arts Center, or EMPAC. The 220,000-square-foot facility has perhaps the highest quality in acoustics, visual presentation, production, and performance technology of any performing arts building in the world. Inside, what looks like a giant wooden egg suspended in an equally giant glass box is actually the main concert hall. It is not until you eye EMPAC a bit that you realize that you are actually entering on the building's seventh level. The rest of the building spills over a long hill on the campus's west side. The fifth floor holds yet another new campus gathering spot, Evelyn's Café.

EMPAC sits on what is essentially a promontory, which means that it is visible from many miles away. Its size on the hill means that it literally redefines the Institute's public face and in effect constitutes a very tangible declaration of the transformation at Rensselaer.

Led by Director Johannes Goebel, the venue inspires experimentation, cross-disciplinary inquiry, and advanced research. In fact, the construction of this extraordinary building has already inspired research that may impact the planning and design of performance venues around the world.

A visitor in 2010 would find that EMPAC is living up to its name with another season of experimentation that crosses the boundaries of the arts and technology. Over a recent semester, for example, choreographer Jeremy Wade performed *there is no end*

Russell Sage Laboratory

to more, a playful solo spectacle delving into Japanese kawaii (cute) culture and mashing together a children's TV show, dances, and animated drawings by manga illustrator Hiroki Otsuka. On the eve of her 80th birthday, French filmmaker Agnès Varda was on hand to discuss her films and life. Margaret Wertheim, a science writer and curator, discussed her work on the poetic and aesthetic dimensions of science and mathematics. A group known as rAndom International played with real-time reactive systems that offer viewers an intuitive body-based experience. In a talk, Rensselaer theoretical neurobiologist Mark Changizi explored why we see what we see, from color to the written word. And a building-wide exhibition featured national and international contemporary artists exploring the condition of weightlessness on earth by deploying techniques such as parabolic flight, rigging, and digital effects.[631]

In short, EMPAC is using this ongoing work to discover and exploit its true potential as it becomes an integral part of Rensselaer. Provost Palazzo says he can envision a day not too far down the road when scientists will use EMPAC's capacities for data projection, visualization, and holographic projection to visualize data in wholly new ways, opening new doors for scientific modeling and simulation. "The important advances will happen at the nexus of traditional disciplines," he says.[632]

For Goebel, one key part of the vision for EMPAC is that, in part, it is intended to bring cultural change to Rensselaer. The idea is not to bring to campus well-known acts that happen to be touring nearby, but rather to offer programming that will challenge common thinking. Thus, EMPAC brings to campus—and commissions— works that are designed to engage participants in news ways of thinking, looking, and knowing. One might not always like what one finds at EMPAC, Goebel says, but visitors will nonetheless know that they will find energy, quality, and a seriousness of purpose there, leading to an experience that will extend one's perspectives.[633]

Walk east from EMPAC and you are in the heart of Rensselaer's research core. In a series of three contiguous buildings to our right is the Materials Research Center, constructed with help from the first facilities grant awarded by NASA in the early 1960s. Here is headquartered Rensselaer's Department of Materials Science and Engineering, one of the oldest materials departments in the country. Today, some 25 laboratories provide facilities for powder metallurgy, polymer, ceramics, ultrasonics, cryogenics, corrosion, and other materials research.[634] Among many other projects, researchers here are exploring ways to improve the power density of conventional batteries, and to create the next generation of solid oxide fuel cell materials. Research groups led by professors Linda Schadler and J. Keith Nelson, for example, recently developed nanofilled polymers with 30 percent higher breakdown strength and orders of magnitude longer endurance times—improvements that could lead to greatly reduced costs to utility companies and more robust delivery of electricity to the consumer. The findings have already attracted commercial interest—emblematic of the type of synergies that Jackson envisioned as taking place under *The Rensselaer Plan*.[635]

Empire State Hall, the second contiguous building, houses the New York State Center for Polymer Synthesis at Rensselaer. Dedicated in 1998, the center provides bridges for companies to work with Rensselaer faculty and students in designing, producing, and testing novel polymers that can change the way people live and work. In 2008, for example, researchers at Rensselaer were part of a team that developed a new, inexpensive, quick-drying polymer that could lead to dramatic cost savings and efficiency gains in semiconductor manufacturing and computer chip packaging.[636] In a potentially important blending of polymer science and biotechnology—again, the kind of interdisciplinary research fomented by *The Rensselaer Plan*—a 2007 finding announced that engineers at Rensselaer had transformed a polymer found in common brown seaweed into a device that can support the growth and release of stem cells at the site of a bodily injury or at the source of a disease.[637]

The third contiguous building, Cogswell Laboratory, completed in 1971, is one of many collections of campus laboratories where disciplines meet in interesting ways. Cogswell is home, for example, to the New York Center for Astrobiology, another product of *The Rensselaer Plan*. Created in 2008 with a $7.5 million grant from NASA, the astrobiology center is part of the NASA Astrobiology Institute, a "virtual" institute of universities that combine their knowledge and expertise to advance our understanding of the origin and distribution of life in the universe. The new center is also another example of where Rensselaer's past intersects with its future, in that it builds on a legacy of NASA-oriented discovery and collaboration developed over the past half-century, which included many significant projects based at Rensselaer.[638]

As we continue our walk, we see behind Cogswell yet another product of the plan, a new parking garage with space for 500 cars. The first major component completed as part of the university's South Campus Development Project, the construction employed some 65 local workers—just one example of tangible evidence of Rensselaer's significant local economic impact.[639]

Across from Cogswell we find the Jonsson-Rowland Science Center, home to the School of Science. Faculty here include a Nobel laureate, as well as members of the National Academies, the American Academy of Arts and Sciences, and other prominent institutions.

The School of Science is the umbrella for several important research centers that came to fruition under *The Rensselaer Plan*. The Baruch '60 Center for Biochemical Solar Energy Research, for example, funded by Trustee and alumnus Thomas R. Baruch and launched in 2008, will work to develop the next generation of solar technology by studying one of the most powerful energy converting machines in world—plants. Researchers will use sophisticated new technologies and techniques to understand how plants convert energy, toward developing new technologies that mimic this extremely efficient natural system.[640]

In 2002, a $1 million grant from the W.M. Keck Foundation established the W.M. Keck Laboratory for Terahertz Science within a new Center for Terahertz Research at Rensselaer. Terahertz waves have the potential to create pictures and transmit information in the same way that visible light can create a photograph, radio waves can transmit sound, and X-rays can "see" shapes within the human body. But "T-rays" paint a picture in more intricate detail and pose few safety risks to biological tissue, making the technology beneficial to many aspects of biomedicine and for earlier detection of disease. The terahertz research team at Rensselaer is known as a world leader in the development and application of terahertz technology.[641]

In 2004, Rensselaer pooled the talents of researchers from several disciplines to establish the Inverse Problems Center, directed by Joyce R. McLaughlin, the Ford Foundation Professor of Mathematical Sciences at Rensselaer. Inverse problems are solved by determining unknown causes based on observations of their effects—studying the surface effects of an earthquake, for example, in order to better understand its root causes.[642] Center researchers create and analyze mathematical models, develop algorithms, and use scientific computing to provide generic solutions that apply to a wide range of diverse and critical problems.[643] Beyond geophysical fault identification, the work of the center applies across a wide range of inquiries, including medical and radar imaging.[644]

The School of Science also takes pride in its support for research by undergraduate students. Student work—encompassing such fields as biology, biomedical engineering, architecture, industrial and management engineering, mechanical engineering, nuclear engineering, applied physics, chemistry, and computer science—is honored in an annual awards ceremony sponsored by Rensselaer's Undergraduate Research Forum.

As yet another example of the interdisciplinarity that is part of the Institute's transformation under *The Rensselaer Plan*, David L. Spooner, Acting Dean of the School of Science, says that Rensselaer's move into biotechnology has helped boost student enrollment in related programs in the school, such as biology, physics, and mathematics. Similarly, he says, the school has also seen an uptick in student interest in its strong programs in bioinformatics and biochemistry/biophysics.[645]

Overall, Spooner says, the reinvigoration of research at Rensselaer has had a very strong positive effect on the School of Science. As evidence, for example, he points to more money for projects, more graduate students, and an increase in the number of publications being produced by investigators based in the school. Just 10 years into *The Rensselaer Plan*, he believes the school's recent progress has bolstered its reputation, strengthening its ability to recruit top-caliber faculty and students. Spooner notes that apart from the positive impact the new focus on biotechnology has had on the biology department, the addition of five constellation faculty has transformed the physics department, bringing new faculty brainpower, helping the department recruit graduate students, and paving the way for increased research funding. Another impact on the school has been Rensselaer's Computational Center for Nanotechnology Innovations, a boon to computer science faculty as well as other researchers whose work relies on computation. Spooner believes that Assistant Professor Joel Giedt, a

Jonsson-Rowland
Science Center

theoretical physicist whose work encompasses a considerable amount of modeling, may be one of the heaviest users of the supercomputer facility.[646]

From the Science Center we head slightly northwest, back to another of the original Ricketts-era structures, the Greene Building. Home to the School of Architecture and completed in 1931, the building was named for Benjamin Franklin Greene, Director of Rensselaer from 1847 to 1859. The names of 15 titans of American architecture—from Bulfinch to McKim to Sullivan—are cut into the stonework on Greene's face. It is a bit incongruous, in a way, that in this 80-year-old Romanesque edifice roam students who will soon be some of tomorrow's most forward-looking architects. The juxtaposition is another reminder of Jackson's tenet that a university's past should always meet its future. Here, in fact, the past animates the future.

The building has its own library, computers for exclusive use by architecture students, and a gallery for showing students' work. In the third-floor Studio 305, students use powerful new technologies that may alter the future of architecture. A professional-quality video editing station allows students to create simulated tours of their proposed buildings, or show their projects within a video image of an actual site. A three-dimensional scanner, for example, can create a computer-based image of physical objects. That is not to say, though, that computers are king here. Rather, computers are another tool—complementing, say, a milling machine that follows computer-created designs to carve three-dimensional objects out of foam or wood.[647]

Much of the focus here is on the connections between design and technology, what Professor Mark Mistur, class of 1983, describes as "a progressive architecture" that "deals not only with environmental issues and sustainability and energy, but also with programmatic issues in terms of understanding how architecture can best serve its clients." Apropos of the ethos at Rensselaer, the School of Architecture advances the principle of "architectural science," with an implication that, as Mistur says, "there should not be a distinction between the art of design and the technology." That is an approach that lends itself well, for example, to collaborations between architects and engineers, physicists, and experts from other disciplines.[648]

As mentioned above, one of the innovations created during *The Rensselaer Plan* is the Institute's collaboration with the architecture firm Skidmore, Owings & Merrill on what has been named the Center for Architecture Science and Ecology (CASE). Headquartered at the firm's offices on Wall Street in lower Manhattan, CASE engages scientists, engineers, and architects toward a common goal of redefining how we build sustainable cities and environments. The idea is to tap and cultivate the talents of a new generation of architects, thinkers, and planners and turn out sustainable and energy-efficient buildings (which today account for more than one-third of energy consumption and nearly 40 percent of carbon production).[649]

CASE anchors one of the School of Architecture's advanced-degree programs, which is framed on the concept of Built Ecologies, or the development of new building strategies with an emphasis on energy-efficiency and sustainability. Approximately 15 master's and doctoral degree candidates share residency between the Rensselaer campus and the CASE offices, working alongside building professionals and postdoctoral researchers as they develop projects and thesis topics tied to specific building challenges.[650] The school's other Ph.D. concentrations, both relatively unique in a universe that tends to emphasize architectural history and both added during the era of *The Rensselaer Plan*, are in lighting research and architectural acoustics.

A visitor to Greene might see a gaggle of students, oblivious to anyone but themselves, critiquing classmates' drawings that paper the floor across a hallway. Step gingerly around the drawings and down the hall to the dean's office and you will find Evan Douglis, an internationally eminent architect who took the reins of the school only in 2009. Douglis had been both chair of the undergraduate department in the school of architecture at New York City's Pratt Institute, and principal of the contemporary architecture and design firm Evan Douglis Studio.

Like other new members of Jackson's administrative team, Douglis took the job in part because of the promise of *The Rensselaer Plan*. Observing that "there are probably a very small handful of visionaries throughout the United States overseeing an academic institution," Douglis says he was intrigued by Jackson's vision for Rensselaer's future. "She is able to identify the value of education in the context of specific challenges globally," he says.[651]

He cites, for example, Jackson's expertise in energy issues, which are also a central focus for today's architects. One of the challenges for educators of architects, he says, is to "reassess a curriculum for the 21st century" so that architecture "engages the environment in a multicultural planet" and proactively "propose[s] different kinds of futures."[652]

A visionary himself, Douglis sees enormous potential in the forum that Rensselaer provides for a discourse about architecture that encompasses "how science and engineering can be integrated" in design research. "I was very interested in coming to a university that has a robust community of scientists and engineers—a whole kind of family of experts that are outside of architecture, but that could be drawn into a circle of architectural research," he says. Douglis says that his ability to draw on expertise from departments across campus, and from industry, creates a "transdisciplinary collaboration" constituting a "fantastic research lab" that can help students assess building components in the context of designs in ways that might not be possible in other architecture schools.[653]

Recognizing that "unfortunately, very few schools have had the opportunity to be able to engage in this practice," he suspects that kind of cross-disciplinary discussion is one of the characteristics that can distinguish the architecture program at Rensselaer. He is also interested in building on the work of his predecessors to intentionally create a vibrant student community and culture within the school.[654]

From Greene's front steps, one can look across '86 Field to another green-roofed building, the Ricketts Building, named for Rensselaer icon Palmer Ricketts. The building is home to the Howard P. Isermann Department of Chemical and Biological Engineering.

In Ricketts, for example, one might find Ravi S. Kane, the P.K. Lashmet Professor at Rensselaer, one of the bright young faculty who joined the Institute during *The Rensselaer Plan*. Kane came to Rensselaer in 2001 and was named a full professor in 2007. As Professor of Chemical and Biological Engineering, Kane conducts innovative research at the intersection of nanotechnology and biology, and is also a gifted mentor to young researchers. Among many other honors, he won the 2008 Young Investigator Award from the American Institute of Chemical Engineers' Nanoscale Science and Engineering Forum, and in 2004 was named to the TR 100, a list of the world's top 100 young innovators sponsored by MIT's *Technology Review*. Affiliated also with the Center for Biotechnology and Interdisciplinary Studies at Rensselaer, Kane works in the area of nanobiotechnology, focused on the applications of nanotechnology to problems in biology or biotechnology.[655]

What motivates Kane? In 2009 he told an interviewer that "a major driving force is the ability to work on important problems, such as designing approaches to treat important diseases, where solutions would have a major impact. In a sense, this is similar to Rensselaer's motto—'Why not change the world?' I also greatly enjoy the process of doing research; it is challenging and a lot of fun. Finally, being a teacher and researcher at a university is even more enjoyable because of the ability to interact with bright and motivated students."[656]

In Ricketts one might also find Shekhar Garde, a rising star in Rensselaer's School of Engineering who was named in 2007 to head the Department of Chemical and Biological Engineering. The department's very name reflects change at Rensselaer: formerly the Department of Chemical Engineering, the department took on its current name in 2003. The move acknowledged the ways in which chemistry and the biological and life sciences had drawn closer together over the past several decades, particularly as ideas for engineering of biological systems have emerged.[657]

Affiliated with Rensselaer's Center for Biotechnology and Interdisciplinary Studies, and the NSF-funded Nanoscale Science and Engineering Center for Directed Assembly of Nanostructures at Rensselaer, Garde collaborates with researchers from a wide range of academic disciplines to further the fundamental understanding of molecular-scale processes that lie at the foundation of bio- and nanotechnologies.[658]

In 2009, for example, Garde and colleagues announced that they had discovered a new, more precise method for measuring hydrophobicity—essentially how much, or how little, nanoscale interfaces love water. The finding could have important applications for the future of drug discovery, Garde says.[659]

Along with Rensselaer colleagues Linda S. Schadler and Richard W. Siegel, Garde is a driving force behind Rensselaer's NSF-funded MOLECULARIUM® Project, which produces animated films designed to get children to think and learn more about atoms and molecules. Molecularium films have combined elements of Garde's research in molecular dynamics simulations with state-of-the-art, computer-generated animation to explore the states of matter—solid, liquid, and gas—and to investigate the inner workings of a living cell.

At the time of his appointment as department head, Garde said the department was on the move. Under *The Rensselaer Plan* it had just hired three top-notch assistant professors, had seen several key faculty members receive major national and international awards, and was engaged in several large, interdisciplinary research projects. "We will continue to increase the intellectual capital of the department by adding brilliant new faculty, graduate students, and undergraduates," Garde says. "Our national ranking is consistently moving up, and our goal is to be listed among the top 20 chemical and biological engineering programs in the nation in the next few years."[660]

Not far from Ricketts, one finds an important campus building along the campus's north corridor, the Heffner Alumni House. Conceived, designed, constructed, and financed by Rensselaer alumni and alumnae, this award-winning building opened its doors in 1989 and is named after Rensselaer Board Chairman Samuel F. Heffner Jr. The building serves an invaluable role as a gateway for one of the Institute's most vitally important constituencies. In fact, more active alumni outreach and the achievements under *The Rensselaer Plan* have brought graduates closer to their alma mater.

Rensselaer had long had an uneven relationship with its graduates, said Trustee Paula Simon, who also served a term as president of the alumni association in the mid-1990s, the first woman to hold that slot. "There was a time when the alumni association was actually based in Manhattan and had no relationship to the institution at all," she says.[661] Rensselaer's harsh student culture from the days of "look to the left, look to the right" often undermined any interest the university might have in maintaining strong bonds with its graduates. As Simon observes, many alumni and alumnae shared the perspective that "when you leave the institution and you say, I cannot wait to get out of there, then why would you have an affinity for the institution?"[662]

Simon recognizes that "you have to have a good student experience to have a good alumni experience." She believes that work under the plan to improve the student experience will inevitably draw alumni closer to the Institute. "That's the only way you are going to get them to come back later," she says. She would also like to see more staff devoted to helping to cultivate relationships with graduates.[663]

Meanwhile, the Institute is finding ways to engage more productively with alumni and alumnae. Rensselaer's Board of Trustees created official communications channels with the Rensselaer Alumni Association Board of Trustees, which meets in Troy three times a year. Jackson has made a point of attending its meetings regularly and reports directly on the Institute's progress. Rensselaer also supports collaboration between the RAA board and Rensselaer's Office of Alumni Relations to deliver programming that includes networking, social events, educational presentations, and student activities.[664] For its part, the RAA has pledged and gifted nearly $900,000 in support of Institute initiatives, including a $300,000 commitment for the East Campus Athletic Village. Every member of the RAA board contributed to the "Renaissance at Rensselaer" campaign.[665]

Catherine Eckart, the immediate past president of the alumni association, has found Jackson to be "really supportive" of the alumni association. "She reaches out to the [alumni] board a lot," Eckart said. "She is very interested in what we think. She doesn't necessarily have to make the time for us, but she does—always."[666]

From Heffner Alumni House, it's a short walk back to Greene. We slip out the side door there and make our way a few steps east to the portico of the J. Erik Jonsson Engineering Center, or JEC. Architecturally speaking, you have just walked into another era, going from the turn of the 20th century to the 1970s. As classes change, the portico handles a flurry of students. A visitor might be struck by the diversity of faces—there is a broad representation of nationalities and ethnic backgrounds. Notable, too, is the number of women. One of Rensselaer's founding fathers, Amos Eaton, wrote pointedly in 1824 about "instructing...sons *and* daughters" [emphasis added]; today, women constitute nearly a third of Rensselaer's freshman class—the result of concerted effort under *The Rensselaer Plan* to enhance student diversity.

JEC is the base for experts who practice across a comprehensive array of engineering specialties: aeronautical, biomedical, chemical and biological, civil, computer and systems, decision sciences, electrical, environmental, industrial and management, materials, mechanical, nuclear, and transportation. Inside the JEC, researchers and students pursue a variety of groundbreaking research in such areas as wind and nuclear energy, nanoscale materials for biomedical applications, and complex mechanical systems for next generation aerospace designs. From the Brooklyn Bridge to the Apollo mission and Mars rovers to solutions for better homeland security, Rensselaer has a long, truly distinguished history in engineering. But by no means does the school rest on its laurels.

For example, Professor Tarek Abdoun led a physical modeling research team that clarified why some of the New Orleans levees failed during Hurricane Katrina. Abdoun and colleagues discovered that the wall in the middle of the earthen structure started to move before the water reached the top. The weak clay directly underneath the peat layer sheared first, causing the whole levee to slide. The work provided critical data that informed the levees' reconstruction.[667] Under the leadership of William A. (Al) Wallace, Professor of Decision Sciences and Engineering Systems, a Rensselaer team is working under a recent grant from the U.S. Department of Homeland Security to investigate how different civil infrastructures—such as roadways, water and power utilities, hospitals, banks, or law enforcement—interact with each other and with the natural environment after a disaster. Using complex systems modeling, they will develop software to help improve emergency response to disasters.[668] And in keeping with Rensselaer's push to become a leader in the life sciences, Professor Jonathan Newell and colleagues, along with a team at Massachusetts General Hospital, led an NIH project to diagnose breast cancer by electrical impedance imaging.[669]

Reflecting another interest of Jackson's and emanating from *The Rensselaer Plan*—that students benefit from a more global educational experience—the engineering school instituted in 2008 what will become a requirement that all undergraduate engineering students participate in an international experience. A new program, Rensselaer Education Across Cultural Horizons, or REACH, was launched to support structured study abroad programs, as well as other international experiences such as internships and exchange programs.[670] Through the campus chapter of Engineers for a Sustainable World, for example, engineering students from Rensselaer have been working to equip a school in the Haitian village of Lascahobas with sufficient solar panels to power computers. Students and faculty were in the village when the 2010 earthquake struck. They were able to drive to the Dominican Republic and fly to New York and get home, but they plan to continue their work in Haiti.[671]

Under *The Rensselaer Plan*, Jackson would like to see international educational and research exchange become a defining aspect of undergraduate education.[672] (Rensselaer's architectural program has long sent students abroad.) In a 2009 speech, she said such experiences point to several dimensions of the educational experience she has advocated under the plan. For one, she says, such experiences show that the Institute's faculty and students "are engaged in activity integral to our founding mission—employing unique educational strategies for engaged, interactive, self-directed learning." Experiences such as students have in Haiti underscore how Rensselaer's academic emphasis is "deliberately global in outlook, intellectually rigorous, sophisticated, and socially nuanced," Jackson says, and also show how the Institute "promotes powerful, mind-opening new experiences" that "foster intellectual agility"—in the context of one of Rensselaer's fundamentals, the application of science for common purposes of life.[673]

David V. Rosowsky, the former chair of civil engineering at Texas A&M University, joined Rensselaer as Dean of the School of Engineering in July 2009. Speaking from his office on the third floor of the JEC just weeks after he had come to campus, Rosowsky said that *The Rensselaer Plan* played a large part in his decision to take on the new assignment. "It was more than just a vision, it was also a strategy for how to get there," he says. Moreover, he says, "when I came on campus and saw the physical manifestation of the plan, the transformation of the campus and the new infrastructure, you cannot help but be impressed."[674]

Rosowsky also appreciates the plan's "potential to bring people together in a truly non-disciplinary way and to "create more core facilities and capacities that transcend traditional school barriers." He says that one of the factors that attracted him to Rensselaer was that "the barriers between schools are actually quite low, partly because of the size of the institution, and partly that is just the culture that has grown up here." Speaking specifically about the Center for Biotechnology and Interdisciplinary Studies, he could be talking about the university as a whole when he recognizes the inherent power in bringing experts from different disciplines together "to work on big problems in an open environment that has clearly been designed for collaboration and multidisciplinary thinking."[675]

The tradition of engineering at Rensselaer has been that of the big kid on the block—engineering tended to overshadow other schools in terms of its overall size and the institutional resources it commanded. It currently enrolls nearly 60 percent of Rensselaer's students. Rosowsky envisions that as other dimensions of the university grow, engineering will likely become proportionately smaller—and he is fine with that. While his school is currently adding faculty, he recognizes that since resources are finite, growth cannot continue at the same pace—which, in turn, will restrict the number of students engineering can add. "I do not want any student who wants to come to Rensselaer and do something related to engineering to not have that opportunity," he says, "but the reality is, we cannot accommodate everyone who wants to be an engineer." He envisions that the engineering school will have to develop more sophistication in managing its enrollments. Mentioning joint degrees in physics, architecture, and management, he suggests engineering may also have to do more to exploit partnerships with other schools.[676]

Meeting with junior-level faculty in the school in his second week on campus, Rosowsky outlined goals that he said applied to all engineering faculty: "I said, my goal is to make you so successful, to enable you to reach a point where you are getting offers from some of the best universities in the world, and you are turning them down. I want you to be that good, that you are that desirable by other schools, and I want you not to take any of them. If I can get you to that point, I will have succeeded. I will have made you realize your greatest potential, and I will have made this an environment you want to remain in for your professional career."[677]

Next door to the Jonsson Engineering Center, students are lined up at yet another university café, Jazzman's, in the lobby of the Darrin Communications Center. Waiting for their next lecture, scores of students sit outside Darrin's large halls, tapping on their laptops and chatting. Representatives of an LGBT student organization promote a fundraiser from a table in the hallway—another symbol of diversity.

The windows that line Thomsen Hall in the Darrin Center are etched with the accomplishments of the members of the Rensselaer Alumni Hall of Fame, a project of the Rensselaer Alumni Association. Among the nearly 30 alumni who have been selected to join this illustrious group during the era of *The Rensselaer Plan* are Hiram F. Mills, class of 1856, a leader in the development of sanitary engineering in America; aircraft designer Robert H. Widmer, class of 1938; and higher education leader Myles N. Brand, class of 1964, who gained national recognition as president of Indiana University from 1994 to 2002 and as president of the NCAA from 2002 until his death in 2009. Brand also had served as an Institute Trustee. Here, too, is Raymond S. Tomlinson, class of 1963, the person who came up with the Internet protocol to enable using the @ sign in email.

In this hallway, past again meets future as today's students—tomorrow's alumni and alumnae—surf the Web in the shadow of some of Rensselaer's greats. One speculates about which students from today will eventually see their stories etched in glass in Thomsen Hall. Perhaps it will be Eben Bayer, class of 2007, and Gavin McIntyre, class of 2007, who created a form of organic insulation, made of agricultural materials, water, and mushrooms, that could replace the foam that is traditionally used in homes.[678] Or perhaps Ari Presler, class of 1987, whose handheld digital movie camera helped the film *Slumdog Millionaire* win eight Academy Awards in 2009, including one for Best Cinematography. According to Presler, the movie was the first movie shot predominantly digitally to win the coveted Best Picture award.[679]

A hallway from Darrin leads directly to the lower lobby of another central point on campus, the Low Center for Industrial Innovation. At nine stories, the CII, as it is known, is the tallest building on campus. Named for past Rensselaer President George Low, the building houses several research centers, student computer labs, and a 10,000-square-foot Class 100 clean room, used for designing computer chips.

The CII is home, for example, to five research labs and some 17 group members associated with the Future Chips Constellation. This group manages Rensselaer's NSF Engineering Research Center to advance "Smart Lighting," work that aims to supplant the common light bulb with next-generation lighting devices. Along with significant energy savings for lighting homes and offices, these technologies will open doors to a diverse spectrum of new applications that will affect everything from biotechnology and transportation to computer networking and displays.[680]

Here, too, is the central office for the Center for Automation Technologies and Systems (CATS), which conducts research and development in both practical and theoretical aspects of automation. As just a small sampling of the work completed here, in 2009 CATS researchers won a $1.6 million federal grant to develop new methods for manufacturing a key fuel cell component.[681] More than 30 faculty members in nine departments at Rensselaer are associated with CATS.

CII also houses the Center for Integrated Electronics, Electronics Manufacturing, and Electronic Media (CIE), created to conduct industry-oriented research in electronics design and manufacturing. True to the principle of interdisciplinary research outlined in *The Rensselaer Plan*, CIE is an umbrella that hosts microelectronics and nanoelectronics research across many disciplines.[682] Another interdisciplinary center located in CII, the Scientific Computation Research Center, develops reliable simulation technologies to help engineers, scientists, and medical professionals evaluate the behavior of physical, chemical, and biological systems of interest.[683]

Upstairs in the CII tower is the office of Rensselaer's relatively new Vice President for Research. The appointment of Francine Berman to that post in 2009 marked further progress in Rensselaer's fast-moving drive to enhance its research capacity. Berman had been High Performance Computing Endowed Chair at the University of California, San Diego, and director of the San Diego Supercomputer Center. She is widely recognized as a pioneer in the effort to build a stronger digital infrastructure in the United States, and had been named as a technology leader by *Newsweek*, *BusinessWeek*, and *IEEE Spectrum*.[684]

Like other administrators recruited to the Institute during the implementation of the plan, Berman was attracted by the plan itself. "*The Rensselaer Plan* is an incredibly well-crafted document," she says. "All of its different components support one another and create something that is beyond the sum of the parts. All of the aspects are there to create the kind of synergy necessary to really change the world."[685]

Like many of her colleagues across campus, Berman speaks of the innate power in Rensselaer's low walls between disciplines and departments. "For a scientist like me, there is nothing more exciting than pondering a really hard question and seeing people with a completely different approach on some aspect of it all of a sudden shed some light in the darkness," she says. Speaking of the unique angles that investigators from different disciplines bring to specific areas of inquiry, Berman says that "many of our hardest problems require different perspectives and different kinds of toolsets that you get in interdisciplinary science. The culture and structure [at Rensselaer] really support interdisciplinary work. In that sense, I get to keep pushing in a direction that the campus is already going in, and that is really exciting."[686]

From the CII, it is just a short walk to one of the crown jewels of *The Rensselaer Plan*, the Center for Biotechnology and Interdisciplinary Studies, or CBIS.

Facts about the building tell one part of the story. At 218,000 square feet, the facility is the third-largest academic and research structure on the Rensselaer campus. With nearly 60,000 square feet of laboratory space and abundant room for offices and meeting and public spaces, CBIS can house some 400 faculty and staff members and graduate students. It is equipped with a state-of-the-art nuclear magnetic resonance core facility, where researchers can characterize, at atomic resolution, the three-dimensional structure, motional dynamics, folding pathways, and binding kinetics and thermodynamics of biomolecules. For biocomputation, shared memory Linux superclusters with multi-terabyte storage are available for large scale data mining, drug design, cheminformatics, molecular modeling, and bioinformatics. In the area of microscopy and imaging, CBIS has several types of electron microscopes; laser scanning, confocal, light and fluorescence, and atomic force microscopes; and other instruments for photometry and microspectroscopy. A fleet of mass spectrometers are available for high throughput protein analysis.[687]

The CBIS creates "a gathering place where scientists and engineers from various disciplines will explore at the intersection of the life sciences with engineering and the physical and information sciences," Jackson said when the CBIS opened, "thereby accelerating discovery and ultimately enhancing the quality of life for all people."[688]

Today, CBIS bustles with ongoing research. With a $4.6 million grant from the National Institutes of Health, for example, Rensselaer researchers are making important final steps toward the development of a safer, synthetic alternative to heparin, a blood thinner that is one of the most widely used drugs in American hospitals. Jonathan S. Dordick, the Howard P. Isermann Professor of Chemical and Biological Engineering and director of the CBIS, is one of the lead researchers for the study, along with Robert Linhardt, the Ann and John H. Broadbent, Jr. '59 Senior Constellation Professor of Biocatalysis and Metabolic Engineering at Rensselaer.[689] Linhardt, Dordick, and colleagues recently received more than $2 million in grants for research on the growth and development of stem cells, work they hope will offer insights into the role specific genes and biological molecules play in stem cell function.[690] Rensselaer Senior Constellation Professor George Makhatadze and his colleagues are using high-powered computers to find ways to increase the stability of proteins.[691] In 2008, theoretical physicist Angel García, the Senior Constellation Professor of Biocomputation and Bioinformatics at Rensselaer, and colleagues uncovered what they believe is the long-sought-after pathway that an HIV peptide takes to enter healthy cells.[692]

Linhardt had enjoyed a successful 21-year career at the University of Iowa, where he had an endowed chair and postings in three departments (chemistry, medicinal

Robert E. Palazzo
Provost

Virginia C. Gregg
Vice President for Finance;
Chief Financial Officer

John E. Kolb, Class of 1979
Vice President for
Information Services
and Technology; Chief
Information Officer

Francine Berman
Vice President for Research

Curtis N. Powell
Vice President for Human
Resources

Claude D. Rounds
Vice President for
Administration

Eddie Ade Knowles
Vice President for
Student Life

chemistry, and chemical engineering). But he saw opportunities at Rensselaer that led him to move. Part of his motivation was based in self-interest, he says. "Rensselaer offered an opportunity to change the trajectory of my career," he says, and he believed there was a good fit between where he wanted to go and the directions the Institute was headed. He perceived that Rensselaer offered unparalleled "low barriers to collaboration [and] interactions between scientists and engineers." He also took notice that Rensselaer "had a very energetic president who was focused on the right questions and had a vision."[693]

Asked about *The Rensselaer Plan* per se, Linhardt says "for me, it's a living plan that has a focus of developing Rensselaer into a world-class university [with] focused areas of strength."[694]

As for the obvious question about leaving a school with a medical school when much of his research was in the realm of biomedicine, Linhardt actually found that a plus. In contrast to environments where the bulk of research funding tends to flow through the medical center and decisions are sometimes weighted in favor of "what's best for the medical school, not what's best for the other disciplines," Linhardt said he liked the fact that Rensselaer "had a president whose vision was technology education, and how to promote it" and who also was an advocate of "diversity in disciplines."[695]

Among other research pursuits, including his work with Linhardt on heparin, Dordick and his group develop high throughput chips that greatly speed the screening of molecules for potential use in drugs and other products. Another area of his laboratory works to incorporate enzymes into materials in what he calls "biocatalytic plastic"—with potential, for example, for creating surfaces that would resist the binding of proteins.[696]

Dordick credits Trustee Howard P. Isermann as an early advocate that Rensselaer stake a position in biotechnology. Dordick remembers that in the early 1980s Isermann, a chemical engineer who developed the ultraviolet absorber that became the most effective and leading sunscreen in the world, "made a very clear statement that said that you can't have a technological institution without biotechnology." Isermann's early support for chemical engineering at Rensselaer, Dordick says, built up the biochemical engineering component of that area and "really became the first true biotechnology on this campus."[697] Jackson, Dordick says, had a similar but much broader vision—which resulted ultimately in the creation of the CBIS.

Dordick says that both design and policies help make the CBIS work. The open laboratories encourage cross-disciplinary conversation. So, too, does the policy that no department would be headquartered in the CBIS—keeping the focus in the CBIS on research and guaranteeing that faculty members would carry ideas back and forth between their laboratory work in the CBIS and their teaching and departmental responsibilities in other buildings. Modularity built into the design makes it relatively easy for laboratory space to be reconfigured as research needs change.[698] Provost Palazzo says the CBIS is distinctive in that it brings investigators, graduate students, and undergraduates from different disciplines "all suddenly under one canopy." As these researchers intermingle, Palazzo said—"looking at each other's data as it's coming out, conversing, reflecting—a new language begins to appear," a broadly cross-disciplinary conversation that elevates "the opportunity for serendipity."[699]

Dordick believes that Rensselaer's traditional focus on engineering gives the CBIS a unique edge. Other major biotechnology facilities, he says, are often aligned with medical centers or are located in life sciences programs, without much historical presence of engineers. In an era when researchers are recognizing that research in the life sciences can benefit greatly from engineering expertise, though, Rensselaer's deep bench in engineering gives research in the CBIS a competitive advantage. Moreover, he says, the Institute's strong grounding in engineering enables researchers in the life sciences to use that perspective to look at problems differently than in labs where engineering is not as strong.[700]

From the Center for Biotechnology and Interdisciplinary Studies, it is a quick walk over to the Rensselaer Union building. Rensselaer has one of the few university student unions run by students. In their third-floor office, we catch up with two student leaders, Michael Zwack, class of 2011, and Alex Franz, class of 2010. As 2009–10 Grand Marshal and President of the Union, respectively, Zwack and Franz proudly carried on a long tradition. Holding the highest elected office in the Rensselaer student government, for example, Zwack was the university's 143rd Grand Marshal. Records are not as clear about the history of the Union president's role, but the two believe Franz is approximately 120th in the lineage. As symbols of leadership, Zwack sported a ceremonial top hat and Franz a derby, well-aged haberdashery that looks as if it could date back to the two leaders' original predecessors.

As the union's chief financial officer, Franz managed a budget of nearly $9 million, raised from a student activity fee, that supports the union itself as well as programs, services, and clubs for students. Professional staff in the union are, in essence, employees of the student government.

Zwack and Franz had monthly meetings with Jackson. They conferred regularly on student life initiatives with members of Rensselaer's cabinet. "Anything we brought to [Jackson] or her cabinet, she was pretty good about responding to," Zwack says. "And she invited our opinions on issues that come across her desk." They also had access through Jackson to the Board of Trustees and met with the Board's student life committee and administration and infrastructure committees. The Trustees, too, Zwack says, "listen to us and to student opinion."[701]

Both student leaders point to *The Rensselaer Plan* as the source of improvements on campus. For one thing, they say, there seems to be less student apathy now than even a few years before. "[Students] over the last few years have been increasingly more active and interested in what's going on," Franz says, a phenomenon that he attributes to Rensselaer's efforts to recruit and enroll higher-quality students. More students now compete for seats in student government. Another sign that Rensselaer is enrolling more highly motivated students, Zwack says, is demand for extracurricular clubs—up from 120 to 185 during the first decade of the plan. "And those clubs are full," Zwack says.[702]

Zwack said changes in the curriculum and the constructions of such facilities as EMPAC and ECAV under *The Rensselaer Plan* are selling points that attract high-caliber students. The push for undergraduates to conduct research is also a plus. For example, he suggests, while undergraduates in cancer research groups at Rensselaer have the chance to do real research, their counterparts elsewhere might be relegated to simply crunching numbers.[703]

The Rensselaer Union is a gateway to Rensselaer's student housing—the beneficiary of substantial renovations during the era of *The Rensselaer Plan*—and to the eastern reaches of campus, with the new East Campus Athletic Village.

The Institute took comprehensive steps under the plan to improve all student residences. Roofs, doors, windows, and carpeting were replaced. Lighting was upgraded. Bathrooms, kitchens, and lounges were renovated. Two residences, Bray Hall and Cary Hall, saw comprehensive renovations that included many new bathrooms, new windows and finishes, and the addition of common rooms. New, more secure building access systems were installed. New sprinkler systems were installed in all residence halls and apartments. The university also purchased and renovated two multifamily houses near campus for use by graduate students. Together with exterior and landscaping improvements, these projects have significantly improved the quality of everyday living in Rensselaer's residence halls and apartment complexes.[704]

An evergreen issue on campus has had to do with rules for sophomore housing and Greek life. Fifteen or 20 years ago, 70 percent of students were affiliated with Greek life, says Eddie Knowles, Rensselaer's Vice President for Student Life. Now just the reverse is true: less than 30 percent are in fraternities and sororities. Under the CLASS initiative, Rensselaer has worked to make the Greek system, which had evolved a certain independence, a more integral part of campus life and the evolving new residential system. Having worked hard to improve student life for first-year students, Rensselaer wanted to extend that experience to sophomores. Since some second-year students are allowed to live in Greek houses, that meant restructuring rules concerning fraternities and sororities to bring them into better alignment with existing Institute policies. All of this is done under the rubric of a "Greek Life Commons" and to improve the physical and health and safety conditions of Greek houses. There are preconditions for allowing sophomores to live in Greek houses. That plan initially met with considerable resistance on the part of the Greeks, who saw some of the rules as impinging on their autonomy. By Fall 2010, however, the Greek Life Commons concept was taking hold, with most fraternities and sororities signing Greek Commons agreements and beginning to improve their houses.[705]

The changes in student living quarters represent a sea change in residential life at Rensselaer. In the place of the old rigidity, *The Rensselaer Plan* has instituted a comprehensive program of nurturing attention to academics and learning in the context of student residential life.

In the student dining halls, a visitor might experience practical evidence of Rensselaer's burgeoning interest in sustainability. Initiatives to support sustainable dining include the use of 100 percent post-consumer napkins, sustainable packaging and recycling options, and new ware-washing sanitizing solutions that are environmentally friendly. A team of civic-minded Rensselaer students can be credited with bringing local and organic foods from the farm to the campus to please the palates of socially conscious students, faculty, and staff. Launched in Fall 2007, Terra Café dishes up a selection of local and organic meals, desserts, and beverages every Wednesday afternoon in the Russell Sage Dining Hall.[706]

Campus interest in sustainability extends far beyond the cafeterias, however. In 2009, Jackson's office sponsored the inaugural Rensselaer Sustainability Charrette—comprised of an interdisciplinary team of Rensselaer students, faculty, and staff—that generated numerous ideas for projects and initiatives that could enhance sustainable practices in the ways Rensselaer operates, educates, researches, and lives.[707] Already, much evidence of sustainability pervades the Institute.

In terms of campus operations, for example, Rensselaer has committed to Leadership in Energy and Environmental Design (LEED) certifications for all new campus building construction. EMPAC is LEED certified and the East Campus Athletic Village is planned to be LEED silver certified. The Center for Biotechnology and Interdisciplinary Studies building is extremely energy efficient with a naturally ventilated atrium, heat recovery in laboratory ventilation, and similar systems. Energy-savings measures also include such innovative technologies as variable speed motor controls, lighting controls, and building management computer systems.[708]

As well, sustainability-related coursework and degree programs are found across the curriculum. For example, the School of Science offers courses assessing the scale of human activities in relation to natural processes. An interdisciplinary program trains doctoral students in fuel cell science and engineering. Classes in engineering design and innovation challenge students to identify global needs, and to create affordable and sustainable technologies for the developing world. Architecture courses focus on performance-driven building technologies to support self-sustaining building environments. Courses in management and humanities, arts, and social sciences encompass ecological economics, values, and policy.[709]

Moreover, Rensselaer research centers—from the Center for Future Energy Systems to the New York State Center for Polymer Synthesis—are developing better hydrogen fuel cells, brighter LEDs, more efficient solar cells, and elements of a more robust electricity distribution grid. Faculty research encompasses a broad spectrum of energy- and sustainability-related research. Some focus on applications for fuel cells, and on fundamental technical issues for hydrogen-related technologies.[710]

Walk from the student residences toward the eastern border of the campus and it will be impossible to miss the new stadium, playing fields, and other athletic facilities that comprise the first completed phase of Rensselaer's East Campus Athletic Village. From high in ECAV's stands, one cannot help but be a little awed as one scans the truly state-of-the-art 5,200-seat stadium, from the press box down to the red RPI logo that marks the center of the brand new FieldTurf playing field. Opened in October of 2009, the facility fast became the envy of many of the athletes—and coaches—from other institutions that come to compete at Rensselaer. Just as fast, it became a new point of pride for members of the Rensselaer community.

One of the most obvious dimensions of the value of ECAV is that it provides outstanding opportunities for athletic endeavors in a university that has a strong athletic tradition. That is certainly true for Rensselaer varsity athletes, but a visitor to ECAV will quickly learn that the facility is intentionally also open to Rensselaer's many intra-mural and club athletes. Jackson was insistent about that, and the reason goes to the fact that as much as ECAV is about sports, it is also about much more than that.[711]

The reference to "village" in ECAV's name, for example, speaks to the notion that the new sports facility is part of a concerted effort to build a sense of community and pride of place at Rensselaer. As one of the defining platforms of *The Rensselaer Plan*, ECAV is yet another physical place where members of the Rensselaer community can gather in a way that was simply not available prior to the plan's implementation. That is true for students who use the facility during a given semester, and ECAV is an important new dimension in Jackson's vision for improving the quality of student life. Beyond that, though, ECAV is also a place where Rensselaer alumni and alumnae can gather. It most decidedly is an asset in attracting new students to the campus. It is also a vital gathering place for Rensselaer's convocations, graduations, and other important ceremonies. Distinctive among other athletic facilities across the northeastern United States, ECAV stands also as a point of pride for the larger Troy community and environs.

ECAV stands with the Biotechnology Center, EMPAC, and many other manifesta-tions of *The Rensselaer Plan* in signaling the dramatic change that defines the new Rensselaer. Appropriately, we will conclude our campus tour here.

CHAPTER 7

LOOKING TO THE FUTURE: OPPORTUNITIES AND ASPIRATIONS

> "We have come a long way in a decade, but we are not done yet. Celebrating where we have come is just a way station to where we are going. We know where we are going, and we are going to keep going."
>
> SHIRLEY ANN JACKSON

Reflecting in the fall of 2009 on the first 10 years of *The Rensselaer Plan*, Jackson recalled that the plan was created out of an intention to "have Rensselaer emerge reenergized, reawakened, refocused." The Institute, she said, had needed to "imagine a different, bolder future." Fundamentally, that meant the Institute had to reform. To be sure, it would honor its rich legacies and accomplishments, and build a new future based on existing strengths—but it needed to change.[712]

"This required us to rethink and reinvent practices and policies across the university," Jackson said, "while also adding important new dimensions that did not exist before."[713]

The hoped-for result of *The Rensselaer Plan*, Jackson said, would be that "we would emerge as an intergenerational community of learners even more strongly engaged—deeply and seriously—in the highest level pedagogy and research, approaching and solving the most important questions and challenges of our time."[714]

Toward that end, Jackson recounted, *The Rensselaer Plan* delineated six broad goals:

- Provide an outstanding and distinctive education

- Expand, dramatically, the research enterprise by creating new initiatives in areas closely aligned with societal and global priorities

- Increase scientific and technological entrepreneurship

- Achieve true intellectual, geographic, gender, and ethnic diversity—garnering the best talent and preparing our students to lead in a global economy

- Draw vitality from, and add vitality to, our multiple and diverse communities

- Redesign and invigorate the processes that would enable it to achieve its goals[715]

In addition, the Institute committed to assuring the academic scope, strength, and relevance of the Institute; enhancing the robustness of its research; elevating the student experience; guaranteeing administrative consistency and financial viability; expanding, managing, and upgrading the physical plant; enlarging Rensselaer partnerships; and bolstering an ever-greater prominence and recognition for the university.[716]

At the heart of Jackson's approach to leadership has been a steadfast commitment to her principle that one can transform an institution—and move that institution from "good" to "great"—by instituting meaningful change across the board in its people, platforms, programs, and processes. One could perhaps also add a commitment to developing pride of place, which Jackson has certainly done at Rensselaer. *The Rensselaer Plan* has provided the framework for that transformation, and the plan's execution has been guided at every step by Jackson's steady and firm hand.

Implicit also in Jackson's success has been the notion that truly important change comes not from incremental or piecemeal modifications of practices and policies but from implementation of change systemically across an enterprise—in this case, on a scale significant enough to lead a large institution, formerly well-entrenched in long-existing ways of doing business, to shift course in significant ways, envision a new future for itself, and start to move with dispatch to realize new possibilities. Thus, for example, the major new platforms that have been constructed and brought online during *The Rensselaer Plan*—the Center for Biotechnology and Interdisciplinary Studies, the Experimental Media and Performing Arts Center, the East Campus Athletic Village, and the Computational Center for Nanotechnology Innovations—are *purposely* significant statements of institutional direction. Designed of course to support new endeavors, their very presence telegraphs strong messages about the importance of those new endeavors. Serving as prominent symbols of new directions, they stand as "intentional anchors," Jackson has said.[717]

History, ultimately, will judge Jackson's performance and the long-term success of *The Rensselaer Plan*. But already, the results of the plan are significant, broad, and indisputable, as this account has detailed. The plan has transformed Rensselaer in ways that energize learning and discovery today, and which, moreover, pave countless new avenues for future pursuits.

The role of Rensselaer's Trustees in the realization of *The Rensselaer Plan* cannot be overstated. In addition to helping secure the financial resources needed to execute the plan and providing oversight critical to helping the plan succeed, strong, unwavering support from the Board for both the plan and the President has been pivotal. Reflecting on this in 2010, Board Chairman Samuel Heffner Jr. observed that the sheer boldness and expansiveness of the plan challenged the Institute's Board to take risks far outside its normal comfort zone. Notably, he recalled, the plan asked the Board to authorize spending and borrowing at levels far above any that the Trustees had previously seen. Moreover, in that it evolved over time as circumstances evolved, the plan also asked Trustees to accommodate more change at a faster pace than lesser plans might have asked of them.[718]

Heffner points out, though, that the Board was fully up to these challenges. Virtually from the moment the plan was first brought to the Board by Jackson for official review, he recalls, Trustees eagerly embraced its promise and were keen to implement its programs as soon as possible. Heffner says the Board made certain that Jackson had their full support as well as the tools she needed to fulfill the plan. Throughout both the implementation of the plan and Jackson's tenure, he says, even when significant stumbling blocks appeared, "the Board has been enormously supportive. There has never been any wavering at any point." The upshot, Heffner says with some understatement, is that by working in tandem, Jackson and the Board "got a lot done in 10 years."[719]

The Board itself deserves considerable credit for having had the courage to stretch its own thinking in order to meet—and capitalize on—the inherent promise of *The Rensselaer Plan*. That point is particularly germane when one considers that the plan's scope and timetable were challenged by not one, but two significant economic downturns. In the face of severe fiscal constraints, boards with less stomach for uncertainty might, for example, have stopped construction or scaled back plans for such defining structures as the Experimental Media and Performing Arts Center and the East Campus Athletic Village. With justifiable pride, Heffner notes that Rensselaer's Board held to its principles in completing both those projects (and others) as originally envisioned.[720]

In retrospect, Heffner says, when they asked Jackson to reform Rensselaer, the Institute's Trustees likely did not imagine the degree of change that would actually take place. Given the significant results of the plan, however, he says that the Board is "extremely pleased" with the way in which, and the degree to which, Rensselaer has been transformed.[721]

The fact that in 2010 Jackson was unanimously offered, and accepted, a 10-year extension of her presidential appointment at Rensselaer attests to the strong belief by the Board of Trustees that she will continue and expand her remarkable record of success under *The Rensselaer Plan*. Heffner says the Board very much looks forward to working with Jackson for the coming decade.[722]

One of the plan's great strengths is that it is a living document—a powerful guide for Rensselaer's daily work, and yet robust enough to also help steer the Institute toward fulfillment of long-term strategies. The plan has been flexible enough to accommodate adjustments as needed, but in ways that did not compromise its fundamental infrastructure or underpinnings. The plan is also evergreen in the sense that it is sufficiently broad in scope and bold in vision to drive progress at Rensselaer—and challenge the Institute to even greater levels of achievement—for a good long time.

In 2010, for example—more than a decade after *The Rensselaer Plan* started—innovations prompted by the plan continue to spark important programs. A good case in point is the new Social Cognitive Networks Academic Research Center, funded through a $16.75 million grant from the Army Research Laboratory and announced in 2010. Drawing on the expertise of researchers from a broad spectrum of fields—including sociology, physics, computer science, engineering, and medicine—the new center will explore how technologies and social behaviors govern the dynamics and evolution of social networks, and the information that can be extracted from them, with implications for homeland and national security, and human cognition. As Jackson observed in announcing the new center, Rensselaer offers a unique research environment to lead this important new center—which will draw, for example, on the capacities of two powerful research platforms constructed during the implementation of *The Rensselaer Plan*, the Institute's Computational Center for Nanotechnology Innovations and the Experimental Media and Performing Arts Center.[723]

Moreover, the plan has positioned the Institute to be at the leading edge of some of today's most crucial areas of inquiry. A brief sampling attests to that. Rensselaer researchers have developed a new way to seek out specific proteins, including dangerous toxins such as anthrax, and render them harmless using nothing but light. They have uncovered small deletions in the genomes of children with autism that strongly correlate to brain function. With colleagues from Rice University, Rensselaer researchers have developed the darkest material known to man, a finding that one day could make solar energy conversion more effective and efficient. Rensselaer faculty and students are modeling Generation IV nuclear reactors to boost the safety and reliability of nuclear power plants. They have created a new laboratory to develop and test next-generation radar systems. They have developed nanosculptures that could enhance new heat pumps and energy converters.[724]

These important findings—and many others that could be cited—reflect both new directions in Rensselaer research and new breakthroughs in areas where the Institute has traditionally been strong. In many cases, the new findings were the product of interdisciplinary investigations that bridged the traditional and the new, and that often linked disciplines in ways that might have been unimaginable just a few years ago.

"Rensselaer people have always changed the world. This is the stuff of what is groundbreaking and important, and it sits at the very root of what we are about as a society," Jackson says.[725] In that context, the new people, programs, and platforms that have become part of the Rensselaer community during the implementation of the plan all advance the fundamental Rensselaerean principle of "the application of science to the common purposes of life."

A decade into *The Rensselaer Plan*, the Institute has been redesigned to be "a unique undergraduate college embedded in a great technological research university," Jackson says. She sees the Rensselaer of today as "an intergenerational cauldron, if you will, of people engaged in the business of learning, growing, discovering, innovating, and impacting the world."[726]

Rensselaer is now well-positioned to consolidate those gains and to build upon them as a springboard to even greater achievements. Given the heightened ambitions and broad vision of the plan, the Institute knows that it is capable of extending its reach even further, and that much more remains to be done. Indeed, even as it celebrates its accomplishments under *The Rensselaer Plan*, the Institute has its eye to the future, and to what must be done now to push forward. "We have come a long way in a decade, but we are not done yet. Celebrating where we have come is just a way station to where we are going," Jackson says. "We know where we are going, and we are going to keep going."[727]

"I think in some respects we have been fixing what was wrong," Trustee John Carr says about the first decade of *The Rensselaer Plan*. "Now we must refine what is here to compete with places that we did not have to compete with before because we were not that good."[728]

In reflecting on achievements to date, Jackson has noted that the path forward is likely to be as challenging, if not more demanding, as the implementation of the first decade of the plan. One challenge will be to sustain Rensselaer's remarkable recent pace and quality of research, while simultaneously pushing forward to identify and stake claims in new areas of intellectual and scientific inquiry. Lest it again fall prey to the kind of stagnation that was a factor in the latter part of the 20th century, the Institute will continue to identify strategies by which it can move forward continually. Having created and implemented countless new policies, Rensselaer will take necessary steps to ensure that the policies continue to do what they are intended to do, to fine-tune them as necessary, and to anticipate needs for next-generation changes.[729]

Key foundational elements are in place. Programs and the physical infrastructure created during *The Rensselaer Plan* were designed with inherent capacity to push Rensselaer in new directions. The biotechnology center is one example, but there are others across campus. The expansion of research has created new domains of knowledge that the Institute can now exploit, and further developed existing domains. For example, the Institute has invested robustly in emerging disciplines that did not exist just a few years ago, such as terahertz science and nanoelectronics. Rensselaer faculty are pioneers in these emerging areas of science, which hold considerable potential in such applications as biomedical imaging, genetics diagnostics, and microelectronics. Rensselaer's alignment with the newly created Collaborative Technology Alliance, under a grant from the U.S. Army Research Laboratory–funded Center for Social and Cognitive Networks that could be worth $36 million over the next 10 years, positions the Institute to continue its work as a leader in the emerging field of network science.[730]

New faculty hired during *The Rensselaer Plan* and their distinguished colleagues already on board certainly have the intellectual wherewithal and drive to sustain and expand what the plan has started. But to achieve true top research university status, the Institute will need to expand its faculty ranks even further.

Under the plan, the Institute has to date invested more than $1 billion in support of its mission. The Institute must build on that financial base, continuing and expanding what has been started under the plan. The Institute will have to build its endowment, which is small compared to peer institutions, some of which have as much as 10 times the endowment per student that Rensselaer has.[731] Clearly capable of winning the most competitive research funding, Rensselaer must sustain its track record in securing significant research grants. Having borrowed significantly to finance elements of *The Rensselaer Plan*, the Institute needs to pay down that debt even as it finances further growth. Steps are being taken in that regard to bolster its credit rating, which was downgraded slightly by Moody's in 2009. (Dartmouth and Georgia Tech were also downgraded.)[732] Upgrading its rating will facilitate borrowing in the future.

Moving forward, the Institute will continue its efforts to maximize the inherent value in its ambitious new buildings. The research space in the Center for Biotechnology and Interdisciplinary Studies, for example, is about two-thirds full. The building could

Work is under way to recruit as many as 10 constellation faculty. The Institute is taking its time here, because Rensselaer wants to make sure that the people they bring in are a good fit.

accommodate another 10 senior faculty members and perhaps three or four junior faculty, according to CBIS director Jonathan Dordick. Work is under way to recruit as many as 10 constellation faculty.[733] The Institute is taking its time here, because Rensselaer wants to make sure that the people they bring in are a good fit.[734] Constellations already in place also seek to add faculty to their teams. Successful faculty recruiting is of course critical to Rensselaer's overarching goals of building the research program, securing as much as $100 million in annual research funding, and continuing to expand the graduate program. If past is prologue, the remarkable research teams that have already produced important findings within the CBIS's laboratories suggest that Rensselaer will attract research groups of similarly high caliber in the future.

Virtually to a person, the scores of Rensselaereans who were interviewed for this book recognize that the Experimental Media and Performing Arts Center holds great potential for the Institute, but that its remarkable capacities will need to be integrated into Rensselaer's academic and research programs in order to fully capitalize on the building's promise. As with the CBIS, the seeds have been planted. It is clear, for example, that EMPAC offers many avenues for truly innovative work across disciplines.

Noting that Rensselaer's master of fine arts program has been ranked 6th in the country, for example, Wayne Gray, the Acting Dean of the School of Humanities, Arts, and Social Sciences, envisions that synergies between that department and EMPAC could lift the department to the top slot in the rankings, especially if natural ties between the two entities are formalized. "The art people say 'imagine if you could do anything you think of,'" Gray says. "Well, if you are an artist in EMPAC, you can." Gray anticipates that faculty in the arts department will continue work that is only just starting to find ways to use EMPAC's remarkable resources to full advantage.[735]

Already, though, the boldness and scope of the Spring 2010 season at EMPAC, outlined earlier, suggests that the Institute is starting to reap interesting benefits from this bold and fascinating experiment. Looking ahead, EMPAC's potential seems virtually limitless.

Beyond making the most of new assets like EMPAC and the CBIS, Rensselaer will continue to invest in its existing assets. Buildings, laboratories, the physical plant as a whole—all will be resourced and equipped so that they serve Rensselaer's academics and research goals optimally. One specific goal in the planning stage is the construction of a new science center, a facility that will double the size of the laboratories and office space it will replace, creating new state-of-the-art science facilities and in the process positioning Rensselaer's science infrastructure in ways that better align with the directions of scientific research in the 21st century.

The knowledge that Rensselaer creates in the future will continue to rely largely on expertise drawn from many disciplines. Rensselaer will continue to foment and nurture interdisciplinary work. Jackson said it best early in the unfolding of *The Rensselaer Plan* when she observed that "low walls must move from being the mantra to the metric if interdisciplinarity and interactivity are to thrive."[736] This is one of Rensselaer's core strengths, evidenced today across campus but especially, for example, in the CBIS.

This point also speaks to a firm belief of Jackson's that students of today—leaders of tomorrow—need broad exposure to the knowledge bases and ways of learning of many disciplines and cultures.[737] New and reengineered programs resulting from the plan provide students with a much broader classroom and co-curricular experience than their predecessors would have received.

Rensselaer has greatly raised its own expectations about the student experience on campus. The Institute has taken on the challenge to sustain and expand work started under *The Rensselaer Plan* to create a much more student-friendly culture. Having launched its concept of commons-based residential living, it is working to deliver on the promise of that approach.

The Institute is sustaining its success in recruiting high-caliber students. It continued its strong trajectory in undergraduate recruiting when it announced in 2010 that more than 13,460 high school students, a record and a jump of more than 8 percent, had applied to be part of the Rensselaer class of 2014. That spring, Rensselaer offered admission to 5,200 applicants into the class of 2014, representing a competitive admit rate of 38.7 percent. Student diversity continues to increase—between 2004 and 2010, Rensselaer has seen a 306 percent growth in applications from underrepresented students and a 188 percent increase in applications from women. In the same period, the university also saw applications from U.S. students outside of the Northeast increase by 306 percent—an important step toward its goal of greatly improving geographic diversity.[738]

Applications for Rensselaer's graduate programs were up 27 percent in 2010 over the previous year, including a 26 percent increase in applications from women, and a 123 percent increase in applications from underrepresented minorities.[739] While the

Institute has made gains in the number of doctoral students it enrolls and graduates, it intends to enroll more Ph.D. candidates in order to meet its goal of being competitive with the very top research universities. To reach the mass of students needed to produce 250 doctoral graduates each year, the Institute is implementing a more aggressive new student recruitment strategy, in the spirit of the transformation that is inherently part of *The Rensselaer Plan*.

Around campus, Rensselaer administrators have many specific ideas for taking Rensselaer forward. To help support Rensselaer's nascent research push into biomedical research, for example, Jonathan Dordick is in talks with several medical centers to establish more robust research collaborations.[740]

Evan Douglis has a broad vision for enhancing the School of Architecture that he heads. He has advocated for and garnered updated resources and more faculty slots. He intends to expand the graduate program by as much as 300 percent. He also has moved to develop improved computer capacities.[741]

"One way to distinguish us from our competitors," Douglis says, "is to say that we have a remarkable and exemplary computation program." By understanding how to use equations, Douglis says, a designer could have a significantly more robust set of capabilities to be able to construct the new world within the computer. "That is a very rarified area of knowledge," he says. Douglis also envisions the possibility of engaging a cadre of international experts in such computation. "I have no doubt that would have a dramatic impact on increasing the [school's] reputation, distinguishing the curriculum and the student experience," Douglis says.[742]

Jonathan S. Dordick
Howard P. Isermann '42
Professor of Chemical and
Biological Engineering;
Director of the Center
for Biotechnology and
Interdisciplinary Studies

David V. Rosowsky
Dean of the School of
Engineering

Evan Douglis
Dean of the School of
Architecture

In the Lally School of Management and Technology, the goals are to continue to build international relationships and the school's visibility as a whole. The school would also like to increase the number of Rensselaer MBA students. Meanwhile, however, Jackson reported in March of 2010 that MBA applications had risen more than 300 percent ahead of the previous year, and that the school had nearly doubled its number of doctoral program applications.[743]

Supporting growth of the entire institution, the Dean of the Engineering School, David Rosowsky, seeks to build the quality of the engineering program as a "platform of excellence" that contributes significantly to Rensselaer's overall quality. "I want to get the teaching loads for my faculty in line with other major research universities, and I want to grow the doctoral program," he says. In part to hold the school's enrollment to manageable and desired levels, he hopes to develop more joint programs with other entities on campus; he mentions opportunities in physics, architecture, and management as just three examples. "These are the things that will elevate the reputation, recognition, and rankings at Rensselaer," Rosowsky says.[744] A number of new faculty slots have been added to the School of Engineering for the 2011 and 2012 fiscal years.[745]

David Spooner, Acting Dean of the School of Science, intends to increase undergraduate enrollment in the school. There is growing interest in science programs related to biotechnology, and the school's computer science program has begun to grow again. Some 308 freshmen enrolled in the School of Science in the Fall of 2010.[746]

The School of Science is also focusing on increasing its graduate enrollments. The school currently has about 350 Ph.D. students and intends to add about 100 more. Spooner thinks there is also room to grow a select few of the school's master's degree programs, such as its M.S. in IT.[747]

As with engineering, the Institute intends to increase the number of faculty in the School of Science. At approximately 110 faculty now, the goal is to reach roughly 150. The Institute also plans to build a new science center by renovating and adding to the Jonsson-Rowland Science Center. This would give the school needed new laboratory space as well as options to configure space more effectively.[748]

Asked to project the future of the School of Science out 25 years, Spooner says, "I have no idea. I would expect that we will not even have the same departments in 25 years." In the short term, though, he says, "I think the interesting things happening now are at the boundaries between the departments in the interdisciplinary areas. That is where the most intriguing issues are, and where the most intriguing work will be done."[749]

Rensselaer will continue to reach out for ways to work with the city of Troy and surrounding environs. In part, the plan's communiversity program was designed to help bolster that sometimes tenuous relationship. The Institute's improvements to its physical plant and to residential units near campus can also be seen as improvements for Troy, as were the relocation of academic and administrative offices to downtown. Because town-gown relations are a key priority under the plan, the Institute has continued to enhance its community relations program, which coordinates and enhances community partnership programs and expands local outreach efforts to local communities.[750]

There is interest across campus in amending select policies set during *The Rensselaer Plan*. Some faculty and administrators feel, for example, that elements of the new graduate tuition and student support policy are too restrictive and they would like to see more flexibility worked into the policy. The policy has improved graduate student support, clarified student matriculation standards, and increased the number of graduate students supported on sponsored research grants. For now, the policy remains in place.

As we have seen, issues regarding faculty governance have been divisive at the Institute during the implementation of *The Rensselaer Plan*. Resolution of those issues has proven elusive. In late 2009, the American Association of University Professors announced an investigation of faculty governance at Rensselaer. Still, the Institute continues to work toward a satisfactory solution of what is a complex set of challenges. In 2007, the Institute's Trustees approved a transitional governance structure to apply during a period of review. In 2008, as part of the review process, nine senior faculty members, representing all of Rensselaer's schools, reviewed faculty governance at peer institutions and identified factors that help create an effective faculty governance system. Jacob Fish, the chair of that committee and the Rosalind and John J. Redfern, Jr. '33 Professor of Engineering, offered this perspective: "We have to understand the faculty governance systems in other great institutions whose ranks we are entering and revise our faculty governance structure accordingly. Despite occasionally harsh rhetoric, I believe the Rensselaer faculty and administration have a common goal of advancing Rensselaer as an influential technological research university and making it an enjoyable and sought-after place to be. I am optimistic that we will get there."[751] All parties seem to agree that it is in Rensselaer's best interests to move beyond the current impasse. As Jackson wrote in 2008, "continued constructive engagement" is needed.[752]

In terms of directions for research and academic programs, where Rensselaer goes from here will unfold as an extension of what has been started under *The Rensselaer Plan*. "The challenge now is to take what we have and what we have done, and what [Jackson's] done, and carry it forth and do it well. And even improve it," says Adjunct Trustee Howard Blitman.[753]

Eventually, of course, Rensselaer will have to find new leadership post-Jackson. Here, too, though, *The Rensselaer Plan* has set the stage for the future. Jackson has shown Rensselaer and its Board how much progress can be realized with a strong leader at the helm. As Trustee Robin Martin puts it, "whenever the transition is, we know what [kind of leadership] we need after [Jackson]" in light of the model of leadership that she has established. That is not to say that Rensselaer will necessarily opt to select a new leader immediately in the Jackson mold, but Jackson's accomplishments certainly establish high benchmarks and elevated expectations. As Martin says, finding Jackson's successor "will be a challenge…but easier because she's been here." The transition will be easier, too, Martin says, because Rensselaer has recruited strong new talent to its Board during Jackson's tenure and found better ways to make the board/president relationship more productive.[754]

There are some who would like to see the Institute push out the edges even further. Using a metaphor from his days as an engineer, for example, Trustee Nicholas Donofrio wants Rensselaer to make sure that it always stays ahead of the power curve. "Once you fall behind the power curve, you can't catch up to it because you're working to try to get to where it is," he says. "And by the time you get to where it is, it's somewhere else."[755]

Donofrio points to EMPAC as a good example of how Rensselaer is charting new ground by looking for links that others haven't yet seen. "You really want innovation? Intersect things that don't normally intersect," he says. "EMPAC is a good intersection point. The more you push yourself to different places, the more opportunity you have to innovate. I want more of that here."[756]

As it pursues further goals that build on the success of *The Rensselaer Plan*, Rensselaer Polytechnic Institute is not the same place it was at the end of the 20th century. The transformation that has taken place under the plan cuts across virtually every dimension of university life. Rensselaer today is engaged in pursuits—technological, intellectual, scientific, artistic, pedagogical—that it would not have even imagined before the turn of this century. As a university, Rensselaer is animated and engaged in wholly new ways, and in wholly new conversations. In short, Rensselaer has raised the bar for itself, setting aggressive standards for how it should fulfill its mission and creating new expectations for itself. Moreover, it has done so on its own terms, with deep respect for its own unique history, and has thus created something new.

The driving force, the difference, in all that Rensselaer has achieved, has been President Shirley Ann Jackson. Obviously aided in a great many important ways by a great number of people, Jackson brought the vision that Rensselaer could achieve greatness on a different scale, countless specific approaches and methods to implement that vision, the ability to raise significant funds to carry out the plan, the requisite courage to engage fully in the many challenges of change, and the wherewithal to ensure that her vision for the Institute would come to life.

"I think Shirley Jackson has taken [Rensselaer] to great heights," says Rep. Paul Tonko, the congressman who represents Rensselaer's district. "As a scientist, she is doubly blessed with having a good mind for management and business. She can work through the minutiae of detail and complexity and get to the heart of the matter, and make very clear the path that you need to follow to achieve results." Both those gifts and Jackson's vision have served Rensselaer well, Tonko says.[757]

Rensselaer Trustee Paul Severino, who as a successful entrepreneur knows a thing or two about new ventures, says, "When you do start-up companies, you've got to do something that's unique. We've done that here. I think [Jackson] has done something completely different. She's transformed us from where we were to a new paradigm. And she's [done] it in a way that is uniquely Rensselaer's. It's not a copy of MIT or Cal Tech or Carnegie Mellon. It's Rensselaer."[758]

Jackson "could arguably be the greatest president this university has ever had," Trustee John Carr believes. "If you look at the history of Rensselaer, there are presidents who have been builders, and presidents who have been internally focused. In all organizations over time, different people bring different things at different times." During her tenure at Rensselaer, he said, Jackson has "brought everything at the same time."[759]

Jackson "has clearly already made a mark of historic proportions," Carr said. "If you put people in their relative times, she would certainly be up there with Amos Eaton and Stephen Van Rensselaer."[760]

Severino clearly believes that Jackson and *The Rensselaer Plan* have set the stage for the Institute to achieve even greater things than have already been accomplished. "I think over the next 10 years, it gets better," he says. "We're going to succeed in our research. We're going to get a much higher level of recognition. [With] the students that we're bringing in today, we're going to get a reputation as having some of the best minds out there."[761]

"We must never forget that the effort we exert drives something bigger than ourselves. All of us—students, faculty, and staff—are agents of innovation, and ambassadors of progress. Our work helps to accelerate the rise and reputation of Rensselaer; contributes to increasing the value of a Rensselaer education to our students and graduates; and better positions our Institute to continue changing the world."

SHIRLEY ANN JACKSON

Today's realities are such that society needs Rensselaer's expertise more than ever. The Institute is at the epicenter of some of the very areas of inquiry that define a remarkable era of scientific and technological discovery. Understanding the interdependence that defines so much of the world today demands the kind of cross-disciplinary expertise that is woven into the very fabric of Rensselaer. The increasing urgency of the world's most pressing scientific questions demands the kind of research expertise that defines Rensselaer today—and precisely the kind of young mindpower that today populates the Institute's classrooms and laboratories.

"No nation can stay a world power or maintain its clout, its muscle, on the global scene if it doesn't continue to provide the human infrastructure of engineers and scientists, mathematicians and architects," Rep. Tonko says. "We need to continue to explore and create and discover and design those sort of activities, which really transition us and allow us to continue to stretch and grow an important bit of value-added to our economy and to our strength as a nation." Rensselaer, he says, has always been precisely that sort of center of inquiry.[762]

One can argue that every individual who is part of the Institute's community has been touched by *The Rensselaer Plan*. Certainly that is true of the faculty, staff, students, and friends who today benefit from the plan's impact. But the plan also connects with all those who came before, from the founders of Rensselaer on, honoring their work by building on their vision and carrying their accomplishments to a new level. And of course the plan creates countless opportunities for those who will be drawn into the Rensselaer community in the future.

In a speech to the Rensselaer community on March 17, 2010, Jackson cast the gains that have been realized under *The Rensselaer Plan* in perhaps their broadest perspective. "We must never forget that the effort we exert drives something bigger than ourselves," she said. "All of us—students, faculty, and staff—are agents of innovation, and ambassadors of progress. Our work helps to accelerate the rise and reputation of Rensselaer; contributes to increasing the value of a Rensselaer education to our students and graduates; and better positions our Institute to continue changing the world."[763]

Energizing the Institute, *The Rensselaer Plan* has inspired Rensselaer to envision a future for itself that has even more possibilities than the future imagined by the most forward-thinking visionaries of earlier generations. Today, well positioned to be competitive in the current decade, Rensselaer is poised to build even further on its current gains in the future.

In launching the campaign that would raise $1.4 billion in support of *The Rensselaer Plan*, Jackson said, "Rensselaer is ready to take its place among the handful of research universities that will shape the course of this century. Our course is set. Our moment is now. Our campaign has begun."[764] And so it has.

ACKNOWLEDGEMENTS

From Samuel F. Heffner Jr. '56, *Chairman, Board of Trustees*

As *The Rensselaer Plan* was being implemented, it became increasingly apparent that, under the guidance of Shirley Ann Jackson, we were making history. I realized that the story of the plan and the work of Dr. Jackson—its visionary, overseer, implementer, and leader—must be documented, for the benefit of the Rensselaer community and those elsewhere who might benefit from the lessons we learned.

President Shirley Ann Jackson was exceptionally generous with her time and perspectives. Nearly a dozen Trustees also shared their thoughts about *The Rensselaer Plan.* My sincere appreciation goes to Cornelius J. (Neal) Barton '58, Adjunct Trustee Howard N. Blitman '50, John W. Carr '77, Gary T. DiCamillo '73, Nicholas M. Donofrio '67, The Honorable Arthur J. Gajarsa '62, Jeffrey L. Kodosky '70, Robin B. Martin '71, Curtis R. Priem '82, Paul J. Severino '69, and Paula Loring Simon '68. Thanks also to Theresa Hobbs, Executive Assistant to the Board, for her help in arranging interviews with Trustees.

We deeply appreciate the foreword written for this book by Dr. Paul E. Gray. As President of Massachusetts Institute of Technology from 1980 to 1990 and Chairman of the MIT Corporation from 1990 to 1997, Dr. Gray was uniquely qualified to offer a relevant perspective on both institutional transformation and the leadership that Dr. Jackson, a Life Member of the MIT Corporation, has brought to bear at Rensselaer.

I congratulate author Steve Pelletier for his thorough job in telling our story and adding his perspective.

From Shirley Ann Jackson, Ph.D., *President*

For more than a decade now I have known Sam Heffner to be an uncommonly wise and generous man. As we share this story of *The Rensselaer Plan*, I am particularly grateful for his support, and for having had him as Chairman of the Board of our Institute and a partner in creating the story of the plan recounted in these pages. I especially thank him for recommending that the story of *The Rensselaer Plan* be told—to become part of the annals of the history of Rensselaer.

I am also grateful to the countless administrators, faculty members, students, staff members, alumni, alumnae, and friends of Rensselaer who have made the transformation of Rensselaer possible, and to the dozens of them who have helped to tell its story. The Institute has built upon its great legacy to completely redesign and reposition itself (over the course of a decade) to be one of the world's leading technological research universities—with global reach and global impact—for the 21st century and beyond.

My thanks also go to Steve Pelletier for the hours of research and writing, and the boundless energy, that enabled him to write a memorable book.

From William N. Walker,
Vice President, Strategic Communications and External Relations
Scores of individuals contributed to this book, but the groundbreaking work of President Shirley Ann Jackson—her envisioning, developing, and implementing of *The Rensselaer Plan*—created the opportunity for a substantive and memorable book.

Samuel Heffner, Chairman of the Board of Trustees, recognized the uniqueness of the transformation that was occurring under President Jackson, and decided that the story of *The Rensselaer Plan* should be told.

Early on, this book was conceptualized in conversations between President Jackson, Ben Wildavsky, senior scholar in research and policy at the Ewing Marion Kauffman Foundation and a leading authority on higher education, and me in my capacity as director of the project. Mr. Wildavsky connected us with a team at the national communications firm Lipman Hearne, led by Robert Moore, that helped to develop the book. Dr. Moore recommended writer Stephen Pelletier for the project. A past vice president for communications at the Council of Independent Colleges who now writes full time, primarily on higher education, Mr. Pelletier brought to this work a broad, seasoned perspective on university leadership and transformation. Through that perspective, and by virtue of his skills as a journalist, he crafted a detailed, engaging story of the transformation of Rensselaer.

In the Rensselaer Strategic Communications and External Relations office, Diane Piester, Tracey Leibach, Meg Gallien, and Dana Yamashita provided invaluable assistance. Our thanks to Lipman Hearne's Annette Stenner, who managed the book's production, and to designer Jerzy Kucinski.

From Stephen G. Pelletier, *Author*

As an author brought in from outside the Rensselaer community, I was faced with the challenge of telling a story of unusual complexity. My ability to do that depended upon the input and cooperation of scores of individuals, whose participation was facilitated by William Walker, Vice President for Strategic Communications and External Relations. I thank him for opening the many doors to interviews required for me to complete the research and writing.

President Jackson sat for long interview sessions over several weekends, answering countless questions patiently and candidly. Her insights were invaluable in telling the complex and intricate story of the vision, process, and implementation of *The Rensselaer Plan*, and therefore in shaping the narrative reflected here.

Chairman Heffner also played a key role. He was extremely gracious with his time, insights, and honest observations, and his perspectives provided a historical view that could come only from his experience of more than three decades as a Trustee.

There are numerous other individuals to thank. Several members of Dr. Jackson's Cabinet provided insights: Robert Palazzo, Provost; Francine Berman, Vice President, Research; Charles Carletta, Secretary of the Institute and General Counsel; Laban Coblentz, Chief of Staff and Associate Vice President for Policy and Planning; Virginia Gregg, Vice President, Finance and Chief Financial Officer; Eddie Ade Knowles, Vice President, Student Life; John Kolb '79, Vice President, Information Services, and Technology and Chief Information Officer; Paul Marthers, Vice President, Enrollment, and Dean, Undergraduate and Graduate Admissions; Curtis Powell, Vice President, Human Resources; and Claude Rounds, Vice President, Administration.

Thanks also to these Rensselaer academic deans who sat for interviews: David Rosowsky, Engineering; Evan Douglis, Architecture; Wayne Gray, Humanities, Arts, and Social Sciences (Acting); and David Spooner, Science (Acting). Other administrators who made time for interviews include Stanley M. Dunn, Vice Provost and Dean of Graduate Education; Prabhat Hajela, Vice Provost and Dean of Undergraduate Education; Johannes Goebel, Director, Experimental Media and Performing Arts Center; and Wolf von Maltzahn, then Acting Vice President for Research.

Rensselaer faculty who were interviewed include Tarek Abdoun, Judith and Thomas Iovino '73 Career Development Professor in Civil Engineering; Selmer Bringsjord, Professor of Cognitive Science and Computer Science; Jonathan Dordick, Howard P. Isermann Professor and Director of the Center for Biotechnology and Interdisciplinary Studies; Angel García, Professor of Physics and Constellation Chaired Professor in Biocomputation and Bioinformatics Areas; Susan Gilbert, Professor and Head,

Department of Biology; James Hendler, Tetherless World Constellation Professor, Department of Computer Science and Cognitive Science Department; Isom Herron, Professor of Mathematical Sciences; Robert Linhardt, Ann and John H. Broadbent, Jr. '59 Constellation Professor of Biocatalysis and Metabolic Engineering and Professor of Chemistry and Chemical Biology, Biology, and Chemical and Biological Engineering; Deborah McGuinness, Tetherless World Constellation Professor, Department of Computer Science and Cognitive Science Department; Achille Messac, Professor of Mechanical, Aerospace, and Nuclear Engineering; Mark Mistur, Associate Professor, School of Architecture; and Gwo-Ching Wang, Professor and Chair, Department of Physics, Applied Physics, and Astronomy.

Other members of the Rensselaer community also contributed to the project. Thanks to the late Lester Rubenfeld, Director of the Center for Initiatives in Pre-College Education and Professor of Mathematical Sciences; Glenn M. Monastersky, Director of Operations, Center for Biotechnology and Interdisciplinary Studies and Clinical Assistant Professor, Biomedical Engineering; Jack Mahoney, Director of Institutional Research; and Richard Hartt '70, Managing Director of the Rensselaer Union. John Dojka, Institute Archivist and Collection Development Coordinator, and Amy Rupert, Assistant Institute Archivist, provided historical background.

Representative Paul Tonko, who serves New York's 21st Congressional District, took time out of an exceptionally busy schedule to share his thoughts about *The Rensselaer Plan*, a conversation that was patiently arranged by Beau Duffy on his staff in conjunction with Deborah Altenburg in the Institute's Washington office. Thanks to Catherine Eckart '85, President of the Rensselaer Alumni Association from 2007 to 2009. Thanks also to Michael Zwack '11 and Alex Franz '10, respectively Rensselaer Grand Marshal and President of the Union during 2009–2010, and to Eben Bayer '07.

Also invaluable was an extensive, detailed account of the genesis and implementation of *The Rensselaer Plan* written by David Haviland '64. The current work was greatly enabled by Mr. Haviland's exceptional research, discerning attention to detail, and astute insights.

This book also draws extensively from another earlier account of Rensselaer history. I am deeply grateful for the perspectives and rich details reported by Father Thomas Phelan, D. Michael Ross, and Carl Westerdahl in *Rensselaer: Where Imagination Achieves the Impossible*, published in 1995. Their work was invaluable in shaping the second chapter of this book.

APPENDICES

PRESIDENTS OF RENSSELAER POLYTECHNIC INSTITUTE

Samuel Blatchford	1824 – 1828
John Chester	1828 – 1829
Eliphalet Nott	1829 – 1845
Nathan S.S. Beman	1845 – 1865
John F. Winslow	1865 – 1868
Thomas C. Brinsmade	1868
James Forsyth	1868 – 1886
William Gurley	1886 – 1887 *(acting)*
Albert E. Powers	1887 – 1888 *(acting)*
John H. Peck	1888 – 1901
Palmer C. Ricketts	1901 – 1934
William O. Hotchkiss	1935 – 1943
Livingston W. Houston	1944 – 1958
Richard G. Folsom	1958 – 1971
Richard J. Grosh	1971 – 1976
George M. Low	1976 – 1984
Daniel Berg	1984 – 1985 *(acting)*
	1985 – 1987
Stanley I. Landgraf	1987 – 1988 *(acting)*
Roland Schmitt	1988 – 1993
R. Byron Pipes	1993 – 1998
Cornelius J. Barton	1998 – 1999 *(acting)*
Shirley Ann Jackson	1999 – present

THE RENSSELAER PLAN

....

1. THE GOAL

Rensselaer pursues this goal: To achieve greater prominence in the 21st century as a top-tier, world-class technological research university with global reach and global impact.

Education and research are inextricably linked in world-class universities.
Excellence in education inspired the founders of Rensselaer, and innovative pedagogy remains a core value of the Institute. To provide leading-edge education, we must be leaders in key research fields, for the creation of the new knowledge is critical to a stimulating learning environment for our students. Cutting-edge research enables us to make our students partners in discovery and open their minds to inquiry. The Institute will, therefore, assign added emphasis to research and scholarship as a key constituent of excellence in education.

A research university is a community of learners.
Research potentiates education, bringing it to full flower. To paraphrase Dr. Paul Gray, President Emeritus and Chairman Emeritus of MIT, a research university is a community of learners—some young, some older—engaged together in creating, disseminating, and applying knowledge, using existing knowledge, skills, and judgment. Research, therefore, is about learning. At the same time, education can be defined as bringing students to the point of self-sufficiency, that is, learning how to proceed when no one knows the answer. Education, therefore, is about research.

Research and education drive reputation.
As it gains greater prominence as a world-class technological research university, Rensselaer will enhance its ability to achieve several interrelated goals—attracting highly talented students and well-respected faculty and staff, expanding geographic reach, and increasing financial support from private and public sources.

Strategic focus is essential to achieving our goal.
Rensselaer will build on its distinctive strengths in interdisciplinary inquiry, interactive learning, and technological entrepreneurship to:

- Enhance national leadership in innovative learning and teaching by providing outstanding and distinctive **Education** for resident undergraduates and graduate students, and for working professionals. Educational programs will incorporate interactive pedagogies, provide an engaging student experience, and create lifetime connections with Rensselaer.

- Dramatically expand the **Research Enterprise**, including associated graduate education, by (i) creating new Institute-wide initiatives in two research arenas closely aligned with societal and global priorities: information technology and biotechnology; (ii) building on and enhancing existing core research strengths; and (iii) supporting additional critical priorities in areas that offer opportunities for research leadership.

- Increase **Scientific and Technological Entrepreneurship** across education, research, technology commercialization, new venture creation, and regional economic development.

- Achieve true intellectual, geographic, gender, and ethnic **Diversity** in our students, faculty, and staff in order to draw upon the best talent available, and to prepare our students to work and lead in a global economy.

- Draw vitality from and add vitality to our diverse **Communities** on campus, among alumni and friends, and in the city, region, state, nation, and around the globe.

- Redesign and invigorate **Enabling Activities** to focus Rensselaer's people, administrative processes, information infrastructure, physical facilities, and financial resources on the realization of strategic goals.

Three fundamental markers will drive our actions: Excellence, Leadership, and Community.

Excellence is the mantra and the metric. Leadership suggests we participate in shaping the agenda and discourse in areas related to our mission and plans. Community compels us to be one Rensselaer as we develop and maintain essential roles and partnerships within local, state, national, and international communities. As we build toward the goal, we insist on excellence, leadership, and community in every aspect of the Institute: in each core enterprise—resident undergraduate education, research and graduate education, education for working professionals, and scientific and technological entrepreneurship; in each academic and administrative unit; and most importantly, in the people of Rensselaer—its faculty, students, staff, alumni, and friends. Finally, we will drive "new" resources—be they substantial new resources or savings from effective use of existing resources—to areas of the highest priority. Under The Rensselaer Plan, discretionary, incentive, and new resources will be directed to identified priorities in research, pedagogy, and other core activities.

We will achieve our goal by embracing our core values, identifying the key characteristics and strengths on which we will build, and understanding the necessity of integrated planning and action.

2.1 Rensselaer Today

Over nearly two centuries, Rensselaer Polytechnic Institute has maintained its reputation for providing an undergraduate education of undisputed intellectual rigor based on exceptional pedagogical innovation. As a research university, Rensselaer has attracted outstanding faculty whose research programs range from microelectronics to computational modeling and simulation, mathematical finance, advanced materials, environmental studies, lighting, and electronic arts. Rensselaer's graduate engineering program ranks 19th in the nation. The Schools of Engineering, Science, Architecture, Humanities and Social Sciences, and Management and Technology, and the interdisciplinary Faculty of Information Technology educate 9,600 students, enrolling 5,000 undergraduates and 1,800 graduate students in residential programs. Rensselaer also enrolls 2,800 students in distance programs and at Rensselaer at Hartford. Rensselaer has earned distinction in interactive learning and the application of information technology to education. New programs have enriched the profile of the student body. The Rensselaer degree is highly regarded, and graduates are aggressively sought by industry, universities, and the public sector. Recent initiatives include new interdisciplinary degree programs in bioinformatics and information technology. Current annual research funding totals $40 million. A significant portion of this support comes from industry, well above the national average, and testimony to the importance of Rensselaer research to the private sector. The Institute is a pioneer in interdisciplinary research and has expanded its programs by making focused research investments supported by strong industry partnerships in such fields as microelectronics, advanced materials, scientific computation, polymer science, industrial automation, and lighting research. In the last 20 years Rensselaer has encouraged technology partnerships and dissemination, developing an internationally recognized incubator center and a flourishing technology park. More recently the Institute has focused on technological entrepreneurship, commercializing leading-edge research and creating new business ventures.

2.2 Unique Strengths

Looking forward, Rensselaer builds on a unique combination of strengths.

Interdisciplinary inquiry. Rensselaer has excelled in employing multidisciplinary and interdisciplinary approaches in curriculum, teaching, research, and outreach. The Institute has been aggressive in building alliances with partners with complementary expertise. Interdisciplinarity is the Institute's most exploitable competitive advantage.

Interactive learning. The value of learning by doing was a central proposition in Rensselaer's first plan of education. At a time when recitation was the dominant educational model, early Rensselaer students were involved in laboratory demonstrations, taking responsibility for discovery and learning. Today, 175 years later, the Institute still is a recognized leader in interactive learning, using technology and teamwork to involve students as active participants in their own educations—both on campus and at a distance.

Technological entrepreneurship. Rensselaer was founded in 1824 "for the purpose of instructing persons...in the application of science to the common purposes of life." Rensselaer people have performed the research, developed the technologies, produced the innovations, and formed the enterprises that defined and accomplished the technological agendas of the 19th and 20th centuries. They will do so in the 21st century. Rensselaer has achieved distinction by focusing its considerable talents and energies on its unique strengths. We will infuse interdisciplinary inquiry, interactive learning, and technological entrepreneurship in all that we do. We will reach our goal by employing strategic focus, energy, agility, comity, and uncommon will.

2.3 Opportunity and Challenge

Focused technological universities in the United States enjoy an extraordinary range of opportunities. Technological innovation is driving national prosperity and is a clearly understood priority of both lawmakers and the public. U.S. high-technology industries, often spun out of universities, have gained international dominance. They have achieved unprecedented support and recognition as the leading industries of the new century. As their investors and creators have acquired wealth, they are increasing their philanthropic contributions to higher education. At the same time, federal research budgets for the physical, information, and especially, biological sciences are growing, spurred by societal priorities, and urged on by industry, which increasingly turns to technological universities as partners in research, in business, and in technological education. As Rensselaer moves forward, so also does its peer group of technological research universities, all intent on enhancing their leadership positions. Among these schools, we are small and under-resourced. While we have achieved international prominence in innovative pedagogy and specific research areas, the pace of growth in research funding, research degrees, and endowment has lagged behind most major research universities, a reality that is reflected in our ranking as a national university. While we have realized extraordinary accomplishments with limited resources, the gap between our aspirations and our means continues to grow. To strengthen education, enhance reputation, and increase the flow of resources, Rensselaer thus must pledge a much deeper commitment to research and graduate education, while extending our excellence in undergraduate education. Our ability to attract and retain the best faculty, and therefore the best students, will be critical for attaining these goals. Rensselaer thus must reflect the diversity of the global community in order to have the best talent as well as the multiple perspectives and innovations necessary for a world-class technological research university.

2.4 Planning and The Rensselaer Plan

Stephen Van Rensselaer and Amos Eaton launched their "magnificent experiment" in 1824 with *The Rensselaerean Plan,* a historic statement that gave form to Eaton's vision for applying science to life's common purposes. The Rensselaer Plan is a 21st-century expression of this tradition. The Rensselaer Plan articulates a strategic vision and delineates the means to achieve it. An "evergreen" plan designed to be revised on a regular basis, The Rensselaer Plan will guide our decisions and provide the framework for school and divisional performance plans that will serve as the basis for each year's operating plan and budget. Performance plans will define means and metrics, and when prioritized, will create the case for major new resources. Integrated effort has created The Rensselaer Plan, and integrated effort will realize its vision. We are a diverse community comprising a broad array of talents and perspectives. Even as we celebrate this diversity, we are united in pursuit of a common goal: greater prominence as a top-tier world-class technological research university with global reach and global impact.

3. RESIDENT UNDERGRADUATE EDUCATION

Rensselaer's educational strength lies in its ability to examine concepts and ideas across disciplines and relate them to the world of practice.

Rensselaer is committed to an undergraduate experience that surpasses all others, combining theory and hands-on experience as the means to educate tomorrow's leaders for technologically based careers. The Institute will enroll outstanding undergraduate students in excellent programs distinguished by interactive pedagogies, partnerships with faculty in research and innovation, seamless customer service, and a campus culture and engaging student experience that create a lifelong relationship with the Institute.

3.1 Undergraduate Programs and Students

Excellence in undergraduate education requires constant improvement in the quality of programs, and the makeup of the student body. We will continue to provide compelling programs that suggest exciting futures; provide a firm grounding in the fundamentals; bridge knowledge to practice; emphasize discovery, reasoning, and action; inculcate a world perspective and cultural understanding; and produce leaders. We will:

- Offer a rich portfolio of traditional and nontraditional choices related to technology, the scientific underpinnings of technology, the technological professions, and the human and social dimensions of technology.

- Create course concentrations, minors, second disciplines, dual degrees, interdisciplinary projects, and other structures that enable students to work at the intersections of disciplines and forge exciting individual career trajectories.

- Update the core curriculum to reflect advances in research strengths, including information technology, biotechnology, and scientific and technological entrepreneurship.

- Offer excellent courses in the arts, sciences, humanities, and social sciences that provide strong foundations and enable students to understand and work within the cultural, social, economic, and political contexts in which they will be expected to lead.

- Integrate outcomes assessment and evaluation into all education programs, ensuring timely and continuous improvement.

Outstanding programs are geared to outstanding students who will be enriched by and add value to Rensselaer. We will:

- Set the undergraduate student body size at approximately 5,000 undergraduate students.

- Increase admissions selectivity, with particular attention to mathematics/science credentials and high school performance (especially in AP and honors courses).

- Seek diversity in its broadest and richest sense, including intellectual and cultural breadth, athletic ability, and entrepreneurial interest.

- Seek greater ethnic and gender diversity by employing new recruiting mechanisms and providing a hospitable climate for all students.

- Recruit nationally, broadening the geographic base of target schools, developing linkages with new schools, especially those enrolling students underrepresented in science and technology, and developing joint education programs with key partners.

- Graduate students known for their abilities as innovative problem-solvers, excellent communicators, interdisciplinary thinkers, team participants, and skilled leaders.

3.2 Interactive Learning

Rensselaer's internationally recognized leadership position in interactive teaching and learning provides an exceptional foundation for excellent and distinctive undergraduate education programs. Given the urgent need to excite and engage a nation of learners about science and technology, and given the importance of distinctive education programs to our success as a top-tier world-class technological university, The Rensselaer Plan nurtures and enhances interactive teaching and learning as an Institute-wide enterprise. We will:

- Investigate new interactive pedagogies across all curricula, forging a deeper relationship between student and teacher.

- Engage students in collaborative learning experiences, taking advantage of technology to facilitate interactivity and teamwork skills to solve problems.

- Customize the learning experience to individual needs, deploying interactive pedagogies to engage a full range of backgrounds and learning styles.

- Use interactive pedagogies to create "virtual environments" that extend the student experience in time and space, sharing courses among universities and creating virtual classrooms, discussion groups, and project settings with faculty and students at other universities, and with researchers, innovators, entrepreneurs, and policy makers around the world.

- Develop continuous and interactive assessment techniques so that testing becomes a tool for learning.

- Pursue leadership in the use of technology in education, developing deeper understanding of how we learn, accelerating the pace of innovation in interactive learning, and providing opportunities to showcase innovative results.

3.3 Participation in Research and Innovation

Rensselaer's educational strength lies in its ability to examine concepts and ideas across disciplines and relate them to the world of practice. Our emphasis on leadership, teamwork, and communication skills transcends traditional courses or even disciplines. To enable our students to attain their full potential in the discovery and responsible application of knowledge, it is essential to involve them in the research work of the Institute. We will:

- Provide incentives for faculty who open their labs to undergraduate students to create research opportunities, facilitate faculty/student interaction, and expand the pipeline of bright, eager students into graduate study.

- Focus participation in research as a means to cultivate women and students of color to expand their representation in our faculty.

- Ensure that all students have a research experience by enlarging the Undergraduate Research Program, and by adding a thesis or comparable major scholarly work requirement for seniors.

- Expand the number of co-op, internship, and project opportunities for students in Rensselaer's innovation enterprises in the incubator program and technology park as well as in programs conducted by other universities, industry, and government. Include opportunities that may be virtual, or short term.

3.4 An Engaging Student Experience

We will provide experiential, residential, and recreational environments that embrace our students and connect them to Rensselaer for life. This begins with a demonstrated commitment to student success that extends from their earliest contact with Rensselaer through the student and alumni years. We will:

- Restructure student orientation programs to build strong affinity groups—including wilderness, community-based, cultural, or other team-building experiences—that will commence before classes begin and continue into the first semester.

- Provide pervasive opportunities for student enterprise, entrepreneurship, community service, and leadership development within academic programs, outside the classroom, in residential settings on campus, and in sororities and fraternities. Utilize the Rensselaer Union and the Archer Center for Student Leadership Development as unique resources in these efforts.

- Empower students as learners and entrepreneurs who design and manage projects, processes, and organizations as students.

- Enliven campus life by creating social activities, competitions, and occasions to celebrate achievement, honor tradition, and create a culture in which students see themselves as belonging to the larger university community.

- Create improved presentation and performance spaces on the campus through renovation or new construction.

- Undertake rolling renovation and/or replacement of residence halls for undergraduates according to an integrated Institute-wide capital plan.

- Replace or renovate athletic facilities according to an integrated Institute-wide capital plan.

- Ensure full-time coaching staff for all women's and men's intercollegiate sports programs.

3.5 Seamless Student Service

The Institute is under an obligation to support students in managing the logistics of their education. These services include outstanding academic advising; career, health, and counseling services; and consolidated, timely, and accurate information on courses and educational opportunities, progress to degree, financial aid, and account status. We will, for all students:

- Increase the accessibility, connectivity, and reliability of information systems affecting student life; this includes upgrading the Institute's Web presence as a constant source of information and interaction with others, and completing the "wiring" of the campus for communication, information, and academic and research needs.

- Provide information proactively, with the goal of enabling students to resolve issues and problems.

- Set standards for providing students and their families and sponsors with professional, competent, efficient, and friendly customer service, and redesign processes to meet these standards.

- Provide the staff and faculty who serve students with the tools, training, and performance metrics required for seamless service.

4. RESEARCH & GRADUATE EDUCATION

A careful strategy to select and pursue areas of focus that match our core strengths will be critical to realizing our opportunity for research growth and influence.

Research, fundamental to a great university, is a public trust. The most significant transformation posited by The Rensselaer Plan is the imperative that Rensselaer create a research portfolio of substantially greater size, quality, prominence, and impact. Rensselaer has long taken great pride in graduates who are highly prized by employers, have immediate impact, and step up to leadership in technology-based careers. In times of very rapid technological change, our graduates cannot do this unless they are educated in an environment of leading-edge research and innovation. By building research programs, and involving students in research activity, we will preserve and enhance our historic strength in undergraduate education. Research is a creative process that generates new principles and spawns new technologies. Such technological innovation stokes the engine of economic growth, and connects the university research enterprise to a cycle that catalyzes the development of new industries and supplies a highly educated up-to-date workforce. Rensselaer will grow from an institution centered on undergraduate education with selected research strengths to a full research university. Rensselaer research in the future will extend over a broad portfolio that puts the Institute in a leadership position both in established fields and in evolving areas of inquiry that hold out great promise and opportunity. The Rensselaer Plan sets its sights on tier-one ranking among U.S. technological research universities, with a goal of expanding research funding from $40 million to $100 million annually in five years, and doubling from 125 to 250 the number of doctorates a year over the next eight to 10 years.

4.1 Enhancing and Growing Research

Greatness demands balance among the range of disciplines that comprise a fully realized technological university. To innovate and to offer the best education, each of Rensselaer's schools must be excellent in research and recognized in its own right. Rensselaer will encourage a full range of individual and group scholarly activity. We will make dramatic investments that substantially increase our involvement in two new arenas vital for national well-being and growth: information technology and biotechnology. We will add emphasis in areas of core strength with important future trajectories. We will invest in a limited number of additional research focus areas, with priorities established in the performance planning process. Looking ahead to dramatic growth, we will build on a track record of success in interdisciplinary research and a long history of technological innovation. We will emphasize careful selection of research problems, do research at interdisciplinary intersections, exploit our "low walls," and build strategic alliances to magnify impact. We will enhance basic research in areas that undergird selected focal areas. We will grow graduate programs associated with research and the education of researchers, and we will improve the infrastructure and resources necessary for research and graduate education. At the end of the day, Rensselaer will advance a rich research portfolio. To support this portfolio, we will:

- Recruit and support world-class faculty in identified priority areas.

- Review the organization of research centers and programs, and restructure and/or sunset them to ensure excellence and sustainability.

- Reorganize research facilities to increase research productivity, creating infrastructure, staff, and research equipment that support several or many research programs.

- Implement research policies (research staff, facilities management, student support, charge-out, cost sharing, and intellectual property policies) sufficient to the task.

- Provide research and researchers with internal and external visibility, including publications, Web features, alumni seminars, and living campus exhibits designed to capture the imaginations of prospective students, staff, and visitors.

- Exploit research results to drive innovation and entrepreneurship.

- Expand and improve inquiry-based graduate programs as an integral aspect of research planning and delivery.

4.2 Core Research Strengths

An essential component of our strategy to increase prominence in research will lie in identifying areas of existing distinction that represent future growth and broad impact in key research areas. These core strengths represent opportunities for the Institute's continuing leadership in fields that promise increased significance, new intellectual challenges, and relevance to broad societal and technological needs. In addition, these core strengths link our existing enterprise to new and exciting research arenas. Three core research strengths on which Rensselaer will build are:

- Microelectronics, photonics, and microsystems technologies.

- Advanced materials and nanotechnology.

- Modeling and simulation of complex systems.

Each core research strength cuts across multiple schools and departments, exemplifies interdisciplinary effort, and holds promise for stimulating the development of new fields of research. Each has achieved distinction. Each serves as a sound foundation for continued progress and deserves priority status for institutional investment.

4.3 New Research Arenas: Information Technology and Biotechnology

As an early and integral component of our strategy to enhance position and distinction, we will focus investment in two Institute-wide research arenas: information technology (IT) and biotechnology. All research and technology indicators suggest that biotechnology and information technology, coupled with the convergence of microsystems and nanotechnologies, are closely aligned with global and societal priorities, and primary drivers of economic growth. They will dominate the future. Biotechnology is already transforming health care and agriculture, and opening up enormous possibilities for sustainable resource management. IT is the driving force in every industry today, transforming many of them and enabling new areas of research, such as the human genome, and enterprise, such as e-business. Both IT and biotechnology are challenging and transforming the world's underlying social, economic, and political structures. Biotechnology and information technology are pervasive in their influence and increasingly dependent on core disciplines such as mathematics, materials, and microelectronics. Rather than Rensselaer moving toward these fields, they are moving toward us. A careful strategy to select and pursue areas of focus that match our core strengths will be critical to realizing our opportunity for research growth and influence. We will exploit important niches in IT and biotechnology. Based on existing building blocks of excellence, working at interdisciplinary intersections, and making carefully selected new investments in faculty and infrastructure, we will achieve research leadership in very selective focal areas within IT and biotechnology. We will follow this process:

- Appoint internal and external task forces to define a small number (most likely, three) of focal areas within IT and within biotechnology. The selection will be based on the identification of important issues and on converging technical themes that build on existing Rensselaer strengths.

- Within each focal area, create a strategy that involves both existing and new faculty. Build or create strengths in basic undergirding areas. We will forge linkages between Rensselaer research projects and programs with other academic institutions, medical centers, state and federal laboratories, and private-sector concerns who offer complementary interests, expertise, staff, and specialized facilities.

- Within each focal area, assemble a critical mass of people who create "constellations" of world-class faculty, staff, and students. A typical constellation will include a senior faculty member and two junior faculty in key areas needed to energize the focal area at Rensselaer. We anticipate a total of six constellations (likely three in each research arena), all or most of whom will be new hires.

- Seek endowment support for "constellation" faculty salaries plus current support for faculty start-up and early term operating costs for approximately three years. New fund-raising efforts and internal redirection and restructuring will provide the needed support.

- Construct specialized research facilities and provide necessary equipment for the focal areas. A new biotechnology and interdisciplinary studies facility will be a necessity in order to create the appropriate synergy among biotechnology, nanotechnology, and microsystems research.

- Expand research and doctoral programs in undergirding disciplines, and create new interdisciplinary graduate programs as required.

4.4 Resident Graduate Education

Because research is the engine that drives most graduate programs and provides their intellectual grounding, dramatic growth in research requires an equally dramatic expansion in inquiry-based graduate programs leading to research-based master's and doctoral degrees. We will:

- Double the production of doctorates awarded over the next eight to 10 years.

- Develop a highly effective enrollment management program for graduate programs, including market research, marketing, relationship-building, admission, orientation, support, and retention activities.

- Enhance student selectivity and quality, ensuring consistency across all graduate programs. Recruit a larger number of excellent students from a national base, as well as the best international students.

- Provide both disciplinary and interdisciplinary doctoral opportunities aligned with areas of research growth.

- Offer a relatively small number of carefully selected residential professional master's programs in sync with the intellectual, research, and education goals of the sponsoring school. We will recruit the very best of our undergraduates interested in professional careers to complete their master's-level professional education at Rensselaer.

- Extend interactive learning across graduate programs. Our distinctive interactive pedagogies allow us to bring studio- and team-based learning to our graduate students.

- Pay systematic attention to the quality of the lives of graduate students, providing an engaging student experience and seamless student service as described in 3.4 and 3.5.

- Create housing options on and off campus for graduate students.

- Examine structure, pricing, and financing of all graduate programs.

5. EDUCATION FOR WORKING PROFESSIONALS

The Rensselaer Plan calls for expanding programs for working professionals targeted at corporate executives, advanced professionals, and entrepreneurs.

We stand at the beginning of a "learning revolution" that will transform higher education. This revolution is characterized by an astonishing pace of technological advancement, expansion of new knowledge at unprecedented rates, shifts to an information-based global economy, and a profound change in the demographics of students. As a consequence, top-tier universities are expanding their scope to include the existing as well as the future workforce, and forging creative partnerships with business, government, and other academic institutions. Programs for working professionals allow universities to transfer research results and innovations directly into the workplace and address the lifelong learning needs of the workforce.

5.1 A Distributed Rensselaer

Rensselaer builds on a strong foundation. Together, Rensselaer at Hartford, Executive Programs, and Professional and Distance Education enroll 2,800 part-time working professionals in graduate academic programs. The RSVP program has received national recognition for leadership in distance education. With 45 years of experience in serving working professionals, Rensselaer at Hartford is a unique asset. The Rensselaer Learning Institute, located within Rensselaer at Hartford, serves over 14,000 working professionals in graduate degree programs and in non-degree training courses. These activities provide the Institute with the foundation to extend research and education beyond the "residential years" and its physical campuses to meet the career-long learning needs of working professionals. The Rensselaer Plan calls for a distributed Rensselaer that operates from campuses in Troy and Hartford while also reaching a much broader audience of working professionals through regional sites, distance education, and international partnerships. A distributed Rensselaer will provide ongoing education to enable professionals in technology-based careers to maintain their leadership positions, and forge lifelong relationships with our alumni. A distributed Rensselaer will serve as the means to transfer research findings to the marketplace while bringing the people and projects of the marketplace to the Troy and Hartford campuses, creating exciting new opportunities for resident students. To consolidate our leadership position in education for working professionals, we will:

- Develop graduate-level, interdisciplinary, and executive programs that flow directly from our leading-edge, interdisciplinary research in such areas as IT, biotechnology, microelectronics, simulation and modeling, and advanced materials. Around these cores, we will customize to meet specific corporate needs.

- Increase, significantly, the involvement of research-active faculty in design and delivery of programs.

- Incorporate interactive pedagogies, both in the classroom and at a distance, as our competitive advantage in providing education to working professionals.

- Target programs toward corporate executives, advanced professionals, and entrepreneurs whose activity exerts significant impact on technology and society.

- Create partnerships with major corporate and government groups to position Rensselaer as the educator of choice in our areas of strategic focus, and with other top-tier technological research universities to broaden our delivery capability.

- Increase, with an eye to quality, the number of students, particularly Rensselaer alumni, in professional and executive programs.

- Recruit students internationally, especially in Asia, South America, Europe, and Africa. Create new sites in strategic locations for the delivery of live and distance-based programs for working professionals.

- Present a strong institutional "common face" to business organizations, government agencies, and individuals when they turn to Rensselaer for their professional education needs via consistent marketing, enrollment management, learner services, and administrative arrangements.

5.2 Rensselaer at Hartford

Rensselaer at Hartford enrolls nearly 2,000 students from over 100 corporations in professional master's programs in management, engineering, and computer science. Courses are offered at Hartford, on site at corporate facilities, and interactively to working professionals across the U.S. and Mexico. As part of a distributed Rensselaer, we will:

- Broaden and increase the base of corporate clients served at Hartford.

- Create a one-year executive MBA program, blending an intensive on-campus experience with distance learning.

- Increase engineering enrollments in degree programs, certificate programs, and courses; and promote the master's degree in high-demand engineering disciplines (e.g., computer and systems engineering) and the dual-degree program with management.

- Expand education opportunities associated with the Institute's core research strengths and the new focal areas in information technology and biotechnology.

- Increase the number of core tenure-track faculty at Hartford engaged in research, balancing teaching and service commitments as appropriate. Create appropriate Institute-wide research alliances with Hartford's corporate partners.

- Expand the reach of interactive pedagogies employed at Hartford, offering a range of interactive campus-based and distance courses and course experiences. Expand experiential and practicum-based (case studies) learning.

- Expand the Rensselaer Learning Institute offerings to technologically focused organizations, adding value, quality, and opportunities for Rensselaer's research, entrepreneurship, and continuing education enterprises.

- Provide outstanding and seamless services to Hartford-based students and their sponsoring organizations.

- Investigate, with Hartford serving as a model, similar operations elsewhere in the U.S. and abroad.

6. SCIENTIFIC & TECHNOLOGICAL ENTREPRENEURSHIP

Technological entrepreneurship will be encouraged with new curricula for students, and new programs to take Rensselaer's intellectual property to market.

For more than 175 years, Rensselaer has exhibited a unique strength in its ability to translate scientific discoveries into practical application, a process that we refer to as technological entrepreneurship. Historically and consistently, faculty, students, and alumni have successfully developed technologies, created innovations, and formed business ventures to bring ideas into practice to create value. Today, the Incubator program, Rensselaer Technology Park, and the Severino Center for Technological Entrepreneurship are national models. Looking ahead, rapid technological change and an emerging global marketplace present outstanding continuing opportunities for scientific and technological entrepreneurship.

6.1 Entrepreneurship Education and Research

Entrepreneurship is a way of life that springs from fundamental education and research programs. We will work to infuse understanding and encouragement of entrepreneurship through all schools and programs. Specifically we will:

- Expand the Institute's fundamental research activity in technological entrepreneurship and the management of innovation.

- Teach the fundamentals of entrepreneurship—and intrapreneurship—to students across all majors, establishing a *general curriculum requirement* in this area.

- Expand opportunities for students to create innovation by increasing the number of hands-on courses such as Introduction to Engineering Design, Inventors Studio, and Multidisciplinary Design Laboratory; programs such as Product Design and Innovation; and competitions such as the Formula SAE car project.

- Provide opportunities for students to work in settings where technology is being commercialized, such as entrepreneurial faculty projects, internships, and co-op experiences.

- Create opportunities in the Rensselaer Union and in the residence halls for students to propose, design, and implement projects, processes, and organizations.

6.2 Intellectual Property and Technology Commercialization

Research is the major driver of science and technology transfer, invention, and innovation. Technological entrepreneurship completes the technology life cycle—from discovery to the creation of impact in the global marketplace. With an expanding research base, we will cultivate a campus culture that provides the spirit and motivation for inventors to pursue commercialization. We will:

- Increase awareness of intellectual property, preserving its value in research agreements and maximizing its value under shared equity arrangements and licensing agreements, covering intellectual property developed in research and materials developed for distance education.

- Create intellectual property policies that encourage entrepreneurship and allow the university to take equity positions in new ventures as appropriate.

- Ensure that intellectual property policies have adequate and appropriate conflict of interest and conflict of commitment provisions.

- Develop an awareness and infrastructure of intellectual property rights policies, incentives, and marketing to support innovation and commercialization.

6.3 Creating and Supporting New Ventures

World-class technological research universities excel in transferring research outputs to the commercial sector. We will create innovative programs targeted at growing major new technological ventures and creating value. We will:

- Enhance the process of matching researchers and entrepreneurs to create new ventures that take Rensselaer intellectual property to market.

- Provide business planning and facilitate venture capital for faculty and students for start-up companies that commercialize leading-edge Rensselaer research.

- Expand the Incubator program to accommodate more start-ups and second-stage incubation.

- Expand the flow of technology, talent, and ventures into the Rensselaer Technology Park and the Capital Region. Bring new focus to the Rensselaer Technology Park as the locus for mature ventures based on the technologies taught and researched at the Institute.

- Work with private and public sources to attract new venture capital and entrepreneurial talent to the Capital Region.

7. RENSSELAER'S COMMUNITIES

As a citizen of the world, Rensselaer must extend its reach and impact beyond present borders. Teaching and research are the starting points.

A university community comprises a collection of communities: The campus community of students, faculty, staff, administration, and trustees lives in a series of larger neighborhood, city, and regional communities, and is supported by a broad national and international community of alumni, friends, business, and professional partners. Rensselaer draws its vitality from, and adds vitality to, each of these communities.

7.1 The Campus Community

World-class people create world-class universities. Students are drawn from the best and the brightest. Faculty are recognized leaders, receiving peer recognition and funding, defining the discourse in their fields, and setting scholarly and professional agendas in national and international arenas. Staff exemplify excellence and commitment; many are leaders in their fields. Institute leaders bring vision, strategic focus, managerial ability, and integrity to their work. The Board of Trustees provides the sustaining stewardship, fiduciary oversight, and financial support that help Rensselaer achieve its plans and aspirations. To achieve Rensselaer's goals, we will:

- Develop recruiting and admissions processes that identify the best students who will succeed at Rensselaer, and provide them an informative, exciting, and seamless process of joining our university.

- Recruit, empower, and compensate staff and faculty at levels commensurate with their skill and contribution.

- Require all faculty to do research/scholarship, innovative teaching, and service, increasing the emphasis on research and scholarship in performance evaluations.

- Strengthen/elevate, significantly, the standards for hiring, promotion, and tenure of faculty with regard to research distinction and teaching quality.

- Expect and assist faculty to garner external research support through competitive grants, fellowships, research centers, research partnerships, and other mechanisms.

- Increase, significantly, the number of women and minority tenure-track faculty.

- Make Rensselaer an employer of choice among faculty and staff by developing uniform policies and approaches to critical human resource activities, and partnering between Human Resources and other academic and administrative divisions to establish optimal strategies, policies, and procedures.

- Provide staff with the tools and the training required as roles and skill sets change.

- Create innovative administrative alignments, organizational arrangements, and reward systems designed to focus energy on goals and strategies, build teams and partnerships, and convert "low walls" to "no walls."

- Strengthen the Institute's leadership at all levels, from department heads to the most senior ranks. Strengthen administrative capabilities in every unit, including planning for leadership development and succession.

- Attract a Board of Trustees that reflects a rich mix of position and influence as well as wealth, work, and wisdom, and is philanthropically oriented.

7.2 A Very Diverse Community

Today's ideas will reach maturity and today's students will be called to lead in a world that is increasingly diverse. The Rensselaer community must be just as diverse, and the Institute must commit to leadership in bringing diversity to science and technology. We will:

- Seek a diverse body of students, via careful attention to excellence and to intellectual, geographical, gender, and ethnic diversity (especially groups underrepresented in science and technology), moving to a resident student body that has a much greater presence of women and underrepresented minority students.

- Expand pipeline programs that provide access for women and underrepresented minority students, especially to research and graduate studies.

- Build a diverse faculty and staff of women and men drawn from all ethnic groups.

- Pursue alliances with historically minority institutions to increase the flow of people and ideas to and from the campus.

- Employ interactive pedagogies to bring together students and researchers from diverse settings, including those at distance from the campus.

- Create a lively discourse on important cultural, social, gender, and ethnicity issues in courses, colloquia, fairs, and festivals as well as in residence halls, student activities, and the research environment.

7.3 Alumni

Rensselaer is fortunate to count many friends and colleagues in the industrial, academic, research, and public sectors. Our 70,000 alumni are foremost in this group. Alumni owe a significant part of their success to Rensselaer; at the same time, Rensselaer's success is coupled with the accomplishments of its alumni and depends on their continued interest, involvement, and support. To forge lifelong partnerships between the Institute and its alumni and friends, we will:

- Direct continuing professional and executive education to alumni on leadership paths.

- Involve alumni as recruiters, visiting lecturers and critics, mentors, and employers of resident undergraduate and graduate students.

- Create services and networks that provide a seamless transition from student to alumni life, assist alumni in career success, and establish linkages among alumni and between alumni and their alma mater.

- Celebrate the achievements of alumni as leaders.

7.4 Neighborhood, City, and Region

Greatness in a university is inextricably linked to the vitality of the region in which it is situated. Rensselaer's campuses are located in regions with a rich tradition of technological innovation, predicated on close and mutually beneficial relationships with the surrounding community. Such mutuality extends from campus edges and gateways to the larger region. We will:

- Develop with the community an extended program for teaching and research in disciplines such as architecture, urban design, ecological economics, environmental policy and management, entrepreneurship and business development, and the human, social, economic, and political dimensions of science and technology.

- Offer to the Capital Region, the Hartford Metropolitan Region, and our other communities, faculty resources and research skills in community development and regional design. Collaboration with established community development efforts will provide an intellectual core as well as a context for action.

- Redevelop community fabric contiguous to and along gateways to the campus by joining in carefully selected neighborhood renewal, housing, hospitality, and commercial projects with private developers and public agencies.

- Expand regional technological entrepreneurship in order to assist in attracting industry, people, and capital to the Capital Region and the Hartford Metropolitan Region.

7.5 National and International Reach

As a citizen of the world, Rensselaer must extend its reach and impact beyond present borders. Teaching and research are the starting points. Students study and experience cultures that expose them to diverse outlooks, expand their ability to communicate across cultural boundaries, and deepen understanding of their own cultural circumstances. Researchers are leaders on the global scene, collaborating with colleagues and placing students in top-tier international organizations. Thus, we seek a broad representation of international students and scholars on campus. We will:

- Enable our students to increase their knowledge and understanding of international issues and cultures, including participation in international exchange programs.

- Forge strategic research partnerships with excellent national and international academic institutions and research laboratories.

- Expand corporate partnerships, adding new multinational technology-based companies and extending current partnerships to include international divisions and global operations.

- Extend education programs for working professionals into the international arena.

- Assume prominent roles in shaping federal and state research and technology agendas.

- Expand global name recognition through international media, corporations, and international alumni.

8. ENABLING CHANGE

Achieving Rensselaer's goal requires a systemic and relentless commitment to change.

Meaningful change, of course, must be driven by well-based and meaningful plans. Thus, as The Rensselaer Plan enables change, change enables The Rensselaer Plan. People are the principal enablers. Rensselaer's communities, discussed above, must have the business processes, information infrastructure, physical facilities, and financial resources to do the job.

8.1 Administrative Processes

A university's programs and initiatives are actualized through administrative processes. The Rensselaer Plan requires that we achieve high performance levels in key administrative processes. We will:

- Identify, as part of Performance Plans, essential and critical administrative processes. We will transform, outsource, or sunset processes that are not essential.

- Execute each chosen process with excellence, emphasizing access, simplicity, outcomes, and appropriate uses of technology at every step.

- Emphasize customer service.

- Create a thoughtful and friendly "electronic Rensselaer" to help knit the Institute and its communities into a seamless whole.

8.2 Information Infrastructure

A leading-edge integrated information environment is integral to teaching, learning, and research. Rensselaer employs a first-rate information culture and a robust information infrastructure. We must sustain this advantage, valuing information literacy at every level and implementing new methods for scholarly communication and electronic interactions. We will:

- Provide an integrated portfolio of education, access, and support technologies, policies, and services for teaching, learning, and research, particularly as we create a ubiquitous environment for mobile computing.

- Provide seamless multimedia access to library, research, and scholarly materials for both on-campus and off-campus use.

- Centralize administrative information systems, while improving distributed decision support throughout the Institute.

- Extend and continually upgrade the inter- and intra-networking infrastructure to support strategic purposes.

- Partner with other universities, companies, and public agencies to augment the Institute's intellectual and capital resources.

- Utilize communication technology to enhance the image of Rensselaer to external audiences, build relationships with key external constituencies, and provide state-of-the-art capabilities, such as online transactions.

- Exploit the full potential of communications technology to build community, enhance employee relations, and serve as a source of vital and interesting campus information.

8.3 Physical Facilities

Rensselaer requires land, buildings, and infrastructure that meet essential research, learning, living and dining, cultural, recreational, and other essential needs. Facilities will be accessible to our diverse population, inviting to the internal and external community, and have a cohesion that emphasizes and complements relationships with the community. Facilities will employ state-of-the-art systems and operate safely, efficiently, and reliably. Academic facilities will be research-ready with modern infrastructure and services, and will be flexible to meet changing research requirements. We will:

- Manage and utilize existing facilities for maximum contribution to the strategic purposes of the Institute.

- Establish annual maintenance levels that provide clean and safe facilities that meet Rensselaer's baseline quality of life requirements.

- Plan investment in deferred maintenance and continuing capital renewal for facilities needed to meet strategic needs.

- Construct a new biotechnology and interdisciplinary studies research facility to support and promote interdisciplinary thrusts in biotechnology, nanotechnology, and microsystems.

- Define and deliver new capital, renewal, and deferred maintenance projects consistent with the academic, research, residential, athletic, and administrative priorities derived from The Rensselaer Plan, and with careful attention to benefits achieved relative to initial and continuing costs incurred.

- Seek creative facilities delivery and financing approaches, including privatization, development partnerships, and other innovative concepts.

8.4 Our Public Face

Rensselaer is a dynamic institution, and expects to step up the pace. Even as we gain prominence, we must project the image of the top-tier technological research university we expect to be. We will:

- Project a cohesive identity, promoting the public's understanding of Rensselaer's accomplishments and increasing the Institute's name recognition and prestige in strategic environments.

- Create a cohesive, creative, timely, and user-savvy Web presence for the institution and its principal programs.

- Improve "front door" and public spaces to ensure a professional, state-of-the-art, and elegant Rensselaer.

8.5 Managing Financial Resources

The Rensselaer Plan has substantial implications for financial resources. While expanding the resource base is paramount, we must first manage existing resources to best advantage, directing expenditures to strategic purposes. We will:

- Derive performance plans and then annual operating plans (budgets) from The Rensselaer Plan.

- Refine or reinvent the budgetary model to focus resources for maximum strategic impact, while maintaining appropriate institutional flexibility.

- Provide managers at every level with accurate, timely, and relevant performance and management information.

- Deploy financial and administrative processes (payroll, billing, payables, collection, purchasing, etc.) that provide a baseline quality of service for students, alumni, families, employees, vendors, and partners.

- Pursue aggressive risk management and internal auditing to assure a safe working and learning environment, appropriate controls, and regulatory compliance.

8.6 Expanding the Resource Base

Garnering substantial additional resources requires a multifront effort led by the President and Board of Trustees, financially supported by the Board of Trustees, and focused and energized by The Rensselaer Plan. We will:

- Mount a comprehensive fund-raising campaign.

- Grow the base endowment via campaign gifts and investment return so that endowment spending can support 20 percent or more of the budget (now 10 percent). Manage the pace and structure of debt financing to strategic purposes.

- Restructure corporate partnerships, adding leadership technology companies in priority areas, meeting partners' criteria for top-tier status, and achieving substantial annual total revenue (research, philanthropy, equipment, and educational programs) and placement of graduates from these companies.

- Pursue major federal and state partnerships that provide facilities, specialized equipment, and maintenance and operating capital to the Institute in exchange for research and technology transfer in areas of national or state need.

- Build philanthropic and other financial support, maximizing alumni and volunteer involvement through long-term mutually beneficial relationships and doubling private investment within five years. We will challenge our major donors to provide "stretch" support as we move forward boldly and quickly.

- Pursue an advancement program that mobilizes and integrates the entire Institute to achieve the financial goals set out in The Rensselaer Plan. This includes coordination of distributed advancement efforts, outreach to students as future alumni, maximum use of technology for communications and commerce, integrated marketing, and focusing policies and programs on maximum return.

9. LEADERSHIP IN THE 21ST CENTURY

Let us look ahead. Let us move forward. We can do this.

The Rensselaer Plan is aimed high. The plan is expansive and ambitious. We will realize the plan by bringing focus, new resources, hard work, and good will—in short by acting together, as a community. Rensselaer has always achieved great things. Together, we can attain greater prominence with the support, intellectual and financial, of all members of the Rensselaer family: faculty, students, staff, alumni, trustees, and friends in corporations, foundations, and government.

BUILDING THE RENSSELAER PLAN

Shirley Ann Jackson, Ph.D.
President
Rensselaer Polytechnic Institute
Troy, New York USA
October 1999

GOAL

The goal for Rensselaer is to be a world-class technological research university with global reach and global impact.

To articulate and implement this goal, we will work together over the next several months to create The Rensselaer Plan.

The Rensselaer Plan will be founded on three markers: excellence, leadership, and community.

The Rensselaer Plan will be given shape and direction by a series of boundary conditions that relate to teaching, research, and outreach programs; students and the student experience; and university activities that enable Rensselaer to achieve its goals.

The process of creating The Rensselaer Plan will involve the entire community in addressing these directive questions:

1. What defines the intellectual core in each key discipline or enterprise at Rensselaer? Is it important, and why? True excellence requires such definition and examination.

2. In these disciplines, are we in a leadership position? Do we set the standard and the agenda? These areas will serve as our foundation.

3. If we are not in a leadership position, do we have the underlying strengths and capabilities necessary to move rapidly into a position of primacy with the proper focus and investment? We will build on these areas of strength.

4. Are there areas that are so vital that we must create a presence in order to stand in the community of world-class universities? We will stake out an identity in these critical disciplines.

5. What areas of current endeavor must we be willing to transform—or to give up—in order to focus our resources and our energies to create the impact we envision? We will make the difficult decisions that are required by a fundamental commitment to our highest ideals.

The fully articulated plan and the process by which it is created and continuously renewed will be the means by which we meet our goal.

PLANS

The Rensselaer Plan addresses fundamentals. When formulated, it will serve as the basis for more detailed performance and operating plans. Planning is a continuing process operating on three levels:

The Rensselaer Plan

The Rensselaer Plan states the aspiration and defines overall parameters for Rensselaer as a world-class technological research university with global reach and global impact. This is an "evergreen" plan that will be reviewed and revised on a regular basis. We will build The Rensselaer Plan this academic year with the expectation that it will be presented to the Board of Trustees in May 2000.

Performance Plans

Within the framework of The Rensselaer Plan, we will create performance plans for each school and administrative division—that is, each of the Institute's "portfolios." Resource requirements will be identified, and plans will be prioritized by the president and the cabinet. The Rensselaer Plan will define the priorities for the university at the highest level; the performance plans will define the means by which we achieve our goals and create the case to secure substantial financial investments from private and government sources, including the next fund-raising campaign. Performance plans will be built beginning summer 2000.

Annual Operating Plans

Each year, results are assessed, performance plans are revised, and the next year's operating plan (budget, capital projects, etc.) is constructed.

PRINCIPLES

The Rensselaer Plan will be founded on a clearly articulated goal for the university, grounded in a definition of the Institute's core enterprises, and guided by several key process principles.

Goal
The goal for Rensselaer is to be a world-class technological university with global reach and global impact.

Core Enterprises

Rensselaer's core enterprises are:

- Resident undergraduate education

- Resident research and graduate education

- Education of working professionals

- Fostering scientific and technological innovation
  (leveraging and maximizing the development, use, and management of intellectual property, technology transfer, entrepreneurship, economic development, etc.)

Markers

Markers are the fundamental "stakes in the ground" established by President Jackson and discussed in her inaugural address: excellence, leadership, community.

Boundary Conditions

A set of boundary conditions established by the president and cabinet shape the enterprise and provide direction for our plans for the future while reflecting and extending Rensselaer's existing strengths.

The boundary conditions give focus to The Rensselaer Plan. We will then ensure that financial resources are raised, and deployed, effectively and efficiently to maximum strategic effect.

Portfolio Planning

The dean or vice president responsible for each portfolio will conduct an assessment, address a series of key directive planning questions, and contribute to the plan being drafted by the president's cabinet with community assistance.

Responsibility for Drafting

Responsibility for drafting The Rensselaer Plan is vested in the provost and vice presidents who comprise the president's cabinet. The cabinet will draft plans based on work material supplied by each of the schools and administrative divisions (institute portfolios), after broad community participation and discussion of the portfolios in university-wide town meetings and workshops.

Community Participation

The campus community will participate in four important ways:

- As **Participants** in town meetings intended to explore the markers and boundary conditions as well as in a series of workshops that will assess individual portfolios against markers. Town meetings and workshops will be organized, moderated, and synthesized by a cross section of campus citizens organized as RealCom (Rensselaer Assessment Leadership Committee).

- As **Responders** to a first draft of the plan that will be created by the president's cabinet. This draft will be published on the Internet, and every community member—faculty,

students, staff, as well as alumni, trustees, and friends of the Institute—will be invited
to contribute. All reactions and recommendations will be reviewed and considered
by the cabinet.

- As **Reviewers** of the final draft of the plan. This final draft will be reviewed by schools
  and departments, administrative divisions, and constituency leadership groups (faculty
  leadership, student leadership, Pillars of Rensselaer, Rensselaer Alumni Association
  leadership, key executives, etc.) before it is approved by the cabinet, president, and
  Board of Trustees.

- As **Implementers** of the plan. The success of The Rensselaer Plan, and the performance and operating plans to follow, depends on implementation. The entire
  Rensselaer community needs to be engaged in plan implementation.

Trustee Approval

The Rensselaer Plan will be substantially completed by April 15, 2000, and presented by
the president for Board of Trustees approval on May 13, 2000 (see timetable).

Performance Plans

When The Rensselaer Plan is approved, the provost, deans, and vice presidents will
create performance plans. Once performance plans are approved by the president, the
provost, deans, and vice presidents will have responsibility for implementation and
accountability for results.

MARKERS

To achieve the goal of establishing Rensselaer as a world-class technological research
university with global reach and global impact, it is necessary to place stakes in the
ground. These "markers" will drive us to our goal. They will be refined in the course of
planning and action, but they cannot be removed.

Excellence

We will insist on excellence in everything we do: education, research, outreach, and
administration. Excellence is the mantra and the metric.

Leadership

We will achieve leadership positions in each of our core enterprises:

- Resident undergraduate education

- Resident research and graduate education

- Education of working professionals

- Fostering scientific and technological innovation

Community

We are one Rensselaer dedicated to intellectual, geographic, gender, and ethnic diversity in the student body, faculty, staff, and administration. We will seek essential roles and partnerships in our local, state, and national "communities." We will be recognized as a leader among technological research universities on the global scene.

BOUNDARY CONDITIONS

Within the framework established by the markers, we set the following bounding, and thus boundary, conditions for assessing and improving every aspect of the Rensselaer enterprise. The boundary conditions provide a starting point in shaping our plans for the future while reflecting and extending Rensselaer's existing strengths.

A. TEACHING, RESEARCH, AND OUTREACH PROGRAMS

Recognized for leadership. Programs are created and conducted by Rensselaer faculty and staff who are recognized leaders in their fields: receiving peer recognition and funding, defining the discourse, setting agendas, chairing high-level study groups, etc.

Designed for sustainability. Programs have well-defined and rigorous intellectual content, are aligned with principal societal and global priorities, and are situated at or near the leading edges of discovery and application.

Potentiate each other. Programs strive to increase the impact of other programs. Examples: teaching/research, graduate/undergraduate, courses inside/outside the major, in the classroom/outside the classroom.

Interdisciplinary. Multidisciplinary and interdisciplinary approaches in curriculum, teaching, research, and outreach are the Institute's most exploitable competitive advantage.

Characterized by partnerships. Strategic alliances with government, industry, other universities, and the community can build critical mass, magnify impact, and accelerate recognition.

Rooted in technology. Programs explore fundamental underpinnings and they develop, assess, and transfer technologies. They emphasize responsible applications for the common good.

A.1 Undergraduate Programs
Boundary conditions for all programs (see A above) plus the following:

Rich mix. Programs present a rich portfolio of opportunities for 5,000 resident undergraduate students (currently 4,800).

Compelling, distinctive fundamental. Programs are compelling (suggesting exciting futures), distinctive (aligned with important societal priorities), and lay foundations for multiple career trajectories.

Content-centered. Programs are content-centered, emphasizing inquiry, discovery, reasoning, and action in complex and changing domains. Programs bridge fundamentals and practice.

Interactive pedagogies. Programs employ a pervasive focus on interactive learning.

Research and innovation partnerships. Programs allow undergraduates to become partners in research and innovation with faculty, alumni, corporate, and government partners.

Residential. Programs take maximum advantage of their residential status, emphasizing both individual and community learning and service while also providing the confidence and leadership skills for a lifetime of success.

A.2 Research and Graduate Programs
Boundary conditions for all programs (see A above) plus the following:

Research activity. Rensselaer attains Carnegie Research I level via dramatically increased government funding and substantial corporate support.

World-class standing. Rensselaer develops and/or sustains several programs with world-class standing. These programs have clear intellectual centers, are aligned with important sustainable societal priorities, attract substantial external interest and funding, and are distributed among the academic schools.

"Must do" areas. Rensselaer strikes out into "must do" areas of research where it has not been well represented, e.g., bioscience and biotechnology.

Ph.D. production. Rensselaer awards at least 250 doctoral degrees each year (currently 115).

Infrastructure. Rensselaer provides and sustains a research infrastructure (faculty, research staff, and facilities; financial aid; charge-out; cost-sharing and intellectual property policies) sufficient to the task.

A.3 Education for Working Professionals
Boundary conditions for all programs (see A above) plus the following:

High-end focus. Develop and offer courses, degrees, and certificates with a high-end, signature focus derived from frontier research and pedagogy.

Leadership orientation. Emphasize special programs for high-level corporate leaders and entrepreneurs, and high-achieving, high-potential professionals.

Geographic distribution. Programs serve the needs of highly qualified working professionals where they are: on campus in Troy, Hartford, or elsewhere in the workplace and around the world.

A.4 Fostering Scientific and Technological Innovation
Boundary conditions for all programs (see A above) plus the following:

Environment for innovation. Rensselaer provides an environment that supplies the advice and critical supporting structures needed to foster and nurture scientific and technological innovation and entrepreneurship.

Value orientation. Members of the Rensselaer community are alert to opportunities for value-added technological innovation in all they do.

Entrepreneurial spirit. Rensselaer fosters the attributes of entrepreneurial creativity, risk taking, and value creation through partnerships, incubators, and other technology transfer mechanisms.

Leveraging intellectual capital. Rensselaer will develop and implement intellectual property rights policies that encourage technological innovation and entrepreneurship, and which are mutually beneficial to the university and those who generate intellectual property.

B. STUDENTS AND THE STUDENT EXPERIENCE

These boundary conditions characterize the students and describe the student experience in Rensselaer's residential undergraduate and doctoral research programs.

Superior qualifications. All students bring top-tier academic credentials, intellect, entrepreneurial drive, and the vision and passion to change the world. Represented in the mix of students are richness of experience and a range of financial capability.

Diversity. Students represent an energizing range of intellectual interests, a broad geographical representation of both U.S. and international students, and a focus on high-achieving women and underrepresented minority students.

Well-rounded experience. The Rensselaer experience deepens capabilities (exploration, risk taking, problem solving, innovation); broadens perspective (beyond the individual to community and global); inculcates responsibility; and creates an integrated view of life and learning.

Leadership education and practice. Students have access to pervasive leadership education complemented by quality opportunities to develop teamwork and leadership skills.

Faculty/student partnerships. Students are seen as colleagues in creating knowledge and in innovation and entrepreneurship. This creates, in turn, a thirst for lifelong learning coupled with enthusiasm for Rensselaer as a partner in that enterprise.

Commitment to student success. There is an Institute-wide commitment to student success—both on campus and later.

C. Enabling Activities

These boundary conditions describe many of the activities the university undertakes to enable its programs and students to achieve the goal of Rensselaer as a world-class technological university with global reach and global impact.

Research and technology agenda. Rensselaer will lead in shaping federal and state research and technology agendas, optimally positioning Rensselaer and expanding our presence in Washington, both within the Administration and on Capitol Hill.

Research programs and partnerships. Rensselaer will identify emerging government research funding trends and programs and build strategic collaborations with other universities and government entities that complement our strengths to magnify influence and increase research support, faculty size, and graduate student enrollment in areas of leadership.

Advancement. Rensselaer will build philanthropic and other financial support, and maximize alumni and volunteer involvement, through long-term mutually beneficial relationships, doubling private investment within five years. Rensselaer will focus on global outreach through international media, corporations, and international alumni. Working with the President, trustees, alumni, and campus leaders, Institute Advancement will focus on strategic priorities of the university to project a cohesive identity and maximize private support.

Corporate partnerships. Rensselaer will build and maintain a portfolio of major corporate partners including leadership technology companies in areas of strategic institutional priority. We will attain the research, recruitment, and other performance metrics that meet these partners' criteria for top-tier status. We will target and obtain substantial annual total revenue (research, philanthropy, equipment, and educational programs) and placement of graduates from these companies. At the same time, we will monitor alumni senior executive status and firms rapidly accumulating wealth in areas of strategic priority.

Regional development. Rensselaer will create mutually beneficial alliances for technology transfer and regional economic development to better integrate Rensselaer into the life of the community. The Institute will secure a leadership role in regional development, helping to attract new industry, people, and institutions.

Community fabric. Rensselaer will participate in the redevelopment of the community fabric (neighborhoods, commerce, entertainment, gateways) especially in areas contiguous to the campus, seeking projects of mutual value to the city and the university. Student and staff housing, as well as lifestyle activities, will consider community-based possibilities.

Information infrastructure. Rensselaer will deploy information technologies and strategies that enable competitive advantage for programs and activities of strategic importance. Rensselaer will sustain an information culture, valuing information literacy and new methods for scholarly communications and electronic interactions.

Facilities complement. Rensselaer will have a complement of real estate, buildings, and infrastructure that meets the essential research, learning, living and dining, cultural, recreational, and other needs of the Institute as required to implement The Rensselaer Plan. Facilities will be accessible to our diverse population, inviting to the internal and external community, and have a cohesion that emphasizes and complements relationships with the community. Facilities will employ state-of-the-art systems and operate safely, efficiently, and reliably. Academic facilities will be research-ready with modern infrastructure and services, and will be flexible to meet changing research requirements.

Facilities maintenance and renewal. Rensselaer will plan investment in a deferred maintenance program ($100 million total) and continuing capital renewal (1.5–3 percent of current replacement value) for Institute facilities meeting strategic needs; and annual maintenance levels that provide clean and safe facilities that meet Rensselaer's quality of life requirements.

Capital projects planning. Capital projects, renewal, and deferred maintenance projects will be scoped and delivered consistent with current and comprehensive academic, research, residential, athletics, and administrative priorities that will drive physical and financial plans, and with careful attention to benefits achieved relative to initial and continuing costs incurred. Rensselaer will be creative in considering privatization, development partnerships, and other innovative delivery approaches.

Financial resources. Rensselaer will grow the endowment via campaign gifts and investment return so that endowment spending increases to 20 percent (from 10 percent) of budget; manage the pace and structure of debt financing to improve our credit rating (to AA); and refine or reinvent the budgetary model so that it focuses resources for maximum strategic impact while maintaining appropriate institutional flexibility.

Staff. Excellence is the expectation for all administrative staff. The staff will be recruited, empowered, and compensated at levels commensurate with their skill and contribution.

Administration and services. Rensselaer will seek very high performance levels in the key administrative positions and processes required to implement The Rensselaer Plan. Rensselaer will provide high-quality services in support of the academic enterprise.

Trustees. A vibrant Board of Trustees provides the sustaining stewardship, fiduciary oversight, and financial support that helps Rensselaer achieve its plans and aspirations. The Board will reflect a rich mix of position and influence as well as wealth, work, and wisdom.

PORTFOLIO ASSESSMENT

The Institute, at present, includes the portfolios listed. While there are many overlaps and cross-cutting issues, each portfolio provides a basis for assessment and planning and, ultimately, a focus of responsibility and accountability for implementation.

- School of Architecture
- School of Engineering
- School of Humanities and Social Sciences
- Lally School of Management and Technology
- School of Science
- Faculty of Information Technology
- Professional and Distance Education
- Computing and Information Services
- The Provost's Office, including academic services and several areas that cut across the schools: faculty, research, undergraduate and graduate programs
- Student Life
- Administration
- Advancement
- Finance
- Government and Community Relations
- Human Resources
- Technology Innovation and Economic Development
- Institute Leadership and Board of Trustees

Each portfolio owner is responsible for doing a portfolio assessment that establishes the current state of the portfolio and that addresses a set of directive questions as they pertain to the portfolio. The portfolio assessment is outlined in the box on the right.

Portfolio owners also will supply performance data in response to requests from the Washington Advisory Group who will be providing, among other services, essential external benchmarking information.

PORTFOLIO ASSESSMENT
to be done for each Institute Portfolio

A. Situation

    1. Objectives: mission, objectives, scale, and current priorities

    2. Status: state of the activities at present; including centrality to the Institute's four core enterprises:

        a. Resident undergraduate education

        b. Resident research and graduate education

        c. Education of working professionals

        d. Fostering scientific and technological innovation

    3. Strengths and weaknesses: self-examination, including an assessment of the importance of the activities in the portfolio

    4. Competition: assessment based on benchmarking and literature

B. Directive Questions

How must the portfolio change, within the framework of the markers and boundary conditions, to achieve the goal of Rensselaer as a world-class technological research university with global reach and global impact?

C. Moving Forward

    1. Strategic plan input: outline general strategies seen as moving the portfolio forward in response to the Directive Questions

    2. Investments: indicate nature and approximate amounts of investment required to mount the strategies and achieve success

    3. Other requirements: implications for and requirements of other portfolios

REALCOM

Broad community assessment will be an essential early step in building The Rensselaer Plan. A cross section of campus citizens, the Rensselaer Assessment Leadership Committee (RealCom), will organize and moderate a series of town meetings and workshops intended to explore the markers and boundary conditions and to help assess each portfolio against the markers. RealCom will synthesize the results of these meetings into a series of summary papers that portfolio owners and the cabinet can use to create the plan draft this fall.

Under the Provost's direction, RealCom will include six faculty members; two students (undergraduate and graduate student); a staff member from Student Life, Advancement, Administration, Finance, and Human Resources; and the President's Chief of Staff/ Assistant Secretary of the Institute.

RealCom will host an initial set of town meetings, open to the university community, where the president will discuss the foundations for The Rensselaer Plan, the Institute's goal, and the markers and boundary conditions.

Working in three teams of approximately four members each, and with each team including at least one faculty member (and more for academic and research portfolios) and a student or the Student Life staff member, RealCom will run a series of workshops devoted to each of the institute portfolios. Meetings will be facilitated by a consultant and/or an assigned cabinet member (but not the portfolio owner). Each meeting will explore the directive questions outlined at the right. Additionally, the meetings will help the community understand the markers and give feedback on the boundary conditions.

DIRECTIVE QUESTIONS FOR EACH PORTFOLIO

Our goal demands the rigor and discipline that underlie all greatness. The Rensselaer Plan will require answers to five questions. These questions are exact and exacting:

1. What defines the intellectual core in each key discipline or enterprise at Rensselaer? Is it important, and why? True excellence requires such definition and examination.

2. In these disciplines, are we in a leadership* position? Do we set the standard and the agenda? These areas will serve as our foundation.

3. If we are not in a leadership position, do we have the underlying strengths and capabilities necessary to move rapidly into a position of primacy with the proper focus and investment? We will build on these areas of strength.

4. Are there areas that are so vital that we must create a presence in order to stand in the community of world-class universities? We will stake out an identity in these critical disciplines.

5. What areas of current endeavor must we be willing to transform—or to give up—in order to focus our resources and our energies to create the impact we envision? We will make the difficult decisions that are required by a fundamental commitment to our highest ideals.

For academic portfolios: position and performance as judged against the moving front of thought and discovery. For administrative portfolios: position and performance as judged against top-tier schools or other world-class enterprises.

TIMETABLE

September 24, 1999
President Jackson establishes markers in inaugural address.

October 5–7
RealCom formed and organized.
This document issued to guide the planning process.

October 11–29
RealCom hosts town meetings (to help the community understand the markers and boundary conditions) and workshops addressing the directive questions for each portfolio.

October 11–29
Deans, vice presidents, and provost assemble performance data as requested by the Washington Advisory Group and other consultants. The Washington Advisory Group will provide external assessments and benchmarks for academic and research activities, and other consultants will provide assessments and benchmarks for administrative activities.

October 16
President begins strategic discussions with the Board of Trustees which will continue throughout the planning process and lead to final discussion and approval of The Rensselaer Plan in May 2000.

October 11–November 15
Deans, vice presidents, and provost conduct portfolio assessments with their staffs and constituents, assembling information for use by the cabinet in preparing the draft plan.

November 1–30
RealCom distills input from town meetings and workshops into summary papers for portfolio areas.

November 15–December 15
Cabinet produces draft plan using markers and boundary conditions, portfolio assessments, the RealCom summary papers, and information provided by the Washington Advisory Group and other consultants.

December 15, 1999–January 31, 2000
Draft plan put out on the Internet for comment.

January 15–February 15
Cabinet revises and develops final draft plan.

February 15–March 15
Final draft plan is vetted by key leadership groups: deans, faculty leadership, student leadership, Pillars of Rensselaer (staff representatives), Rensselaer Alumni Association leadership, key executives, etc.

March 1–31
Cabinet writes and approves The Rensselaer Plan.

April 1–10
President reviews and approves The Rensselaer Plan.

April 15
The Rensselaer Plan is sent to the Board of Trustees.

May 13, 2000
The President presents The Rensselaer Plan to the Board of Trustees for approval.

June 2000 and beyond
Performance plans are developed in each portfolio area.
Performance plans are prioritized.
Case for next fund-raising campaign is developed.

The Rensselaer Plan and the performance plans (prioritized and resource-loaded) become the basis for budget formulation and execution.

THE RENSSELAER PLAN: PERFORMANCE PLANNING GUIDELINES
JULY 2000

I. PERFORMANCE PLAN OUTLINE

Each portfolio Performance Plan (see Attachment A) *must address each* of the *first year highest priorities* that affect or are affected by that portfolio. The expectation is that essentially *all* portfolios will have a role to play in advancing these priorities. Below is the listing of the *first year highest priorities* developed during the retreat and workshop of the Performance Planning Leadership Group. In addition, *other commitments* in The Rensselaer Plan, and *ongoing activities* within your portfolio are to be *prioritized* for the first, second, and third years, while insuring that the *first year highest priorities* are addressed.

FIRST YEAR HIGH PRIORITY INITIATIVES

University Positioning
Biotechnology and Information Technology Initiatives
    1. Constellations
    2. Building (Center for Biotechnology and Interdisciplinary Studies)
First Year Experience
    1. Freshman Orientation
    2. Graduate Orientation
    3. New Hires (Faculty and Staff)
Electronic Media & Performing Arts Center/Building

Process and Management
Revised Budget Process
Review/revise Intellectual Property policies
Tenure standards (faculty), and hiring and promotion criteria (faculty and staff)

The portfolio Performance Plan should be organized as follows:

Executive Summary

The Executive Summary should concisely communicate the key messages of the Performance Plan. The format should capture the essence of the Performance Plan and the Executive Summary should serve as a benchmark against which to measure the overall message. The Executive Summary should be limited to two pages.

Section I. Mission, Vision of The Rensselaer Plan

During the assessment phase of The Rensselaer Plan process, each portfolio discussed and developed mission and vision statements, and analyzed in depth its internal strengths and weaknesses, and external opportunities and threats. This need not be redone. A brief restatement of the results of the analyses with respect to the completed Rensselaer Plan should be included here in an effort to frame the actions and performance measures outlined in the following sections.

Section II. Strategic Goals, Strategies, and Action Plans: How do we get there?

Strategic goals of The Rensselaer Plan ("the Plan") are Targets that guide the performance planning of *all* Institute portfolios. *Strategies* are the high level means whereby the organization intends to realize its goals. For example, one of the Plan's *strategic goals* is to expand the research enterprise. One of the Plan's *strategies* to achieve this goal is "to make dramatic investments that substantially increase our involvement in two new arenas vital for national well being and growth; *information technology and biotechnology.*" In turn, *action plans* detail the activities and initiatives that specific offices or individuals must undertake to carry out the strategy.

Each portfolio should examine the relationship between the commitments in the Rensselaer Plan and the six Institute-wide goals in the following way:

In addition to the first year Institute-wide highest priorities listed on page 1:

- Which of the Plan's other commitment statements (or cluster of related commitments) are the portfolio's *additional* highest priorities? On what basis is this prioritization established?

- How do the portfolio priorities align with the overarching goal and the six Institute-wide goals of The Rensselaer Plan?

- Which of these will create the greatest change at Rensselaer?

- How does the attainment of these priorities contribute to the success of other Institute portfolios?

Specific portfolio *action* plans should consider the following:

- Which *related* commitments already in the Plan act as drivers to produce change in the portfolio high priority commitment areas?

- Are there other drivers that are necessary and critical to produce change in the portfolio high priority commitment areas?

- What specific steps/actions will be undertaken (year 1, year 2, year 3) to meet the portfolio high priority commitments?

- What specific steps/actions will be undertaken (year 1, year 2, year 3) to rationalize *existing* activities to the portfolio *high priority commitments*? (This should result in an overall *rank ordering* of *all* activities, while *insuring* that the portfolio's highest priorities [including the *first year highest priorities*] are addressed.)

- What are the specific intermediate milestones for implementation for year 1, year 2, year 3?

- Which steps/actions require corresponding actions by other portfolios?

- What unit or individual within the portfolio is responsible? (Who owns it?)

- How will the collection and use of performance measure be incorporated into the action plan?

Strategies for implementation at the portfolio level should consider the following:

- What current programs, functions, or activities will be "sunset" to free up resources for reallocation?

- What other measures will be taken to redirect resources from low to higher priorities, e.g., program or process redesign/improvement?

- What changes in organizational structure or reporting relationships are required to implement the strategy?

- What new initiatives or activities are proposed?

- Where are collaborations with other portfolios required?

- How do the strategies build on strengths and address weaknesses?

- How do the strategies respond to, or how are they impacted by, external opportunities and threats?

Section III. Performance Measures

Once the portfolio highest priority commitments and action plans have been determined, a methodology by which progress can be measured should be developed.

Performance measures:

- Provide a mechanism for measuring the portfolio's success in channeling its resources toward achieving its strategic goals.

- Provide actionable, real-time data and use targets for operational excellence in critical processes to create the incentive for improvement and proper allocation of resources.

- Align the objectives of individuals with the overall strategy of the organization, thereby ensuring a universal commitment toward common goals.

Performance measures include outcome measures, output measures, and process measures:

- *Outcome measures* determine whether the desired state (vision) has been achieved and should *assess* quality (e.g., success rate with competitive proposals or professional recognition—individual, department, school, university).

- *Output measures* quantify "how much" (e.g., the total number of submitted research proposals, or number of doctoral degrees awarded).

- *Process measures* are used to monitor implementation (e.g., performance against action plan milestones).

Questions to consider in developing performance measures include:

- What comparative benchmarks (external and internal) will form the basis of outcome measures?

- How effectively do the proposed measures assess progress against benchmarks, rather than the current state of affairs?

- How effectively do the proposed measures serve as measures for assessing progress in achieving Institute-wide goals?

Each performance measure therefore should:

- Be a direct measure of progress toward a goal

- Be a measure of status relative to external and internal benchmarks

- Be SMART: specific, measurable, attainable, reliable, and timely

- Be easy to understand, communicate, and use

Section IV. Resource Plan

Ultimately, the Institute's budget process will require each portfolio to develop a zero-based budget for all of its functions and programs. However, as a prelude to the portfolio budget proposal, each portfolio should include in its Performance Plan a preliminary resource estimate that explores the resource implications of its strategies and action plans. The resource estimates should specify resource requirements, including personnel, space, etc., and propose sources of funding, selected from, but not limited to:

- Internal portfolio reallocation resulting from program or function closure, reduction, or redesign

- Redirection or reallocation of personnel and facilities

- Increases from general operating dollars

- Increases in extramural grant and contract funding

- Revenues from Endowment or new capital campaign funds

II. PERFORMANCE PLANNING PROCESS

- *Timelines and reports:* Performance Plans should be prepared as three-year rolling plans, with the first year's plan being the most comprehensive (approximately 20 pages in length). Updates of the performance plans in years two and three (approximately 10 pages in length) should assess progress against Performance Plans and measures, establish modifications in goals, strategies, and action plans based on progress, and reconsider the resource implications of these modifications.

- *Pre-planning fundamental baseline questions:* At the outset of the performance planning process, units may have fundamental baseline questions the answers to which portfolio administrators believe will have significant import on the directions of the unit. These questions should be presented by the portfolio administrators to the President for early consideration. The answers to some of these questions *may* be most appropriately addressed in the performance planning process.

- *Consultation and involvement:* As each portfolio prepares its performance plans, consideration should be given to the appropriate levels of consultation and involvement of faculty and students, and of other portfolios. This is the reason for the inclusion of a step in which the draft Performance Plans will be distributed to other portfolio administrators. Factors to consider include current consultation mechanisms and governance structures, and the functions of the portfolio. Clear expectations of process participants should be established at the outset.

- *Submission and review process:* Performance Plans for *all* portfolios should be submitted to the Office of the President, which will coordinate the review process. Administrators of schools and administrative units reporting to the Provost should consult with the Provost during the formulation of their portfolio Performance Plans, who will also coordinate the cross-cutting reviews of the academic portfolios. The Provost and Administrators of units reporting directly to the President should consult with the President during the formulation of their portfolio Performance Plans.

INSTITUTE PORTFOLIOS

The following portfolios are responsible for developing performance plans:

Schools

- School of Architecture
- School of Engineering
- School of Humanities and Social Sciences
- Lally School of Management and Technology
- School of Science
- Rensselaer at Hartford

Academic Functions

- Undergraduate Education
- Graduate Education
- Education for Working Professionals
- Enrollment Management
- Faculty of Information Technology

Vice Presidential Divisions

- Information Technology Infrastructure and Services
- Research (including interdisciplinary center/activities)
- Student Life
- Administration
- Advancement
- Finance
- Government and Community Relations
- Human Resources
- Economic Development and Technological Entrepreneurship

TIMELINE (JULY 2000–JULY 2001)

The timetable (with process milestones) for completing the Performance Plans is as follows:

Milestones with specific deliverables associated with them have an (*)

2000

- Distribute performance planning guidelines — Friday, July 28

- Complete Review of Portfolio with respect to The Rensselaer Plan — Friday, September 1

- Distribute review guidelines (from Provost Office) to Faculty Senate Planning and Resources Committee (FPRC) for academic programs — Friday, September 1

- Complete initial draft and distribute to other portfolio owners (to identify crosscutting issues and to insure a coordinated approach to joint efforts.) — Friday, October 27

- Distribute draft of academic performance plans to FPRC to review and provide feedback to academic administrators. — Friday, October 27

- Crosscutting reviews within the academic portfolios; Student reviews of Student Life Performance Plan; Crosscutting reviews among research centers — Friday, November 10 / Tuesday, November 21

- Portfolio owners submit performance plans to the Office of the President — Friday, December 1

- President's Cabinet meets with portfolio owners for comprehensive review of all portfolio Performance Plans — Monday, December 4 / Wednesday, December 20

2001

- Feedback process and resource loading begins; Fiscal Year 2002 budget instructions issued — Friday, January 5

- Zero-based budgets submitted to the Office of the President — Friday, January 19

- Resource Allocation & overall prioritization completed — Friday, February 2

- Budget submission to Board of Trustees — Friday, February 16

- Assessment against benchmarks/performance measures — June–July

- Begin year 2 of Performance Planning Process — July

THE FOUNDING DOCUMENT

To the Rev.d D.r Blatchford Lansingburgh

Dear Sir:

I have established a school at the north end of Troy, in Rensselaer county, in the building usually called the Old Bank Place, for the purpose of instructing persons, who may choose to apply themselves, in the application of science to the common purposes of life. My principal object is, to qualify teachers for instructing the sons and daughters of farmers and mechanics by lectures or otherwise, in the application of experimental chemistry, philosophy, and natural history, to agriculture, domestic economy, the arts, and manufactures. From the trials which have been made by persons in my employment at Utica, Whitesborough, Rome, Auburn, & Geneva during the last summer, I am inclined to believe that competent instructors may be produced in the school at Troy who will be highly useful to the community in the diffusion of a very useful kind of, knowledge, with its application to the business of living. Apparatus for the necessary experiments has been so much simplified, and specimens in natural history have become subjects of such easy attainment, that but a small sum is now required as an out fit for an instructor in the proposed branches of science. Consequently any school district may have the benefit of such a course of instruction about once in two or three years, as soon as we can furnish a sufficient number of teachers. I prefer this plan to the endowment of a single public institution for the resort of those only whose parents are able and willing to send their children from home or to enter them for several years upon the Fellenberg plan. It seems to comport better with the habits of our citizens and the genius of our government to place the advantages of useful improvement equally within the reach of all. Whether my expectations will ever be realized or not, I am willing to hazard the necessary expense of making the trial. Having procured a suitable building advantageously located among farmers and mechanics, and having furnished funds which are deemed sufficient by my agents in this undertaking for procuring the necessary apparatus etc. it now remains to establish a system of organization adapted to the object. You will excuse me if I attach too much consequence to the undertaking. But it appears to me that a board of trustees to decide upon the manner of granting certificates of qualifications, to regulate the government of students etc. is essential. I therefore take the liberty to appoint you a member and president of a board of trustees for this purpose.

I appoint the following gentlemen trustees of the same board. The Rev.d D.r Blatchford, Mr. E. Parmalee, of Lansingburgh, Guert Van Schoonhoven, John Cramer of Waterford Simeon DeWitt, T. R. Beck of Albany, John D. Dickinson and Jedediah Tracy of Troy.

And I appoint o. L. Holley Esq. of Troy, T. R. Beck, of Albany first and second vice-presidents of said board.

As a few regulations are immediately necessary, in order to present the school to the public, it seems necessary that I should make the following orders, subject to be altered by the trustees, after the end of the first term.

Order 1.ˢᵗ The board of trustees is to meet at times and places to be notified by the president, or by one of the vice-presidents in the absence or disability of the president. One half of the members of the board are to form a quorum for doing business. A majority of the members present may fill any vacancy which happens in the board; so that there may be two members resident in Troy, two in Lansingburgh, two in Waterford, and two in Albany. The powers and duties of the trustees to be such as those exercised by all similar boards, the object of the school being always kept in view.

Order 2.ⁿᵈ I appoint Dr. Moses Hale, of Troy sect. & H. N. Lockwood treasurer.

Order 3.ʳᵈ I appoint Amos Eaton of Troy professor of chemistry and experimental philosophy, and lecturer on geology, land surveying, & the laws regulating town officers and jurors. This office to be denominated the senior professorship.

Order 4.ᵗʰ I appoint Lewis C. Beck, of Albany, professor of mineralogy, botany and zoology and lecturer on the social duties peculiar to farmers and mechanics. This office to be denominated the junior professorship.

Order 5.ᵗʰ The first term is to commence on the first Monday in January next, and to continue fifteen weeks. For admission to the course, including the use of the library and reading-room, each student must pay twenty-five dollars to the treasurer, or give him satisfactory assurances that it will be paid in one year. In addition to this, each section of students must pay for the chemical substances they consume and the damage they do to apparatus.

Order 6.ᵗʰ All the pay thus received by the treasurer, as for parts of courses of instruction, is to be paid over to said professors as the reward of their services.

Order 7.ᵗʰ In giving the course on chemistry, the students are to be divided into sections not exceeding five in each section. These are not to be taught by seeing experiments and hearing lectures, according to the usual method. But they are to lecture and experiment by turns, under the immediate direction of a professor or a competent assistant. Thus by a term of labor, like apprentices to a trade, they are to become operative chemists.

Order 8.ᵗʰ At the close of the term each student is to give sufficient tests of his skill and science before examiners, to be appointed by myself, or by the trustees, if I do not appoint. The examination is not to be conducted by question and answer, but the qualifications of students are to be estimated by the facility with which they perform experiments and give the rationale; and certificates or diplomas are to be awarded accordingly.

Order 9.th One librarian, or more, to be appointed by the professors, will be keeper of the reading-room. All who attend at the reading room are to respect and obey the orders of the librarian in regard to the library and conduct while in the room.

Order 10.th Any student who shall be guilty of disorderly or ungentlemanly conduct is to be tried and punished by the president or vice president & two trustees. The punishment may extend to expulsion and forfeiture of the school privileges, without a release from the payment of fees. But a student may appeal from such decision to the board of trustees. This instrument, or a copy of it, is to be read to each student before he becomes a member of the school; and be is to be made to understand that his matriculation is to be considered as an assent to these regulations.

S. Van Rensselaer

Albany, Nov. 5, 1824.

To the Rev'd Dr. Blatchford, Lansingburgh

Dear Sir:

I have established a School at the North end of Troy, in Rensselaer County, in the building usually called the old Bank Place, for the purpose of instructing persons who may choose to apply themselves, in the application of Science to the common purposes of life. My principal object is to qualify teachers for instructing the sons and daughters of Farmers and Mechanics by lectures or otherwise, in the application of experimental chemistry, philosophy and natural History, to agriculture, domestic economy, the arts and manufactures. — From the trials which have been made by persons in my employment at Utica, Whitesborough, Rome, Auburn & Geneva, during the last summer, I am inclined to believe, that competent instructors may be produced in the School at Troy who will be highly useful to community in the diffusion of a very useful kind of knowledge, with its application to the business of living. — Apparatus for the necessary experiments has been so much simplified, and specimens in natural History have become subjects of such easy attainment that but a small sum is now required as an outfit for an instructor in the proposed branches of Science. — Consequently any School district may have the benefit of such a course of instruction about once in two or three years, as soon as we can furnish a sufficient number of teachers. I prefer this plan to the endowment of a single public institution, for the resort of those only whose parents are able and willing to send their children from home, or to enter them for several years upon the Fellenberg plan. It seems to comport better with the habits of our citizens and the genius of our Government to place the advantages of useful improvements, equally within the reach of all. — Whether my expectations will ever be realized or not I am willing to hazard the necessary expense of making the trial.

Having procured a suitable Building, advantageously located among farmers and Mechanics, and having furnished funds, which are deemed sufficient by my agents in this undertaking, for procuring the necessary apparatus &c it now remains to establish a system of organization

See p. 46. memorandum

4)

adapted to the object. You will excuse me, if I attach too much consequence to the undertaking. That it appears to me, that a board of Trustees to decide upon the manner of granting certificates of qualifications, to regulate the government of Students &c is essential. I therefore take the liberty to appoint you a member and President of a board of Trustees for this purpose.

I appoint the following Gentlemen Trustees of the same board The Rev. D. Blatchford, Mr. E. Parmelee of Lansingburgh. Gueri Van Schoonhoven, John Cramer of Waterford Simeon DeWitt, T. R. Beck of Albany, John D. Dickinson, Jedh. Tracy of Troy. And I appoint O. L. Holley Esq. of Troy, T. R. Beck of Albany first and second Vice Presidents of said board.

As a few regulations are immediately necessary, in order to present the School to the public; it seems necessary that I should made the following orders, subject to be altered by the Trustees, after the end of the first term.

Order 1st The board of Trustees is to meet at times and places to be notified by the President, or by one of the Vice Presidents in the absence or disability of the President. one half of the Members of the board are to form a quorum for doing business: A majority of the Members present may fill any vacancy which happens in the board: So that there may be two members residents in Troy, two in Lansingburgh, two in Waterford, and two in Albany, The powers and duties of the Trustees to be such as those exercised by all similar bodies — the object of the school being always kept in view.

Order 2nd I appoint Dr. Moses Hale of Troy Sec. & I. N. Lockwood Treasurer.

Order 3rd I appoint Amos Eaton of Troy Professor of Chemistry and Experimental Philosophy, and lecturer on Geology, Land Surveying & the Laws regulating Town officers and Jurors. This office to be denominated the Senior Professorship.

Order 4th I appoint Lewis C. Beck of Albany, Professor of Mineralogy, Botany and Zoology and lecturer on the social duties peculiar to Farmers and Mechanics: This office to be denominated the junior Professorship.

Order 5.ᵗ. The first term is to commence on the first Monday in January next, and to continue fifteen weeks. For admission to this course including the use of the Library and reading room, each Student must pay twenty five Dollars to the Treasurer or give him, satisfactory assurances that it will be paid in one year. In addition to this, each section of Students may pay for the chemical substances they consume and the damage they do to apparatus.

Order 6.ᵗʰ. All the pay thus received by the Treasurer, or for parts of courses of instruction, is to be paid over to said Professors, as the reward of their services.

Order 7.ᵗʰ. In giving the course on Chemistry, the Students are to be divided into sections not exceeding five in each Section. These are not to be taught by seeing experiments and hearing lectures, according to the usual method, But they are to lecture and experiment by turns, under the immediate direction of a professor, or a competent assistant. Thus by a term of Labour, like apprentices to a trade they are to become operative chemists.

Order 8.ᵗʰ. At the close of the term, each Student is to give sufficient tests of his skill and science before examiners to be appointed by myself, or by the Trustees, if I do not appoint. The examination is not to be conducted by question and answer, but the qualifications of Students are to be estimated by the facility with which they perform experiments and give the rationale, and certificates or diplomas are to be awarded accordingly.

Order 9.ᵗʰ. One Librarian, or more, to be appointed by the Professors, will be keeper of the reading room. All who attend to the reading room, are to respect and obey the orders of the librarian, in regards to the Library and conduct while in the room.

Order 10.ᵗʰ. Any Student who shall be guilty of disorderly or ungentlemanly conduct, is to be tried and punished by the President, or a vice President, & two other Trustees. The punishment may extend to expulsion and forfeiture of the School privileges, without a release from the payment of fees. But a Student may appeal from such decision to the board of Trustees.

This instrument, or a copy of it, is to be read to each Student before he becomes a member of the School; and he is to be made to

6]

understand that his matriculation is to be considered as an assent to these regulations.

Albany Nov. 5th 1824.   S. Van Rensselaer

City of Troy, Rensselaer County, Dec. 29. 1824.
On this day at eleven O'clock. A.M. a quorum of the trustees

[Form of the degree and device for the seal. Continued from page 25.] The common seal of this school shall be — Rensselaer School in an outer circle — incorporated 1826 in an inner circle — and March 21 in the centre. And the form of the degree shall be as follows.

The President And Trustees
of
Rensselaer School.

Founded in the year 1824 by the Hon. Stephen Van Rensselaer, in the City of Troy and State of New York. To all patrons of Science, of Agriculture, and of the Arts.

Be it known to you, That _____ has passed through a course of experimental and demonstrative exercises at this School, in Chemistry, Natural Philosophy and Natural History, with their application to Agriculture, Domestic Economy, and the Arts, together with Land Surveying, and General Mensuration; and has given satisfactory evidence of his qualifications, and of his title to the honors of the School.

Therefore by the authority vested in the President and Trustees of said School, by an act of the Legislature of the State of New York and in conformity with the constitution and by-laws of said school he is admitted to the degree of Bachelor of Arts, or Master of Arts, in Rensselaer School; and is presented to the public as competent to perform duties or to enter upon employments which will aid farmers, mechanics, and manufacturers, in the application of Science to their respective vocations, and which will contribute to the dissemination of useful knowledge among the industrious part of the rising generation.

In testimony whereof the seal of said School, together with the signatures of the President and Professors, is hereunto annexed.— Done at the School, by order of the Board of Trustees on the ____ day of ____ in the year 18__

President

Secretary

Professors

Examined   Amos Eaton Senr

THE RENSSELAER POLYTECHNIC INSTITUTE
MISSION STATEMENT

Rensselaer educates the leaders of tomorrow for technologically based careers. We celebrate discovery, and the responsible application of technology, to create knowledge and global prosperity.

NOTES

1   Shirley Ann Jackson, "Perpetuating a Tradition of Excellence" (speech, 12/11/98).

2   David Haviland, "The Rensselaer Plan Report," unpublished manuscript hereafter known as "RPR."

3   Jackson, "Renaissance at Rensselaer: 10-Year Retrospective" (speech, Rensselaer Polytechnic Institute, Troy, NY, 12/5/09), http://www.rpi.edu/president/speeches/ps120509-transformation.html.

4   Jackson, "The Process of Academic Transformation" (speech, Aspen Symposium of the Forum for the Future of Higher Education, Aspen, CO, 10/1/02).

5   David Haviland, "RPR," chapter 1A, p.3.

6   Samuel F. Heffner Jr., personal interview, September 2009.

7   "RPR," chapter 1, p. 1.

8   Jackson, personal interview, September 2009.

9   Ibid.

10 Ibid.

11 Ibid.

12 Ibid.

13 Ibid.

14 Ibid.

15 Ibid.

16 Ibid.

17 Ibid.

18 Thomas Phelan, D. Michael Ross, and Carl Westerdahl, *Rensselaer: Where Imagination Achieves the Impossible* (Troy, NY: Rensselaer Polytechnic Institute, 1995), pp. 88–115; 159–170.

19 Ibid., p. 171.

20 Ibid., p. 172.

21 Ibid.

22 Ibid., p. 175; Anderson Center website, http://www.ciue.rpi.edu/aboutTheCenter.html.

23 Rensselaer website, http://www.lib.rpi.edu/dept/library/html/Archives/history/presidents/schmitt,r.html.

24 Phelan, Ross, and Westerdahl, *Rensselaer: Where Imagination*, pp. 175–179.

25 Ibid.; http://www.rpi.edu/dept/facsen/1997-1998/4-7-1998Minutes.htm.

26 Rick Karlin, "Pipes Resigns from RPI," Albany *Times Union*, 4/2/98.

27 Pipes faculty site at Purdue, https://engineering.purdue.edu/MSE/People/ptProfile?id=1436.

28 John Carr, personal interview, October 2009.

29 Paul Severino, personal interview, October 2009.

30 Jeffrey Kodosky, personal interview, November 2009.

31 Paula Simon, personal interview, October 2009.

32 Heffner, personal interview.

33 Ibid.

34 National Academies website, http://sites.nationalacademies.org/pga/step/PGA_045491.

35 Heffner, personal interview.

36 Various Trustee interviews.

37 Heffner, personal interview.

38 Arthur Gajarsa, personal interview, October 2009.

39 Various Trustee interviews.

40 Heffner, personal interview.

41 Various Trustee interviews.

42 Neal Barton, personal interview, September 2009.

43 Nicholas Donofrio, personal interview, October 2009.

44 Gajarsa, personal interview.

45 Heffner, personal interview.

46 Barton, personal interview.

47 Gary DiCamillo, personal interview, October 2009.

48 Donofrio, personal interview.

49 Jackson, personal interview.

50 Diane O'Connell, *Strong Force: The Story of Physicist Shirley Ann Jackson* (Washington, DC: National Academies/Joseph Henry Press, 2006), pp. 4–5.

51 Jackson, "L'Oreal for Women in Science Luncheon Keynote" (speech, 5/22/2008).

52 O'Connell, *Strong Force*, pp. 1–3.

53 Ibid., p. 5.

54 Jackson, personal interview.

55 O'Connell, *Strong Force*, p. 5.

56 Ibid.; Jackson, personal interview.

57 Jackson, personal interview.

58 Ibid.

59 Ibid.

60 Ibid.

61 Ibid.

62 Jackson, personal interview; O'Connell, *Strong Force*, p. 33.

63 Jackson, personal interview.

64 Ibid.

65 Ibid.

66 Ibid.

67   Jackson, personal interview; O'Connell, *Strong Force*, p. 96.

68   Jackson, personal interview.

69   Ibid.

70   Council on Competitiveness, "Council Member, Leader in Higher Education and Government, to Receive the Vannevar Bush Award: Shirley Ann Jackson Recognized for Contributions to Science and Technology Fields," press release, 3/22/07.

71   Jackson, personal interview; Jackson, "L'Oreal."

72   Jackson, personal interview.

73   Ibid.

74   Jackson biography, Rensselaer website, http://www.rpi.edu/president/profile.html.

75   Jackson, personal interview.

76   Ibid.; Jackson biography, Rensselaer website.

77   Ibid.

78   Jackson, personal interview.

79   Ibid.

80   Jackson biography, Rensselaer website.

81   Ibid.

82   Ibid.

83   Heffner, personal interview.

84   Jackson biography, Rensselaer website; Rensselaer press releases.

85   Jackson, "Perpetuating a Tradition of Excellence" (speech, 12/11/98).

86   Ibid.

87   Ibid.

88   Jackson, "Honoring Tradition, Changing the World" (inaugural speech, Rensselaer Polytechnic Institute, Troy, NY, 9/24/99).

89   Ibid.

90   Rensselaer, "Dr. Shirley Ann Jackson Becomes Rensselaer Polytechnic Institute's 18th President on July 1, 1999," press release, 6/30/99.

91   "RPR," chapter 2, pp. 1–2.

92   *Rensselaer Review*, "Campus Welcomes Dr. Jackson," July 9, 1999, as quoted in "RPR," chapter 2, p. 2.

93   Rensselaer, "Dr. Shirley Ann Jackson Becomes."

94   Phelan, Ross, and Westerdahl, *Rensselaer: Where Imagination*, pp. 15–16.

95   Ibid.

96   Ibid., pp. 23–25.

97   Ibid., pp. 16–21.

98   Ibid., pp. 21–22.

99   Ibid., pp. 22–23.

100   Ibid., p. 26.

101   Ibid., p. 28.

102   Ibid., pp. 28–29.

103   Ibid., pp. 29–30.

104   Ibid., pp. 30.

105   Ibid., p. 38.

106 Ibid., p. 40.

107 Ibid., p. 36.

108 Ibid., pp. 38 and 45.

109 Rensselaer website, http://www.rpi.edu/about/hof/roebling.html.

110 Phelan, Ross, and Westerdahl, *Rensselaer: Where Imagination*, p. 61; Rensselaer website, www.rpi.edu/about/alumni/inductees/roebling2.html.

111 Rensselaer website, http://www.rpi.edu/about/alumni/inductees/ferris.html.

112 Ibid., http://www.rpi.edu/about/alumni/inductees/horsford.html.

113 Ibid., http://www.rpi.edu/about/alumni/inductees/mills.html.

114 Ibid., http://www.rpi.edu/about/alumni/inductees/bedford.html.

115 Ibid., http://www.rpi.edu/about/alumni/inductees/praeger.html.

116 Ibid., http://www.rpi.edu/about/alumni/inductees/cluett.html.

117 Ibid., http://www.rpi.edu/about/alumni/inductees/dumont.html.

118 Ibid., http://www.rpi.edu/about/alumni/inductees/jonsson.html.

119 Ibid., http://www.rpi.edu/about/alumni/inductees/loewy.html.

120 Ibid., http://www.rpi.edu/about/alumni/inductees/tomlinson.html.

121 Phelan, Ross, and Westerdahl, *Rensselaer: Where Imagination*, pp. 48–49.

122 Ibid.

123 B.F. Greene, *The Rensselaer Polytechnic Institute: Its Reorganization in 1849–50, Its Condition at the Present Time, Its Plans and Hopes for the Future* (Troy, NY: D.H. Jones & Co, 1855), pp. 3–4.

124 Greene, *Rensselaer*, p. 4.

125 Phelan, Ross, and Westerdahl, *Rensselaer: Where Imagination*, pp. 50–52.

126 Ibid.

127 Ibid.; Rensselaer website, http://www.rpi.edu/about/history.html.

128 Phelan, Ross, and Westerdahl, *Rensselaer: Where Imagination*, pp. 65–68.

129 Ibid.

130 Ibid., pp. 68–72 and 196.

131 Ibid., pp. 73–75.

132 Ibid., pp. 78–79.

133 Ibid., p. 79.

134 Ibid., pp. 80–81.

135 Ibid., pp. 82–85.

136 Ibid., pp. 88–93.

137 Ibid., p. 96.

138 Ibid., p. 97.

139 Ibid., p. 111.

140 Ibid., p. 113.

141 Ibid., pp. 109–110.

142 Ibid., p. 115.

143 "President Ricketts," *New York Times*, December 12, 1934.

144 Phelan, Ross, and Westerdahl, *Rensselaer: Where Imagination*, pp. 118–120.

145 Ibid., pp. 120–122.

146 Ibid., p. 125.

147   Ibid., pp. 126–135.

148   Ibid.

149   Ibid., p. 131.

150   Ibid., p. 145.

151   Ibid., p. 144.

152   Ibid., p. 147–150.

153   Ibid., pp. 151–154.

154   Ibid., pp. 154–158.

155   Ibid., p. 158.

156   Ibid., pp. 159–160.

157   Ibid., pp. 160–161.

158   Ibid., p. 161.

159   Ibid., pp. 163–165.

160   Ibid., pp. 166–167.

161   Rensselaer Technology Park website, http://www.rpitechpark.com/aboutpark.php.

162   Phelan, Ross, and Westerdahl, *Rensselaer: Where Imagination*, p. 168.

163   Ibid., pp. 168–169.

164   Jackson, personal interview.

165   Heffner, personal interview.

166   DiCamillo, personal interview.

167   Phillip A. Sharp, "Life Sciences at MIT: A History and Perspective," MIT Faculty Newsletter, Vol. XVIII, No. 3, January/February 2006.

168   Carnegie Mellon website, http://www.cmu.edu/about/history/history.pdf.

169   E.J. Vettel, "The Protean Nature of Stanford University's Biological Sciences, 1946–1972," *Historical Studies in the Physical and Biological Sciences*, September 2004, Vol. 35, No. 1, Abstract.

170   DiCamillo, personal interview.

171   Jackson, personal interview.

172   Jackson, "Honoring Tradition."

173   Ibid.

174   Jackson, personal interview; video "Rensselaer: A Journey of Transformation," Rensselaer Polytechnic Institute, December 2009.

175   Jackson, "Honoring Tradition."

176   Ibid.

177   David Haviland, personal interview, August 2009.

178   Jackson, personal interview.

179   Haviland, personal interview.

180   Ibid.

181   Jackson, personal interview.

182   "RPR," chapter 3, p. 2.

183   Ibid.

184   Jackson, "Building The Rensselaer Plan" (Initiating Document), October 1999.

185   Ibid.

186   "RPR," chapter 3, p. 4.

187   Jackson, "Building The Rensselaer Plan."

188 Haviland, personal interview.

189 Jackson, personal interview.

190 Ibid.

191 Jackson, "Building The Rensselaer Plan."

192 "RPR," chapter 3, p. 6.

193 Jackson, "Building The Rensselaer Plan."

194 Ibid.

195 Ibid.

196 Ibid.

197 Ibid.

198 Ibid.

199 Ibid.

200 Ibid.

201 Ibid.

202 Ibid.

203 Ibid.

204 Ibid.

205 Ibid.

206 Ibid.

207 Ibid.

208 Ibid.

209 "RPR," chapter 3, p. 13.

210 Haviland, personal interview.

211 Ibid.

212 Jackson, personal interview.

213 Online biographies of principals.

214 Jackson, personal interview.

215 Ibid.

216 Ibid.

217 Ibid.

218 Ibid.

219 Ibid.

220 Ibid.

221 Ibid.

222 "RPR," chapter 4, pp. 1–2.

223 Ibid.

224 Ibid., p. 2.

225 "The Rensselaer Plan" (Draft Plan), December 1999.

226 Ibid.

227 Ibid.

228 Ibid.

229 Ibid.

230 Ibid.

231 Ibid.

232 Jackson, personal interview.

233 Severino, personal interview.

234 Jackson, personal interview; Jackson, "Honoring Tradition."

235 Jackson, personal interview.

236 Haviland, personal interview.

237 "The Rensselaer Plan" (Draft Plan).

238 Jackson, personal interview.

239 Ibid.

240 "RPR," chapter 4, p. 6.

241 Ibid., p. 7.

242 Jackson, "Letter from the President," 12/15/99.

243 "RPR," chapter 4, p. 8.

244 Ibid.; Haviland, personal interview.

245 Rensselaer Assessment Leadership Committee (RealCom), "Final Report Summarizing Community Response to the Draft Plan," February 2000.

246 Ibid.

247 Ibid.

248 "RPR," chapter 4, p. 11.

249 Ibid.

250 "The Rensselaer Plan" (Final Draft), February 2000.

251 "RPR," chapter 4, p. 12.

252 "The Rensselaer Plan" (Final Draft).

253 "RPR," chapter 4, p. 12.

254 "The Rensselaer Plan" (Final Draft).

255 Jackson, personal interview.

256 Ibid.

257 "RPR," chapter 4, p. 14.

258 Ibid., pp. 14–15.

259 Jackson, personal interview.

260 "RPR," chapter 4, p. 16.

261 Jackson, personal interview.

262 "The Rensselaer Plan, as Proposed to the Board of Trustees," 5/12/00.

263 Ibid.

264 Ibid.

265 Jackson, personal interview.

266 Jackson, "Process of Academic Transformation."

267 "RPR," chapter 4, pp. 16–17.

268 Severino, personal interview.

269 Jackson, personal interview.

270 Jackson, Introduction to the Publication of *The Rensselaer Plan* ("Let Us Move Forward: Institute's New Strategic Plan Approved by Board of Trustees"), *Rensselaer Review*, 5/22/2000.

271 Jackson, "Process of Academic Transformation."

272 DiCamillo, personal interview.

273 Jackson, personal interview.

274 "RPR," chapter 5, p. 7.

275 Jackson, personal interview.

276 Ibid.

277 Ibid.

278 Ibid.

279 *The Rensselaer Plan*, May 2000 (reprinted in 2003), p. 10.

280 Ibid., p. 5.

281 Ibid.

282 Ibid., p. 2.

283 Ibid., p. 10.

284 Ibid., p. 2; fourfold rationale from "RPR," chapter 7, p.1.

285 "RPR," chapter 7, pp. 11–14.

286 Ibid., p. 10.

287 Ibid., p. 11.

288 DiCamillo, personal interview.

289 *The Rensselaer Plan*, p. 11.

290 Ibid., p. 10.

291 Jackson, "10-Year Retrospective."

292 "*The Rensselaer Plan*: Let Us Begin," *Rensselaer* magazine, June 2000, http://www.rpi.edu/dept/NewsComm/Magazine/dec99/inaug1.html.

293 Office of Research, FY02 Performance Plan, 12/1/00, p. 2.

294 "RPR," chapter 7, pp. 7–8.

295 Ibid.

296 Ibid.

297 Rensselaer, "Office of Research Offers Grant-Related Workshops for Faculty," press release, 9/30/02; Rensselaer, "$1 Million Grant from the W.M. Keck Foundation Establishes the Keck Laboratory," press release, 8/26/2003; "RPR," chapter 7, p. 13.

298 "RPR," chapter 8, p. 5.

299 *Rensselaer Review*, 5/1/00; *Campus News*, 12/18/00.

300 Internal Strategic Planning Committee for Biotechnology, Final Report.

301 Ibid.

302 Ibid.

303 Rensselaer, "Final Steps: Rensselaer Leads Effort to Replace One of the Most Widely Used Drugs in American Hospitals," press release, 9/16/2009.

304 *The Rensselaer Plan*, p. 13.

305 "RPR," chapter 8, pp. 18–19.

306 Rensselaer, "IT Master's Program Catches Eye of *Computerworld*," press release, 8/19/08.

307 Rensselaer website, http://www.rpi.edu/dept/IT/.

308 "RPR," chapter 8, p.19.

309 Rensselaer website, http://www.rpi.edu/research/constellations/computation.html.

310 Ibid.

311 Ibid.

312 Rensselaer, "Rensselaer, IBM, and New York State Unveil New Supercomputing Center," press release, 5/21/07.

313 John Kolb, personal interview, September 2010.

314 *Campus News*: "IT Research Strengths Identified in Committee Report," 11/27/00.

315 Ibid.

316 Rensselaer, press releases.

317 Rensselaer website, http://www.rpi.edu/futurechips/index.htm.

318 Rensselaer, "Smart Lighting: New LED Drops the 'Droop,'" press release, 1/12/09.

319 Rensselaer website, http://tw.rpi.edu/wiki/Tetherless_World_Constellation.

320 Rensselaer, "The eScience Revolution: Rensselaer Researchers to Create Semantic Web Platforms for Massive Scientific Collaboration," press release, 10/1/09.

321 Rensselaer website, http://msec.rpi.edu/.

322 Rensselaer, "Rensselaer Researchers Receive $1 Million To Model Metal Maladies," press release, 10/15/09.

323 Rensselaer, press releases.

324 Jackson, "Beyond the Price at the Pump: A Comprehensive Energy Security Roadmap" (speech, Museum of Science and Industry, Chicago, 11/20/08).

325 Ibid.

326 Rensselaer, press releases.

327 Jackson, "Beyond the Price at the Pump."

328 Rensselaer, "Darrin Fresh Water Institute Earns $1.5 Million Gift for Research Professorship," press release, 9/18/06.

329 Rensselaer, "Database Shows Effects of Acid Rain on Microorganisms in Adirondack Lakes," press release, 6/23/08.

330 Rensselaer website, http://green.rpi.edu/archives/zebra_mussels/index.html.

331 Rensselaer, "Studying the Mighty Hudson," press release, 9/1/03.

332 Rensselaer, press releases.

333 Rensselaer website, http://smartlighting.rpi.edu/.

334 Jackson, "Beyond the Price at the Pump"; Rensselaer website, http://www.case.rpi.edu/home.html.

335 Rensselaer website, http://www.rpi.edu/dept/nsec/.

336 Rensselaer, "Adding Nanotubes Makes Ordinary Materials Absorb Vibration," press release, 2/13/06.

337 Rensselaer Research Report 2007, p. 36.

338 Rensselaer, "New Hybrid Nanostructures Detect Nanoscale Magnetism," press release, 12/8/08.

339 Rensselaer, "On the Boil: New Nano Technique Significantly Boosts Boiling Efficiency," press release, 7/7/08.

340 Rensselaer, "Researchers Develop Nanoblade," press release, 9/24/07.

341 Rensselaer Research Report 2007, p. 12; Robert Linhardt, personal interview, September 2009.

342 *Rensselaer* magazine, March 2009.

343 Curtis Priem, personal interview, October 2009.

344 Rensselaer website, http://www.arts.rpi.edu/; related press releases.

345 *The Rensselaer Plan*, various pages.

346 Ibid., p. 23.

347 Jackson, "10-Year Retrospective."

348 *Campus News*: "Committee to Plan for New Biotechnology Center," 12/11/00.

349 Rensselaer, "Ground Broken for Biotechnology Center at Rensselaer," press release, 5/17/02.

350 *Campus News*: "Trustees Approve $255 Million Construction Project; Initiative Features New Buildings for Biotechnology and Electronic Arts," 12/11/00.

351 *Campus News*: "Ceremony to Break Ground for the New Center for Biotechnology and Interdisciplinary Studies," 5/20/02.

352 Rensselaer, "Top-Tier Scientists, Policymakers, Government Officials To Join Rensselaer in Marking the Opening of the Center for Biotechnology and Interdisciplinary Studies Sept. 9–11," press release, 9/2/04.

353 CBIS website, http://biotech.rpi.edu/index.php/about.

354 Ibid.; Jackson, personal interview.

355 Jackson, personal interview.

356 "RPR," chapter 8, p. 14.

357 *Campus News*: "Ribbon-Cutting Ceremony Marks Opening of Rensselaer's Center for Biotechnology and Interdisciplinary Studies," 9/13/04.

358 Biotechnology Symposium: Biological Discoveries That Will Change the World, 9/9/04.

359 Presidential colloquy: "Opportunities at the Interface of Bioscience and Bioengineering," 9/10/04.

360 Ibid.

361 "RPR," chapter 8, p. 17.

362 Jackson, "10-Year Retrospective."

363 Rensselaer, "Cyberinfrastructure Expert James Myers to Lead the Computational Center for Nanotechnology Innovations at Rensselaer Polytechnic Institute," press release, 8/30/10.

364 Kolb, personal interview.

365 Ibid.; Rensselaer website, http://www.rpi.edu/news/events/ccnifactsheet06.html.

366 Kolb, personal interview.

367 Rensselaer, "Rensselaer, IBM, and New York State Unveil New Supercomputing Center," press release, 5/15/07; "Rensselaer Celebrates Grand Opening of World-Class Supercomputing Center, press release, 9/7/2007; "Cyberinfrastructure Expert James Myers."

368 Kolb, personal interview.

369 Rensselaer, "Rensselaer Polytechnic Institute Appoints Cyberinfrastructure Expert James Myers."

370 Kolb, personal interview.

371 Ibid.

372 Rensselaer, "Rensselaer, IBM, and New York State Unveil New Supercomputing Center," press release, 5/15/07.

373 Ibid.

374 Kolb, personal interview.

375 "Rensselaer: A Journey of Transformation."

376 *The Rensselaer Plan*, p. 6.

377 Jackson, personal interview.

378 *Campus News*: "Task Force Named to Plan for Electronic Media and Performing Arts Center," 11/13/00.

379 Rensselaer website, http://www.eng.rpi.edu/soe/index.php/faculty/154?soeid=tichyj.

380 Rensselaer, "Innovative in Form, Pioneering in Function, An Electronic Media and Performing Arts Center Takes Shape at Rensselaer," press release, 7/5/02.

381 Jackson, "Envisioning EMPAC," (speech, 10/4/03).

382 Ibid.

383 DiCamillo, personal interview.

384 The Electronic Media and Performing Arts Center Task Force Final Report, 2/22/01.

385 Ibid.

386 Ibid.

387 Jackson, personal interview.

388 Rensselaer, "Innovative in Form, Pioneering in Function, An Electronic Media and Performing Arts Center Takes Shape at Rensselaer," press release, 7/2/02.

389 Ibid.

390 Jackson, personal interview.

391 Ibid.

392 Ibid.

393 Jackson, "Groundbreaking for the Experimental Media and Performing Arts Center (EMPAC), (speech, 9/19/03).

394 *Campus News*: "EMPAC's New York City Debut," 12/1/03.

395 Priem, personal interview.

396 "Rensselaer: A Journey of Transformation."

397 Priem, personal interview.

398 Ibid.

399 Rensselaer, "Rensselaer Opens the Curtis R. Priem Experimental Media and Performing Arts Center (EMPAC)," press release, 10/3/08.

400 Ibid.

401 Ibid.

402 Rensselaer website, http://empac.rpi.edu/building/.

403 Rensselaer, "DANCE MOViES Commission Launched by EMPAC," press release, 12/4/06.

404 Rensselaer, "Rensselaer Unveils Its Plans for EMPAC, The Experimental Media and Performing Arts Center," press release, 11/17/03.

405 Dennis Overbye, "Art and Science, Virtual and Real, Under One Big Roof," *New York Times*, 9/22/08.

406 Priem, personal interview.

407 Jackson, "Groundbreaking."

408 Priem, personal interview.

409 Rensselaer website, http://www.lib.rpi.edu/dept/library/html/Archives/buildings/87_gym.html.

410 Rensselaer website, http://www.rpi.edu/dept/aux_serv/fieldhouse/history.html.

411 Rensselaer website, http://www.lib.rpi.edu/dept/library/html/Archives/buildings/alumni_recreation.html.

412 "RPR," chapter 11, p. 17.

413 Rensselaer website, http://www.rpi.edu/tour/mueller/index.html; *Rensselaer Review*, 5/15/00.

414 Jackson, personal interview.

415 Rensselaer, "Rensselaer Breaks Ground for East Campus Athletic Village; First Phase to be Completed by Fall 2009," press release, 8/31/07.

416 Ibid.

417 Rensselaer, "Rensselaer Polytechnic Institute Hosts East Campus Athletic Village Grand Opening," press release, 10/3/09.

418 Ibid.; Jackson, personal interview.

419 Rensselaer, "Rensselaer Breaks Ground for East Campus Athletic Village; First Phase to Be Completed by Fall 2009," press release, 9/4/07.

420 Ibid.

421 DiCamillo, personal interview.

422 Donofrio, personal interview.

423 Jackson, Eddie Ade Knowles, personal interviews, August and September 2009.

424 Rensselaer website, http://www.rpi.edu/tour/barton/index.html; *Campus News*, 9/18/2000.

425 Jackson, personal interview.

426 Ibid.

427 Ibid.

428 Rensselaer, "Rensselaer Polytechnic Institute Dedicates Newly Renovated Academy Hall," press release, 12/17/04.

429 Jackson, personal interview.

430 Rensselaer, "Rensselaer Polytechnic Institute Dedicates Newly Renovated Academy Hall."

431 "Engineering Light and Motion," *Rensselaer* magazine, December 2000, http://www.rpi.edu/dept/NewsComm/Magazine/Dec00/atRensselaer.html.

432 "RPR," chapter 11, pp. 9–10.

433 Jackson, "10-Year Retrospective."

434 Ibid.; "RPR," chapter 11, p. 24.

435 Heffner, personal interview.

436 Rensselaer, "Rensselaer Names Local Man Vice President for Administration," press release, 5/14/01.

437 Claude Rounds, personal interview, October 2010.

438 Ibid.

439 Ibid.

440 Ibid.

441 Ibid.

442 Ibid.

443 Ibid.

444 *Campus News*, 12/3/2001.

445 Jackson, "2009 State of the Institute" (speech, 10/02/09).

446 Jackson, "10-Year Retrospective."

447 Rensselaer, "Rensselaer Announces Initiative to Support Advancement of Female Academics," press release, 3/27/07.

448 *Campus News*, 9/17/01.

449 Jackson, personal interview.

450 *Campus News*, 2/18/03.

451 Rensselaer, "Renowned Scientist Angel E. García Will Lead New Biocomputation and Bioinformatics Research Constellation," press release, 11/10/04.

452 Rensselaer, "Renowned Scientist to Join Rensselaer Biocomputation and Bioinformatics Group," press release, 9/14/07.

453 Rensselaer, "Semiconductor Expert to Head Future Chips Research at Rensselaer," press release, 9/4/2002.

454 Rensselaer website, http://www.rpi.edu/dept/phys/faculty/profiles/schubert.html.

455   Rensselaer, "Future Chips Constellation Completed with Two New Faculty Appointments," press release, 3/8/04.

456   Rensselaer, "Web Visionary James A. Hendler Will Lead Tetherless World Research Constellation," press release, 6/19/06.

457   Rensselaer, "Web Language and Artificial Intelligence Expert Joins Tetherless World Research Constellation," press release, 10/16/07.

458   Deborah McGuinness, personal interview, November 2009.

459   Ibid.

460   Rensselaer, "Data Scientist Joins Rensselaer Tetherless World Research Constellation," press release, 11/13/08.

461   Rensselaer, "Renowned Physicist Named Kodosky Constellation Chair at Rensselaer," press release, 2/4/08.

462   Rensselaer, "Nanotechnology Expert to Lead Rensselaer's Materials Science and Engineering Department," press release, 11/5/07.

463   Rensselaer, "Nanoscience Expert and Experienced Academic to Head Rensselaer Biology Department," press release, 8/22/07.

464   Rensselaer, "New Professor's Research Involves Heart and Eye Modeling, Smart Satellite Imaging," press release, 1/8/08.

465   Rensselaer, "New Chair of Chemistry and Chemical Biology Working to Strengthen Department," press release, 10/4/04.

466   Rensselaer, "Three New Faculty to Join Chemical and Biological Engineering Department," press release, 10/31/07.

467   Jackson, "10-Year Retrospective."

468   Ibid.

469   Jackson, "Honoring Tradition."

470   School of Engineering brochure, http://www.eng.rpi.edu/mse/MSE_Fall2009.pdf.

471   Rensselaer website, http://www.rpi.edu/president/accomplishments.html; Jackson, "10-Year Retrospective."

472   Jackson, "10-Year Retrospective."

473   Rensselaer, "Stellenbosch University and Rensselaer Polytechnic Institute Announce Collaboration to Expand Science and Engineering Capacity," press release, 3/17/09.

474   Jackson, "10-Year Retrospective."

475   Jackson, "Moving Forward in Challenging Times" (speech, 2010 Presidential Spring Town Meeting, 3/17/10).

476   *The Rensselaer Plan*, p. 14.

477   Ibid., pp. 14–15.

478   "Graduate Education Performance Plan," Fall 2000.

479   Ibid.

480   "RPR," chapter 7, p. 16.

481   Ibid.

482   Ibid.

483   Rensselaer website, http://www.rpi.edu/president/accomplishments.html.

484   Jackson, "10-Year Retrospective."

485   Ibid.

486   *Rensselaer Review*, Feb. 7, 2000.

487 Rensselaer websites, http://www.rpi.edu/president/accomplishments.html; http://www.rpi.edu/about/communiversity/hartford.html.

488 Jackson, personal interview; Graduate Education Performance Plan FY2004, Fall 2002.

489 "RPR," chapter 7, p. 18.

490 Ibid.

491 Ibid.; *Campus News*, 2/18/02.

492 "RPR," chapter 7, p. 18.

493 Ibid., p. 19; *Campus News*, 2/18/02.

494 *Campus News*, 2/18/02.

495 Graduate Tuition and Student Support Policy; "RPR," chapter 7, p. 19.

496 "RPR," chapter 7, p. 19.

497 Ibid.

498 Ibid., p. 20.

499 Ibid.

500 Ibid.

501 Ibid., p. 24.

502 Ibid., pp. 23–24; Rensselaer institutional research.

503 Knowles, personal interview.

504 Ibid.

505 Ibid.

506 Ibid.

507 Ibid.

508 Jackson, personal interview.

509 Jackson, "10-Year Retrospective."

510 Ibid.

511 First-Year Experience website, http://www.fye.rpi.edu/update.do?artcenterkey=49.

512 Rensselaer, "Rensselaer's First-Year Experience Program Recognized among Best in the Country," press release, 2/21/07; FYE website.

513 "Rensselaer's CLASS Initiative: A Transformation in the Making," paper provided by Eddie Knowles.

514 *Inside Rensselaer*, "Rensselaer's CLASS Program: A Transformation in the Making," 12/5/08.

515 Jackson, "Signs of Progress: Rensselaer Vignettes" (speech, The 2009 Presidential Fall Town Meeting, Troy, NY, 11/4/09).

516 *Inside Rensselaer*, "Launching Rensselaer's CLASS Program: A New Vision for Student Life," 9/11/09.

517 Knowles, personal interview.

518 Ibid.

519 Ibid.

520 *The Rensselaer Plan*, p. 10.

521 Howard Blitman, personal interview, October 2009.

522 Ibid.

523 Jodi Ackerman Frank, "Plan for Success," *Rensselaer* Magazine, Winter 2005–06, http://www.rpi.edu/magazine/winter2005-06/features/feature1-pg1.html.

524 Phelan, Ross, and Westerdahl, *Rensselaer: Where Imagination*, p. 175.

525 Jackson, "Unlimited Opportunities: 2009 State of the Institute" (speech, EMPAC Concert Hall, Troy, NY, 10/2/09).

526 Campaign summary document, http://www.rpi.edu/giving/print/CampaignClose.pdf.

527 Ibid.

528 Data from Rensselaer Institutional Research.

529 Ibid.

530 Rensselaer, "Rensselaer to Create Center for Bioengineering and Medicine," press release, 12/1/02.

531 "RPR," chapter 5, p. 2.

532 Jackson, "Process of Academic Transformation."

533 Ibid.

534 *The Rensselaer Plan*, p. 5.

535 "RPR," chapter 5, p. 1.

536 Jackson, "Process of Academic Transformation."

537 "RPR," chapter 5, p. 1.

538 Jackson, personal interview.

539 Ibid.

540 Ibid.

541 Jackson, personal interview; Virginia Gregg, personal interview, September 2010.

542 Gregg, personal interview.

543 Jackson, Gregg, personal interviews.

544 Gregg, personal interview.

545 Jackson, Kolb, Gregg, personal interviews.

546 Jackson, Gregg, Curtis Powell, and Kolb, personal interviews.

547 Ibid.

548 Powell, personal interview, November 2009.

549 Jackson, "Responding to the Global Economic Crisis: Challenge and Opportunity" (speech, 1/14/09).

550 Ibid.

551 Simon, personal interview, October 2009.

552 Ibid.

553 Robert Palazzo, personal interview, August 2009.

554 Ibid.

555 "RPR," chapter 17, pp. 7–8.

556 Minutes of the General Faculty, 11/3/04.

557 "RPR," chapter 17, p. 10.

558 Achille Messac, "Open Letter to the Faculty, included in Minutes of the Faculty Senate," 2/22/06.

559 Jackson, personal interview; "RPR," chapter 17, p. 11–12.

560 Rensselaer, "Board of Trustees Enthusiastically Endorses Leadership and Presidency of Dr. Shirley Ann Jackson," press release, 5/3/06.

561 Jackson, "President Shirley Ann Jackson's Remarks at Meeting with Rensselaer Faculty" (speech, 4/28/06).

562 Ibid.

563 Ibid.

564 Ibid.

565 Ibid.

566 Ibid.

567 Jackson, personal interview.

568 Robin Martin, personal interview, October 2009.

569 Carr, personal interview.

570 Donofrio, personal interview.

571 Jackson, "Process of Academic Transformation."

572 Martin, personal interview.

573 Carr, personal interview.

574 Jackson, "Process of Academic Transformation."

575 Ibid.

576 Palazzo, personal interview.

577 Ibid.

578 Rensselaer website, http://www.rpi.edu/president/accomplishments.html.

579 Jackson, "2009 State of the Institute."

580 Ibid.

581 Ibid.

582 Data from Rensselaer Institutional Research.

583 Ibid.

584 Ibid.

585 Ibid.

586 Rensselaer online archives, http://www.rpi.edu/library/archives/buildings/winslow.html;
     Amy Rupert, personal communication, January 2011.

587 Jackson, personal interview.

588 Ibid.

589 Jackson, "Signs of Progress: Rensselaer Vignettes" (speech, The 2009 Presidential Fall Town
     Meeting, 11/4/09).

590 Jackson, personal interview.

591 Ibid.

592 Rensselaer, "Rensselaer Unveils Newly Renovated Residence Commons in Downtown Troy,"
     press release, 5/15/09.

593 Blitman, personal interview.

594 Rensselaer, "Rensselaer Unveils Newly."

595 Ibid.

596 Gurley Precision Instruments website, http://www.gurley.com

597 Rensselaer, "Rensselaer Unveils Newly."

598 LRC website, http://www.lrc.rpi.edu/aboutUs/history.asp.

599 Rensselaer, "Lighting Research Center Develops Framework for Assessing Light Pollution,"
     press release, 9/8/08.

600 Rensselaer, "New Approach Sheds Light on Ways Circadian Disruption Affects Human Health,"
     press release, 7/16/08.

601 Rensselaer, "Exposure to Early Evening Sunlight in Spring Creates Teenage Night Owls,"
     press release, 7/26/10.

602 Rensselaer, "Lighting Research Center Named Recipient of U.S. Green Building Council's 2008 Green Building Research Fund Grant," press release, 9/11/08.

603 David Gautschi, personal interview, September 2009.

604 Ibid.

605 Ibid.

606 Ibid.

607 Ibid.

608 Ibid.

609 Ibid.

610 Rensselaer, "Rensselaer Launches Five-Year Collaboration with Leading Chinese University," press release, 8/5/08.

611 Gautschi, personal interview.

612 "A Message to RPI Alumni from Dean Gautschi," undated letter, http://www.lallyschool.rpi.edu/Members/nashj2/news-items/a-message-to-rpi-alumni-from-dean-gautschi/.

613 William Patrick, "West Hall Revival," *Rensselaer* magazine, Winter 2004, http://www.rpi.edu/magazine/winter2004/feature3-pg1.html.

614 Rensselaer website, http://www.arts.rpi.edu/; Jackson, "Moving Forward."

615 Patrick, "West Hall Revival."

616 Rensselaer website, "Folsom Library Renewal," http://www.lib.rpi.edu/images/renovation/Folsom_Renewal_Details_Handout.pdf; *Campus News*: "Dedication Ceremony Celebrates the New Face of Folsom Library," 12/5/05.

617 *Campus News*, "Dedication Ceremony."

618 School Designs website, http://schooldesigns.com/Project-Details.aspx?Project_ID=2538.

619 Rensselaer website, "Folsom Library Renewal," http://www.lib.rpi.edu/images/renovation/Folsom_Renewal_Details_Handout.pdf.

620 Jackson, personal interview.

621 Ibid.

622 Ibid.

623 Wayne Gray, personal interview, November 2009.

624 Ibid.

625 Ibid.

626 Rensselaer, "Bringing *Second Life* to Life: Researchers Create Character with Reasoning Abilities of a Child," press release, 3/10/08.

627 Rensselaer, "Economist's Model Forecasted Current Economic Slowdown One Year in Advance," press release, 9/23/08.

628 DIS website, http://www.sts.rpi.edu/pl/design-innovation-society-dis.

629 Rensselaer website, http://www.rpi.edu/about/campustour/vcc/.

630 Jackson, personal interview.

631 EMPAC programming schedule, Spring 2010.

632 Palazzo, personal interview.

633 Johannes Goebel, personal interview, November 2009.

634 Rensselaer websites, http://www.eng.rpi.edu/mse/research_centers.cfm; http://www.rpi.edu/tour/mrc/index.html.

635 Departmental newsletter, http://www.eng.rpi.edu/mse/MSE_Fall2009.pdf.

636 Rensselaer, "New Polymer Could Improve Semiconductor Manufacturing, Packaging," press release, 1/28/08.

637 Rensselaer, "Seaweed Transformed into Stem Cell Technology," press release, 11/8/07.

638 Rensselaer, "Rensselaer Opens Center Dedicated to the Search for Life in the Universe," press release, 11/24/08.

639 Rensselaer, "Rensselaer's New Parking Garage to Open Today," press release, 1/12/04.

640 Rensselaer, "Trustee Makes Donation to Start New Solar Energy Research Center at Rensselaer," press release, 10/31/08.

641 Rensselaer, "$1 Million Grant from the W.M. Keck Foundation Establishes the Keck Laboratory," press release, 8/26/10.

642 University of Alabama website, http://www.me.ua.edu/inverse/whatis.html.

643 Rensselaer, "Rensselaer Merges Talents to Tackle Complex Global Problems," press release, 4/5/04.

644 IPC website, http://www.iprpi.rpi.edu/.

645 David Spooner, personal interview, September 2009.

646 Ibid.

647 "'Studio 305' Adds New Technologies to Architect's Toolbox," *Rensselaer* magazine, March 2001, http://www.rpi.edu/dept/NewsComm/Magazine/mar01/atRensselaer.html.

648 Mark Mistur, personal interview, September 2009.

649 Rensselaer, "Rensselaer Polytechnic Institute and Skidmore, Owings & Merrill LLP Announce Launch of Center for Architecture Science and Ecology," press release, 11/14/08.

650 Ibid.

651 Evan Douglis, personal interview, September 2009.

652 Ibid.

653 Ibid.

654 Ibid.

655 Kane website, http://www.rpi.edu/~kaner/; Rensselaer, "Kane Wins 2009 ACS Young Investigator Award," press release, 4/7/09.

656 Michael Mullaney, "3° with Ravi Kane," *The Approach*, 4/15/09.

657 *Campus News*, 7/14/03.

658 Garde group website, http://boyle.che.rpi.edu/.

659 Rensselaer, "Loves Me, Loves Me Not: Researchers Discover New Method for Measuring Hydrophobicity at the Nanoscale," press release, 12/3/09.

660 Rensselaer, "Rensselaer Names Garde New Head of Chemical and Biological Engineering," press release, 10/17/07.

661 Simon, personal interview.

662 Ibid.

663 Ibid.

664 Jackson, personal interview; Rensselaer Alumni website, http://www.alumni.rpi.edu/board/index.html.

665 Rensselaer Alumni Association annual reports 2004–2005 and 2005–2006; "Renaissance at Rensselaer: The Campaign," *Rensselaer* magazine, Winter 2004, http://www.rpi.edu/magazine/fall2004/difference.html.

666 Catherine Eckart, personal interview, November 2009.

667 Rensselaer, "U.S. Army Corps of Engineers Honors Rensselaer Researchers for Work on New Orleans Levee Modeling," press release, 11/28/07.

668 Rensselaer, "New $1.1M Grant: Restoring Basic Needs after Hurricanes, Disasters," press release, 9/3/08.

669 School of Engineering brochure, http://www.eng.rpi.edu/soe/images/stories/PDFs/soe_overviewbrochure_fall_2009.pdf.

670 Rensselaer, "Rensselaer Launches International Experience for All Engineering Students," press release, 4/11/08.

671 Jackson, "Signs of Progress: Rensselaer Vignettes"; Scott Waldman, "Students get disaster survival lesson in Haiti," Albany *Times Union*, 1/21/10.

672 Jackson, "Signs of Progress."

673 Ibid.

674 David Rosowsky, personal interview, September 2009.

675 Ibid.

676 Ibid.

677 Ibid.

678 Rensselaer, "Rensselaer Graduates Win Top Environmental Prize in Oxford University Business Plan Competition," press release, 12/5/07.

679 *Inside Rensselaer*, "Camera Created by Graduate Helps Nab Oscar for Best Picture," 3/13/09.

680 Rensselaer, "Outshining Edison: New NSF Engineering Research Center to Advance 'Smart Lighting,'" press release, 10/6/08.

681 Rensselaer, "Faster, Cheaper Fuel Cells: New $1.6 Million DoE Grant Supports Fuel Cell Manufacturing Innovations," press release, 3/24/09.

682 MANE website, http://mane.rpi.edu/research_centers_details.cfm?rcID=CIE.

683 SCOREC website, http://www.scorec.rpi.edu/about_us.html.

684 Rensselaer website, http://www.rpi.edu/president/cabinet/berman.html.

685 Francine Berman, personal interview, September 2009.

686 Ibid.

687 CBIS, Biochemistry and Biophysics program websites, http://biotech.rpi.edu/; http://www.rpi.edu/dept/bcbp/facilities.html.

688 Rensselaer, "Top-Tier Scientists, Policymakers, Government Officials to Join Rensselaer in Marking the Opening of the Center for Biotechnology and Interdisciplinary Studies Sept. 9–11," press release, 9/2/04.

689 Rensselaer, "Final Steps: Rensselaer Leads Effort to Replace One of the Most Widely Used Drugs in American Hospitals," press release, 9/16/09.

690 Rensselaer, "Rensselaer Receives More Than $2 Million from New York State to Fund Stem Cell Research," press release, 3/23/09.

691 Rensselaer, "Building a Better Protein," press release, 2/23/09.

692 Rensselaer, "Researchers Reveal HIV Peptide's Possible Pathway into the Cell," press release, 1/17/08.

693 Robert Linhardt, personal interview.

694 Ibid.

695 Ibid.

696 Dordick group website, http://enzymes.che.rpi.edu/.

697 Rensselaer website, http://www.rpi.edu/about/alumni/inductees/isermann.html; Jonathan Dordick, personal interview, November 2009.

698 Dordick, personal interview.

699 Palazzo, personal interview.

700 Dordick, personal interview.

701 Michael Zwack and Alex Franz, personal interview, November 2009.

702 Ibid.

703 Ibid.

704 Jackson, Rounds, personal interviews.

705 Jackson, Knowles, personal interviews.

706 *Inside Rensselaer*, "Green@Rensselaer: Order Up—Sustainable Dining Options at Rensselaer," 3/5/10.

707 Rensselaer website, http://www.rpi.edu/about/sustainability/index.html.

708 Rensselaer website, http://www.rpi.edu/about/sustainability/operations/index.html.

709 Rensselaer website, http://www.rpi.edu/about/sustainability/president/index.html.

710 Ibid.

711 Jackson, personal interview.

712 Jackson, "10-Year Retrospective."

713 Ibid.

714 Ibid.

715 Ibid.

716 Ibid.

717 Jackson, personal interview.

718 Heffner, personal interview, April 2010.

719 Ibid.

720 Ibid.

721 Ibid.

722 Ibid.

723 Rensselaer, "Rensselaer Polytechnic Institute Launches $16.75 Million Center to Research Social Cognitive Networks," press release, 5/4/10.

724 Examples from Jackson, "2009 State of Institute" and "10-Year Retrospective."

725 "Rensselaer: A Journey of Transformation."

726 Ibid.

727 Ibid.

728 Carr, personal interview.

729 Jackson, personal interview.

730 *Inside Rensselaer*, "Rensselaer to Lead Multi-Million Dollar Center for Social and Cognitive Networks," 10/23/09.

731 Jackson, "Process of Academic Transformation."

732 *Inside Higher Ed* website, http://www.insidehighered.com/news/2009/06/18/bonds.

733 Dordick, personal interview.

734 Jackson, personal interview.

735 Gray, personal interview.

736 Jackson, "Process of Academic Transformation."

737 Jackson, personal interview.

738 Jackson, "Moving Forward."

739 Ibid.

740 Dordick, personal interview.

741 Douglis, personal interview.

742 Ibid.

743 Jackson, "Moving Forward."

744 Rosowsky, personal interview.

745 Jackson, personal interview.

746 Spooner, personal interview.

747 Ibid.

748 Ibid.

749 Ibid.

750 Rensselaer, "Rensselaer Appoints New Director of Community Relations," press release, 6/20/08.

751 Rensselaer, "Rensselaer Announces Makeup of Committee to Review Faculty Governance," press release, 9/24/07.

752 Jackson, letter to faculty, 3/4/08.

753 Blitman, personal interview.

754 Martin, personal interview.

755 Donofrio, personal interview.

756 Ibid.

757 Rep. Paul Tonko, personal interview, November 2009.

758 Severino, personal interview.

759 Carr, personal interview.

760 Ibid.

761 Severino, personal interview.

762 Tonko, personal interview.

763 Jackson, "Moving Forward."

764 Rensselaer, "Rensselaer Announces $1 Billion Capital Campaign—the Largest in the University's History," press release, 9/11/04.

INDEX

203–4; international experience, 155, 222; signature thrusts, 109–23; sustainability, 231; technology in classroom, 155

degrees, 9; B.S. in biomedical engineering/M.D., 159, B.S. in electronic arts, 122; B.S. in engineering/MBA, 159; B.S. in games and simulation arts and sciences, 122; co-terminal, 155; joint degrees, 223; MBA, 159, 205, 244; M.S. in law, 159; M.S. in IT, 244; Ph.D., 7, 119, 159, 160–61, 207, 217, 244; Ph.D. in electronic arts, 122

departments (*see also* programs *under* Rensselaer Polytechnic Institute); Biology, 154, 215; Chemistry and Chemical Biology, 154; Economics, 210; Electrical, Computer, and Systems Engineering, 152, 154; Howard P. Isermann Department of Chemical and Biological Engineering, 218; iEAR (Integrated Electronic Arts at Rensselaer), 122, 207; Language, Literature, and Communication, 122; Materials Science and Engineering, 154; Science and Technology Studies, 210

diversity, 7, 24, 45, 76, 90, 98, 122, 221; faculty, 78, 81, 150–51; geographic, 242; LGBT student organization, 223; students, 196, 242; women, 221

entrepreneurship, 64–65, 75, 101, 203–4 (*see also* entrepreneurship)

faculty, ix, xiv, 5–6, 195, 240; awards, 150; constellation concept, 114–16, 150–55; diversity, 150–51; expanding, 42, 114–15, 150–55; faculty governance, 245; faculty senate, 9, 43, 69, 85, 88, 89, 161, 163, 182–83, 186; grants, 108; policy making, 41; reaction to Jackson, 182–84; recruitment, 114–15, 150–155, 204; rejection of *Holley Commission*, 38; research, 41, 159, 182 (*see also* research at Rensselaer Polytechnic Institute); student-faculty ratio, 150; tenure, 176

finances, 65, 66, 170–72; alumni support, 220; assets, 42; campaign for Rensselaer Polytechnic Institute, 170–72, 177–78; capital budgets, 148; compensation system, 179; credit rating, 240; economic climate, 180; economic development, 78; endowments, 39, 46, 66, 102, 177; grants and philanthropic support, ix, 106, 108, 115, 116, 138, 140, 159, 163, 171, 172, 203, 209–10, 213, 214, 221, 225, 226, 238, 240; investments, 147, 240; operating budget, 177; tuition, 160–61

global reach, 81, 156, 205–6, 222

Hartford campus, 159–60

historical overview, vii, 29–49; alumni inventions, 33–36; Civil War, 36, 38–39; decline in late 20th century, 5–6, 46–49; fires, 38, 39; founding, 29–33; leadership, 8–11, 36–49; name change, 37; opening to women, 33; reputation, 5–6, 47

innovation, 62, 64, 101, 204, 206; Anderson Center for Innovation in Undergraduate Education, 8; Center for Industrial Innovation (CII), 126, 193, 224–25; Computational Center for Nanotechnology Innovations (CNNI), *113*, 113–14, 116, 129–32, 152, 215–16; Design, Innovation, and Society (DIS), 210; interdisciplinary inquiry, 91, 122, 154, 204–5, 215, 225, 228, 241, 242; IT (information technology), 111–16

mission, 104, 109, 119

physical resources, xiv, 7, 66, 101, 124–49, 241–42; acquisitions, 43; Approach, The, 201–3, *202*; clean room, 224; computers, 45, 112–13, *113*, 129–32, 210, 216, 224; goals, 65–66; Hartford campus, 159–60; labs, 147, 214, 224; land footprint, 40, 43, 147; Ned Harkness Field and Track, 141; parking, 214; Ricketts campus, 40; Robison pool, 141; South Campus, 125, 147, 214; video equipment, 210; writing center, 210

programs, 7, 40, 41, 42, 63 (*see also* curriculum *under* Rensselaer Polytechnic Institute; departments *under* Rensselaer Polytechnic Institute); biotechnology and life sciences, 109–11, 225–29; computational science and engineering, 111–16; design, 210; energy and the

This book is printed on SFI-certified paper.

Produced by Lipman Hearne, Inc., Chicago, Washington
Printed by Dynagraf, Inc., Canton, MA